Writing Time

signale
_____
modern german letters, cultures, and thought

Series Editor: Paul Fleming, Cornell University
Peter Uwe Hohendahl, Founding Editor

Signale: Modern German Letters, Cultures, and Thought publishes new English-language books in literary studies, criticism, cultural studies, and intellectual history pertaining to the German-speaking world, as well as translations of important German-language works. *Signale* construes "modern" in the broadest terms: the series covers topics ranging from the early modern period to the present. *Signale* books are published under a joint imprint of Cornell University Press and Cornell University Library in electronic and print formats. Please see http://signale.cornell.edu/.

WRITING TIME

Studies in Serial Literature, 1780–1850

SEAN FRANZEL

A Signale Book

CORNELL UNIVERSITY PRESS AND CORNELL UNIVERSITY LIBRARY
ITHACA AND LONDON

Cornell University Press and Cornell University Library gratefully acknowledge the College of Arts & Sciences, Cornell University, for support of the Signale series.

Copyright © 2023 by Cornell University

All rights reserved. Except for brief quotations in a review, this book, or parts thereof, must not be reproduced in any form without permission in writing from the publisher. For information, address Cornell University Press, Sage House, 512 East State Street, Ithaca, New York 14850.

First published 2023 by Cornell University Press
and Cornell University Library

Library of Congress Cataloging-in-Publication Data

Names: Franzel, Sean, author.
Title: Writing time : studies in serial literature, 1780–1850 / Sean Franzel.
Description: Ithaca [New York] : Cornell University Press, 2023. | Series: Signale: modern German letters, cultures, and thought | Includes bibliographical references and index.
Identifiers: LCCN 2023015243 (print) | LCCN 2023015244 (ebook) | ISBN 9781501772443 (hardcover) | ISBN 9781501772450 (paperback) | ISBN 9781501772467 (epub) | ISBN 9781501772580 (pdf)
Subjects: LCSH: Time in literature. | Time—Philosophy—History—19th century. | Serial publications—Europe—History—19th century. | Authors and readers—History—19th century.
Classification: LCC PN56.T5 F73 2023 (print) | LCC PN56.T5 (ebook) | DDC 070.1/7509034—dc23/eng/20230509
LC record available at https://lccn.loc.gov/2023015243
LC ebook record available at https://lccn.loc.gov/2023015244

For Mae and Louis

Contents

List of Illustrations	xi
Acknowledgments	xv
Introduction	1
Temporalization and Seriality	7
Writing Time	11
The Timeliness and Untimeliness of Serial Forms	14
Elements of Serial Print	24
Tableaux mouvants, Miscellanies of Time, and *Zeitgeschichten*	36
Part I *Tableaux mouvants*	41
1. Bertuch's *Modejournal*: Cultural Journalism in an Age of Revolution	53
More than "Merely a Fleeting Page"?	57
"Interesting" and "Frightening" Tableaus	63

"Drawings of Every New Fashion and Invention": The Journal's Fashion Plates	70
Small Print Luxury	79
An "Archive of the Fashions of Body and Mind"	86
2. Goethe's *The Roman Carnival* and Its Afterlives	92
A First View of *The Roman Carnival*	99
Second (and Third) Views of Carnival: Republication, Print Luxury, and Consumable Classicism	119
After Goethe's *Carnival*	134
3. Caricature and Ephemeral Print in *London und Paris*	143
Canalizing the Flow	148
"Friends of the Art of Uglifying"	154
Les Cris de Paris	158
"Ephemeral Favorites"	167
Linen Monuments	171
The Monument as Caricature and as Ephemeral Event	179
Part II Miscellanies of Time	**191**
4. Jean Paul's Paper Festivals	199
Figures of Time	203
Preaching at Twilight	207
Writing the Present, Writing the Future	214
Paper Monuments, Paper Festivals	224
Ends and Beginnings	232
5. Jean Paul's Incomplete Works	238
Before and after Death	243
Opera Omnia	253
The *Papierdrache*	261
Jean Paul's Literary Afterlives	267

Part III Contemporary Histories (*Zeitgeschichten*) 273

6. Waiting for the Revolution (Ludwig Börne) 283

   Diaries of the Times 286
   Letters from Paris 297
   "Adieu until the Next Revolution" 305
   The History of the Coming Revolution 309

7. Heine's Serial Histories of the Revolution 316

   Various Conceptions of History 323
   Interrupting the History of the Revolution 326
   Heine's Anti-Portraiture 334
   Rhetoric after the Revolution 339
   After 1848: Literary Afterlives and the Death
     of the Author 346

Afterword: Serial Literature's Untimely Afterlives? 355

Bibliography 371

Index 399

Illustrations

0.1 Jean-Henri Marlet, "Lecture des Journaux aux Thuileries." *Tableaux de Paris* (1821–1824).   43

1.1 "1. Ein Officier in der berühmten National-Garden-Uniforme. 2. Eine junge Dame im Demi-Negligé von neuester Mode zu Paris." *Journal des Luxus und der Moden* (1790).   73

1.2 "Maskenzug in Weimar am 30. Januar 1810 (Prinzessin. Rother. Brunhild. Siegfried)." *Journal des Luxus und der Moden* (1810).   75

1.3 "Neujahrsgeschenk der Mode." *Journal des Luxus und der Moden* (1790).   83

1.4 "Venus mit Grazien." *Journal des Luxus und der Moden* (1796).   85

1.5 "Janus." *Journal des Luxus und der Moden* (1794). 87

1.6 "Die beyden Calender, der neuheidnische und altchristliche. (En parallèle)." *Journal des Luxus und der Moden* (1794). 90

2.1 Anonymous, "Suovetaurilien-Prozession." In Karl Philipp Moritz, *Anthousa, oder Roms Alterthümer. Ein Buch für die Menschheit* (1791). 108

2.2 Georg Melchior Kraus, after drawing by Christian Georg Schütz, "Aufzug des Pulcinellen-Königs." In Johann Wolfgang von Goethe, *Das Römische Carneval* (1789). 113

2.3 Johann Heinrich Lips, title page illustration. *Das römische Carneval* (1789). 117

2.4 Title page. *Masken des römischen Carnevals* (1790). 122

3.1 Cover. *London und Paris* (1798). 150

3.2 Johann Heinrich Meyer, "Attempt in the Art of Uglifying, Dedicated to the Great Eulogist of It." 155

3.3 "Les Cris de Paris." *London und Paris* (1799). 162

3.4 "Liberté de la presse." *London und Paris* (1799). 169

3.5 Page view. *London und Paris* (1799). 177

3.6 "Die Colonne der grossen Armee auf dem Place Vendôme zu Paris," *Paris, Wien und London* (1811). 184

3.7 "Monument des Generals Desaix auf dem Place Victoire zu Paris." *Paris, Wien und London* (1811). 185

4.1 Jean Paul's *Werkchen* and their republication in anthology and works edition formats. 230

4.2 Page view. *Morgenblatt für gebildete Stände* (1809). 235

5.1 Page view. *Morgenblatt für gebildete Stände* (1807). 248

5.2 Page view. *Intelligenzblatt zum Morgenblatt für gebildete Stände* (1826). 254

6.1 Title page. Ludwig Börne, *Gesammelte Schriften* (1833). 291

6.2 Title page. Ludwig Börne, *Briefe aus Paris* (1834). 301

6.3 Page view. Ludwig Börne, *Briefe aus Paris* (1832). 303

Acknowledgments

Completing this book during the global pandemic has helped me appreciate colleagues, friends, and family in new ways. I have had the good luck of workshopping this manuscript with many colleagues, and I'd like to first and foremost thank my colleagues at the University of Missouri for helping me with and through this project: Roger Cook, Noah Heringman, Seth Howes, and Carsten Strathausen all gave me feedback on multiple chapters; thanks as well to Sean Ireton, Monika Fischer, Martha Kelly, Kristin Kopp, Tim Langen, Megan McKinstry, Megan Moore, Brad Prager, and Dan Sipe. I'd also like to thank the University of Missouri library staff, who helped me obtain materials for the book at every turn despite ongoing austerity budgeting.

I am also particularly grateful to friends and colleagues who have offered feedback on parts of the book: André Bank, Mike Barrett, Michael Bies, Tobias Boes, Vance Byrd, Mary Helen Dupree, Samuel Frederick, Ilinca Iurascu, Bryan Klausmeyer, Trudy Lewis, Malika

Maskarenic, Petra McGillen, Mattias Pirholt, Michael Swellander, Birgit Tautz, and Stefan Uhlig. My thanks as well to Stefani Engelstein, Matt Erlin, Stefan-Ludwig Hoffmann, Craig Howes, Catriona MacLeod, Jim Mussell, Daniel Purdy, Nicholas Saul, Lynne Tatlock, and Mark Turner for productive conversations over the years.

This project wouldn't have materialized the way it did without the input and encouragement of colleagues in the Journalliteratur research group at the Universities of Bochum, Marburg, and Cologne. Special thanks to Nicola Kaminski, Nora Ramtke, and Sven Schöpf at Bochum; Daniela Gretz, Marcus Krause, and Nicolas Pethes at Cologne; and David Brehm, Vincent Fröhlich, Volker Mergenthaler, Alice Moran, and Jens Ruchatz at Marburg. It was a real treat to be so warmly welcomed into your many debates about periodicals and into your cultures of collaborative inquiry!

I have fond memories of presenting early versions of material from this book at the Universities of Basel, Bochum, British Columbia, Cologne, Copenhagen, Erfurt, Marburg, Michigan, and Notre Dame; at the University of California, Davis; at the Free and Humboldt Universities in Berlin; and at Dartmouth College. I am thankful for all the kind invitations and feedback. A special thanks to Michael Gamper and Wolfgang Struck for their support of my application for the Alexander von Humboldt Fellowship, which helped me complete research for the book in 2019 and 2020.

Even though this is my second book, I still proudly feel the influence of my graduate school mentors. A special thanks to Peter Uwe Hohendahl, Peter Gilgen, and Neil Saccamano for their inspiration and kindness over many years.

A special thanks to the two anonymous readers for their many helpful suggestions for improving the manuscript and to Kizer Walker, who has helped see the project through to fruition. Thanks as well to Liv Cordray, who designed the book's table, and to Judy Metro, who helped immensely with the final polish of the manuscript.

Parts of this book had an earlier gestation in book chapters, and I wish to acknowledge the editors of the following publishing houses who have given me kind permission to adapt these previous publications. Part of a section of chapter 3 appeared under the title "*Les*

Cris de Paris: Lebendigkeit, Neuigkeit und Intermedialität in der urbanen Tableauliteratur um 1800," *Belebungskünste: Praktiken lebendiger Darstellung*, edited by Nicola Gess, Annette Kappeler, and Agnes Hoffmann (Munich: Fink, 2019), 83–103. Parts of chapter 4 appeared under the title "Jean Paul's Incomplete Works," in *Reading Miscellanies—Miscellaneous Readings*, edited by Daniela Gretz, Markus Krause, and Nicolas Pethes (Hanover: Wehrhahn, 2022), 167–94. Parts of chapter 7 appeared under the title "Heine's Serial Histories of the Revolution," in *Truth in Serial Form: Serial Formats and the Form of the Series (1850–1930)*, edited by Malika Maskarenic (New York: de Gruyter, 2023), 25–55. All previously published work has been substantially revised for this book.

Finally, I'd like to thank my parents, Kathy and Jack, and parents-in-law, Judy and Alex (now deceased), for their long-standing support. And finally, I'd like to thank Rose, Mae, and Louis for all that we have shared as a family in Missouri; the Pacific Northwest; Washington, DC; Berlin; Leipzig; and places in between over the past eight years.

Introduction

Musing on periodicals and their relationship to time, journal editor Ludwig Börne combines the commonplace notion of the periodical as a timepiece with the assertion that journals have a very material effect on the world and our experience of it. According to Börne, journals do not merely measure time like the hands of a clock; rather, they are akin to the clock's "engine itself, that keeps the gears of time moving regularly and that measures their progressions."[1] The idea that newspapers and journals affect the perception and structure of time was quite familiar to nineteenth-century authors, editors, and readers; in this book I expand on this idea and explore how a range of experiments in literary and journalistic writing shapes temporal awareness. If, as Marshall McLuhan argues, "the 'message' of any medium or technology is

---

1. Ludwig Börne, "Einleitung," *Die Wage, Eine Zeitschrift für Bürgerleben, Wissenschaft und Kunst* 1 (1818): 1.

the change of scale or pace or patterns that it introduces into human affairs," then one of the key messages of nineteenth-century print media is that they shape readers' sense of time.[2] Like other transformative technologies such as the telegraph and railway, periodicals create new forms of communication and "new kinds of work and leisure" (as McLuhan puts it) with corresponding alterations in the experience of these activities' temporal components.[3] The period under study—the 1780s to the 1850s, sometimes called the age of European revolution—is commonly characterized as ushering in a modern or "new" time, *die Moderne* or *Neuzeit*. From a media-historical perspective, though, the nineteenth century is first and foremost a "news and newspaper modernity" (*Zeitungsmoderne*), as Gerhard von Graevenitz has put it.[4] In this book, I seek to center format and genre conventions characteristic of this news and newspaper modernity—fashion reporting, miscellaneous urban sketches, serialized correspondence reports, recurring new year's greetings, caricatures, and more—and show how they both thematize and structure time itself, how, in other words, they *write* time.

Across Europe and in German-speaking lands in particular, the late eighteenth and early nineteenth centuries witness the emergence of recognizably modern cultural and political journalism as it appears in new types of literary magazines and political reporting based in the daily newspaper. The periodical press had grown in earnest in the seventeenth century with the first scholarly journals and newspapers, while the eighteenth century delivered to broader reading audiences a diversified array of journals, including mid-century moral weeklies, which in German were often modeled on English predecessors such as Addison and Steele's *Spectator* (1711–1712) or *The Tatler* (1709–1711). A range of Enlightenment journals, including review and popular-scientific or scholarly publications such as *Die Berlinische Monatsschrift* (The Berlin monthly)

---

2. Marshall McLuhan, *Understanding Media: The Extensions of Man* (Cambridge, MA: MIT Press, 1994), 8.
3. McLuhan, *Understanding Media*, 9.
4. Gerhart von Graevenitz, *Theodor Fontane: ängstliche Moderne. Über das Imaginäre* (Konstanz: Konstanz University Press, 2014), 345.

(1783–1996), as well as fashion and cultural journals such as C. M. Wieland's *Der Teutsche Merkur* (The German mercury) (1773–1790), played an instrumental role in expanding the number of publications for lay readers and shifting reading habits toward the "extensive" consumption of new material. It is the French Revolution, though, that precipitates the rise of newly influential cultural and political journals, magazines, and newspapers. The 1790s is a decade of tremendous growth in journal publication, building on the accelerated emergence of new journals in previous decades relative to the early and mid-eighteenth century.[5] In German-speaking lands, this period witnesses the rise of modern newspapers, including the Augsburg-based *Allgemeine Zeitung* (General newspaper) (1798–1929), with correspondent reports from European capitals promising the latest political and cultural news. The 1790s also witnesses the emergence of leading (if in certain cases short-lived) literary and art-historical journals, including F. Schiller's *Die Horen* (The Horae) (1795–1797), F. and A. W. Schlegel's *Athenäum* (Athenaeum) (1798–1800), and J. W. von Goethe's *Propyläen* (Propylaea) (1798–1800). Such journals break with the mid-century weeklies' repertoire of moral lessons and instead task themselves with responding to the unprecedented events of the present through new literary and philosophical undertakings. This period likewise witnesses the founding of leading cultural journals such as the *Journal des Luxus und der Moden* (Journal of luxury and fashion) (1798–1823), the *Morgenblatt für gebildete Stände* (Morning pages for the educated classes) (1807–1865), the *Zeitung für die Elegante Welt* (Paper for the elegant world) (1801–1859), and the slightly later Viennese publication the *Wiener Zeitschrift für Kunst, Literatur, Theater und Mode* (Viennese journal for art, literature, theater, and fashion) (1817–1849), whose title encapsulates the thematic range of these journals. Serialized across multiple daily, weekly, or monthly installments, such journals shape the way readers encounter literary, journalistic, and critical texts in proximity to other miscellaneous contents.

---

5. See Joachim Kirchner, *Das deutsche Zeitschriftenwesen. Seine Geschichte und seine Probleme*, vol. 1 (Wiesbaden: Harrassowitz, 1958), 267.

In this book, I refer to serial literature primarily as the contents and reporting of both cultural journals (*Zeitschriften*) and daily newspapers (*Zeitungen*), though I largely focus on literary-leaning examples of the former. These journals and newspapers share certain key features, including a heterogeneous mixture of textual (and in many cases visual) forms and the assumption that more installments are to come, in contrast to the self-contained book. Print historians commonly refer to such installment-based publications as serial print or serials. Serial formats play an outsize role in the period under study because they are well suited to keeping up with changing circumstances and they generate a sense of movement through time; indeed, this sense of movement leads to the common perception of new installments of printed literature as a kind of watery "flow" that adds to an ever-growing "sea" of print.[6] Readers come to be trained in the expectation that the latest news will come with the next day's, week's, or month's installment, that various events are taking place simultaneously, and that the future will likely bring something unexpected. Cultural journals are associated with urban life and developments in politics, fashion, the arts, commerce, science, and other aspects of society that depend on and generate time-specific information. Over time, periodicals come to rival the book "as the dominant textual medium of intellectual exchange, social commentary, and entertainment," for they offer currentness (*Aktualität*), newness, and a varied mixture of information and entertainment.[7] For readers in provincial locations—that is, most of the German-speaking public—journal editors and authors seek to make their readers' encounters with correspondence reports and literary entertainment a weekly or even daily routine. This routinized, temporally punctuated media landscape can be characterized

---

6. As Thomas Carlyle puts it in 1831, "Literature, Printed Thought is the molten sea and wonder-bearing Chaos, into which mind after mind casts forth its opinion, its feeling to be molten into the general mass, and to work there." Thomas Carlyle, "Review of William Taylor, *Historic Survey of German Poetry*," *Edinburgh Review* 53, no. 105 (1831): 179-180.

7. James Wald, "Periodicals and Periodicity," in *Companion to the History of the Book*, ed. Jonathan Rose and Simon Eliot (Hoboken, NJ: Wiley, 2008), 424.

as a kind of "serial culture" that spans Europe and the world and that morphs and expands as the century progresses.[8]

The French Revolution observed at a distance is a key feature of this serial culture: as Hannah Arendt points out, modern German thought originates in the observation of the revolution "from the standpoint of the spectator who watches a spectacle."[9] Journals function as sites to process the unfolding of the transformative events in the wake of the revolution, to look back at the recent past, and to conjecture about the future. Indeed, the goal of many new journals founded in this era is to provide readers with a cultural "history of the present," or *Zeitgeschichte*, and experiment with how to write the history of revolutionary events that are still perceived to be ongoing. Throughout the nineteenth century, journals—"our fortifications," as Heinrich Heine called them—would remain key vantage points from which to offer political and cultural commentary.[10] Writers don the mantle of *Zeitschriftsteller*, a late eighteenth-century neologism connoting a writer (*Schriftsteller*) who writes for journals (*Zeitschriften*) and in the service of "the times" (*die Zeit*). Like the revolution itself, journals and newspapers become symbolic not only of what is current but of temporal complexity and of the confrontation between the old and new.

Journals are also essential and tangible commodities in the print marketplace of the period, especially with the rising demand for illustrated fashion journalism from a German audience eager for the latest fashions from Paris and London. With their hand-colored fashion plates, these journals serve as sites for the delectation of luxury objects and other commodities, but they are also forms of print luxury in their own right and compete with pocketbooks (*Taschenbücher*), other seasonal gift books, and literary annuals. The increasingly diverse range of formats and venues to which writers could contribute leads to new styles of authorship based in both multiauthor journals and

---

8. Mark W. Turner, "The Unruliness of Serials in the Nineteenth Century (and in the Digital Age)," in *Serialization in Popular Culture*, ed. Thijs van den Berg and Rob Allen (London: Taylor and Francis, 2014), 12.

9. Hannah Arendt, *On Revolution* (New York: Penguin, 2006 [1963]), 43.

10. Heinrich Heine to Gustav Kolb, November 11, 1828. HSA, 20, 350.

single-author books. In the process, writers rethink the function of miscellaneous formats vis-à-vis the status and desirability of single-author editions. Throughout this book I explore different reflections on the commodity status of serial print at the intersections of periodical literature and more bookish, single-author modes of writing, and I foreground writers who bring the logic of journal-based authorship to bear on their oeuvre.

I thereby hope to remedy certain limitations of book-centered literary history in which the contexts and conventions of journal publication disappear. Serial forms diverge from the temporal footprint of the stand-alone literary work and visual image and call out for new approaches to crafting literary- and cultural-historical narratives. It can be easy to forget that most literary works of the period first appeared in serialized form in journals or anthologies, such as pocketbooks or almanacs. Book-centric scholarship reinforces canonization and the retrospective editorial decisions that put writings into critical editions. In calling for this shift in focus, I draw on book- and media-historical scholarship that examines the historical specificities of publication formats and the poetics of collective groupings of texts rather than the hermeneutics of single works, while also trying to avoid a certain amount of lingering bias in favor of the book. To be sure, book and print history have tracked the role of periodicals in shifting reading practices, disseminating revolutionary ideas, and overconfidently spreading visions of the book's obsolescence. However, at the same time that scholars conclude that the book as such does not exist, many continue to privilege stand-alone works as normative textual units.[11] I seek instead to recenter serial forms in our understanding of the literary and media history of the period. As a result, the sections of this book gravitate toward smaller forms predicated on open-ended continuation rather than toward self-contained forms such as the novel, novella, or lyric poem. Serial forms create conditions for "writing time" by profiting off a sense of incomple-

---

11. "Das Buch, wie wir es zu kennen glauben, hat in der Epoche, die rückblickend als geistesgeschichtliche Großepoche des Buchs verstanden wird, so gar nicht existiert." Carlos Spoerhase, *Das Format der Literatur: Praktiken materieller Textualität zwischen 1740 und 1830* (Göttingen: Wallstein, 2018), 45.

tion and embracing contingent relationships of proximity. Of course, there are also challenges to writing literary and media history that focus on serial forms: the corpus is potentially unlimited, and the conundrums of selection and focus are frequent and daunting. The methodological choice to view textual units or images as part of a series brings with it the awareness that coordinates for mapping serial literature can be established on the basis of different factors. As Frank Kelleter remarks, "one and the same text can be regarded as simultaneously serial and non-serial, depending on the perspective from which it is seen—or, more properly, depending on the historical situation in which its textual activities are mobilized in one way or another."[12] Dives into the sea of serial print seem destined primarily to resurface with case studies, and this fact informs the structure of this book, which is organized around several author- and journal-focused studies. At the same time, I also present some generalizable conclusions about how serial forms shape the understanding of time in the period in question and beyond.

Temporalization and Seriality

Serial formats are both caught up in and agents of what Reinhart Koselleck has described as the "temporalization" of social, cultural, and political experience. Temporalization names the process of concepts and metaphors being infused with coefficients of movement and change, as the semantics governing a range of realms of life become historicized and linked to specific temporal frameworks. Temporalization generates characteristically modern shapes of time, including forms of linear progression (time's arrow) that supplant patterns of cyclical return (time's cycle) or moments of transition and transformation between past and future, as in Koselleck's *Sattelzeit*, which refers to the period between 1770 and 1830.[13] For Koselleck, the

---

12. Frank Kelleter, "Five Ways of Looking at Popular Seriality," in *Media of Serial Narrative*, ed. Frank Kelleter (Columbus, OH: Ohio State University Press, 2017), 15.
13. See Karol Berger, *Bach's Cycle, Mozart's Arrow: An Essay on the Origins of Musical Modernity* (Berkeley: University of California Press, 2007).

geographical metaphor of a saddle or pass between two points of higher elevation also entails a "Janus-faced" gaze backward into the past and forward into the future.[14] As many historians have noted, the *Sattelzeit* is a transitional era when different historiographical regimes come into conflict amid the emergence of history writing as an academic discipline. In the process, the present comes to be perceived to contain multiple competing times, to manifest the contemporaneity of the noncontemporaneous (*Gleichzeitigkeit des Ungleichzeitigen*).[15] Literature and criticism play a particularly central role in this process; as Dirk Göttsche writes, "one of the most striking stylistic features of the new, critical sense of time and history in German literature during the 1790s is the emergence of a metaphoric of time, a system of metaphors which express the period's heightened awareness of historical crisis and of both political and epistemological challenge in terms of temporal experience."[16] In delving into the particular status of seriality and serial literature as "techniques of temporalization" (to use Wolf Lepenies's term[17]), I build on what Christopher Clark has referred to as historical and literary studies' recent "temporal turn."[18]

---

14. Reinhart Koselleck, "Einleitung," in *Geschichtliche Grundbegriffe. Historisches Lexikon zur politisch-sozialen Sprache in Deutschland*, vol. 1 (Stuttgart: Klett-Cotta, 1972), xv.

15. See Helge Jordheim, "'Unzählbar viele Zeiten.' Die Sattelzeit im Spiegel der Gleichzeitigkeit des Ungleichzeitigen," in *Begriffene Geschichte. Beiträge zum Werk Reinhart Kosellecks*, ed. Hans Joas and Peter Vogt (Frankfurt: Suhrkamp, 2011), 449–80. François Hartog, for example, describes this period in terms of the confrontation between historiographical regimes while other historians talk of the "oscillation" (Christopher Clark) between different conceptions of historical time or of modernity's characteristic "pluritemporality" (Achim Landwehr). See François Hartog, *Regimes of Historicity: Presentism and Experiences of Time*, trans. Saskia Brown (New York: Columbia University Press, 2015); Christopher Clark, *Time and Power: Visions of History in German Politics, from the Thirty Years' War to the Third Reich* (Princeton, NJ: Princeton University Press, 2019); Achim Landwehr, *Geburt der Gegenwart. Eine Geschichte der Zeit im 17. Jahrhundert* (Frankfurt: Fischer, 2014).

16. Dirk Göttsche, "Challenging Time(s): Memory, Politics, and the Philosophy of Time in Jean Paul's Quintus Fixlein," in *(Re-)Writing the Radical: Enlightenment, Revolution, and Cultural Transfer in 1790s Germany, Britain, and France*, ed. Maike Oergel (New York: De Gruyter, 2012), 221.

17. Wolf Lepenies, *Das Ende der Naturgeschichte. Wandel kultureller Selbstverständlichkeiten in den Wissenschaften des 18. und 19. Jahrhunderts* (Munich: Hanser, 1976), 19.

18. Clark, *Time and Power*, 4.

Scholars across a variety of disciplines have shown how serial forms undergo significant expansion in the nineteenth century, an era, as Benedict Anderson notes, when the "logic of seriality" gives rise to "a new grammar of representation."[19] On a general level, a series is a set or sequence of multiple entities organized on the basis of the relationships of these different parts; the Latin *serere* means to join together or bind. *Reihe* (row), the German term for series, has clear spatial connotations and evokes a sense of sequential viewing. A common distinction is between series with a closed set of terms and those with open-ended and ongoing terms; Anderson, for example, describes how the nineteenth-century census is based on a conception of a "bound" series—x number of inhabitants, no more, no less—and identifies newspapers and popular performances as sites of "unbound" seriality.[20] Cultural history is familiar with closed episodic forms such as cycles of poems, song, and images.[21] The print landscape is also a particularly important catalyst for unbound seriality, wherein writers, editors, and readers are all constantly involved in placing ensembles of texts and images into various serial "constellations."[22] Prominent studies of the nineteenth-century literary landscape have foregrounded the effects of serialization on the novel and other self-contained narrative structures,[23] while others have focused on quintessentially small forms that reveal the intermedial resonances of print and performance.[24] Scholars have examined the European rise of the illustrated periodical and explored the

---

19. Benedict Anderson, "Nationalism, Identity, and the Logic of Seriality," in *The Spectre of Comparisons: Nationalism, Southeast Asia, and the World* (London: Verso, 1998), 34.
20. Anderson, "Nationalism, Identity, and the Logic," 29.
21. On the aesthetics of narrative cycles and their relation to seriality, see Christine Mielke, *Zyklisch-serielle Narration: Erzähltes Erzählen von 1001 Nacht bis zur TV-Serie* (Berlin: De Gruyter, 2006).
22. See Nicola Kaminski, Nora Ramtke, and Carsten Zelle, "Zeitschriftenliteratur/Fortsetzungsliteratur: Problemaufriß," in *Zeitschriftenliteratur/Fortsetzungsliteratur*, ed. Nicola Kaminski, Nora Ramtke, and Carsten Zelle (Hanover: Wehrhahn, 2014), 15.
23. See Helmut Müller-Sievers, *The Cylinder: Kinematics of the Nineteenth Century* (Berkeley: University of California Press, 2012).
24. See Angela Esterhammer, *Print and Performance in the 1820s: Improvisation, Speculation, Identity* (Cambridge: Cambridge University Press, 2020); and

popular seriality at the heart of the mass press of the second half of the nineteenth century and the afterlives of the writings of popular male and female authors across various print formats.[25] Seriality has been explored as a central feature of technical and industrial manufacturing and the mechanical production of multiple identical items.[26] Scholars have thereby examined the media-based preconditions of nineteenth-century realism, including the technology of the steam-powered rotary printing press (invented in 1843), advances in mechanized image reproduction, and the mass distribution of late-century family journals such as the *Gartenlaube*.[27] More recently, theories of twentieth- and twenty-first-century popular entertainment have described serial television and video in terms of ongoing, episodic storytelling based in the repetition and alteration of genre conventions such as the cliff-hanger, which is commonly traced back to nineteenth-century print.[28]

Building on this work, I am particularly interested in the effects serial forms have in modeling the passing of time, creating new senses of the present, and allowing new points of access to the past, present, and future. The genres and format conventions that I situate at the heart of serial print and cultural journalism—urban sketches, correspondence reports, fashion plates and caricatures,

---

Clare Pettitt, *Serial Forms: The Unfinished Project of Modernity: 1815–1848* (Oxford: Oxford University Press, 2020).

25. See Patricia Mainardi, *Another World: Nineteenth-Century Illustrated Print Culture* (New Haven, CT: Yale University Press, 2017); Claudia Stockinger, *An den Ursprüngen populärer Serialität: Das Familienblatt "Die Gartenlaube"* (Göttingen: Wallstein, 2018); and Lynne Tatlock, "The Afterlife of Nineteenth-Century Popular Fiction and the German Imaginary: The Illustrated Collected Novels of E. Marlitt, W. Heimburg, and E. Werner," in *Publishing Culture and the "Reading Nation": German Book History in the Long Nineteenth Century*, ed. Lynne Tatlock (Rochester, NY: Camden House, 2010), 118–53.

26. See Christine Blättler, "Überlegungen zu Serialität als ästhetischem Begriff," *Weimarer Beiträge* 49, no. 4 (2003): 504–5.

27. On the concept of medial realism, see Daniela Gretz, ed., *Medialer Realismus* (Freiburg: Rombach, 2011).

28. See Umberto Eco, "Interpreting Serials," in *The Limits of Interpretation* (Indiana University Press, 1990), 83–100. See also recently Vincent Fröhlich, *Der Cliffhanger und die serielle Narration. Analyse einer transmedialen Erzähltechnik* (Bielefeld: Transcript, 2015).

miscellanies and proliferating continuations, and more—are instrumental in shaping the pace and scale of modern life and worth examining more closely. Following other projects that return to nineteenth-century small forms such as the feuilleton or the operetta to find traces of an emergent modernity, whether Walter Benjamin's archaeologies of the nineteenth-century urban landscape or Siegfried Kracauer's rediscovery of Jacques Offenbach's Paris, I explore how sometimes quotidian or unassuming forms had an outsize effect on nineteenth-century experience and allow for the past to be reencountered in new ways.[29] That said, examining the earlier nineteenth century runs the risk of simply framing it as a prequel to later developments such as the mass press in the second half of the nineteenth century or the birth of cinema. This book's case studies linger with this earlier pretechnical period leading up to the eve of mass printing as key for reflections on seriality and time, while also suggesting ways that this period is attuned to concerns familiar to other historical epochs and media constellations such as information overload, the inundation of images, and the attempt to find historical perspective in ephemera. Focusing on the German-speaking context of European news and newspaper modernity brings to light the unique and sustained contributions that German writers, editors, artists and readers make in reconceptualizing cultural journalism, the serialized flow of images, the literary work, and the task of history writing.

Writing Time

Throughout this book, and indeed in its title, I use the term "writing time" not only as shorthand for experiments by authors, editors, and artists in writing about and depicting time but also for the function of serial forms to organize and structure time itself. In calling this structuring potential "writing," I take my lead in part from the

---

29. On Kracauer's rediscovery of the operetta and on nineteenth-century small forms more broadly, see Ethel Matala de Mazza, *Der populäre Pakt: Verhandlungen der Moderne zwischen Operette und Feuilleton* (Frankfurt: Fischer, 2018).

programmatic imbrication of time and writing at the heart of the self-understanding of nineteenth-century writers and journalists via terms such as *Zeitschriftsteller*, "history writer" (*Geschichtsschreiber*), and "journalist." The association of the act of writing with a permanently unfolding chronicle of the times is at the heart of a variety of journalistic and literary endeavors. This common use of writing as shorthand for print publication underlies the fact that print is the dominant storage medium of the time.[30] Techniques of writing and print publication play a central part in influential studies of eighteenth- and nineteenth-century transformations of literary, scholarly, and bureaucratic institutions, and Friedrich Kittler's media-theoretical work is perhaps the most prominent (and provocative) of these.[31] Kittler places a notion of writing as "serial, that is temporally transposed, data flow" at the heart of his account of the Romantic system of writing, or *Aufschreibesystem*.[32] Kittler shows how around 1800 writing is central for displaying competence both as a civil servant and as an author of original literary works. He thereby defines writing more generally as an inherently temporalizing technique, for it fixes language, speech, and visual imagery in external forms and allows these components to be stored, circulated, and reencountered at different times: writing and other media are, as Sibylle Krämer puts it, "modalities of time management" that alter "the irreversibility of the flow of time."[33] For

---

30. Though it should not lead us to ignore the period's many important "scenes" of writing by hand. See Rüdiger Campe, "Writing; The Scene of Writing," *MLN* 136, no. 5 (2021): 971–83.

31. See Albrecht Koschorke, *Körperströme und Schriftverkehr. Mediologie des 18. Jahrhunderts* (Munich: Fink, 1999); Ian McNeely, *The Emancipation of Writing: German Civil Society in the Making, 1790s–1820s* (Berkeley: University of California Press, 2003); William Clark, *Academic Charisma and the Origins of the Research University* (Chicago: University of Chicago Press, 2007). For recent work on writing's place in more general media history, see John Durham Peters, *The Marvelous Clouds: Towards a Philosophy of Elemental Media* (Chicago: University of Chicago Press, 2015).

32. Friedrich A. Kittler, *Gramophone, Film, Typewriter*, trans. Geoffrey Winthrop-Young and Michael Wutz (Stanford, CA: Stanford University Press, 1999), 3.

33. Sibylle Krämer, "The Cultural Techniques of Time Axis Manipulation: On Friedrich Kittler's Conception of Media," *Theory, Culture & Society* 23, nos. 7–8 (2006): 96.

Kittler, nineteenth-century literature is a transformative culmination of writing's potential for creating a hallucinatory flow of imaginary sounds and images, though it is destined to be supplanted by twentieth-century analog recording media and their ability to store and transmit sound and image.[34] Kittler's vision of media as modes of manipulating time encourages us to examine the varied, and at times countervailing, functions of print in shaping the experience of time. However, taking a more careful look at the literary landscape requires going beyond Kittler's rather undifferentiated account of print formats, an account that results from his guiding concern with the break between print and technical media such as radio and film rather than with the diverse modalities of nineteenth-century print.

The work of the United States–based art historian George Kubler (1912–1996) helps us to explore in more detail how print formats put various sorts of information into conjunctive and disjunctive constellations and how these constellations have varied temporal significances. Kubler proposes that we understand different series of similar material things produced over time—iterations of a particular style of pottery, a particular literary genre, a particular architectural feature, or a particular publishing rubric across multiple decades or centuries—as generating different "shapes" or forms of time.[35] Such series develop according to their own time frames, which can span multiple generations or be short bursts. As a historian of premodern art, Kubler is interested in, among other things, forms of pottery and building styles that in certain cases are stylistically consistent across multiple centuries.[36] Differently structured sequences have different temporal shapes, and in many cases such shapes are in operation simultaneously. Kubler likewise foregrounds the role of historiography in constellating different objects and creating retrospective shapes of time. Glossing Kubler, Siegfried Kracauer suggests that the

---

34. See Friedrich A. Kittler, "Die Laterna magica der Literatur: Schillers und Hoffmanns Medienstrategien," *Athenäum* 4 (1994): 219–37.

35. See George Kubler, *The Shape of Time: Remarks on the History of Things* (New Haven, CT: Yale University Press, 1962).

36. On recent scholarship that has adapted Kubler's contributions to theorizing seriality, see Simon Rothöhler, *Theorien der Serie zur Einführung* (Hamburg: Junius, 2020), 92–101.

coexistence of such shapes unsettles the construct of time as a diachronic, linear flow: "The shaped times of the diverse areas overshadow the uniform flow of time."[37] At stake, as Kracauer puts it, is not the "March of Time," but the "march of times."[38] Kubler thus gives us tools for analyzing how various series can model linear succession and synchronic simultaneity. Print in particular lends itself to this kind of analysis, for individual serial forms aggregate component parts but they also operate in a landscape where other serial aggregations proliferate.[39] Seriality comes into view not just as one particular shape of time created by a sequence of similar things but also as an enabling feature, a template of sorts for the generation of multiple, often divergent shapes of time.

The Timeliness and Untimeliness of Serial Forms

Serial print's effects on temporal awareness can be further accessed from a variety of perspectives, and in the remainder of this introduction, I consider two in particular. First, I'd like to explore from an intellectual-historical perspective how serial patterning competes with certain predominant models of time based in the natural world and history writing, respectively. Second, I'll turn to a more print- and media-historical account of the constitutive elements of serial print.

Patterns of biological life and historical eventfulness are perhaps the most fundamental frameworks human beings have used to make sense of their temporal existence, and they have given rise to some of the most enduring figures through which we conceive of time. That said, conceptions of life and human history both undergo significant transformation in the nineteenth century. This transformation includes the natural sciences' discovery of the "deep time" of

---

37. Siegfried Kracauer, "Time and History," *History and Theory* 6, no. 6 (1966): 67–68.
38. Kracauer, "Time and History," 69.
39. On assemblages of component parts leading to temporal figures, see Lucian Hölscher, *Zeitgärten. Zeitfiguren in der Geschichte der Neuzeit* (Göttingen: Wallstein, 2020), 29.

the planet and the human species, the natural sciences' discovery of the microtemporalities of the climate and of biological organisms, and the early social sciences' exploration of physiognomy and social types. The temporalization of concepts of biological, cultural, and political life also entails a growing awareness of the historical situation of all peoples, and the nineteenth century is of course when the philosophy of history, historicism, and modern academic historiography emerge. Seen against this backdrop, serial media come into view as both timely and untimely, as alternately integral parts of projects of nineteenth-century knowledge production and countervailing irritants to such projects. To be sure, serial formats are key tools for producing timely, new knowledge about life: serialized novels help narrate the course of an individual's life, and episodic travelogues of scientific exploration and discovery, culminating in Darwin, help to reimagine the lives of nations and of the human race.[40] National literary canons rely not only on a broad sense of the "life" of the nation but also on the connection of a sequence of works to the lives of individual authors. Historians, in turn, have likewise long depended on serial forms to lend structure to historical time, whether by the year-to-year chronicling of historical events or by leaning on concepts of linear unfolding or modernizing progression. Through segmentation and the promise of continuation, historians use serial forms to break the past into distinct epochs and manage expectations about the future. However, serial forms can also generate shapes of time that break with temporal figures of monodirectional historical unfolding and can thus be seen as untimely counterpoints to predominant organicist and historicist shapes of time. Considering the particularities of serial form reveals specific media times that cannot be subsumed into natural or historical time.

---

40. See Noah Heringman, *Deep Time: A Literary History* (Princeton, NJ: Princeton University Press, 2023). On seriality's role in nineteenth-century science, see Nick Hopwood, Simon Schaffer, and Jim Secord, "Seriality and Scientific Objects in the Nineteenth Century," *History of Science* 48, nos. 3–4 (2010): 251–80. On seriality's role in addressing epistemic uncertainty, see Malika Maskarinec, "Introduction," in *Truth in Serial Form: Serial Formats and the Form of the Series (1850–1930)*, ed. Malika Maskarinec (Berlin: De Gruyter, 2023).

Ephemerality and the Time of Life

The association of serial print with ephemerality has been ubiquitous since the early days of print and remained a commonplace in the nineteenth century.⁴¹ In Ancient Greek, *ephemeros* means daily or lasting a single day; it is also the word for insects and plants with short life spans. The association of print with the impermanence of life builds on long-standing traditions of meditating on the transience (*Vergänglichkeit*) of the world. Sixteenth- and seventeenth-century genre painting, for example, depicts the decay of biological life in still-life, memento mori, and vanitas motifs and allegorical scenes of everyday life through a variety of interchangeable tropes evocative of the fleetingness of human affairs: skulls, dust and smoke, instruments of time measurement, natural objects in various states of decay, various features of the seasons, and various kinds of paper, writing, and print. At the same time as they encourage viewers to contemplate frames of time, though, these images operate within an abiding detemporalized Christian religious-philosophical worldview. From the perspective of divine eternity, all worldly transience is a repetition of the same. To the extent that worldly life is equivalently transient, individual scenes remain "irredeemably ahistorical," for they represent archetypal structures rather than unique historical events.⁴²

Various scholars have shown how modern understandings of time revalue the Christian concept of *Vergänglichkeit*. Sociologists have dated the beginnings of modern conceptions of time to the sixteenth and seventeenth centuries, when, as Niklas Luhmann argues, the functional differentiation of social life starts to decouple experiences of time from the individual life cycle.⁴³ Elena Esposito

---

41. See Joachim Krausse, "Ephemer," in *Ästhetische Grundbegriffe*, ed. Karlheinz Barck et al., vol. 2 (Stuttgart: Metzler, 2001), 242.

42. As Koerner puts it, human activities are represented as "ongoing in the always present, and therefore permanently timeless, here and now," "suspended between the beginning and the end but irredeemably *ahistorical*." Joseph Leo Koerner, *Bosch and Breugel: From Enemy Painting to Everday Life* (Princeton, NJ: Princeton University Press, 2016), 186.

43. Niklas Luhmann, "Temporalisierung von Komplexität: Zur Semantik neuzeitlicher Zeitbegriffe," in *Gesellschaftsstrukur und Semantik*, vol. 1 (Frankfurt: Suhrkamp, 1980), 257.

shows how the emergent discourse of fashion in particular frees tropes of transience from religious connotations of permanence and impermanence.[44] Similarly, Hans Blumenberg has described how modern science discovers micro- and macrotemporal scales incommensurate with the time of individual life. In his far-reaching study of conceptions of the times of life (*Lebenszeit*) and of the world (*Weltzeit*) and their shifting interrelation throughout history, Blumenberg explores the effects of diverse systems of knowledge on temporal awareness and the ambivalent relationships of these systems to experiences of time anthropologically grounded in individual life.[45] Blumenberg's study includes a consideration of how Enlightenment scholars come to terms with scientific progress as something that transcends the time span of individual scientists' lives, for example, and how the nineteenth century historicizes the understanding of world time. It is a consensus view in this scholarship that various print formats play a central role in shaping perceptions of time, whether in the realm of fashion journalism, yearly calendars and almanacs, or scientific journals.[46] Serial formats are commonly tied to seasonal, calendrical, or otherwise cyclical shapes of time but also open onto more indeterminate temporal frameworks. To take one example, we might consider the common journal title *Ephemerides*. This term originally referred to the movement of planets and stars over the course of the year before becoming, in the eighteenth century, a general synonym for a periodical that tracks ongoing events across a variety of realms, including theater, the literary market, and commerce. In effect, the periodical landscape's calibration with calendrical time is loosened as it comes to track the logics of different social and cultural realms.

Serial print's propensity for going quickly out of date and being quickly discarded is the basis for associating it with the brevity of life. Yet the figure of print ephemerality is likewise a point of contrast to

---

44. Elena Esposito, *Die Verbindlichkeit des Vorübergehenden: Paradoxien der Mode*, trans. Allesandra Corti (Frankfurt: Suhrkamp, 2004).

45. Hans Blumenberg, *Lebenszeit und Weltzeit* (Frankfurt: Suhrkamp, 1986).

46. On fashion journalism, see Esposito, *Die Verbindlichkeit des Vorübergehenden*, 107; on periodicals as catalysts of the temporalization of the natural sciences, see Lepenies, *Das Ende der Naturgeschichte*, 103.

a different life-related metaphor at work in the literary realm, namely that of the literary work as an organic whole, which pits ephemerality against the notion of a fully realized, "living" form. As it develops in the late eighteenth century, the notion of the work as organism posits the coherent relation of component parts of the work and its formation, genesis, or *Bildung*.[47] This sense of the work is a cornerstone of idealist aesthetics and is often associated with the place in the author's biographical development that the work represents. Furthermore, the concept of the work helps critics, authors, and readers to distinguish the works of canonical authors from the heterogeneity of periodical literature and to valorize classicizing shapes of time organized around notions of completion and monumentality. Nineteenth- and twentieth-century theories of the bildungsroman are informed by the intertwining concepts of formation and development favored by so many novelists, philosophers, historians, and scientists of the period.

The term *Entwicklung* (development, unfolding) shows how certain concepts can be associated both with life and its inanimate media-based alternatives. On the one hand, the term connotes the development of an individual person, providing a shape of time proper to the bildungsroman and other realist genres: the story is over when the hero's formation is complete or when all knots have been disentangled.[48] On the other hand, though, writers apply connotations of unwrapping, unfolding, and disentangling to the print landscape, envisioning it as a complexly knotted or entangled system made up of unrelated materials.[49] In the 1798 introduction to

---

47. See Wolfgang Thierse, "'Das Ganze aber ist das, was Anfang, Mitte und Ende hat.' Problemgeschichtliche Beobachtungen zur Geschichte des Werkbegriffs," in *Ästhetische Grundbegriffe. Studien zu einem historischen Wörterbuch*, ed. Karlheinz Barck, Martin Fontius, and Wolfgang Thierse (Stuttgart: Metzler, 1990), 378–414.

48. On development as a nineteenth-century temporal figure, see most recently Hölscher, *Zeitgärten*, 234–43. On the trope of narrative disentanglement, see Sabine Mainberger, *Die Kunst des Aufzählens. Elemente zu einer Poetik des Enumerativen* (Berlin: De Gruyter, 2003), 9.

49. Kubler describes cultural activity as "cultural bundles consisting of variegated fibrous lengths of happening, mostly long, and many brief." Kubler, *The Shape of Time*, 111.

their journal *London und Paris* (London and Paris), for example, F. J. Bertuch and K. A. Böttiger call upon readers to imagine the current "age of paper" as a "thousandfold intertwined knot [*Knäuel*] of written and oral traditions," yet they defer the project of "disentangling" (*entwirren*) this knot to some future historian.⁵⁰ Gerhard von Graevenitz's account of the late nineteenth-century's cultural imaginary likewise invokes the metaphor of a knot. For Graevenitz, the temporal awareness of the epoch is a "grotesque chronotope" made up of the coexistence of multiple images of historical time: "a knot of time [*Zeitknäuel*] that is without direction . . . and that is made up of discontinuities, of things that don't fit together, and of quick labile and explosive alternations; and at the knot's core [is] a zone of coldness and anxiety."⁵¹ For Graevenitz, this shape of time is grounded in the media culture of the period: illustrated journals, exhibitions and world's fairs, and novels and other literary genres. It is the media landscape, in other words, rather than the time of individual life, that generates this knotted, entangled time and that serves as an unruly backdrop for the many attempts to posit coherence and organic unity in the period.

Scholars have come down differently on the question of seriality's timeliness in reconceptualizing human life in the nineteenth century. In their study of the Victorian serial, for example, Linda Hughes and Michael Lund argue that serial forms offer new ways of representing the temporalities of individual lives, with uncertainty about how fictional narratives will end paralleling readers' uncertainties about their own futures.⁵² Carl Gelderloos's work on early twentieth-century modernist photobooks also shows how artists and writers use mechanical media technologies to "privilege biological

---

50. Friedrich Justin Bertuch and Karl August Böttiger, "Plan und Ankündigung," *London und Paris* 1, no. 1 (1798): 4, 3.
51. Graevenitz, *Theodor Fontane: ängstliche Moderne*, 703.
52. As Linda K. Hughes and Michael Lund argue, "the serial embodied a vision, a perspective on stories about life, intrinsic to Victorian culture." Linda K. Hughes and Michael Lund, *The Victorian Serial* (Charlottesville: University of Virginia Press, 1991), 12. See also Kelleter's discussion of "neo-vitalist" poststructuralist and posthumanist approaches to popular seriality that portray seriality as a "fundamental life force of culture." Kelleter, "Five Ways of Looking," 11.

and natural temporalities."⁵³ Helmut Müller-Sievers takes a different tack, exploring how serial forms transcend the parameters of individual life and "natural" time. Serialized fiction, like the serial television of the early twenty-first century, generates the sense that multiple series are going on simultaneously: "The series allows for an experience of time that is not the supposedly personal time of the individual, the time that is broken up into daily segments."⁵⁴ In occurring without our awareness and even potentially continuing after our own deaths, series give readers and viewers a sense of the difference between "our time" and "time without us": "[the series] will continue like the world on the day after our death."⁵⁵ Building on Blumenberg's reflections on disjunctions between *Lebenszeit* and *Weltzeit*, Müller-Sievers encourages us to think about how the times of serial media have recursive effects on times that we think of as our own, times proper to our own lives.⁵⁶ More generally, Müller-Sievers prompts us to consider how serial media create shapes of time that point to structures that are more expansive—or more miniscule—than those contained by any notion of life. I return to serial formats' divergences from patterns of natural time at key moments throughout my book, for these divergences help to structure the coordinates upon which the authors and editors I discuss write time.⁵⁷

---

53. Carl Gelderloos, *Biological Modernism: The New Human in Weimar Culture* (Evanston, IL: Northwestern University Press, 2020), 67.
54. Helmut Müller-Sievers, "Kinematik des Erzählens: Zum Stand der amerikanischen Fernsehserie," *Merkur* 64, no. 794 (2015): 29.
55. Müller-Sievers, "Kinematik des Erzählens," 29.
56. John Rieder pursues a similar line of thought in the context of the genre system of science fiction: "Seriality, one could say, constructs a set of continuities in the generic world that simultaneously accentuate its discontinuity from other domains of experience. It establishes a periodicity that punctuates the other routines and duties of the mass audience by separating itself from them and asserting a life, or at least a temporality, of its own. Thus the topic of seriality leads from repetition to collective fantasy, on the one hand, and to the temporal rhythms of mass culture, on the other." John Rieder, *Science Fiction and the Mass Cultural Genre System* (Middletown, CT: Wesleyan University Press, 2017), 57.
57. The work of Wolfgang Ernst, who tells a story of how the microtemporalities of electric and electronic media withhold themselves from human perception, is also instructive here. Wolfgang Ernst, *Chronopoetics: The Temporal Being*

"Untimely" Histories?

The nineteenth century likewise witnesses the competition of multiple modes of historiography ahead of the consolidation of history as an academic discipline. As Reinhart Koselleck has shown, the early to mid-nineteenth century is not only a time in which contemporary history writing flourishes but also a time in which academic history writing increasingly breaks with an understanding of history writing as writing the history of the present in favor of an ideal of writing histories of the past and of "completed" historical events.[58] Serial forms—the lectures, journals, and book series of which scholars, journalists, critics, and would-be politicians make ample use to address current events—are both timely and untimely: they propel developments in history writing and in the processing of the recent past, yet they are disparaged by the gatekeepers of historical knowledge production. G. W. F. Hegel, for example, dismisses journalism as a venue for writing history for it lacks the proper overview and "transforms all events into reports."[59] Hegel's rejection of historical journalism is based on an ideal of systematic coherence, or *Zusammenhang*, related to the concept of the organic work. Throughout the book, I will return to historical projects at the margins of academic history writing that trouble both Hegel's idealist philosophy of history and the historicist emphasis on completed events and that embrace the contingencies of serial formats. These projects include reporting about the revolution through the lens of fashion and popular culture, returning to archived newspapers and journals of past decades, and reactualizing the past by republishing anonymously published newspaper articles.

Koselleck's work proves particularly useful in exploring how various projects of history writing might offer alternatives to the

---

and *Operativity of Technical Media*, trans. Anthony Enns (London: Rowman and Littlefield, 2016).

58. On shifts in concepts of *Zeitgeschichte*, see Reinhart Koselleck, "Constancy and Change of All Contemporary Histories. Conceptual-Historical Notes," in *Sediments of Time: On Possible Histories*, trans. and ed. Sean Franzel and Stefan-Ludwig Hoffmann (Stanford, CA: Stanford University Press, 2018), 100–117.

59. G. W. F. Hegel, *Vorlesungen über die Philosophie der Geschichte*, vol. 12 of *Werke* (Frankfurt: Suhrkamp, 1970), 14.

shapes of time particular to the modern philosophy of history. Much of his early and mid-career work is dedicated to showing how modern social and political concepts emerge in tandem with the philosophy of history, which posits modernity's teleological directionality. In Koselleck's account, nineteenth-century history writing breaks with the earlier rhetorical-humanist model of multiple histories; this earlier model assumes that historical events can be understood on the basis of a set inventory of interpretive topoi and that the lessons of the past remain applicable because human life and experience remain constant. By contrast, the Enlightenment and especially the French Revolution erode the expectation that the past will repeat itself, a process that represents the "destruction of natural chronology."[60] The philosophy of history responds to uncertainty about the future with a linear model of time based in concepts of progress, revolution, Enlightenment, the state, and more, as well as in a vision of singular "world history" corresponding to the movement of the human race toward a common goal. For Koselleck, such an orientation envisions the future on the basis of philosophical concepts rather than historical experience, and it runs the risk of misunderstanding the present and past.

Koselleck then faces the challenge of keeping sight of a plurality of historical times in an age when history in the singular is ascendant. As part of his broader theory of history, or *Historik*, he tracks how divergent experiences of events lead to divergent historical representations, how modernity's emphasis on the new obscures patterns of repetition and recurrence, and how longer-term structures cut across individual generations and historical epochs alike, drawing on Fernand Braudel's notion of *longue durée*.[61] In contrast to the historiographical ideal of systematic coherence and totality, Koselleck turns to the realm of geology for imagining the succession and simultaneity of multiple times. The term he uses is *Zeitschich-*

---

60. Reinhart Koselleck, "On the Need for Theory in the Discipline of History," in *The Practice of Conceptual History: Timing History, Spacing Concepts*, trans. Todd Samuel Presner et al. (Stanford, CA: Stanford University Press, 2002), 8.

61. See Koselleck, "Sediments of Time."

ten, or sediments or layers of time, which he defines as "multiple temporal levels of differing duration and varied origin that are nonetheless simultaneously present and effective."[62] Presented as shorthand for the contemporaneity of the noncontemporaneous, the concept of *Zeitschichten* envisions the accumulation and storage of different temporalities: natural times, historical times, technical times, cultural and political times, and more. Koselleck thereby casts his own theory of historical time as untimely to a certain extent, for he takes aim at the self-conception of modernity even while being a product of it. Koselleck places particular importance on literary and visual forms as techniques of visualizing and representing time, and he identifies Goethe in particular as a kindred spirit. Goethe's approach to history is open-ended and provisional, and his oeuvre comes into view as a set of interrelated texts that produces a sense of overlapping frames of time.[63] Goethe is "untimely" in his resistance to the systematic thrust of idealist philosophy, his disregard for a singular "world history," and his pursuit of multiple histories in a variety of different forms of writing.[64] Despite being a rather clichéd scholarly mode (what male German *Bildungsbürger* has not at one time compared himself to Goethe?), Koselleck's valorization of Goethe helps us to envision how literary experiments can write time in variegated ways that resist the teleology of the philosophical concept and that resist being reduced to metahistorical tropes based on

---

62. Reinhart Koselleck, "Einleitung," in *Zeitschichten: Studien zur Historik* (Frankfurt: Suhrkamp, 2000), 9–19, 9. On Koselleck's theory of historical times, see especially Helge Jordheim, "Against Periodization: Koselleck's Theory of Multiple Temporalities," *History and Theory* 51 (2012): 151–71; and John Zammito, "Koselleck's Philosophy of Historical Time(s) and the Practice of History," *History and Theory* 43, no. 1 (2004): 124–35.

63. In a way, Koselleck's approach to Goethe is in line with other recent revaluations of Goethe's protean oeuvre; see most recently Michael Bies and Wolfgang Hottner, *"(Ist fortzusetzen.)" Anschlüsse, Fortführungen und Enden in Goethes späten Werken* (Freiburg: Rombach, 2024).

64. See Reinhart Koselleck, "Goethe's Untimely History," in *Sediments of Time: On Possible Histories*, trans. and ed. Sean Franzel and Stefan-Ludwig Hoffmann (Stanford, CA: Stanford University Press, 2018), 60–78. For a more extended version of my discussion here of Koselleck's view of Goethe, see Sean Franzel, "Koselleck's Timely Goethe?" *Goethe Yearbook* 26 (2019): 283–99.

literary genre.[65] Yet his study of Goethe also calls for examining other nineteenth-century historiographical projects that are in critical dialogue with the philosophy of history. The figures under exploration in my book share an interest in venturing out into the sea of print in search of shapes of historical time, provide us with more differentiated visions of the temporal awareness of the age, and help us to rethink the format conditions of modes of history writing more generally.

Elements of Serial Print

I turn now to a more print- and media-historical consideration of the basic techniques through which print formats organize distinct elements into serial patterns. Again, the term "serial" connotes linking and joining together, and I am interested in how serial forms can link both unlike and like things. On the one hand, through genre rubrics such as the miscellany, the notion of the journal as archival repository, and the conceit that journals present readers with a "flow" of multiple images readers are encouraged to explore the accidental, incidental, or disjunctive relationships of mixed contents. These conventions are all based in periodicals' status as quintessentially mixed media that place unrelated texts, images, and reports into different relations of coming before or after. On the other hand, serial forms model coordinated, conjunctive relationships of different parts in a series through structures of regular and irregular periodicity, continuation, and republication. The periodic return of the same journal or the continuation of the same story or report across multiple issues can be understood as techniques of marking time that establish continuity and duration. Taken together, disjunctive and conjunctive format conditions and the genre conventions that rely on them give readers templates for observing order as well as disorder, permanence as well as impermanence.

---

65. As in Hayden White's account of the nineteenth-century historical imagination; see Hayden White, *Metahistory: The Historical Imagination in Nineteenth-Century Europe* (Baltimore: Johns Hopkins University Press, 1973).

Miscellaneity, Archival Storage, and Sequential Viewing

It is common for scholars to use *miscellaneity* as a shorthand for periodicals' "nonlinear assemblage of parcels of text."[66] As James Mussell puts it, miscellaneity and seriality are "the means through which readers engage with newspapers and periodicals."[67] As a technical term of periodical studies, "miscellaneity" is based in the longstanding literary genre and format convention of the miscellany, with roots in early modern notions of the florilegium and eighteenth-century moral-satirical traditions. This tradition flourished in eighteenth-century moral weeklies (the so-called *moralische Wochenschriften*) and in related anthology and pocketbook formats, all of which presented readers with a deliberately varied mixture of edifying and entertaining material. "Miscellany" (*Miscelle*) can be the title of a specific rubric in a given journal, but it can also be a journal or anthology's title or guiding principle. The interest in miscellaneous material remains constant into the nineteenth century, but the principle of miscellaneity takes on new cultural authority around 1800, as expanded reading audiences grow ever more eager for ever more material. Indeed, in a piece commissioned for the inaugural issue of the *Morgenblatt für gebildete Stände*, Jean Paul states that miscellaneity is the essence not merely of the *Morgenblatt* or of all periodicals more broadly but of the age itself.

The miscellany is a quintessential small form, and formats that assemble smaller forms mirror the reading practices of audiences awash in printed matter. As propagators of miscellaneous contents, authors and editors function as much as compilers and collectors as genial creators of original content.[68] Miscellaneity also involves techniques of temporal juxtaposition. Dated in different ways and containing texts written by different authors, nineteenth-century journals place different times into relation and promote miscellaneous

---

66. Wald, "Periodicals and Periodicity," 422.
67. James Mussell, *The Nineteenth-Century Press in the Digital Age* (London: Palgrave Macmillan, 2012), 50.
68. On nineteenth-century adaptations of techniques of compiling, see Petra S. McGillen, *The Fontane Workshop: Manufacturing Realism in the Industrial Age of Print* (New York: Bloomsbury, 2019).

styles of reading.⁶⁹ Readers are required to move from one text's or image's context and presuppositions to another at varying speeds and rhythms, aided by various format and typographic conventions that facilitate transitions.⁷⁰ Though all print entails a strong tendency to nonlinearity, periodicals and other serial texts make nonlinear encounters possible in a particularly salient way.⁷¹ The dual dynamic of these articles' internal (diegetic, if you will) depictions of distinct frames of time, on the one hand, and of readers moving (extradiegetically) through an open-ended sequence of articles, on the other, is always at play. The "under the line" feuilleton section of newspapers, developed in the 1790s, comes to function as a key motor for topical and temporal juxtaposition, working in tandem with other sorts of regular supplements and addenda. Furthermore, miscellaneous cultural journalism undergoes a process of temporalization during this period. In mid-eighteenth-century moral weeklies, miscellaneous modes commonly negotiated stock virtues and vices from the religious and humanistic tradition with equal parts didacticism and satire. As miscellaneous formats come to function as a privileged mode of reporting from revolution-era European capitals, they become increasingly urgent and time specific. This can be seen in the publisher Cotta's twin journals, titled *Englische Miszellen* (English miscellanies) and *Französische Miszellen* (French miscellanies) (1803–1806), which he would combine in founding the *Morgenblatt für gebildete Stände*. Parts I and II of *Writing Time* explore this cultural journalism and its temporalization of the miscellany.

The understanding of journals as sites of *archival storage*—a key topic in recent book and media history—works hand in hand with miscellaneity. Throughout the eighteenth and nineteenth centuries (and up to the present day), it has been common to name journals

---

69. See Daniela Gretz, Marcus Krause, and Nicolas Pethes, ed., *Reading Miscellanies—Miscellaneous Readings* (Hannover: Wehrhahn, 2022).

70. On the transitional function of the feuilleton, see Gustav Frank and Stefan Scherer, "Zeit-Texte. Zur Funktionsgeschichte und zum generischen Ort des Feuilletons," *Zeitschrift für Germanistik* 22, no. 3 (2012): 524–39.

71. See John Durham Peters's critique of Lev Manovich's widely discussed distinction between "narrative," and hence linear, print media and nonlinear, "database" digital media; Peters, *The Marvelous Clouds*, 290.

Archive, Magazine, Library, or *Museum,* thus envisioning periodicals as repositories for differently timed, often expired, yet reactualizable items, not unlike the reading rooms and lending libraries in which they were commonly read. As archives, journals can be more or less organized, more "museum" than "magazine," and they rely on various techniques of creating rubrics and indexing to manage information overload. Journals' statuses as small or larger archives apply both to individual issues and to the collecting and binding together of a yearly set of issues, a practice intended by many editors, as evidenced by many journals' continuous pagination.[72] Journals and other serial forms are thus analogous to other quintessentially nineteenth-century sites of collection and preservation: the libraries, museums, and exhibitions that Jürgen Osterhammel calls the era's "memory strongholds, treasures of knowledge, and storage media."[73] However, in contrast to more stable archives, the close connection of journals to current events lend their archival quality a certain precarity.[74]

The status of cultural journals as literal and figural archives has clear temporal ramifications, as readers are called upon to negotiate a variety of coexisting frames of time. Radical temporal heterogeneity—what Michel Foucault calls "heterochronia"[75]—is just one option for journals, with some conveying an aspiration to a panoramic historical or geographical overview, as expressed in the titles of mid-nineteenth-century German journals such as *Panorama* (Panorama), *Über Land und Meer* (Across land and sea), or *Das Universum* (The universe). It is also common for authors and editors to state that the

---

72. See Gustav Frank, Madleen Podewski, and Stefan Scherer, "Kultur—Zeit—Schrift. Literatur- und Kulturzeitschriften als "kleine Archive," *Internationales Archiv für Sozialgeschichte der Literatur* 34 (2009): 1–45.

73. Jürgen Osterhammel, *Die Verwandlung der Welt. Eine Geschichte des 19. Jahrhunderts* (Munich: Beck, 2011), 31.

74. As Scherer and Stockinger put it, the "tension between currentness ... and stabilization, order, and archivization" is always at play. Stefan Scherer and Claudia Stockinger, "Archive in Serie. Kulturzeitschriften des 19. Jahrhunderts," in *Archiv/Fiktionen. Verfahren des Archivierens in Kultur und Literatur des langen 19. Jahrhunderts,* ed. Daniela Gretz and Nicolas Pethes (Freiburg: Rombach, 2016), 253–276, 256.

75. See Michel Foucault, "Of Other Spaces," *Diacritics* 16 (1986): 22–27, 26.

jumbled contents of their writings are intended for future readers, in particular readers in possession of the proper historical overview, to sort out, as we saw in the quote from Bertuch and Böttiger (see note 50). Directing archival material toward future readers—"future historians"—casts their journal as an archive that makes reencounter possible. Journals thus partake of a certain kind of permanence despite their common association with impermanence.[76] Serial print shares this dynamic with a range of other storage media, including web-based digital media. The ability to rediscover the currency of old materials bases the experience of the new as much in repetition and nonsimultaneity as in real-time diachronic unfolding and enables untimely afterlives of now-expired representations of the present.

Rubrics that foreground *sequential viewing* likewise facilitate the encounter with serialized forms. A set of largely synonymous terms casts the small forms of journals and anthologies in expressly visual terms; these include "tableau," "sketch," "physiognomy," "portrait," piece (*Stück*) and counterpiece (*Gegenstück*), "panorama," "travel" or "fleeting images" (*flüchtige Bilder*), "images of time" (*Zeitbilder*), and more. The late eighteenth century witnesses a rise in small forms that present flexible, mosaic-like snapshots of modern life, a conceit well suited for serial publication, as periodicals offer readers partial "views" of fleeting moments and promise that more will come. Such forms lend themselves to repetitive proliferation and continuation, as ongoing, serialized observation is seen as necessary to understanding a changing world. It is in this context that contemporaries register a sense of multiple images rushing or passing by (*Bilderflut*). The metaphor of flow has long been associated with tropes of transience and is a central part of the nineteenth-century engagement with time and the dynamic movement of the urban landscape. This metaphor maps onto the long-standing Heraclitean figure of time as a diachronic

---

76. As Richard Taws reminds us, "the 'ephemeral' names both that which is fleeting and that which remains, the object to be destroyed, but also the mass-reproduced, collected, and preserved." Richard Taws, *The Politics of the Provisional: Art and Ephemera in Revolutionary France* (University Park, PA: Penn State University Press, 2013), 168.

stream (which Blumenberg has called an absolute metaphor for time and historicity[77]), but like the miscellany and the archive, flow also can evoke disjunctive structures of syncrisis (the comparison of opposites) and rearrangement, as in conceits of the journal as "museum" or "gallery" of "images." The genre conceit of the tableau is especially important for generating a sense of sequential viewing. Louis-Sebastien Mercier's multivolume *Le Tableau de Paris* (The tableau of Paris) (1781–1788) pioneers a style of short vignettes about urban life and the changing city; in calling these sketches tableaus, he relies on metaphors of visualization and theatrical scenery. His work has a large influence on German cultural journalism—part I of this book foregrounds the *tableau mouvant*—and the genre rubric of the urban sketch proves to be an extremely malleable literary and historiographical form.

The notion that serial print enables visual observation profits from the reciprocity between literary writing and the visual arts, but it is also based in the important fact that so many journals and anthologies include images. Prior to the rise of illustrated periodicals in the 1830s, most journals place images at the end of individual issues, and illustrations and elaborate title vignettes are key attractions of literary *Taschenbücher*. Printed images help ground a "pedagogy of observation" (as Vance Byrd terms it), as readers are tasked with negotiating a variety of images and literary visualizations.[78] Plates depicting fashions in clothing and interior design are a key part of the broader realm of cultural entertainment, serving as markers of moral and cultural standing. These images document new fashions and luxury products and help readers visualize historical differences and change over time. Caricatures, political propaganda, and time-specific "image journalism" all become staples of serial print in the revolutionary era, as publishers embrace techniques of image production that are less time-consuming than painting or engraving,

---

77. Hans Blumenberg, *Quellen, Ströme, Eisberge*, ed. Ulrich von Bülow and Dorit Krusche (Frankfurt: Suhrkamp, 2012), 103.

78. See Vance Byrd, *A Pedagogy of Observation: Nineteenth-Century Panoramas, German Literature, and Reading Culture* (Lewisburg, PA: Bucknell University Press, 2017).

which includes etching and, later, lithography.[79] Though much of the time frame I address in this book predates the technological advances that would enable the late nineteenth-century illustrated press, the late eighteenth and early nineteenth centuries witness a significant expansion of the market for printed images both as literary illustrations and as political and cultural catalysts in their own right. The visual imaginary of the period thus calls out for analytical tools that are not predicated on absorption in single works and instead invites a focus on how techniques of connecting, contrasting, and transitioning amid a profusion of different images help readers process the "flood."

A sense of being overwhelmed by images leads to the search for techniques of selecting certain ones out of the ephemeral flow and channeling them into forms of repetition and recurrence. Take the example of the writer, journal editor, and antiquarian Karl Philipp Moritz, who laments the chaos of modern life, where the pace of images rushing by rivals that of time's passing: "In the flight of time, it is all we can do just to capture the outlines of the images that rush pass us."[80] The desire to find points of normative orientation in a crowded media landscape goes hand in hand with an appreciation of printed images as consumer items to be preserved. Selecting images from the flow can be a process of the figural imagination, but it also is a strategy of lending value to specific print products intended to make a visual impression on consumers. Printed images are an important part of the discourse of luxury around 1800, and classicizing formal and stylistic conventions are often used to establish value. Part I of this book explores questions of neoclassicism and print luxury under the sign of serial form; like the Wedgwood vases and sculpture reproductions so popular at the time, certain printed images are meant to instantiate classicizing norms of beauty, yet they are also produced en masse through serial repetition.

Selecting and preserving texts or images is very much a gesture of consolidating the flow of data into clearly identifiable works. But

---

79. On the concept of "image journalism," see Rolf Reichardt and Hubertus Kohle, *Visualizing the Revolution: Politics and Pictorial Arts in Late Eighteenth-Century France* (London: Reaktion, 2008).

80. Karl Philipp Moritz, *Anthousa, oder Roms Alterthümer. Ein Buch für die Menschheit* (Berlin: Maurer, 1791), 6.

as soon as one starts to consider works as part of a series, the idea of the work's singularity appears suspect.[81] Throughout *Writing Time*, I return to how the disjunctive features of serial forms—based in writers' and readers' propensities to juxtapose heterogeneous material—challenge emphatic concepts of the individual work. In addition to being an era of expanding serial culture, the early and mid-nineteenth century sees the emergence of idealist aesthetics of the autonomous work. The idea of the work as an organic totality dates back to antiquity but also finds new expression in the aesthetics of Moritz, Goethe, Hegel, and the Romantics. Moreover, scholars have tracked the rise of this aesthetics of autonomy to the shifting copyright laws and the expansion of the literary marketplace around 1800, which leads authors to develop strategies of distinguishing certain kinds of literary works from the broader flow of print and paper. It is in this context that serial formats are commonly disparaged for lacking coherence (*Zusammenhang*) and being merely pieced together (*zusammengestückelt*). Throughout *Writing Time*, I show how serial print's tendency to take form in loosely coordinated assemblages and unbound continuations serves as an uncanny other to the ideal of coherence and unity of parts that come to be asserted ever more emphatically in this period.

Periodicity, Continuation, Irregular Periodicity, and Republication

Along with producing disjunctive textual and visual constellations, serial formats likewise facilitate the conjunction of similar entities. *Periodicity* is an essential feature of the print landscape and a defining characteristic of periodicals, for it sets in motion patterns of

---

81. "Looking back, it is not the notion of seriality [*das Serielle*] that seems paradoxical, but rather the idea that one could observe something as singular as existing in itself apart from any plurality." Elisabeth Bronfen, Christiane Frey, and David Martyn, "Vorwort," in *Noch einmal Anders. Zu einer Poetik des Seriellen*, ed. Elisabeth Bronfen, Christiane Frey, and David Martyn (Zurich: Diaphanes, 2016), 9–10.

similar items following each other at varying paces.[82] Rhythms of production, consumption, and distribution structured the systems of recurring book fairs and postal networks, the latter being the dominant mode of delivering journals and newspapers to readers well into the nineteenth century.[83] Periodic recurrence generates the expectation that more will come at a predictable pace and pattern, organizing the time of the new and of the pause between issues. Periodicity can thus inform a successive, additive sense of time, in which the release of each installment makes the previous one out of date. From the moment the periodical press emerged in the seventeenth century, it was common to calibrate journals' periodicities with readers' daily routines and seasonal turning points. The explicitly temporal connotations of "Journal" or *Zeitschrift* suggest the diaristic recording of time, and daily periodicity is referenced in titles such as *Morgen-* or *Abendblatt*. Patterns of cyclical recurrence are evoked by periodical titles such as *Calendar, Almanac, Yearbook*, and *Zodiac*, as well as titles based on the seasons, like Schiller's *Horen*, which references the Greek goddesses of time and the seasons. The seasonal recurrence of trade fairs and other commercial patterns likewise shapes a sense of newness and repetition, particularly in the fashion world, which is predicated on the rapid succession of different trends. In addition, the church calendar plays a central role in people's lives, structuring certain key rhythms of reading and writing, and serves as the backdrop for journals' recurring discussions of carnival and other popular festivities. Periodicities of varying sorts create what we might call, with Kubler, related "families of shapes of time."[84]

Periodicity is at the heart of the promise of *continuation*: the sense that another issue or installment is to come. Of course, articles, novellas, poems, and individual journals inevitably end, but even when a story or correspondence report concludes or when a

---

82. "The essence of periodicals is periodicity." Wald, "Periodicals and Periodicity," 422.

83. See Will Slauter, "Periodicals and the Commercialization of Information in the Early Modern Era," in *Information: A Historical Companion*, ed. Ann Blair et al. (Princeton, NJ: Princeton University Press, 2021), 128–50.

84. Kubler, *The Shape of Time*, 91.

journal closes shop, there is always more textual material to consume, other papers to read (at least until newspapers cease to exist). There is a certain fragility to shapes of time based on unbound continuation—the awareness that the sea of print will continue to ebb and flow—but there is also something reassuring. As with periodicity, patterns of continuation can evoke both diachronic movement—as "irresistible, forward moving stor[ies] in a linear shape"[85]—and cyclical structures of repetition, showing basic similarities between these shapes of time.[86] Structures of daily, monthly, or yearly repetition and continuation take on particular relevance in the wake of the French Revolution, which is paradoxically cast both as a break with the old and as an inaugural moment for new traditions, with revolutionaries going so far as to propose that the revolution redefines the way time is measured. Revolutionary cultural politics is wont to overlay the time of national popular life with the time of print publication. In part I I explore how representations of Roman carnival coexist with reports on revolutionary festivities in the cultural journals of the 1790s, with Goethe and other German writers turning to carnival's relative permanence as an anchor for finding continuity and structure in chaotic times. Representations of the recurrence of antiquity into the present and future share an interest with revolutionary cultural politics in classicizing shapes of time, but, as we will see, journal-based depictions of such festivals also serve as sites of critical observation, with month-to-month or year-to-year commentary on festival culture subjecting new cultural forms to scrutiny. Bringing political, social, and cultural life into resonance with the media times of print can complicate models of predictable repetition.

Irregular periodicity represents a particular challenge to patterns of regular, quasinatural recurrence. Many of the literary experiments under examination throughout this book partake of the irregularity

---

85. Hughes and Lund, *The Victorian Serial*, 73.
86. As Koselleck argues, cyclicality, too, is based in a conception of linear direction: "Cyclical movement is a line directed back into itself." Reinhart Koselleck, "Sediments of Time," in *Sediments of Time: On Possible Histories*, trans. and ed. Sean Franzel and Stefan-Ludwig Hoffmann (Stanford, CA: Stanford University Press, 2018), 3–4.

and temporal "unruliness" of nineteenth-century serial forms.[87] To be sure, this is an epoch of the regularization and mechanization of print, as Müller-Sievers has shown in his study of the rotary press, with time taking on regularized, cyclical, and indeed cylindrical shapes.[88] Rationalization and mechanization likewise condition the emergence of cinematic time.[89] At the same time, though, patterns of irregular temporal unfolding proliferate in the nineteenth century, including in the practice of publishing a given journal or an open-ended works edition in installments not yet on a regularized, preset schedule (what in German is referred to as *zwanglose Hefte*). Anthology collections frequently appear in serialized installments, yet their periodicity is often not predetermined or on track. The irregular appearance of similar items in a series reveals where the time of print runs on a schedule that differs from the predictable patterns of seasonal, diachronic time or commercial life. Irregular periodicity is just one example of how media rather than natural pregivens model expectations toward the future.[90]

Republication is a special case of irregular periodicity. It is common for newspapers and journals to cut and paste copy from other periodicals and for more established writers to try to profit from the same text being published multiple times if they can get out ahead of the often-inevitable pirated reprints. The republication of texts by established writers usually proceeds from a multiauthor journal version (sometimes referred to as prepublication or *Vorabdruck*) to a single-author anthology or works edition. It is easy to forget that such format migration is a standard feature of the nineteenth century, not least because twentieth-century critical editions often neglect publication contexts, a process of "stripping, disciplining and

---

87. As Turner argues, "we ought to celebrate the serial's unruliness and explore further its stuttering, uncertain, nonlinear and often unpredictable qualities." Turner, "The Unruliness of Serials," 20.
88. See Müller-Sievers, *The Cylinder*.
89. See Mary Ann Doane, *The Emergence of Cinematic Time: Modernity, Contingency and the Archive* (Cambridge, MA: Harvard University Press, 2002).
90. Irregular publication patterns cultivate "reader experiences with nonlinearity, simultaneity, contiguity and incoherence." David Brehm et al., *Zeit/Schrift 1813–1815 oder Chronopoetik des 'Unregelmäßigen* (Hanover: Wehrhahn, 2022), xiii.

institutionaliz[ing]" texts, as Laurel Brake puts it.[91] Evaluating the format migrations characteristic of the period involves taking a skeptical glance at the sometimes-spurious additions of subsequent critical editions. Either way, it is a deliberate philological choice to deal with journal versions or later single-author anthologies.[92] To be sure, republication in book form was and is part and parcel of the business of print. Nineteenth-century authors and publishers capitalize on the same writings multiple times, and republication helps writers evade the censors who police journals and newspapers more strictly. But, in the hands of certain writers, republication also establishes patterns of temporal unfolding. Jean Paul, for example, invests the typically pejorative terms prepublication (*Vorabdruck*) and pirated reprinting (*Nachdruck*) with poetic and historiographical significance, and I seek to visualize the effects of republication in chapters 4 and 5 (see figure 4.1). The activity of marking different versions, whether performed by authors and publishers or by subsequent readers, emphasizes each version's place in a series of distinct publication events, and writers draw attention to this kind of medial and historical eventfulness in promoting their works. Imprinting multiple dates on the same text models how texts and images can be rediscovered and reactualized at different times. Writers calibrate patterns of history with the time of publication and republication, lending new meanings to the saying that "history repeats itself."

Republication is also reconstellation, as the migration of texts from one more-or-less miscellaneous repository to another places them in new textual environments. At first glance, format migration from journal to book and/or works editions would seem to reinforce the book-centric logic and canonical standing of the individual work, a logic commonly supported by works editions and the subsequent organization of critical-scholarly editions according to a sense of

---

91. Laurel Brake, *Print in Transition, 1850–1910: Studies in Media and Book History* (London: Palgrave, 2001), 29.

92. Andreas Huyssen addresses this point, for example, in his choice to base his analysis of the mediality of the modernist miniature on anthology editions rather than on the versions in newspaper feuilletons. Andreas Huyssen, *Miniature Metropolis: Literature in an Age of Photography and Film* (Cambridge, MA: Harvard University Press, 2015), 300n9.

"complete," "bound" seriality. As my case studies show, however, the temporal patterns established by republication do not always necessarily elide the unruly temporalities of the periodical. Though my studies are largely organized around individual author figures, I explore ways in which these figures' activities in republishing and envisioning the open-ended future rediscovery of their works are not primarily tied to notions of completeness, wholeness, or organic unity. Serial formats prompt us to reconsider or at least expand our concept of authorship. Republication is also an interesting test case for the fragility of certain shapes of time, for placing different versions of the same or similar texts into a series is a choice that only some readers make. Authorial control and intention can be asserted through republication and recirculation, yet works can be dissociated from an author's life and oeuvre through the same processes, as texts float back into the sea of print to be reissued, reencountered, and rearchived.

Just as it is a feature of author-based literary history to isolate and philologically secure authoritative versions of individual texts, it is a feature of periodical studies to look more closely at textual environments and format migration. Literary history faces the challenge of discerning the relationships between various kinds of more and less interrelated texts. This is a challenge, I would propose, of discerning different kinds of retrospective shapes of time, and it is one that must be constantly renegotiated by new generations of scholars. Serial forms offer us concrete tools for addressing these historiographical challenges and for crafting new kinds of literary-historical narratives guided by the material features of the traditions and historical contexts in question. If literary history is concerned with different afterlives of literary and cultural objects, serial print offers us important coordinates through which to orient ourselves when facing the sea of print.

Tableaux mouvants, Miscellanies of Time, and *Zeitgeschichten*

The three parts of my book are organized around specific formal and generic conceits—the tableau, the miscellany, and the contemporary history (*Zeitgeschichte*)—and around adept practitioners of serial literature in each of these categories. In part I, I look at how fashion and cultural journals of the 1780s and 1790s are predicated on notions of sequential viewing, focusing on Bertuch's *Journal des Luxus und der Moden* and *London und Paris*, two pioneers of cultural journalism in the period. Bertuch's journals deliberately adapt Mercier's ethnographic sketches of urban life, commerce, and fashion, or tableaus. Bertuch is certainly not alone in German letters in embracing the tableau as a formal conceit, but he is a forerunner in aggressively including images in his journals. Bertuch's journals work with shapes of time characteristic of the discourses and businesses of fashion and print, associating both with the ever-changing generation of the new and with historical reemergence. Chapter 1 sketches the organizing conceptual and format conditions of Bertuch's *Journal des Luxus und der Moden* and his response to the "new time" of the French Revolution. I explore how Bertuch, his coeditors, and their correspondents attempt to chronicle the present and identify patterns of historical duration at work. I also explore the journal's prominent use of fashion plates as part of its broader engagement with the genre conventions of the tableau. Fashion imagery plays a central role in the journal's representation of luxury, but it is also an important part of the journal's aspiration to be itself a form of print luxury. Chapter 2 examines Goethe's representation of the Roman carnival, which was published in the *Journal des Luxus und der Moden* and accompanied by a series of images that strongly recall the journal's fashion plates. I read Goethe's piece against the backdrop of reporting on features of postrevolutionary popular life characteristic of Bertuch's and his coeditors' cultural journalism. The multiple versions of Goethe's piece in luxury book, journal, and works editions represent a compelling case of how different print formats shape the awareness of time. Chapter 3 turns to the place of caricature in Bertuch's journals and these journals' critique of the cultural politics of the Napoleonic era. Here I look at caricature as both a type of printed image and, more broadly, a mode of cultural journalism. Caricature mobilizes a variety of shapes of time, including fleeting public interest and the subversion of self-serious claims to monumental timelessness. Although associated with the history of ancient satire and classicizing line drawing, caricature diminishes neoclassical forms. Exploring Bertuch's journals' satirical treatment of recurring popular festivities, I show how his journals remain skeptical of the historical vision of revolutionary cultural politics, even while helping readers orient themselves historically.

In part II, I look at the *miscellany*, a form that epitomizes the heterogeneous appearance of the literary journal. In particular, I focus on Jean Paul's embrace of miscellaneity as an organizing principle of his works and as an inroad to reflections on time. Jean Paul is a central figure in this book who operates at the intersection of periodical literature and more book-centered, single-author modes of writing. In Jean Paul's hands, the convention of juxtaposing unrelated textual units becomes a way to model temporal heterogeneity. At the same time, he is an outlier vis-à-vis the nascent philosophy of history, incessantly reminding readers of the transience of human affairs. Chapter 4 looks at how he responds to the chaos of Napoleonic occupation; the fundamental question of this chapter is how miscellaneous, occasional writings can comment on the present day and historicize it in productive ways. Jean Paul seeks to relativize the upheaval of the Napoleonic Wars, adopting a future vantage point from which to cast present suffering as fleeting. In envisioning possible futures, he also embraces logics of publication and republication, playfully staging the reencounter with past works. Chapter 5 turns from politics to authorial persona and autobiography, examining how Jean Paul imagines the completion of his oeuvre. The works edition is a key place where the time of writing and the time of life (*Lebenszeit*) are intertwined. The fundamental question of this chapter is how an utterly miscellaneous body of work can come to an end. As I show, Jean Paul's reflections on the end of his life and the end of his works actually serve as a way of imagining serial continuation, as he filters his approach to cultural permanence through the precarious temporalities of the small, miscellaneous literary work, or *Werkchen*. In this context, I compare Jean Paul's and Goethe's approaches to their collected works editions. Jean Paul ironizes the process of authorial canonization and monumentalization when he presents readers with a body of miscellaneous works in a state of incessant continuation, bringing the finitude of the author as living person into an ambivalent relationship to an ever-growing body of work. In effect, Jean Paul makes the challenge of encountering an unmanageable sea of print into a condition of possibility for his works edition.

In part III I explore Börne's and Heine's commentaries and correspondence reports from Paris in the 1820s, 1830s, and 1840s as experiments in writing contemporary history. First publishing many of these writings in newspapers and journals, Börne and Heine cull the larger trends of the times from what appear to be insignificant, fleeting occurrences. This interpretive strategy takes on additional importance when both authors rework their journal articles into book form. Both authors hope that their serialized histories of the present and recent past can provide continued insight into the past, present, and future. Paradoxically, for Börne and Heine, now out-of-date accounts of forgotten events take on new kinds of urgency through republication and encourage readers to identify previously unseen structures of duration over time, including those that might intimate the coming of future revolutions on the basis of the failures of 1789 or 1830. Questions of republication figure prominently in my exploration of works editions written under the sign of ephemeral print forms, as Börne and Heine experiment with open-ended, ongoing editions that consist of writings for periodicals and that model different historiographical afterlives. Chapter 6 focuses on Börne's editorial projects, his *Briefe aus Paris* (Letters from Paris) (1832–1834), and his reflections on print format, historical time, and the future of the revolution. Chapter 7 explores Heine's two most important attempts at serial history writing in *Französische Zustände* (Conditions in France) (1833) and *Lutezia* (1854), including his juxtaposition of historical reflections and journalistic reportage, his critique of academic historians of the revolution, and his engagement with portraiture and caricature. Reconsidering Heine's and Börne's history writing through the question of seriality sheds new light on how they construe an awareness of historical time on the basis of textual and medial formats rather than on the basis of a philosophical-historical telos.

The book's epilogue returns to questions of the historiographical stakes of foregrounding serial literature, considering the timely as well as untimely afterlives of serial forms.

Part I

Tableaux mouvants

Ludwig Börne is one of the most adept practitioners of the cultural journalism that is the focus of part I of this book. Active as both an author and editor of some of the most influential periodicals of the 1820s and 1830s, Börne was notably abreast of trends in French and other European forms of publication, and he would end up living in Parisian exile for the latter portion of his adult life. In his early career, Börne was a correspondent for the *Morgenblatt für gebildete Stände* and wrote a series of short accounts, or tableaus, of Parisian life that appeared intermittently and anonymously in the journal over several years in the early 1820s. Such series were a typical genre of urban correspondence and cultural reportage, beginning in the 1780s and stretching into the mid-nineteenth century, and they built on the pioneering work of Louis-Sébastien Mercier in works such as *Le Tableau de Paris* (1781–1788). In a piece titled "From Paris: Reading-Cabinets [*Lese-Kabinette*]," Börne sketches the relative continuity of French reading practices from 1789 to the present. Despite the rollback of many of the revolution's achievements, "reading in general, but especially reading political newspapers, has taken deep root in the mores of the people, and one would have to dig up the French soil from the very bottom if one wanted to wipe out the universal participation in civic affairs. . . . Everyone is reading, every person is reading [*alles liest, jeder liest*]."[1] Running parallel to the ups and downs of the previous thirty years' revolutionary experiment is the basso continuo of the daily and weekly periodicities of journals and newspapers. Portraying reading as a popular national pastime, Börne turns to an outdoor scene:

> For a painter of [French] mores, there is no richer view than the garden of the Palais Royal in the hours before midday. Thousands hold newspapers in their hands and present themselves in the most varied positions and movements. The one sits, the other stands, the third walks, sometimes more quickly, sometimes more slowly. Now a report grabs his attention and he forgets to place his second foot on the ground, and for several seconds he stands on one leg like an ascetic on a pillar. Some lean up against trees, others on the railings that enclose the flowerbeds, others on the columns of the arcades. The butcher's apprentice wipes his bloody hands so as not to turn the paper red and the peripatetic pastry seller lets his cakes go cold because he is reading.[2]

Börne enacts in miniature the model of multiple ongoing scenes of contemporary life that characterizes the larger series of his correspondent reports, as he describes—"paints"—a sequence of figures, each with a journal or paper in their hands. Collected and republished in 1829 under the title "Depictions" or "Tableaus of Paris" (*Schilderungen aus Paris*), these pieces are just one of the many ubiquitous literary and graphic accounts of present-day city life in circulation at the time. Indeed, a contemporaneous book of colored lithographs titled *Tableaux de Paris* may well be a template for Börne's outdoor scene; there the artist Jean-Henri Marlet depicts outdoor reading as an exercise of civic duty but also as a pleasant and fashionable pastime (figure 0.1).[3]

---

1. Ludwig Börne, "Aus Paris. Die Lese-Kabinette," *Das Morgenblatt für gebildete Stände*, 17, no. 206 (August 28, 1823): 821.
2. Börne, "Aus Paris. Die Lese-Kabinette," 821.
3. Jean-Henri Marlet, *Tableaux de Paris* (Paris, 1821–1824), NP.

Figure 0.1. Jean-Henri Marlet, "Lecture des Journaux aux Thuileries." *Tableaux de Paris* (Paris, 1821–1824), NP. Bibliothèque nationale de France. 10 5/8 × 13 ½ inches.

Börne's sketch of the Palais Royal's garden lends his historical topography of modern French reading habits more fine-grained detail, capturing the diverse, uncoordinated movements of multiple readers as they are entwined with different journals and papers and caught up in other daily habits (which, in Marlet's image, includes intermittently resting one's eyes).

This sketch of the present affords a glimpse of patterns of cultural continuity across several decades, but Börne extends this thought experiment a step further by adopting a hypothetical vantage point in the distant future:

> If Paris ever were to perish in the same way as Herculaneum or Pompeii, and one were to uncover the Palais Royal and find the people there in the same position in which death surprised them—the paper pages in their hands would be disintegrated—the antiquarians would be at a loss for what these people actually were doing when the lava enveloped them. It is clear that there was no market, no theater at this location. There was no single spectacle to draw their attention, for the heads are turned in all different directions and their gazes directed at the earth. What were they doing? one will ask, and no one will answer: they were reading newspapers.[4]

Zooming out even further from the present moment and its connection to 1789, Börne positions himself as something of a future paleoarchaeologist, reconstructing the daily life of the 1820s as it recedes into an almost inaccessible past. He thereby amplifies the familiar trope of print ephemerality, for the papers are the one thing not entombed by this hypothetical natural disaster. The ephemerality of newsprint is also a sign of its relative newness and modernity, for the more traditional social spaces of the theater and market retain a certain archaeological legibility. Construing the strange poses of modern readers as foreign through historical distance, Börne likewise raises the prospect that it is the lack of the physical trace that holds the truth of the now-past present. As something of an absent archive, these imaginary incinerated papers are both "that which is fleeting and that which remains" (as Richard Taws puts

---

4. Börne, "Aus Paris. Die Lese-Kabinette," 821.

it), at least for the (media) archaeologist in the know.[5] Börne's hypothetical memorialization of the print artifacts of the present projects a time of the media landscape beyond individual life and raises the question of what the writing of the future will be after the demise of print (or if there will be writing at all).

This thought experiment brings key features of the era's cultural journalism and its self-reflective discourse on serial print into striking relief. On the one hand, Börne's gesture of likening the present to an antiquity rediscovered is clearly classicizing. The implicit assertion is that current reading practices prove that certain democratic aspects of civic life from the 1790s persist and that these practices and the serial print that enables them point beyond the individual lives of Börne's contemporaries, extending into the past (at least to 1789) and the future. This is a characteristic strategy of revolutionary cultural politics, which turns to classicizing shapes of time to project permanence—shapes of time, in other words, that are defined by a structure of predictable repetition and by reference back to republican origins. On the other hand, Börne relativizes this sense of duration: from a vantage point far enough into the future, French civic life is just as transient as anything else. The visual humor of his sketch amplifies this point, for the poses of the entombed readers are drawn more from the world of caricature and fashion journalism than from iconic classical sculpture. In Börne's reportage, realistic accounts of daily life converge with caricature, and the sequential viewing of disparate figures takes precedence over any absorption in classical form. As we will see, this coexistence of classicism and caricature in the characterization of popular life is a recurrent theme in the period's cultural journalism. In adapting the form of the tableau as a visual and literary genre, Börne's piece deploys seriality both as a tool of literary representation (e.g., the row of newspaper readers) and as a defining format condition of print. Serial continuation generates a more complicated shape of time than that of the ceaseless production of the new. Additionally, Börne involves contemporary readers in these shapes of time: don't readers of the *Morgenblatt*, despite their spatial and temporal

---

5. Taws, *The Politics of the Provisional*, 168.

remove, partake indirectly in a kind of democratic activity, a contemporaneity with Parisians? Börne's future history of newspapers must include the journals that his readers hold in their hands and their eventual disintegration, but also their continuation into an uncertain future. This emphasis on the material side of print is typical of cultural journalism and its attempts to survey the range of print on offer, from texts and images meant for careful preservation to out-of-date newspapers discarded for the ragpickers. Throughout this book, we will repeatedly encounter the specific conceptual and metaphorical moves that Börne avails himself of here, including the emphasis, via the literary genre of the tableau, on visual observation in tandem with an archive of assumed or actual images; the notion that the accumulation of multiple sequential sketches of the present can and should access multiple times; the idea that Paris is a central stage for the culture and politics of the postrevolutionary era; the parallel evocation and parodying of classicism; and a keen sense of print's materiality.

Contemporaries of the French Revolution realize what later historians would confirm: that, as Lynn Hunt puts it, "a new relationship to time was the most significant change, and perhaps the defining development, of the French Revolution."[6] It is common for observers in the 1790s to conclude that unprecedented contemporary events follow each other ever more rapidly and that the past is no longer a reliable template for predicting the future. F. J. Bertuch and K. A. Böttiger, for example, introduce their new journal *London und Paris* in 1798 via a sense of accelerated, disjunctive time: "The new has never become old so quickly and the old of all centuries has never become new so frequently than in the last decade, since revolution has become the catchword of southwestern Europe."[7] Acceleration is just one temporal figure available to observers after they realize that earlier cyclical models of time and history have become tenuous and that the past, even when it becomes new again, is relegated to an ambivalent sort of transience

---

6. Lynn Hunt, *Measuring Time, Making History* (Budapest: Central European University Press, 2008), 68.
7. Bertuch and Böttiger, "Plan und Ankündigung," 3.

in the face of events perceived to be unprecedented and historically unique as well as in the face of an unpredictable future. From its inception, print had always been associated with the perception of time, but the French Revolution heightens the sense that print media enable and shape the experience of historical events. As Bertuch and Böttiger note, the age of revolution is also "the age of paper" and of "newspaper scribbling" (*Zeitungsschreiberei*), and it "nearly drowns under all the journals and newspapers," with newspapers having become "the sole form of literature" in France.[8] Later scholars have deemed the revolution as much a "media event" as a social and political event, and this is especially evident in the mark made on German observers.[9] German-speaking lands had long had a flourishing network of periodicals and a strong readerly interest in travel writing but the 1790s witness a boom in reporting on the revolution, a clear prelude to Börne's *Scenes from Paris*. Periodicals in particular let readers follow the unfolding of events through time.

Along with documenting the revolution's latest speeches, decrees, and executions, serial print likewise processes the age's upheaval through the lens of theater, art and architecture, festivity and popular spectacle, fashion, interior design, and more. The cultural journalism pursued by the likes of *London und Paris* becomes particularly important for spreading news about the times to broader lay audiences, as correspondent reports detailing the latest political, scholarly, or cultural fashions fuel the sense that readers are holding "the times" in their own hands. The late eighteenth and early nineteenth centuries witness the founding of many of the most successful German-language journals of the period such as the *Journal des Luxus und der Moden* (1786), the *Zeitung für die Elegante Welt* (1801), and the *Morgenblatt für gebildete Stände* (1807). These cultural and fashion journals are particularly apt for capturing the temporal spirit of the age of revolution, for they provide a space for the kind of reflective undertaking of Börne's on broader cultural trends, on what is new

---

8. Bertuch and Böttiger, "Plan und Ankündigung," 3.
9. See Rolf Reichardt, "The French Revolution as a European Media Event," *European History Online* (*EGO*), Leibniz Institute of European History (IEG), August 27, 2012, last accessed January 27, 2021, http://www.ieg-ego.eu/reichardtr-2010-en.

and what persists, on what will change permanently as a result of this turbulent time, and on what will remain a fleeting fashion. Though many of these journals demonstratively claim that they do not deal with politics, the oblique treatment of political topics through a cultural lens is an effective way to engage readers and avoid excessive scrutiny from censors. Cultural journals do the work of "translating" between different realms and spaces of experience that Birgit Tautz has shown to be so central to the literary culture of the era.[10] These journals call on readers to negotiate the interconnected temporalities of commerce, politics, theater, the literary market, fashion, and more, and they establish patterns of continuity through serialized articles that revisit recurring events or places—especially cities, which condense experiences of actuality and noncontemporaneity.[11] Bertuch and Böttiger thereby contribute to a style of historical-cultural journalism that mixes historical scholarship and entertaining diversion and that would prove influential in the so-called *Bildungspresse* of the later nineteenth century.[12] These journals also present readers with a range of different kinds of texts, archival documents, images, and advertisements, training them to be consumers of various kinds of print, including newly emerging forms of print luxury. All the while, such journals have a strong sense of the effects of various print media on the age. As writers and editors self-consciously add yet one more new journal to an oversaturated market, the avid consumption of serial forms comes into view as a sign of the times and a trend that rivals the fashionable ideas and styles of the revolution.

Many of the journals edited by the literary luminaries of the late eighteenth century have been amply studied for how they process the upheaval of the 1790s and its aftermath. These include Wieland's

---

10. See Birgit Tautz, *Translating the World: Toward a New History of German Literature Around 1800* (State College, PA: Pennsylvania State University, 2018).

11. As Bernhard Fischer puts it, cities are "spatial condensation points of noncontemporaneity"; Bernhard Fischer, "Paris, London und Anderswo. Zur Welterfahrung in Hermann Hauffs *Morgenblatt* der 1830er Jahre," *Jahrbuch der Deutschen Schillergesellschaft* 51 (2007): 330.

12. See Gerhart von Graevenitz, "Memoria und Realismus: Erzählende Literatur in der deutschen 'Bildungspresse' des 19. Jahrhunderts," in *Memoria: Vergessen und Erinnern*, ed. Anselm Haverkamp and Renate Lachmann (Munich: Fink, 1993), 286–87.

prescient commentaries on the lead-up to the revolution in *Der Teutsche Merkur* (1773–1790); Schiller's *Horen* (1795–1797) and its turn to the aesthetic realm as an antidote to the terror; the *Athenäum* (1798–1800) of the Jena Romantics, in which Friedrich Schlegel proclaims Fichte's philosophy, Goethe's *Wilhelm Meister*, and the French Revolution to be the three greatest tendencies of the day (a provocative statement that affirms the cultural journal's typical juxtaposition of politics and culture); and Kleist's *Berliner Abendblätter* (1810–1811), which weaponizes cultural reportage against Napoleonic occupation. In suggesting that we take another look at the period's literary and journalistic milieu, I propose that there is still much to learn from specific journals and the different ways that they shape the perception of time. The tools of media history and periodical studies allow us not merely to address the conceptual and aesthetic advances of leading figures as they happen to be articulated in periodicals but also to attend to how serial formats themselves generate shapes of time. Cultural journals are sites where different periodicities and temporal rhythms coexist, where the temporal footprints of individual literary works enter into tension with their textual environments, and where key metaphors such as print ephemerality, tableau-like image flow, and the journal as an archival repository are negotiated.

Bertuch, a publishing pioneer with multiple commercial endeavors—"a regular Citizen Kane of the eighteenth century," as Seifert notes—was known for having a keen sense of the business of print and was adept at profiling his journals in the contemporary landscape.[13] He had the luck (and at times misfortune) of straddling pre- and postrevolutionary periods and living through the Napoleonic period, and played a key role in establishing Weimar as a literary hub and as a home for periodicals in particular, founding fifteen journals in eighteen years. In taking a closer look at the projects of Bertuch and his coeditors, the artist Georg Melchior Kraus, and the journalist and antiquarian Böttiger, I draw on recent

---

13. Hans-Ulrich Seifert, "Die Französische Revolution im Spiegel der deutschen periodischen Zeitschriften," in *La Révolution Française vue des deux côtés du Rhin*, ed. André Dabezie (Aix-en-Provence: University of Provence Press, 1990), 170.

scholarship that recenters Bertuch's journals in the publishing and intellectual landscape of the day.

Founded in 1786, Bertuch's *Journal des Luxus und der Moden*—the fashion journal (*Modejournal*), as contemporaries call it—is particularly well suited for exploring reflections on time and the temporal spirit of the age of revolution. Like serial print, fashion is intimately associated with newness and ephemerality. With its rise in the seventeenth and eighteenth centuries, fashion played a key role in gradually loosening the semantics of the new from the pejorative, religious-philosophical connotations of transience, or *Vergänglichkeit*. Fashion discourse emerged hand in hand with different print formats, which aided readers in visualizing new fashions and fashions reemerging from the past. The eighteenth-century discourse of fashion prepared the ground for the subsequent development of nineteenth-century historicism, and fashion's manifestation of the contemporaneity of the noncontemporaneous has been frequently noted.[14] At the same time, though, the term *Modejournal* risks being misleading, for the *Journal des Luxus und der Moden* takes on many features of what German-language scholarship calls the cultural journal (*Kulturzeitschrift*), a point that Angela Borchert makes abundantly clear in her work on Bertuch.[15] The *Modejournal*'s cultural and fashion journalism is intimately intertwined with travel writing; political reportage; the writing of contemporary history; satirical entertainment; theater, literary, and art criticism; and writing about nature.[16] Indeed, this journal and other contemporaneous serial print contribute greatly to the sense that reading about the revolution was

---

14. See Timothy Campbell, *Historical Style: Fashion and the New Mode of History, 1740–1830* (Philadelphia: University of Pennsylvania Press, 2016), 26.

15. See Angela Borchert, "Einleitung," in *Das "Journal des Luxus und der Moden": Kultur um 1800*, ed. Angela Borchert and Ralf Dressel (Heidelberg: Winter, 2004), 19. On the cultural journal more generally, see Alphons Silbermann, "Die Kulturzeitschrift als Literatur," *Internationales Archiv für Sozialgeschichte der deutschen Literatur* 10 (1985): 94–112.

16. On the more capacious conception of fashion in this time and its relevance for notions of the natural world, see Hopwood, Schaffer, and Secord, "Seriality and Scientific Objects," 261. In the German context, see especially Daniel L. Purdy, *The Tyranny of Elegance: Consumer Cosmopolitanism in the Era of Goethe* (Baltimore, MD: Johns Hopkins University Press, 1998).

perhaps the most fashionable thing to do. Bertuch's flagship journal comes into view as a forerunner of the topics and format conditions of key strands of nineteenth-century periodical literature, of what was understood at the time under the broad heading of "belletristic" entertainment.[17] So many writers who publish in leading journals are invested in the discourse of fashion and its intersections with the arts, whether it is Jean Paul and Börne publishing in the *Morgenblatt*, or Heine in the *Zeitung für die Elegante Welt*, and Bertuch is quite clear about staking out a scope for the journal that is deliberately broader than mere fashion reporting.

You might note that I gravitate toward journals founded on notions of open-ended serial unfolding—the flow and disjunctive juxtaposition of never-ending *tableaux mouvants*, as we will see in the *Modejournal* and *London und Paris*—rather than on the conceit of a select community of discussants, as with the *Athenäum* journal and its ideal of editorial and authorial "symphilosophy" or as with Goethe's art journal *Propyläen*, whose title evokes a portal into an enclosed space for discussion among likeminded friends of the arts.[18] It also stands out that figures of miscellany, serial flow, and the transience or persistence of certain styles depart from the trope of intimate, directed, and cumulative conversation and are more aligned with a sense of heterogeneity and empty diversion (*Zerstreuung*); as Goethe put it in a letter to Schiller, most journals usually only "add more distraction to distraction."[19] Though Goethe and other leading figures published multiple pieces in the *Modejournal*, they also looked down on it as unserious and "confusedly pieced together" (*konfus zusammengestückelt*), that is to say, as departing from any sense of

---

17. Sibylle Obenaus, *Literarische und politische Zeitschriften 1830–48* (Stuttgart: Metzler, 1986), 7.
18. See J. W. Goethe, "Einleitung," *Die Propyläen. Eine Periodische Schrift* 1, no. 1 (1798): iii.
19. "All pleasures, including the theater, are intended to merely distract, and the great desire of the reading public for journals and novels emerges because these writings always and most often add more distraction to distraction" (*Alle Vergnügungen, selbst das Theater, sollen nur zerstreuen und die große Neigung des lesenden Publicums zu Journalen und Romanen entsteht eben daher, weil jene immer und diese meist Zerstreuung in die Zerstreuung bringen*). Goethe to Schiller, August 9, 1797. WA, IV.12, 217.

organic totality characteristic of the self-standing literary artwork.[20] This disdain, along with a healthy dose of envy—the journal had a long, successful run, in contrast to many short-lived, more aesthetically ambitious projects—has colored the reception of the journal.

For our purposes, Bertuch's commercial orientation and his emphasis on the business side of fashion, literary production, and the book market illuminate the commodity status of literary texts, something that authors around 1800 can be prone to downplay via the aesthetics of the autonomous work. Bertuch draws pragmatically and self-interestedly on a range of collaborators, eschewing a conception of the author or editor as solitary genius and instead embracing collaborative, commercial practices of reproduction, copying, and serial production. These collaborators include the antiquarian Böttiger, the artist Kraus, the Weimar drawing school that Kraus ran and that Bertuch was instrumental in founding, and their various correspondents and contributors. Bertuch and his coeditors deliberately situate their journal as part of a spectrum of different kinds of print luxury, thereby mobilizing temporal logics of permanence and impermanence and tapping into a highly competitive market for illustrated print. Indeed, the *Modejournal* and its "foreign sister" *London und Paris* both came to be known for their inclusion of multiple images and image commentaries in each installment, including fashion plates (discussed in chapter 1), representations of popular festivities (discussed in chapter 2), and caricatures (discussed in chapter 3). Even though the technologies enabling the easy inclusion of multiple images on the newspaper or journal page were still several decades away, Bertuch's journals innovatively experiment with text-image ensembles. Presenting readers with series of different images modeled on the visual and literary conceit of the tableau is a key part of how these journals seek to process the age of revolution and, indeed, to write a provisional account of the times.

---

20. This is from an 1814 piece in Goethe's "Invektiven" titled "Journal der Moden." WA, I.5, 170.

1

BERTUCH'S *MODEJOURNAL*

Cultural Journalism in an Age of Revolution

By the time he founded the *Journal des Luxus und der Moden* in 1786, Friedrich Justin Bertuch was already a successful publisher and businessman, and in 1791 he consolidated his business endeavors together in the city of Weimar in an overarching private institution (or corporation, in today's parlance), the Landes-Industrie-Comptoir. These endeavors included a paper factory; a paper flower factory; a printing shop; publishing offices; a drawing school founded in 1776, whose graduates made illustrations for his journals and books; and the manufacture and sale of physical tools, ceramics and baskets, fabrics, chocolate, wine, and more.[1] He routinely

---

1. Gerhard R. Kaiser, "Friedrich Justin Bertuch—Versuch eines Porträts," in *Friedrich Justin Bertuch (1747–1822). Verleger, Schriftsteller und Unternehmer im klassischen Weimar*, ed. Gerhard R. Kaiser and Siegfried Seifert (Tübingen: Niemeyer, 2000), 21. On Bertuch's involvement in the business of paper in particular, see Cornelia Ortlieb, "Schöpfen und Schreiben: Weimarer Papierarbeiten," in *Weimarer*

employed more than ten percent of the Weimar population, and he took it upon himself to promote regional artisans and manufacturers and the economic development of specific principalities (the "Land" in Landes-Industrie-Comptoir) more broadly. A proponent of British free market economics, Bertuch sought to catch up to the more economically advanced English and French, and his journals and newspapers provided ongoing commentary on what did and didn't work across various branches of manufacturing, trade, and the business of print. The semantics of the *comptoir*, *Kontor*, or "counter" exhibit Bertuch's keen sense of exposing readers to new consumer items and trends. The word's original meanings range from a counting table or enclosed box to a writing room where papers and money were stored, and the term came to be a common designation for publishing houses in Bertuch's day.[2] The Comptoir was thus conceived as a physical location and an abstract commercial entity, synonymous with the *Handlung*, *Handel*, or *Institut*. As Bertuch devised it, the bundling of different artisanal projects provided a place for various artisans to "collect their work or patterns in a common magazine [*gemeinschaftliches Magazin*], where the rich enthusiast and buyer can survey with a single glance and pick something out."[3] Bertuch's mercantile worldview thus involved a keen sense of physical locations that would bring together heterogeneous products and the imperative that customers would be provided tools for gaining an overview thereof. An underlying logic of publicizing the Comptoir's products cut across the physical shop and print objects such as journals, books, and catalogues, which

---

Klassik: Kultur des Sinnlichen, ed. Sebastian Böhmer et al. (Berlin: Deutscher Kunstverlag, 2012), 76–85.

2. "Das Contör, des -es, *plur.* die -e, gleichfalls aus dem Italiän. *Contoro*, bey den Kaufleuten, die Schreibstube. In Ostindien führen auch die Niederlagen und Handlungshäuser der Europäer in fremden Gebiethe diesen Nahmen. Nach dem Franz. *Comptoir*, lautet dieses Wort auch zuweilen im Deutschen Comptor oder Comtor." Johann Christian Adelung, *Grammatisch-kritisches Wörterbuch der Hochdeutschen Mundart*, vol. 1 (Leipzig: Breitkopf, 1793), 1348.

3. F. J. Bertuch, "Über die Wichtigkeit der Landes-Industrie-Institute für Teutschland," *Journal des Luxus und der Moden* 8, nos. 8 and 9 (August and September 1793): 458.

serve to list, preview, organize, and display mixed contents. Even as the Comptoir came to function more as a conventional publishing house, the focus on visual encounters and the materiality of goods would remain a key focus of his commercial endeavors.

The *Journal des Luxus und der Moden* (1786–1827) was Bertuch's flagship publication for many years and played a central role in promoting the visual encounter with various kinds of products and art objects. The 1780s were a boom time for periodicals covering fashion and related topics, and Bertuch sought to capitalize on growing consumer interest and buying power in Germany.[4] With its "fire colored soft cover" (*feuerfarbenen Einband*), as Goethe puts it, the *Modejournal* figured prominently in establishing the reputation and brand of Bertuch's Comptoir. Initially modeled on what many deem the first modern fashion journal, the *Cabinet de Mode* (1785–1793), Bertuch's journal bore traces of the "well-bred tone" of early eighteenth-century galant fashion journalism, but it also spoke to the tastes of a growing and younger-skewing middle-class reading public.[5] In advocating for functional, "pragmatic" forms of luxury accessible to the middle class, the journal incorporated aspects of the revolutionary critique of the excesses of the ancien regime. Amid shifting Enlightenment-era debates about acceptable luxury (modest, functional, and middle-class) and unacceptable luxury (excessive, wasteful, self-indulgent, and aristocratic), Bertuch's journal sought to expose readers to new goods, and it relied on ample imagery to do so. Indeed, Georg Melchior Kraus, the director of the Weimar Princely Free Drawing School, served as coeditor of the journal for many years and oversaw the production of its images.

---

4. The *Cabinet de Mode* (1785–1793) is widely regarded as the first modern European fashion journal and served as a model for the *JLM* and for many of the fashion journals of this time. See Annemarie Kleinert, *Die frühen Modejournale in Frankreich: Studien zur Literatur der Mode von den Anfängen bis 1848* (Berlin: Erich Schmidt, 1980).

5. On galant journalism, see Daniel Roche, *The Culture of Clothing: Dress and Fashion in the "Ancien Régime,"* trans. Jean Birrell (Cambridge: Cambridge University Press, 1994), 478–79. See also Joseph Vogl, "Luxus," in *Ästhetische Grundbegriffe. Historisches Wörterbuch in sieben Bänden*, ed. Karlheinz Barck et al., vol. 3 (Stuttgart: Metzler, 2001), 703.

The *Modejournal* was one of the most successful serial publications of the period, with average print runs of 1,000 to 1,200 issues.[6] A typical issue ran from fifty to seventy-five pages and contained six to eight short articles and three to four fashion plates and other images. Articles included reports on the visual and decorative arts, on popular and high society festivities in foreign cities, on new monuments throughout Europe; theater reviews; descriptions of specific clothing and domestic accessories; reviews of various new inventions and products; and reviews of yearly trade and book fairs, including ample discussions of the growing market for luxury books and other print media. As scholars have noted, the journal's contents are considerably broader than initially advertised (another indicator that "cultural" is a better modifier for Bertuch's journal than "fashion").[7] Articles serialized across multiple issues were common, as were recurring rubrics geared toward ongoing commentary such as "fashion news from . . ." (*Moden-Neuigkeiten aus* . . .), which report on trends and current happenings in Vienna, Paris, London, and other European cities.[8] Correspondents, often anonymous, were important parts of the enterprise and help guarantee the journal's currentness; this was especially the case with the Parisian correspondent.[9] Each issue also contained an advertising supplement, or *Intelligenzblatt*, that listed manufacturers' and publishers' products for sale. The journal also expressly considered historical fashions and domestic accoutrements, frequently turning to a comparison with antiquity, more of which we will see in chapter 2. In describing a variety of different objects, some of which were purchasable, the journal created a sense of both actual

---

6. Johann Wolfgang von Goethe to Friedrich Schiller, January 30, 1796, in MA, 8.1, 157.

7. See Geoffrey Winthrop-Young, "Introduction to the *Journal of Luxury and Fashion* (1786)," *Cultural Politics* 12, no. 1 (2016): 29. See also Paul Hocks and Peter Schmidt, *Literarische und politische Zeitschriften 1789–1805* (Stuttgart: Metzler, 1975), 21.

8. On the connection of the *Modejournal* to the German discourse about Paris in particular, see Boris Roman Gibhardt, *Vorgriffe auf das schöne Leben: Weimarer Klassik und Pariser Mode um 1800* (Göttingen: Wallstein, 2019).

9. As Martha Bringemeier has noted, scholars have yet to discover the identity of this Parisian correspondent; see Martha Bringemeier, *Ein Modejournalist erlebt die Französische Revolution* (Münster: Coppenrath, 1981), 15.

and vicarious or wishful consumption that was attractive to a growing lay, mixed-gender reading public.

More than "Merely a Fleeting Page"?

The journal's foremost immediately apparent temporal point of reference is fashion's "thirst for newness and variety" and its "transient and quickly changing" nature, as Bertuch and Kraus announce in their introduction.[10] They emphatically connect the journal's format to actuality and newness, an association all too typical in fashion journalism.[11] The journal is to serve as a fleeting, "flying page" (*fliegendes Blatt*) or flyer (*Flugblatt*) that can keep up with the new:

> Fashion is a fickle goddess that changes her appearance almost as frequently as the moon; and it is with this in mind that we have made our journal merely a fleeting page [*daß wir dies Journal blos zum fliegenden Blatte machen*], so as to deliver timely updates and exact descriptions, colors and drawings of every new fashion and invention, regardless of what branch of luxury they belong to.[12]

The monthly appearance of the journal and its advertising supplement are calibrated with the diachronic unfolding of the new and with the cyclical rhythms of the fashion market centered on trade fairs and other recurring commercial events.[13]

The journal also makes a point of juxtaposing fashions past and present, offering a perspective onto the broader arc of history through the lens of fashion. As Bertuch states in an advertisement for the journal,

---

10. F. J. Bertuch and G. M. Kraus, "Einleitung," *Journal der Moden* 1, no. 1 (January 1786): 11.
11. See Borchert, "Einleitung," 15; see also Karin A. Wurst, *Fabricating Pleasure: Fashion, Entertainment, and Cultural Consumption in Germany, 1780–1830* (Detroit: Wayne State University Press, 2005), 138.
12. Bertuch and Kraus, "Einleitung," 12.
13. As Timothy Campbell puts it, the diverse media of fashion journalism adapted the "regular rhythms sustained by commercial life [as] a generative matrix for historical reflection." Campbell, *Historical Style*, 2.

In fact, a nation is characterized by nothing more strikingly and more clearly than by the sort of luxury it pursues and by the spirit of its fashions, and an accurate history of the fashions of just several of the most important peoples over the past few hundred years would certainly be a most interesting contribution to a future philosophical history of the human spirit.[14]

Fashion's ubiquity makes it a prime candidate for providing unique insight into the history of different peoples. As Georg Simmel would observe over a hundred years later, fashion is such a compelling topic because of "the contrast between its extensive, all embracing distribution and its rapid and complete transience [*Vergänglichkeit*]."[15] Bertuch's method of juxtaposing different historical fashions is grounded in Enlightenment conjectural philosophy and its proto-ethnographic interest in the customs and manners of so-called primitive peoples, as well as in the revaluing of sociability, vanity, and self-regard (Rousseau's amour propre or Kant's unsocial sociability) in defense of certain forms of fashion and luxury. Bertuch's original plan was to house historical inquiries in offshoots from the monthly journal, including a yearly fashion calendar titled *Pandora* (three volumes of which appeared between 1787–1789), and a yearly *Annalen des Luxus und der Moden* (Annals of luxury and fashion), but he ended up integrating this historical scope into the journal itself. This historical side of Bertuch's journalism is concerned with patterns of reactualization (of "the old of all centuries becoming new" as the introduction to *London und Paris* reads or of "ebb and flow") and of linear progress or decline implied in the gesture to universal history.

Inventorying contrasting fashions is a central tool in the journal's aim of compiling material for an expansive future cultural history. The introduction calls upon readers to "collect" and submit their own examples of past and present fashions and inventions.[16] The February 1790 issue provides a good example of this style of history

---

14. "Ankündigung [des Journals der Moden]," *Anzeiger des teutschen Merkurs* (November 1785): clxxxvii.

15. See Georg Simmel, "The Philosophy of Fashion," in *Simmel on Culture: Selected Writings*, ed. David Frisby and Mike Featherstone (London: Sage, 1997), 205.

16. Bertuch and Kraus, "Einleitung," 15.

writing, as the editors direct readers to consider two adjacent articles as "counter-" or "companion pieces" (*Gegenstücke*) and "archival pieces" (*Akten-Stücke*): "We deliberately place [this and the following article] next to each other to offer a gauge of the luxury of different times and nations."[17] The terms "piece" (*Stück*) and "companion piece" (*Gegenstück*) are common in the journal literature of the period, applying both to articles and images. Underlying these terms is the presumption that the individual contents of serial print will be juxtaposed with other more or less similar kinds of texts or images. The first of these companion pieces is titled "Measure of the Fashion and Domestic Needs at the Beginning of the Seventeenth Century in Germany," and it presents an excerpt of receipts of the Duke Johann Ernst von Sachsen-Eisenach from the years 1591 to 1603, which is intended to exhibit the presumably modest taste of a prominent nobleman of the region. This list is a good example of how inventories of commercial goods are integrated into the journal's broader historical profile.[18] There is an archival quality to this list, which documents and memorializes particular fashions and tastes, some of which may have become obsolete. The second piece, titled "Revenues of a French Court Dentist up to the Year 1789," is a relic of a much more recent past, detailing the unfathomably high pension (*survivance*) of a court dentist and the cost of the royal family's weekly teeth cleanings.[19] This is a past that was still the present as recently as six months earlier, in the spring and early summer of 1789. To be sure, the takeaway from these "counterpieces" is rather predictable—the corrosive excesses of the French ancien régime make the German nobility appear modest in their tastes—yet readers are also given a detailed glimpse of the material objects that filled

---

17. "Maasstab der modischen und häuslichen Bedürfnisse Anfange des XVII Jahrhunderts in Teutschland," *JLM* 5, no. 2 (February 1790): 73. The editors refer to the pieces as *Gegenstücke* in a footnote on 77.

18. On Bertuch's broader gestures of inventorying, see Sean Franzel, "Serial Inventories: Cataloguing the Age of Paper," in *Network@1800: Non-linear Transatlantic Histories*, ed. Birgit Tautz and Crystal Hall (Liverpool: University of Liverpool Press, 2023).

19. "Revenüen eines Französischen Hof-Zahn-Arztes bis ins Jahr 1789 (Ausz. Eines Schreibens aus Paris vom 6. Jan. 1790)," *JLM* 5, no. 2 (February 1790): 77–78.

the domestic life of the past. At this early stage in the revolution, Bertuch and his anonymous French correspondent are still relatively friendly to its aims; like many moderates in Germany, they turned against the Revolution after the Reign of Terror.[20] Yet this rather whimsical treatment of royal dentistry occasions a more serious reflection on time and history: as the article notes, "a gap opened up in between June 1789 and January 1790 that is wider than a century."[21] The juxtaposition of these two articles prompts readers to evaluate historical breaks and continuities and to scale frames of time up and down: in certain circumstances, the present might bear more similarity to a period two hundred years ago than to one six months ago. Lingering with lists of material objects, taking stock for future historical evaluation, and juxtaposing various partial inventories are thus central to Bertuch's stated historiographical aims.

Bertuch expands on this juxtapositional aesthetic in the 1798 founding of *London und Paris* with Böttiger as coeditor. It was their original intention to shift much of the *Modejournal*'s ever-growing material on England and France into this new journal, what they call the *Modejournal*'s "foreign sister."[22] Published eight times a year, *London und Paris* shared the *Modejournal*'s size and appearance and would prove to be equally profitable. Both were important forerunners to the double-columned *Unterhaltungsblätter* (journals for literary entertainment) of the early nineteenth century, which were shorter and published multiple times a week. *London und Paris* reinforces the *Modejournal*'s focus on England and France as the most important hubs of modern cultural and political life and indeed as the period's most important "counterpieces." The parallel depiction of contrasting examples has roots in Plutarch's accounts of Greek and Roman lives, and the contrast of past and present is a mode of historical and journalistic writing favored by Böttiger, who is himself an antiquarian.[23] Calling on the reader to compare different times and

---

20. On the politics of the anonymous correspondent, see Bringemeier, *Ein Modejournalist*, 15.
21. "Reveniien eines Französischen Hof-Zahn-Arztes," 78.
22. Bertuch and Böttiger, "Plan und Ankündigung," 9.
23. Böttiger's short-lived two-volume anthology *Zustand der neusten Litteratur, Künste, und Wissenschaften in Frankreich* (Condition of the newest literature,

places had been a long-standing form of historical reflection, but it also is well suited to modern serial formats, which present readers with an ongoing stream of various kinds of artifacts and reports. The parallel discussion of antiquity and modernity is one possible permutation of this kind of historical journalism, but other variants were possible: the author and antiquarian Karl Philipp Moritz, for example, founded a journal comparing modern Italy and Germany titled *Italien und Deutschland, in Rücksicht auf Sitten, Gebräuche, Litteratur, und Kunst* (Italy and Germany, regarding mores, customs, literature, and art) (1789–1792), and the historian and journalist Johann Wilhelm von Archenholz published a multivolume anthology titled *England und Italien* (England and Italy) (1785–1787).

Juxtaposing "counterpieces" is just one technique of writing cultural history at the disposal of the *Modejournal*. The "fashion news from..." (*Mode-Neuigkeiten aus...*) rubric likewise plays an important role in including political news in the journal and contextualizing it historically.[24] The fact that many of these pieces are dated with day, month, and year lends them journalistic actuality. It is a common refrain that current events make any discussion of fashion impossible. The *Modejournal*'s very first July 22, 1789, report on the revolution is prefaced by the following disclaimer: "Do not expect any report from the realm of fashion from me this issue."[25] The Parisian correspondent usually would bring the subject back to fashion, especially to the dress and behavior of revolutionary actors, including the "fashionable political colors" (*politische Modefarben*) of revolutionary insignia or clothing items that typify the moment in some way. The interest in contemporary trends extends to the consumption of political news. As Bertuch notes in a short 1792 article on "Fashionable Reading Material," "the reading of newspapers and

---

arts, and sciences in France) (1796) contains a piece titled "Two Parallels" that addresses "revolutionary women in modern Paris and in ancient Rome," and "revolutionary courts in Athens and Paris."

24. On the increased influence of political debates on fashion during the revolution, see Wolfgang Cilleßen, "Modezeitschriften," in *Von Almanach bis Zeitung. Ein Handbuch der Medien in Deutschland 1700–1800*, ed. Ernst Fischer, Wilhelm Haefs, and York-Gothart Mix (Munich: Beck, 1999), 209–10.

25. "Mode-Neuigkeiten," *JLM* 4, no. 8 (August 1789): 345.

political flyers and pamphlets" has become an all-consuming fashion in its own right: "From the regent and ministers down to the woodcleaver in the street and the farmer in the village tavern, from the lady in the dressing room to the servant girl in the kitchen, everyone now is reading newspapers."[26] Reading comes into view as something more than just vicarious involvement in distant events: if reading about politics is a specifically revolutionary fashion, then German readers are as à la mode as anyone.

The trope of the revolution as *the* ultimate fashion of the day is also never far from the minds of editors, correspondents, and readers. As the *Modejournal*'s Parisian correspondent writes, political news is a proper topic for the journal because politics is itself an expression of fashion: "In France, politics is now the only universal fashion that exists, it is that through which everything courses and from which an entirely new spirit of the luxury of the nation and its pleasures is developing."[27] This statement reveals a bit more of Bertuch's attempt to track historical time via the practices of foreign peoples, trends in manufacturing and entertainment, and the circulation of ideas. To this end, the journal presents readers with excerpts from a new French dictionary of political terms (a "Revolutionary Fashion Dictionary") and its redefinition of terms such as "nation," "people," "citizen," or "state," or with a copy of the French revolutionary calendar, calibrated for reader reference with the Gregorian calendar, to which I'll return later in this chapter.[28] Yet pejorative inflections of the topos of the revolution as (mere) fashion are always close at hand. Amid the growing political violence in 1792 and 1793, the journal starts carrying satirical articles about being cured of the "French fashion fever" (*fränzosische Mode-Fieber*).[29] The association of revo-

---

26. This appears as a supplement Bertuch wrote for a piece on reading fashions in Germany. "Ueber Mode-Epoken in der Teutschen Lektüre, mit einem Zusatz der Herausgeber," *JLM* 7, no. 11 (November 1792): 557.
27. "Mode-Neuigkeiten aus Frankreich," *JLM* 5, no. 8 (August 1790): 460.
28. See "Neustes Revolutions-Mode-Wörterbuch," *JLM* 7, no. 2 (February 1792): 57–74; and "Die beyden Kalender, der neuheidnische und altchristliche," *JLM* 9, no. 1 (January 1794): 3–20.
29. See Jean Claude Gorgy, "Meine Genesung vom französischen Modefieber," *JLM* 7, no. 7 (July 1792): 333–42.

lutionary ideas with a passing fever brings us back to intersecting tropes of fashion and print ephemerality.[30] Is reading about the revolution a sign of something more permanent, or is the revolution simply fated to be superseded by the next new thing? Is an archive of snapshots of the present sufficiently durable for the writing of history at some point in the future? The manifestations of fashion as a broader index of cultural history come into view as an ambivalent historiographical template, for changes in fashions reveal something about different historical presents, yet they rarely fail to be supplanted by the new and unexpected.

"Interesting" and "Frightening" Tableaus

In addition to being keenly aware of the temporalities of fashion, the *Modejournal* is also very involved in the inherently visual aspects of fashion, which has long been based in scenes of display, self-presentation, and conspicuous as well as vicarious consumption. Historians have described the fashion imagery of the late eighteenth century and the serial formats that disseminate it both as the "apogee of [the aristocratic] civilization of the visual" and as catalysts of decidedly modern forms of spectatorship.[31] This visual project is at the heart of the *Modejournal*; as its introduction states, the journal is to "deliver" to readers, "from time to time," an "interesting tableau [*Tableau*] that is to . . . entertain but also to teach readers to more accurately judge and make use of this giant ebb and

---

30. As Siegfried Seifert notes, in the mid-1790s, "the political concept of fashion is used by Bertuch ever more strongly and clearly and even almost identically to describe the French Revolution itself." Siegfried Seifert, "*Archiv der Moden des Leibes und des Geistes*. Zur Wiederspiegelung der Französischen Revolution von 1789 bis 1795 im Weimarer *Journal des Luxus und der Moden*," *Leipziger Jahrbuch zur Buchgeschichte* 23 (2015): 114.

31. Roche, *The Culture of Clothing*, 475–76. See also Nicola Kaminski and Volker Mergenthaler's more recent work on the visual appearance of nineteenth-century journals, pocketbooks, and almanacs, which, as they show, guide the reader's gaze toward different consumer objects and "market scenes." Stephanie Gleißner et al., *Optische Auftritte. Marktszenen in der medialen Konkurrenz von Journal-, Almanachs- und Bücherliteratur* (Hanover: Wehrhahn, 2019).

flood through the more general overview [*allgemeinere Überblick*] that they gain from it."[32] Bertuch and Kraus link the Horatian maxim of *prodesse et delectare* to serial form, with the journal's periodicity allowing for ongoing tableaus "from time to time." As the news of the revolution sweeps across Europe, the journal's Parisian correspondent often urges readers to prepare themselves for "great, most interesting, in part also terrifying tableaus."[33] In an 1794 article on the guillotine, Bertuch describes the device as a "gruesome object" (*schauerlicher Gegenstand*); the journal's discussion of it "places it sternly in our gallery next to images that awaken much sweeter feelings."[34] Construing the consumption of cultural journalism as a form of serial viewing is at the heart of conceits both of attaining overview and of lingering with individual objects, whether they are tools of political terror and/or justice or more benign domestic accoutrements.

The frequent reference to the tableau and its historiographical potential builds explicitly on the work of Louis-Sébastien Mercier, whose *Le Tableau de Paris* (1781–1788) and *Le Nouveau Paris* (1798) pioneered the genre of the literary tableau as a short urban sketch, a textual object emphasizing visual observation and a sense of the city as a quasi-stage. With earlier templates in seventeenth- and eighteenth-century depictions of social types, Mercier deploys the format of an ongoing collection of short observations to document a rapidly changing city. He publishes one installment after another of his twelve *Tableau* volumes, with his six-volume *Le Nouveau Paris* addressing the "new" postrevolutionary age, and he positions himself as a social critic with an unsparing eye for the hypocrisies of the pre- and post-1789 eras.[35] The *Modejournal* like-

---

32. Bertuch and Kraus, "Einleitung," 10.
33. "Die großen, äußerst interessanten, zum Theil auch schrecklichen Tableaux." "Mode-Neuigkeiten," *JLM* 4, no. 8 (August 1789): 345–46.
34. F. J. Bertuch, "Über Erfindung und Alter der Guillotine," *JLM* 9, no. 4 (1794): 193.
35. As Karl Riha puts it, "The consciousness of the metropolis corresponds to the stylistic principle of seriality [*das Stilprinzip der Reihung*]." Karl Riha, *Die Beschreibung der "Großen Stadt." Zur Entstehung des Großstadtmotivs in der deutschen Literatur (ca. 1750–1850)* (Bad Homburg: Gehlen, 1970), 73.

wise straddles these two periods, and Bertuch, Böttiger, and their correspondents extensively refer readers to Mercier's pre- and post-revolutionary work.[36] The political stakes of the "new" tableaus and the *Modejournal* are relatively similar, with Mercier opposing the radicalism of the Reign of Terror and remaining a political moderate throughout the 1790s; as we will see, though, Bertuch and Böttiger critique Mercier's *Le Nouveau Paris* for its datedness during the rise of Napoleon.[37]

The tableau is of particular interest to me in the context of the broader issues of this book because it is an inherently serial form and thus a flexible vehicle for generating more writing. Though Mercier is the sole author of his tableaus, his approach encourages multiple perspectives: as he writes, "if a thousand people followed the same route, if each one were observant, each would write a different book on this subject, and there would still be true and interesting things for someone coming after them to say."[38] The tableau genre thus lends itself to scaling up and out for a variety of single- and multiauthor forms of writing characteristic of the periodical press. Indeed, the literature of the urban sketch continues unabated into the mid-nineteenth century, with figures such as Honoré de Balzac, Charles Dickens, Charles Baudelaire, and more embracing the form, and multiauthor anthologies such as *Les Français peints par eux-mêmes* (The French, painted by themselves) (1840–1842) proliferating.[39] The tableau is also of central interest to me because it is a telling example of the temporalization of format and genre conventions. The conceit of offering readers tableaus draws on the characteristic use of visual tables in previous centuries to inventory different kinds of information in written and visual forms, placing objects and phenomena in static,

---

36. On the relationship of the two works see Joanna Stalnaker, "The New Paris in Guise of the Old: Louis Sébastien Mercier from Old Regime to Revolution," *Studies in Eighteenth-Century Culture* 35 (2006): 223–42.

37. See Jeremy D. Popkin, "Editor's Preface," in Louis-Sébastien Mercier, *Panorama of Paris: Selections from Mercier's Tableau de Paris*, ed. Jeremy D. Popkin (University Park, PA: Pennsylvania State University Press, 1999), 16.

38. Louis-Sébastien Mercier, "Preface," in *Panorama of Paris*, 24.

39. On aspects of this immense body of literature, see Martina Lauster, *Sketches of the Nineteenth Century: European Journalism and Its Physiologies, 1830–50* (New York: Palgrave MacMillan, 2007).

detemporalized categories.[40] In contrast, the literary-journalistic tableau and its project of documenting the transience of urban life is based more on the temporal unruliness of serial print and the sense of a dynamic city. As Mercier writes in the preface to his *Tableau de Paris*, he has eschewed earlier topographical descriptions of the city, "the story of every castle, college, and alleyway," to instead "concentrate on customs and their rapidly changing nuances."[41] He goes on: "I have made no *inventory* or *catalogue*. I have sketched what I saw; I have varied my *Tableau* as much as possible. I have depicted the subject from many points of view."[42] There is clear evidence of this temporalization in the fact that other journalists like Bertuch and Böttiger criticize Mercier's writings for depicting the city as it no longer currently is. If the tabular inventory functioned in early centuries as a tried-and-true, largely detemporalized means of presenting information in both written and visual forms, the temporalized literary-journalistic tableau relies more on the temporal unruliness of serial print than on any aspiration toward stable classification.

Mercier's writings are quite influential in the world of German letters in the 1790s. German journals and serial anthologies of the period commonly invoke scenic viewing in their titles, such as *Der Pariser Zuschauer* (The Parisian spectator), *Pariser Laufberichte* (Paris walking reports), *Zeichnungen zu einem Gemälde des jetzigen Zustandes von Paris* (Sketches for a painting of the current condition of Paris), and more.[43] Such collections continue long into the nineteenth century and expand to other cities, with the emergence of tableaus of Leipzig, Berlin, Vienna, and more.[44] Along with

---

40. This is a well-known story told by Foucault and others; see Annette Graczyk, *Das literarische Tableau zwischen Kunst und Wissenschaft* (Munich: Fink, 2004). See also Wolf Lepenies, *Das Ende der Naturgeschichte. Wandel kultureller Selbstverständlichkeiten in den Wissenschaften des 18. und 19. Jahrhunderts* (Munich: Hanser, 1976), 26.
41. Mercier, "Preface," 23.
42. Mercier, "Preface," 23.
43. On these and related titles, see Seifert, "Die Französische Revolution im Spiegel," 173.
44. See Kai Kauffmann, *"Es ist nur ein Wien!" Stadtbeschreibungen von Wien 1700–1873. Geschichte eines literarischen Genres der Wiener Publizistik* (Vienna: Böhlau, 1994).

Mercier's collections, another important template for this emphasis on viewing and observation is Addison and Steele's *The Spectator*, which was imitated by the German-language so-called moral weeklies of the mid-eighteenth century. Notions of newness and the image converge in the semantics of spectatorship, with many of the terms closely associated with periodicals—"novella," *Neuigkeit*, "novel," "story," "image," "piece" (*Stück*), "painting," "sketch," and more—functioning as synonyms and shaping reader expectations for more.[45] At the same time, though, the cultural journalism of the 1790s bears the trace of an essential temporalization, with writers and readers sensing what they are observing as unprecedented and new rather than as instantiations of long-standing moral truths.

The tableau is likewise a central conceptual anchor of the "foreign sister" to the *Modejournal*, the journal *London und Paris*. As Bertuch and Böttiger put it in their programmatic introduction,

> But the pictures [*Gemälde*] of the mass of people, as they drive each other around daily, amid these consequential world events in London and Paris, whipped on by thousands of desires and needs, a scene [*Scene*] of the most lively human life that is renewed with every morning that reddens the gallery of the Louvre and the gothic towers of Westminster Abbey, in short, a *tableau mouvant* of these two cities, composed and copied down by adept observers on location and at the very place, captured in the moment of the most lively movement: [it would be a worthwhile undertaking] to arrange this periodically and therefore to place, in quick succession, in the hands of the German newspaper reader and observer of ongoing world affairs, an ever-rejuvenating sketch of the two theaters that corresponds ever anew to the times.[46]

Echoing the introduction to the *Modejournal*, Bertuch and Böttiger cast the journal's ephemerality as a virtue, suggesting that its periodicity synchronizes it with "ongoing world affairs" and that the journal approximates the "scenes" its correspondents are observing in real time. Though *London und Paris* is published only eight

---

45. See Reinhart Meyer, *Novelle und Journal: Titel und Normen. Untersuchungen zur Terminologie der Journalprosa, zu ihren Tendenzen, Verhältnissen und Bedingungen* (Stuttgart: Steiner, 1987), 236.

46. Bertuch and Böttiger, "Plan und Ankündigung," 5.

times a year, the editors invite readers to imagine the journal's correspondents setting out into the city each day as walking tour guides or cicerones.⁴⁷ In this model, new tableaus appear diachronically, both in sync with daily and seasonal times and with the rhythms of serial publication. The movement of the *tableau mouvant* corresponds both to the movements of peripatetic correspondents through the city and to the forward movement of the journal itself through time. Like Mercier, Bertuch and Böttiger evoke earlier topographical travel writing focusing on iconic architecture, while offering a more temporalized vision of the city: both the city's and the journal's correspondents are on the move, changing with the times.

It is in this context that Bertuch and Böttiger argue that Mercier's model of the tableau requires medial updating, as they once again raise the question of the best format for representing the present. Mercier's writings run the risk of presenting readers with out-of-date accounts of the times: "How eagerly have we waited the past two years for his second tableau, which was only delayed because the skillful painter of scenes had his newest paintings grow old under his pen?"⁴⁸ Mercier's single-author, serialized books risk portraying the city as it appeared yesterday rather than "today":

> But who could even think himself capable of capturing this fermenting and brewing, this burning and dissipating, this precipitation and sublimation of the most dissimilar substances in a *fixed* description, and a *completed* depiction [*eine* feststehende *Beschreibung, und eine* geschlossene *Schilderung*]? I certainly can say: *this is how it is today*. But in just a few weeks, the actors, decorations, and audience are often new and the old piece is performed with new settings and for new audiences. Whoever wants to write a *book* about this only lays gravestones. But a regularly recurring *periodic* writing [*Schrift*] rejuvenates itself with that which is rejuvenating, flies with the flying genius of the times, and delivers ever fresh paintings, just as it itself is fresh.⁴⁹

---

47. See Christian Deuling, "Early Forms of Flânerie in the German Journal *London und Paris* (1798–1815)," in *The Flâneur Abroad: Historical and International Perspectives*, ed. Richard Wrigley (Newcastle: Cambridge Scholars Press, 2014), 94–117.
48. Bertuch and Böttiger, "Plan und Ankündigung," 5.
49. Bertuch and Böttiger, "Plan und Ankündigung," 6–7.

In a flurry of mixed metaphors evocative of an ever-changing present, the editors describe the present day as a "retort" (a glass container used in distilling liquids and other chemical operations) in which heterogenous materials ferment, transmute, and potentially settle. Even though Mercier himself came down on the side of open-ended literary reportage rather than of the completed work, Bertuch and Böttiger cast his bookish works as insufficiently fresh and dynamic. This passage also draws on the association of the tableau with the theater and its many moving parts, an association that Mercier himself cultivated as an author of plays. Though Bertuch's and Böttiger's emphasis is on the new, they also recognize how the past can still remain at work in the present, with some aspects— "the old piece" (*das alte Stück*)—being continued while other aspects are switched out. This temporal figure evokes the sense of a limited, repetitive theater repertory, suggesting that the periodical's format allows it to be ever attentive to the persistence of the old in the present. Yet if Bertuch was comfortable accessing a notion of history repeating itself according to predictable patterns when contemplating the "ebb and flow" of historical fashions in the early 1790s, here the return of the old seems much less predictable. The best the journal can do is keep up, to stay aloft with the "flying genius of the times."

I have already mentioned Goethe's indictment of Bertuch's fashion journalism as being "confusedly pieced together" (*konfus zusammenstückelt*).[50] Yet, like Mercier, Bertuch and Böttiger treat such confusion as a virtue, framing their journal more as a receptacle for ever-shifting contents than as a site of coherence and permanence. The conceit of the tableau allows for the juxtaposition of multiple representations of the present that also stand in an open-ended relationship to one another. Multiple Parisian and London tableaus stand side-by-side, "together" but not in any necessary or logical relationship other than one governed by the notion that things are happening at the same time. This takes us back to the logic of the "counterpiece" or "parallel." The aspiration to offer an overview inherent in the historical tableau is at best limited to a

---

50. Johann Wolfgang von Goethe, "Journal der Moden," WA, 5, 170.

series of different overviews of multiple presents—"this is how it is today"—and the task of collating multiple tableaus is left to the reader. At the same time, Bertuch and Böttiger are attuned to how the rhythms of serial print shape a sense of time and history. Despite coming out only eight times a year, the periodicity and sequence of articles at work in *London und Paris* simulate to some extent the day-to-day flow of time and impart a sense of the coexistence of multiple temporalities. In the introduction to *London und Paris*, though, Bertuch seems to temper his bullishness ten years earlier about the *Modejournal*'s ability to provide philosophical-historical overview, noting here that it is too early to pursue any kind of "serious history" of the present epoch, to "untangle" the "thousandfold knot of intertwining written and oral traditions" (*dem tausendfach verschlungenen Knäuel schriftlicher und münndlicher Traditionen*) to which the journal itself contributes.[51] In the service of accelerated cultural journalism, the tableau is an all too incomplete form of historical knowledge, but it also has the potential of being as up-to-date as possible.

"Drawings of Every New Fashion and Invention": The Journal's Fashion Plates

As a journalistic conceit and literary genre, the tableau's purchase on the visual imagination remains mediated through language. Of course, actual images do figure quite prominently in Bertuch's various publishing projects—the *Modejournal* alone contained over 1,500 images across its forty-year run—and such images were at the heart of Bertuch's efforts to shape the public's taste in fashion, design, and the visual arts.[52] His publishing house aggressively intervened in the contemporary market for illustrated print that cut across journals, pocketbooks, almanacs, art books, lexica, scholarly

---

51. Bertuch and Böttiger, "Plan und Ankündigung," 4.
52. For a useful registry of these images, see Doris Kuhles and Ulrike Standke, *Journal des Luxus und der Moden. Analytische Bibliographie mit sämtlichen 517 schwarzweißen und 976 farbigen Abbildungen der Originalzeitschrift* (Munich: Saur, 2003).

journals, and more and built on the popularity of print imagery in other European countries.[53] This also included children's literature: the twelve-volume, encyclopedic *Bilderbuch für Kinder* (Picturebook for children) (1790–1830) was the most successful product of the Landes-Industrie-Comptoir and is a telling example of an ongoing anthology based in serial imagery—"instruction for the eye" (*Unterricht für das Auge*), as Bertuch puts it.[54] The reading boom at the time, described as a passion or frenzy for reading (*Leselust, Lesewuth*), was accompanied by a concomitant *Schaulust*, or passion for viewing, and Bertuch sought to tap into this to the best of his abilities, not least by according fashion plates a prominent place in the *Modejournal*.

The fact that the artist Georg Melchior Kraus was listed as the coeditor of the *Modejournal* until his death in 1806 shows how the journal's identity is firmly anchored in the "drawings [*Zeichnungen*] of every new fashion and invention," as he and Bertuch put it, that are part of each issue.[55] This "image factory" (*Diers*) played an instrumental role in establishing the brand of the *Modejournal*, for it was responsible for producing the journal's distinctive fashion plates.[56] The images were commonly placed in a section at the end of each issue, except in the case of the occasional title plate (*Titelkupfer*), and range in size from single pages to gatefolds opening to the side or the bottom. The plates were made through drypoint line etching on copper plates and commonly feature one or more figures or objects etched in outline and isolated on a blank background, as we see in the image of an officer's uniform of the new revolutionary National Guard and a young woman wearing an informal

---

53. On aspects of this market in England, see most recently Pettitt, *Serial Forms*.
54. See Silvy Chakkalakal, *Die Welt in Bildern: Erfahrungen und Evidenz in Friedrich J. Bertuchs Bilderbuch für Kinder* (Göttingen: Wallstein, 2014).
55. Bertuch and Kraus, "Einleitung," 12. See also Purdy, *The Tyranny of Elegance*, 10.
56. See Diers, "Bertuchs Bilderwelt. Zur populären Ikonographie der Aufklärung," in Kaiser and Seifert, *Friedrich Justin Bertuch*, 435; and Birgit Knorr, "Georg Melchior Kraus (1737–1806). Maler-Pädagoge-Unternehmer" (PhD diss., University of Jena, 2003), 174.

yet "elegant demi-negligé" (figure 1.1).⁵⁷ Even though this is one of the earliest traces of the uniforms and accoutrements of revolutionary actors in the journal, there is already a trace here of the deprecating caricature-like treatment of the revolution as flippant fashion—is the National Guard officer possibly flirting with the young woman?—that comes in later issues. The documentation of particular fashions associated with the revolution and its excesses blurs the lines between journalistic reporting and social critique. Most issues contain several fashion plates exhibiting ladies' and men's dress. The journal also includes drawings of furniture and decoration for the home and workplace, as well as representations of monuments, statues, and other artworks. These plates' uncluttered style focuses the viewer's attention on individual products, design objects, or works of art, abstracting them from their immediate environment. Such images likewise sometimes show the same item from different sides, functioning in effect like something of a product catalogue. Many images are adapted from French and British sources and are accompanied by commentaries by the journal's editors or correspondents. This penchant for copying and "image translation" brings into clear view the role of Kraus and the Drawing School in image reproduction. Bertuch and Kraus make the most of the techniques on offer in the period that Mattias Pirholt has recently called "pre- or semi-technical reproducibility," and their images evoke a sense of functional use and circulation rather than an aspiration to artistic originality (indeed, it was common for Bertuch to include the same image in multiple journals).⁵⁸

---

57. "Ein Officier in der berühmten National-Garden-Uniforme. 2. Eine junge Dame im Demi-Negligé von neuester Mode zu Paris," *JLM* 5, no. 1 (January 1790): plate 1. It was common not to differentiate between etching (*Radierung*) and engraving (*Kupferstich*) when using the term *Kupfer*, as Bertuch and Kraus do for the journal's images. See Renate Müller-Krumbach, "'Da ich den artistischen Theil ganz zu besorgen habe.' Die Illustrationen für das *Journal des Luxus und der Moden* von Georg Melchior Kraus," in *Das "Journal des Luxus und der Moden": Kultur um 1800*, ed. Angela Borchert and Ralf Dressel (Heidelberg: Winter, 2004), 218.

58. See Mattias Pirholt, *Grenzerfahrungen. Studien zu Goethes Ästhetik* (Heidelberg: Winter, 2018), 129–75. On the importance of French sources for German reproduction, see Annemarie Kleinert, "Die französische Konkurrenz des *Journal des Luxus und der Moden*," in Borchert and Dressel, *Kultur um 1800*, 198.

Figure 1.1. "1. Ein Officier in der berühmten National-Garden-Uniforme. 2. Eine junge Dame im Demi-Negligé von neuester Mode zu Paris." *Journal des Luxus und der Moden* 5, no. 1 (January 1790): plate 1. Hezogin Anna Amalia Library Weimar (HAAB Weimar). 7 ½ × 4 ½ inches.

The fashion plate witnessed a tremendous rise in the second half of the eighteenth century amid the self-assertion of middle-class cultures of visual representation. Predecessors of the *Modejournal* in this regard included more developed fashion journalism in Britain and France, representations of national costumes, and seventeenth- and eighteenth-century "ceremonial" literature that offered positive and negative examples of dress and comportment for "young cavaliers."[59] The fashion plate organizes and "directs" (as Kaminski and Mergenthaler would say) vision in specific ways, focusing readers' attention on discrete clothing items and design objects, temporarily removing them from the flow of other objects.[60] At the same time, though, the *Modejournal* also trains readers to process an ongoing series of images. This dual technique of lingering with one object and moving through multiple fashions, objects, articles, and more is characteristic of this instructional approach. Fashion images fix the transience of current fashions in place, but they also help readers to visualize historical difference and gain "new alertness to the location of all dress in time."[61] Readers' activities in making their way through the journal help to establish patterns of serial viewing, as, for example, in the sequential appearance of figures as readers unfold specific images (many of which were commonly larger than the journal's octavo pages). Gatefold images such as the one in figure 1.2 from 1810 give readers a large image to enjoy; this image depicts figures from a Weimar masked procession put on by Goethe for Duchess Anna Amalia, and an article in the same issue discusses this event in detail.

This procession is organized around the history of Romantic poetry and depicts figures from the medieval romances of King Rother

---

59. See Karin A. Wurst, "Fashioning a Nation: Fashion and National Costume in Bertuch's *Journal des Luxus und der Moden* (1786–1827)," *German Studies Review* 28, no. 2 (2005): 367–86. On the "ceremonial" tradition and its influence on print of the later eighteenth century, see Werner Busch, *Das sentimentalische Bild. Die Krise der Kunst im 18. Jahrhundert und die Geburt der Moderne* (Munich: Beck, 1993), 312–17.

60. See Gleißner et al., *Optische Auftritte*.

61. Campbell, *Historical Style*, 1, 15.

Figure 1.2. "Maskenzug in Weimar am 30. Januar 1810 (Prinzessin. Rother. Brunhild. Siegfried)." *Journal des Luxus und der Moden* 25, no. 3 (March 1810): plate 7. HAAB Weimar. 7 ½ × 8 ¼ inches.

and the *Niebelungenlied*.[62] Each opening of a fold in the plate reveals a new figure, aiding in the effect of imagining the procession, and readers could learn more about it and the female figures' clothing in a supplemental article. Image commentaries are another tool for guiding reader attention, as they call on readers to flip back and forth between texts and illustrations located elsewhere.[63] It is common for images in journals and anthologies of the period to be separated from corresponding text, and the *Modejournal* is a good example of how

---

62. Friedrich Mayer, "Die romantische Poesie. Maskenzug, aufgeführt zum Geburts-Feste der Durchlauchtigsten Herzogin von Sachsen-Weimar am 30.Januar 1810," *JLM* 25, no. 3 (March 1810): 139–54.

63. "Costume der Brunehild und der Prinzessin (als Erklärung zum Maskentafel)," *JLM* 25, no. 3 (March 1810): 197–98.

readers are called on to navigate their way through various kinds of print objects.

Fashion imagery is also in dialogue stylistically and thematically with other contemporaneous forms of visual culture. This includes the moral-satirical prints of the mid-eighteenth century. With their street scenes and depictions of daily life, the print series of William Hogarth (1697–1764) resonated strongly in Germany, aided by Georg Christian Lichtenberg's adept commentaries on them.[64] Artists such as Daniel Chodowiecki (1726–1801) or Johann Heinrich Ramberg (1763–1840) modeled themselves on Hogarth and were kept quite busy providing prints to accompany novels, pocketbooks, and almanacs.[65] Such illustrations share a basic affinity to fashion journalism, with representations of the dress and behavior of different social classes and professions fueling many series. Indeed, the fact that the term *Kupfer* is applied universally to fashion plates and literary illustrations, with the term "illustration" becoming widespread in Germany only in the 1830s, speaks to this affinity.[66] Readers clearly respond positively to the task of navigating a series of related texts and images, which Bertuch and his coeditors promote with their image commentaries.

The *Modejournal* and Bertuch's other publications are also swept up in a flurry of pro- and anti-revolutionary imagery, as we saw with the representation of the uniform of the newly founded National Guard. Though the majority of the journal's images remain in the realm of fashion and decorative arts, images that deal more or less obliquely with current events are not uncommon in the journal.[67]

---

64. As Lichtenberg put it, Hogarth and artists like him, such as Chodowiecki, whose images Lichtenberg likewise wrote commentaries on, offer readers "scenes from the play [*Schauspiel*] that we see daily and in which we, not infrequently, play a role." Cited in Busch, *Das sentimentalische Bild*, 309.

65. On images in *Taschenbücher*, see Catriona MacLeod, "The German Romantic Reading Public: *Taschenbücher* and Other Illustrated Books," in *The Enchanted World of German Romantic Books 1770–1850*, ed. John Ittmann (New Haven, CT: Philadelphia Museum of Art and Yale University Press, 2017).

66. Doris Schumacher, *Kupfer und Poesie. Die Illustrationskunst um 1800 im Spiegel der zeitgenössischen deutschen Kritik* (Cologne: Böhlau, 2000), 18.

67. See Kuhles and Standke, *Journal des Luxus und der Moden*, for a systematic bibliography of the journal's images.

Copied images (*Nachstiche*), including caricatures, from France and England play a central role in the German reception of the revolution. *London und Paris* focuses on the abundant pro- and anti-Napoleonic imagery more systematically (as we will see in chapter 3), but the *Modejournal* also contains some caricatures, especially those that treat contemporary fashions and national types, as well as typical songs associated with the revolution, such as "Ah, ça ira!" (1790) or "La Marseillaise" (1793). Caricature and other forms of political propaganda are commonly produced via etching rather than the more laborious procedure of engraving. Simple line etching is favored by journalists and propagandists and comes to be increasingly associated with contemporaneity.[68] Caricature and fashion journalism share certain stylistic similarities, including the focus on dress and bodily features and the use of outline drawing and underdeveloped backgrounds. Poking fun at the silly excesses of certain clothing styles is part and parcel of the world of fashion and fuels certain clichés about gender and national types.[69] Exaggerated bodily gestures, ostentatious dress, and the depiction of facial features remain key features of anti-Napoleonic caricature and continue to play a central role in the satirical press of the later nineteenth century. As we will see in more detail in chapter 3, Böttiger is also keen to stress the roots of the representation of comic and grotesque types in ancient satire, peppering his commentaries on modern caricature with antiquarian references.

Outline drawing is where fashion journalism, caricature, and classicizing style intersect.[70] Popular classicism is a defining feature of the *Modejournal*'s visual aesthetic, which builds on a more general predilection of German print iconography of the mid- and late eighteenth century. The period's taste for antique dress and ornamentation draws

---

68. See Reichardt and Kohle, *Visualizing the Revolution*.

69. See Peter McNeil, "Fashion and the Eighteenth-Century Satirical Print," in *The Fashion History Reader: Global Perspectives*, ed. Giorgio Riello and Peter McNeil (London: Routledge, 2010), 257–62.

70. See Catriona MacLeod, "Schattenriß (Silhouette)," *Goethe-Lexicon of Philosophical Concepts* 1, no. 1 (2021): 74–82; see also Robert Rosenblum, "The Origin of Painting: A Problem in the Iconography of Romantic Classicism," *Art Bulletin* 39, no. 4 (1957): 279–90.

on the Enlightenment critique of baroque excess and profits from the "rediscovery" of antiquity by the likes of Winckelmann, Herder, Goethe, and others. This classicizing visual language cuts across decorative illustration and self-standing images meant to accompany the growing number of luxury editions.[71] In turn, the *Modejournal*'s interest in consumer items at the intersection of art and interior design skews toward the classical; as Böttiger notes in 1796, "the editors [of the journal] . . . eagerly seek to do the proper justice to the taste of the ancient Greeks and Romans in everything pertaining to the arts, costumes, and decoration."[72] This dedication to classical style extends to an interest in features of daily life in antiquity. The journal's valorization of contemporary classicizing design, including furniture and monuments and the reproduction of sculpture, busts, medallions, antique vases, ornaments, and more, is very much caught up in the pragmatic classicism of the age.[73] As Catriona MacLeod has shown in connection with the *Modejournal*, manufacturers such as Wedgwood and G. M. Klauer take part in a realm of cultural production where the serial production of identical objects predominates over the uniqueness of the art object and where classical taste is domesticated and commodified.[74] Bertuch and his coeditors attempt to tap into the growing market for printed representations of classical—or classically inspired—architecture, sculpture, bas reliefs, ancient gems and coins, and more. Art and cultural journals are important organs for the eighteenth-century popularization of Greek and Roman antiquity, and print imagery is an important ersatz for the grand tour (the antiquarian Böttiger, for example, never set foot in Italy). Even Goethe, who was able to travel to Rome, relies extensively on drawings,

---

71. See Peter-Henning Haischer and Charlotte Kurbjuhn, "Faktoren und Entwicklung der Buchgestaltung im 18. Jahrhundert," in *Kupferstich und Letternkunst. Buchgestaltung im 18. Jahrhundert*, ed. Peter-Henning Haischer et al. (Heidelberg: Winter, 2017), 69.

72. Karl August Böttiger, "Venus und die Grazien, zum Glückswunsche für das Jahr, 1796," *JLM* 11, no. 1 (January 1796): 6.

73. On classical style in bourgeois monuments, see Peter Springer, "Denkmalsrhetorik," in *Historisches Wörterbuch der Rhetorik*, ed. Gert Ueding, vol. 2 (Berlin: De Gruyter, 2013), 533.

74. See Catriona MacLeod, "Skulptur als Ware. Gottlieb Martin Klauer und das *Journal des Luxus und der Moden*," in Borchert and Dressel, *Kultur um 1800*, 267.

etchings, wood cuts, lithographs, and plaster castings as sources for his experience of sculpture, painting, and other artworks that he is not able to see in person.[75]

Small Print Luxury

Bertuch's attempts to capitalize on this strong market for reproductions and print imagery bring us to a key, final point regarding fashion plates, for they are implicated in both terms of the title *Journal des Luxus und der Moden*: these plates are necessary for the visualization of new fashions, but, as material objects, they are themselves a form of luxury. Literary products are very much at the heart of contemporary debates about luxury; as Matt Erlin notes, books are "one of the most widely circulated luxury commodities in the period."[76] The German market for luxury books had lagged behind other countries at the time, and the 1790s represents a period of significant expansion, with the 1794 Göschen edition of Wieland seen by contemporaries and later observers alike as a key turning point.[77] Along with costly works editions such as the Wieland edition—illustrated, in the Antiqua font—the period also witnesses a boom in ample "luxury articles in miniature" (as Bernhard Fischer put it) in the form of calendars and pocketbooks.[78] Bertuch's role in centering various kinds of print in this discourse cannot be overstated: as he and Kraus write in an advertisement for the journal, the journal's founding occurs at a boom time for "luxury in every form of life and pleasure," which includes the "industriousness of our scholarly and non-scholarly manufacturers," that is, those scholarly "fabricants" trained in putting letters, lines, and

---

75. See Pirholt, *Grenzerfahrungen*, 132.
76. See Matt Erlin, *Necessary Luxuries: Books, Literature, and the Culture of Consumption in Germany, 1770–1815* (Ithaca, NY: Cornell University Press, 2014), 54.
77. See Haischer and Kurbjuhn, "Faktoren und Entwicklung der Buchgestaltung," 46.
78. Bernhard Fischer, "Johann Friedrich Cottas *Damencalender* ('Taschenbuch für Damen')," in Haischer et al., *Kupferstich und Letternkunst*, 558.

color to the page.[79] The *Modejournal* profiles itself as a key site for advertising and reviewing luxury books, going out of its way to discuss new books, lexica, journals, and anthologies and giving readers a little bit of print luxury to hold in their hands with each issue.[80] There is certainly a healthy dose of self-promotion here, with Bertuch attempting to shape the criteria according to which classicizing print objects are evaluated, but it must be said that hand coloring the fashion plates is by far the most expensive part of publishing the journal.[81]

This association of print with luxury is on clear display in advertisements for the book version of Goethe's *Das römische Carneval*, which Bertuch was instrumental in producing in the late 1780s. In a 1789 advertisement in the *Modejournal*, he describes this book as "a small, interesting work" and "perhaps the first and only of its kind in this well-known branch of newer luxury."[82] The advertisement describes the paper, the typeface, the images, the title vignette, the colored cover, and more. The reference to the work's smallness aligns this product with other forms of serial print, including the diminutive, often duodecimo *Taschenbücher* or annual pocketbooks, which would commonly contain multiple illustrations.[83] The practice of offering more and less elaborate editions of the same text likewise presented readers with a choice between modest and more opulent products, and such books were a sizeable part of the market for holiday gifts. Smallness could be both a positive and negative quality, as an

---

79. "Geschäftigkeit unserer gelehrten und ungelehrten Fabrikanten." "Ankündigung [des Journals der Moden]," *Anzeiger des teutschen Merkurs* (November 1785): clxxxvi.

80. As Fischer puts it, Bertuch and Cotta "embody a new type of publisher, who, rather than simply waiting for manuscripts that they can then circulate as books, themselves become producers of texts through the array of publication forums that they put on offer." Bernhard Fischer, "Friedrich Justin Bertuch und Johann Friedrich Cotta. Die 'Phalanx' der Buchhändler," in Kaiser and Seifert, *Friedrich Justin Bertuch*, 395.

81. See Knorr, "Georg Melchior Kraus," 162.

82. "Das Römische Carneval," *Intelligenzblatt des Journals des Luxus und der Moden* 2 (February 1789): xvii.

83. See Multigraph Collective, "Anthologies," in *Interacting with Print: Elements of Reading in the Era of Print Saturation* (Chicago: University of Chicago Press, 2018), 41–43.

article in the *Modejournal* assumed to be written by the artist J. H. Meyer shows. Meyer was close to Goethe and would become the director of the Weimar Drawing School after Kraus died, and his 1800 article takes aim at the "etchings that every book or little book [*jedes Buch oder Büchlein*] receives as a dowry." Meyer is critical of "all the little etchings and etchings [*die Kupferstichlein und Kupferstiche*] that our pocketbooks and novels are teeming with," distinguishing, it would seem, between full-fledged etchings and more diminutive ones, and he criticizes the propensity of young artists to try to make money through rough etchings for this market before they have matured as artists, producing "grimacing faces [*Menschen-Fratzen*] *en portrait* and *migniature* [*sic*]."[84] Meyer operates here with classicizing criteria that contrast artistic permanence and monumentality with smallness, coherent visual form with caricature, and worthwhile "books" and "etchings" with "little" products on the print market. The association of pejorative smallness with the representation of faces is an integral part of a related contemporaneous discourse about miniature porcelain busts—another form of "small" luxury discussed by the *Modejournal*.[85] We will return to Goethe's book and its republication in the *Modejournal* in chapter 2, but I would like to hold on to the fact that the journal serves as a site for commenting on and promoting (as well as disparaging) diminutive forms of luxury while at the same time presenting itself as a modest luxury good competing for readers in the contemporary marketplace.

Bertuch's attention to print objects as luxury items also extends to more elaborate and expensive texts. In a 1793 article on "typographical luxury" in the *Modejournal*, he calls for more editions that imitate the Antiqua "Didotian letters, plates, and vignettes" of the

---

84. Johann Heinrich Meyer [presumed], "Genügen uns die Kupferstiche deren jedes Buch oder Büchlein in unsern Zeiten einige zur Mitgift bekommt?" *JLM* 15, no. 3 (March 1800): 116.

85. See Catriona MacLeod, "Sweetmeats for the Eye: Porcelain Miniatures in Classical Weimar," in *The Enlightened Eye: Goethe and Visual Culture*, ed. Evelyn K. Moore and Patricia Anne Simpson (Amsterdam: Rodopi, 2007), 41–72. See also Michael Yonan, "Porcelain as Sculpture: Medium, Materiality, and the Categories of Eighteenth-Century Collecting," in *Sculpture Collections in Europe and the United States 1500–1930: Variety and Ambiguity*, ed. Malcolm Baker and Inge Reist (Amsterdam: Brill, 2021), 174–93.

Wieland edition and for more editions of "our classical writers whose works will last centuries" that will function as "a series of . . . *national-monuments*" (*eine Reihe* . . . National-Monumente).[86] Here the aspiration for print luxury and a kind of monumental permanence go hand in hand and depend on the book taking on certain qualities of the work of art, something that Bertuch traces directly to the illustrations, which, as he notes, can transcend their typical decorative function (as *Bücherdekorationskupfer*) and "become genuine beautiful artistic pages" (*wahre schöne Kunstblätter*).[87] The discourse of print luxury also points to ways that, despite being tied to the transience of fashion, Bertuch's journal partakes of the desire for collection, preservation, and permanence. Luxuriousness can dissipate in the sensuous enjoyment of the moment, but luxury items can also call out for preservation and extended enjoyment and for being selected from the flood of consumer items on offer. The sense of the journal as a registry of different fashions as they come and go encourages readers to preserve fashion images as items with a documentary, memorializing, or quasi-historiographical function.

The use of the fashion plate to represent obsolete historical fashions amplifies this archival function, as does the use of plates to commemorate historical and seasonal events and turning points. The *Modejournal* partakes of the convention, firmly established in calendars, almanacs, and pocketbooks, of including commemorative illustrations to mark a new issue, the twelve months (*Monatskupfer*), or the seasons.[88] Such images are particularly common in marking the new year, which, in the case of yearly calendars and almanacs, coincides with their being published in the fall, in time to be available as Christmas or new year's gifts. Bertuch and Kraus's take on this convention can be seen in the supplemental plates that accompany each January issue, which they call "New Year's Presents of Fashion." In the early days of the journal, these began as fashion vignettes—figure 1.3 is one from 1790—but they later take

---

86. F. J. Bertuch, "Ueber den Typographischen Luxus mit Hinsicht auf die neue Ausgabe von Wielands sämmtlichen Werken," *JLM* 8 (November 1793): 605–6.
87. Bertuch, "Ueber den Typographischen Luxus," 606–7.
88. See Fischer, "Johann Friedrich Cotts *Damencalender*," 544.

Figure 1.3. "Neujahrsgeschenk der Mode." *Journal des Luxus und der Moden* 5, no. 1 (January 1790): frontispiece. Gotha Research Library, University of Erfurt. 7 ½ × 4 ½ inches.

on a classicizing appearance, as with this "New Year's Present" evocative of reproductions of antique gems. A "New Year's Present" from 1809 (see image 1.4) lends a classical theme topical relevance, as readers are presented with a scene of Greek heroes deliberating before the siege of Troy, an altogether timely evocation of military strategizing at a time of the Napoleonic occupation of German-speaking lands. By calling these images "presents," the editors emphasize practices of distribution and circulation, but they also suggest that readers might be more likely to hold onto these images, even if they might neglect other images of clothing or design objects included in the journal. The marking of a particular time or year can take on increasing urgency in a period of turmoil, with the gesture of preservation taking on a commemorative, even historiographical function; indeed, Clare Pettitt describes these expressly miniaturized depictions of historical sites and events in nineteenth-century serial print as the material objects or "equipment of history" that readers and authors use to make sense of historical time.[89] Drawing on Bertuch's valorization of luxury editions as "national-monuments," we might also consider these texts as smaller, more modest quasi-monumental objects—"paper monuments," to anticipate a coinage of Jean Paul's—that enable certain memorializing practices in line with other products for domestic consumption popular at the time, products discussed by Christiane Holm and Günter Oesterle as "serially produced commemoration."[90] Viewed in light of such practices of memorialization, the association with classical themes functions as a gesture toward patterns of continuity, repetition, and duration. With their new year's presents and the journal's other images more generally, Bertuch and Kraus display an awareness that print objects provide temporal orientation by helping readers consider different patterns of transience and continuity in a time of flux.

---

89. See Pettitt, *Serial Forms*, 239.
90. Christiane Holm and Günter Oesterle, "Andacht und Andenken. Zum Verhältnis zweier Kulturpraktiken um 1800," in *Erinnerung, Gedächtnis, Wissen, Studien zur kulturwissenschaftlichen Gedächtnisforschung*, ed. Günter Oesterle (Vandenhoeck und Ruprecht, 2005), 434–35.

Figure 1.4. "Venus mit Grazien." *Journal des Luxus und der Moden* 11, no. 1 (January 1796): title plate. HAAB Weimar. 7 ½ × 4 ½ inches.

An "Archive of the Fashions of Body and Mind"

In closing, we might linger on a specific issue of the *Modejournal* that brings the logic of the journal as both archive and tableau into resonance with questions of (small) print luxury and the marking of time. The first issue of 1794 comes at a dramatic point in the revolution, for the preceding year witnessed an intensification of the Reign of Terror, with the execution of Marie Antoinette and many others. As the commentary on the *Titelkupfer*, or frontispiece, notes, "never has Germany and humanity yearned so much for a happy turn of the year as this year.... The wounds inflicted by the madness and lunacy of the robber hordes of France... still bleed, and German bravery, manliness, and moral rectitude [*treuer Biedersinn*] alone will be able to resist them."[91] The journal's editors seek to mark this turn to a new year with a "new year's wish" that incorporates the desire to commemorate but also turn the page on the previous year: "It is completed, this year of horrific, murderous, and disgraceful actions, which will be eternally written, in human blood, into the annals of the world and will stand there as a warning memorial [*Warnungs-Mal*] for the nations of the world."[92] To this end, the editors present readers with an image of Janus, "the two-headed, symbolically rich god of the turn of the year among the ancients" (see figure 1.5). The head on the left looks back directly at the numerals 1793, and as the authors note, in a westward direction (i.e., toward France). It is shrouded in a black veil, which is intertwined with a cypress branch, a symbol of mourning. The second, unveiled head is turned east, into the new year, and it is wearing the "white tunic of quietude and civil affairs" (*bürgerliche Geschäfte*). As the commentary notes, the ornamental wreath on this side intertwines "the palm branch of peace and the rose of joy—Germany, may this be your horoscope this year!"[93] The classicizing imagery serves as a counterpoint to the commemorative function of the year's violence and its place in

---

91. "Erklärung der Kupfertafeln," *JLM* 9, no. 1 (January 1794): 63.
92. "Erklärung der Kupfertafeln," 64.
93. "Erklärung der Kupfertafeln," 64.

Figure 1.5. "Janus." *Journal des Luxus und der Moden* 9, no. 1 (January 1794): title plate. HAAB Weimar. 7 ½ × 4 ½ inches.

human memory, where it should persist negatively as a *Warnungs-Mal* rather than as a more positive monument, or *Denkmal*. This image also delineates multiple frames of time. The line between the two heads establishes a vertical plane that divides the years from each other, and the gaze of the head on the right gazes into the new year and also forward into the pages of the journal. The layout of the image connects practices of reading to the forward march of time: a new issue for a new year.

Directly following this image is an article titled "Two Calendars, the Neo-pagan and the Early Christian *en Parallèle*," which details the enactment of the French Republican calendar, likewise an event of the previous year.[94] The revolutionary calendar occurs under the sign of the "old" and the "new"—it is typical of the French, as the Parisian correspondent notes, "to make everything new, and to tear down all of the old" (*alles neu zu machen und alles Alte nieder zu machen*).[95] Here the line between old and new unfolds not on the divide of the new year but rather on the divide between revolutionary and pre-revolutionary time and between modernity and antiquity (here represented by the "*altchristlich*" Gregorian calendar established in 1582 but based in part on the calendar used in ancient Rome). "Since their heads have started to become dizzy or fall off, every day of the New French [*Neufranken*] produces ten new idiocies along with each new atrocity."[96] This tendency to generate ever new things calls for their documentation and for "a prophetic and witty observer" to collect all the "scurrilities, pasquinades, rhodomatades, and ridiculous national traits of the New French that they have exposed to the world during their new revolutions."[97]

It is the *Modejournal*, then, that takes on this documentary task, providing readers with an explanation of how the new calendar works, a summary of its months, its new festival dates, and more:

---

94. On this article, see Seifert, "*Archiv der Moden des Leibes*," 114–19.
95. "Die beyden Kalender, der neuheidnische und altchristliche," *JLM* 9 (January 1794): 4, italics in original. The alternative title ("Zwei Kalender, der neuheidnische und altchristliche, *en parallèle*") is what is listed in the table of contents at the end of the journal.
96. "Die beyden Kalender," 4.
97. "Die beyden Kalender," 5.

"As our journal, according to its purpose and conception, should be the *archive of the fashions of the body and mind of our age*, it is also our duty to preserve for posterity this strange phenomenon of French folly and to at the same time provide our readers with a necessary table for comparison [*Vergleichungs-Tafel*] so as to keep this New French anomaly in order."[98] Here the journal's archival function goes beyond merely documenting the new calendar as a historical curiosity; indeed, after summarizing how the calendar is organized, the editors present readers with a tabulated comparison of the two calendars, *en parallèle* (or facing), as the title states (see figure 1.6). One can only imagine that this document had various kinds of use values that would prompt readers to set it aside or perhaps cut it out and use it as a reference tool. As the editors note, having this handy tool is necessary to keep "all transactions of trade and computation" (*aller Handels- und Rechnungsgeschäfte*) from "entering into paralysis."[99] This print object, running across eleven pages, provides the informative service of offering the German equivalent of translating the names of each day in the new calendar, but the object is also a gesture of rebuke, marking the continued existence of the Christian holidays that had been expunged from the revolutionary calendar.

Here again, we see the journal page divided up in the service of marking time (though the position of the old and the new has switched from the Janus image's, with the old calendar now on the right). The tabular presentation of the days of the year and other relevant information (feast days, planting and harvest months, and more) is a typical feature of eighteenth-century almanacs and calendars, including Bertuch's short-lived fashion calendar *Pandora*, and is a feature of serial print that would have been immediately legible to contemporary readers. Seen in the light of this familiar convention, this archived print object has value both as a reference tool and as a visual curiosity, or as one more example of a peculiar fashion. Though this calendar has just been implemented across France, the question how long it would last remains open—is it just another scurrile thing thought up by the revolutionaries currently in power? In chapter 3 I

---

98. "Die beyden Kalender," 5.
99. "Die beyden Kalender," 4–5.

L'An II de la Republ. Française.		Altchristlicher
Neuheidnischer Calender. BRUMAIRE.	Teutsch. Nebelmond.	Calender 1793.
I. Decad.		
1 P. Pomme.	Apfel.	D. 22 Octbr. 1793.
2 D. Celeri.	Sellerie.	M. 23 Severin.
3 T. Poire.	Birn.	D. 24. Salome.
4 Q. Petexave.	Rothe Rübe.	F. 25. Wilhelmine.
5 Q. Oye.	Gans.	S. 26. Job.
6 S. Heliotrope.	Sonnenblume.	S. 27. 22 n. Trin.
7 S. Figue.	Feige.	M. 28. Sim. Jud.
8 O. Scorzonere.	Haferwurz.	D. 29. Narcissus.
9 N. Alisier..	Elsbeer.	M. 30. Claudius.
10 D. Charrue.	Pflug.	D. 31. Ref. Fest.
II. Decad.		
11 P. Salsifis.	Bocksbart.	F. 1. Novbr. 1793.
12 D. Cornuette.	Stachelnuß.	S. 2. Aller Seel.
13 T. Poireterre.	Erdbirne.	S. 3. 23 n. Trin.
14 Q. Endives.	Endivien.	M. 4. Carolus.
15 Q. Dindon.	Truthahn.	D. 5. Blandina.
16 S. Chiroui.	Chiroui.	M. 6. Leonhard.
17 S. Cresson.	Kresse.	D. 7. Erdmann.
18 O. Dentilaire.	Zahnkraut.	F. 8. Emerich.
19 N. Grenades.	Granatapfel.	S. 9. Theodor.
20 D. Herse.	Egge.	S. 10. 24 n. Trin.
III. Decad.		
21 P. Bacchante.	Tollkraut.	M. 11. Mart. Bisch.
22 D. Olive.	Olive.	D. 12 Modestus.
23 T. Garance.	Grapp.	M. 13. Arcadius.
24 Q. Orange.	Pommeranze.	D. 14. Levinus.
25 Q. Iars.	Gänserich.	F. 15. Leopold.
26 S. Pislache.	Pistazien.	S. 16 Edmund.
27 S. Marjone.	Gentile.	S. 17. 25 n. Trin.
28 O. Coing.	Quitte.	M 18. Hesychius.
29 N. Cormier.	Sperling.	D 19. Elisabeth.
30 D. Rouleau.	Walze.	M 20. Aemilia.

Figure 1.6. "Die beyden Calender, der neuheidnische und altchristliche. (En parallèle)." *Journal des Luxus und der Moden 9*, no. 1 (January 1794): 9. Gotha Research Library, University of Erfurt. 7 ½ × 4 ½ inches.

explore various satirical gestures at work in Bertuch's journals in more detail, but here we might note that this object's commemorative function and use function are both based in readers being presented with a material object that in some way marks and organizes time. This goes back to the conception of the journal as a form of tabulating, inventorying presentation and as a format that presents readers with multiple sequential tableaus. This calendar is one more permutation of a counterpoint or parallel to fuel historical reflection. Like the Janus image, the calendar operates through visual juxtaposition based on the layout of the page and the format of the journal.

In effect, the journal presents readers with two different kinds of print luxury and two print objects, each with different uses and aesthetic values and each with different claims on readers' attention and on readers' motivation to preserve such artifacts. I could extend this consideration of different "archival" objects to the rest of this specific issue, but these two objects already give a sense of how the journal marks different shapes of time through its status as material object. Its series of images, both metaphorical and actual, help readers to create certain temporal matrices, to renegotiate the old and the new, the fleeting and the permanent, and the cyclical and the synchronic. Part of the way that the journal prompts readers to view print objects as consumer commodities is to lead readers into the activity of observing themselves observing time. Commemorative gestures of marking historical time are connected to the interaction with specific print objects, and these gestures access, but are not limited to, classicizing visual language. The tableau comes into view as a malleable form existing at the intersection of various kinds of "large" and "small" print formats and, indeed, "large" and "small" articles of print luxury. This imbrication of the tableau, print luxury, and the marking of time leads us to the topic of the next chapter on Goethe's account of Roman carnival across book and journal versions and the different work these formats do in visualizing competing shapes of time established by the recurrence of certain similar phenomena or events. These shapes include the classical permanence and organic unity associated with the stand-alone work as well as the more jumbled temporalities of cultural journalism that unfold according to the patterns of the literary and fashion marketplaces, contemporary political affairs, and patterns of domestic life.

2

GOETHE'S *THE ROMAN CARNIVAL* AND ITS AFTERLIVES

Goethe's account of the Roman carnival was published first in 1789 as a book, *Das römische Carneval* (The Roman carnival), then in the *Modejournal* on the eve of the Lenten season in the first 1790 issue of the *Journal des Luxus und der Moden*. Bertuch and Kraus are involved in both versions, and Böttiger refers back to it in various antiquarian articles after he becomes coeditor of the *Modejournal*. As I argue, Goethe's text plays a central role in crafting the journal's reputation as a promulgator of neoclassical taste and as a site for exploring how antiquity persists in the present. Goethe's text likewise is a telling example of how contemporaries engage with the cultural politics of the revolution through the logics of visual spectatorship. This chapter therefore presents multiple "views" of Goethe's carnival piece, its shifting locations in the orbit of the *Modejournal*, and the multiple serial structures in which the piece is implicated. Different horizons open up if we view Goethe's text as a stand-alone work, as one in a series of articles about Rome and antiquity in *Modejournal*, as part of a broader journalistic and historiographical fascination with Rome vis-à-vis contemporary France, or as one of many single-author writings later incorporated into collected works editions. A case study of Goethe's carnival publications foregrounds how print formats shape the temporal imaginary both via the individual work and via constellations of print objects that resist consolidation into a single unified form.

Goethe traveled in Italy between 1786 and 1788, with two separate extended stays in Rome. While there, he corresponded extensively with friends and colleagues in Weimar and around Germany and contributed multiple short pieces of travel writing for Bertuch's journals, including the *Der Teutsche Merkur* and the *Modejournal*. His experience of the Roman festival unfolded sequentially, in line with his two visits in the city; as he later notes, it was only after attending a second time that he overcame his initial wish to never participate again: "It was the second time that I saw the carnival, and it inevitably soon struck me that this popular festival followed its decisive course like every other recurring life activity and pattern [*daß dieses Volksfest, wie ein anderes wiederkehrendes Leben und Weben seinen entscheidenden Verlauf hatte*]."[1] This double viewing plays a formative role in his more general understanding of how experiences and impressions settle properly into place through repetition.[2] Goethe's 1789 account of Roman carnival is an important example of how he explores the manifestations of serial forms across the arts and the natural world. For Goethe, serial structures cut across natural phenomena and cultural artifacts alike, and he describes carnival as a mixture of both, a "product of nature and a national-event" (*Naturerzeugnis und National-Ereignis*).[3]

---

1. MA, 15, 611–12.
2. On the theme of repeated seeing in Goethe's Italian writings, see Frank Fehrenbach, "'Bravi i morti!' Emphasen des Lebens in Goethes *Italienischer Reise*," in *Vita aesthetica. Szenarien ästhetischer Lebendigkeit*, ed. Armen Avenessian, Winfried Menninghaus, and Jan Völker (Berlin: Diaphanes, 2009), 65.
3. MA, 15, 612. As Eva Geulen has highlighted, exploring such a mixture troubles the distinction between seriality as a quality of phenomena themselves and as a mode of representation and is a feature of Goethe's broader approach to serial form. "The currently dominant mode of ordering different types of seriality privileges the distinction between series composed of already given phenomena that are, as it were,

He casts his carnival piece as an achievement both of empirical observation and aesthetic form-giving: he recalls composing the text by "noting the individual happenings in sequence [*der Reihe nach*]," and he structures it as a series of multiple short sketches with twenty accompanying illustrations.[4]

A double view structures how Goethe came to orient himself vis-à-vis carnival, but it also echoes his short text's complex publication history. He initially pitched it to Bertuch for the *Modejournal*, but the two ended up doing a limited-run book version in the spring of 1789 first, reversing in a peculiar way the usual pattern of literary works being prepublished (*vorabdegruckt*) in a periodical before coming out as a single-author, stand-alone work,[5] a pattern that would become typical for literary material throughout the nineteenth century. In turn, most modern readers encounter the carnival piece in Goethe's autobiographical *Italienische Reise* (Italian journey), but it only took up this place in 1829 after being republished and reconstellated some fourteen times. Goethe's double viewing of carnival and his piece's complex publication history prompt reflection on the temporal connotations of multiple formats, including the association of journals with ephemeral fashions, commerce, and current events; the associations of the luxury book with classicizing permanence; and the association of works editions with practices of collecting individual works according to a provisional or final order determined by the author.

Goethe and Bertuch knew each other well in Weimar, but their relationship grew more distanced over the course of the 1790s as their approaches to the business of print and the literary field diverged (Goethe even reverted to addressing Bertuch with the formal *Sie* (you) after earlier addressing the publisher with the less formal *du*).

---

inherently predisposed to being grouped together, vs. series as tool, technique, and a mode of construction—in short, the distinction between series conceived as grounded in substance or considered a method." Eva Geulen, "Serialization in Goethe's Morphology," *Compar(a)ison* 2 (2008): 53.

4. MA, 15, 612.

5. As Siegfried Unseld notes, the piece is longer than most articles in the journal; he also cites Bertuch's ambition to try his hand at a more profitable luxury edition. See Siegfried Unseld, *Goethe and His Publishers*, trans. Kenneth J. Northcott (Chicago: University of Chicago Press, 1996), 88.

That said, the carnival piece is clearly modeled on some of the *Modejournal*'s basic formal and thematic conceits, including its appeal to the visual imagination and its interest in foreign costumes. The images, drawn by Christian Georg Schütz and etched by Kraus, are strikingly reminiscent of the *Modejournal*'s fashion plates. Carnival and its costumes are featured in the journal before and after the January 1790 journal publication (which does not contain the images from Goethe's text but directs readers to purchase a supplemental booklet featuring them), and later issues refer readers back to his text, even citing specific images, leading to the conclusion that the piece is a key text in establishing the journal's brand at the intersection of popular antiquarianism and cultural journalism. As the epitome of transient eventfulness and patterned recurrence, carnival is a topic well suited for the journal, both an expression of popular energies and an important date in the social calendar of high society.[6] Even after becoming disdainful of Bertuch's commercialism and his promotion of applied arts and manufacturing,[7] Goethe continued to turn to the *Modejournal* to publish his pieces documenting the masked processions that he intermittently organized for the Weimar court (see figure 1.2).[8]

Despite the nearly identical textual content of the book and journal versions, certain differences between the two are readily apparent. Bertuch frames the 1789 book version as a beautiful work meant to last given its paper, type, and hand-colored images, and he enlists his joint venture with the authors, artists, and other printers as a

---

6. Readers were presented with a "tableau" of the "public revelries" (*öffentliche Lustbarkeiten*) of Venetian carnival just months after Goethe's carnival piece. See J. P. Siebenkees, "Ueber die öffentlichen Lustbarkeiten in Venedig," *JLM* 5, no. 5 (May 1790): 229–41.

7. See Michael Bies, "Wieder das Fabrikenwesen. Goethe und das Handwerk der Klassik," in *Der Streit um Klassizität: Polemische Konstellationen vom 18. Zum 21. Jahrhundert*, ed. Daniel Ehrmann and Norbert Christian Wolf (Munich: Fink, 2021), 47–66.

8. See Wolfgang Hecht, "Goethes Maskenzüge," in *Studien zur Goethezeit*, ed. Helmut Holtzhauer and Bernhard Zeller (Weimar: Böhlau, 1968), 127–42; and Georg Schmidt, "Inszenierungen und Folgen eines Musensitzes: Goethes Maskenzüge 1781-84 und Carl Augusts politische Ambitionen," *Ständige Konferenz Mitteldeutsche Barockmusik* (2002): 101–18.

prime example of classicizing print luxury. At first glance, journal publication would seem to invite the contrast between lasting book and ephemeral journal. Additionally, journal publication integrates Goethe's carnival scenes into a broader series of visual material and juxtaposes his account with representations of other unrelated times and places. Goethe's piece thereby builds on the ever-growing reader interest in popular festivity, with the costumes of carnival in particular as models for serial entertainment and cultural journalism. The satirical journal *Der hinkende Teufel zu Berlin* (The limping devil of Berlin) (1827), for example, presents its contents "in a colorful series like a masked procession in carnival" (*in Bunter Reihe wie ein Maskenzug im Karneval*), and pocketbook and calendar publications depicting carnival scenes abound, in several cases reproducing Goethe's piece without his permission.[9] At the same time, the 1790 republication appears as a high-water mark for information and imagery from revolutionary France.[10] In the January 1790 issue, his account of the festival appears alongside reports from Paris, including news of the revolutionary National Guard and its uniforms (discussed in chapter 1), news from the theater season in various cities, and more.[11] Journal publication brings the time of carnival into relation with other patterns of repetition and recurrence, including patterns of political, cultural, and commercial eventfulness that straddle pre- and postrevolutionary periods; the pace of bringing news of the revolution to German readers on a daily, weekly, monthly, or yearly basis; and patterns of cultural entertainment that pass readers by "in a colorful series." Multiple "views" of Goethe's carnival piece are warranted because the text and its images are implicated in a range of divergent print formats and because they resonate with a variety of significant external events.

---

9. Ursula E. Koch, *Der Teufel in Berlin. Von der Märzrevolution bis zu Bismarcks Entlassung. Illustrierte politische Witzblätter 1848–1890* (Cologne: Leske, 1991), 31.

10. Like most German journals, the *Modejournal* began covering the events of the summer of 1789 in August of the same year and continued to do so unabated throughout the fall and winter.

11. "Mode-Neuigkeiten," *JLM* 5, no. 1 (January 1790): 62.

In particular, Goethe's account of carnival can reveal a larger story about alterations to the awareness of time in the revolutionary period—what is new? what persists from the past?—and a story about the development of different kinds of classicisms in the literature, journalism, and arts of Germany in the 1790s.[12] Goethe's role in promoting the renewed consideration of the art and culture of ancient Greece and Rome is well-known. The orientation to art objects in particular helped him and Karl Philipp Moritz to develop an aesthetics of autonomous, organically unified form and to explore in theory and practice heteronomous, serial forms such as the ornament and arabesque.[13] Antiquity remained a significant point of reference in the literary and art market of late eighteenth-century Germany, with growing middle-class audiences contrasting classicizing style and forms with the baroque excesses of the aristocracy.[14] As we have seen in the preceding chapter, the *Modejournal* participates quite actively in this renewed interest in antiquity, foregrounding design objects, furniture, clothing, and more that rely on neoclassical patterning and decorative lines. The journal also features frequent articles on the customs of antiquity. The juxtaposition of ancient and modern customs and practices is an important way in which the *Modejournal* registers the temporalization of fashion. This is a style of journalism that looks for traces of antiquity in the present and that helps to write the ongoing history of the present. Bertuch and Böttiger share with Goethe a skepticism toward the revolution that all three filter through

---

12. As Larry F. Norman argues, the study of the reception and perpetuation of classical styles reveals the coexistence of what he calls "multiple classicisms." Larry F. Norman, "Multiple Classicisms," in *Classicisms*, ed. Larry F. Norman and Anne Leonard (Chicago: Smart Museum of Art, 2017), 15.

13. See David Wellbery, "Form und Idee. Skizze eines Begriffsfeldes um 1800," in *Morphologie und Moderne. Goethes 'Anschauliches Denken' in den Geistes- und Kulturwissenschaften seit 1800*, ed. Jonas Maatsch (Berlin: De Gruyter, 2014), 1; on Goethe's productive approach to the heteronomy of the ornament, see Pirholt, *Grenzerfahrungen*, 103–27.

14. "The new doctrine disapproved of baroque and rococo as the art of the ephemeral, stimulating fleeting impressions according to the inconstant whims of fashion." Jean Starobinski, *1789: The Emblems of Reason*, trans. Barbara Bray (Cambridge, MA: MIT Press, 1988), 76.

their engagement with modern and ancient festivities. That said, their relationship is likewise characterized by "dissenting views about literature and divergent publicational strategies."[15] Of Goethe's aesthetically high-minded allies (among them Schiller and the artist J. H. Meyer), Herder is perhaps the most ill-disposed to Bertuch's commercially oriented journalism, claiming that the "pernicious fashion journals" (verderbliche Modejournale) corrupt "true Greek taste."[16] One of my tasks here is to revisit these perhaps familiar differences about the commercial orientation of the literary market in light of questions of serial forms and temporal structures that evoke classical antiquity, what I am referring to as "classicizing" shapes of time.

As we saw in the preceding chapter, different manifestations of popularized classicism are an integral part of the material culture of the age, and these manifestations address the full range of the senses.[17] Along with luxury print editions, a popular classicizing style likewise reigns in many of the era's popular design and art objects, including vaseware, sculpture reproductions, furniture, and other domestic accoutrements. As Catriona MacLeod and Stephan Pabst have shown, the aesthetics of these design objects is rooted in serial fabrication rather than in the production of singular, unique works.[18] Bertuch, Kraus, and Böttiger firmly align this aesthetics of copying and reproduction with the commercial side of publishing. Here, too, contrasting approaches to the art object reveal another side to the period's "multiple classicisms" and the "polemical constellations" in which it developed around 1800.[19] Goethe's per-

---

15. Siegfried Seifert, "Goethe/Schiller und die 'nivellirenden Naturen.' Literarische Diskurse im 'klassischen Weimar,'" in Das Schöne und das Triviale, ed. Gert Theile (Munich: Fink, 2003), 80.
16. Cited in Ruth Wies, "Das Journal des Luxus und der Moden (1786–1827), ein Spiegel kultureller Strömungen der Goethezeit" (PhD diss., University of Munich, 1953), 63.
17. As a recent exhibition on Weimar classicism as a "culture" of "the sensuous" has shown. See Sebastian Böhmer et al., ed., Weimarer Klassik. Kultur des Sinnlichen (Berlin: Deutscher Kunstverlag, 2012).
18. See MacLeod, "Skulptur als Ware"; Stephan Pabst, "Kultur der Kopie. Antike im Zeitalter ihrer Reproduzierbarkeit," in Böhmer et al., Weimarer Klassik.
19. On classicism's rootedness in such polemical confrontations, see Daniel Ehrmann and Norbert Christian Wolf, "Einführung," in Ehrmann and Wolf, Der Streit um Klassizität, 1–29.

ception that culture is "threatened by serial mass goods" puts him at odds with the smaller, more occasional forms of material culture and art objects propagated by the likes of the *Modejournal*, even though publishing the text in the journal brings the text into the orbit of such entertainment.[20] The gesture to classicizing form can aid in the selection and isolation of certain works as self-standing, coherent wholes, but gestures to antiquity can also help to make sense of the proliferation of shifting serial forms. Seen against the backdrop of the "fundamental seriality" of invocations of classical form—classicism's "inevitable placement in a vast chronological sequence of succeeding variants," as Larry F. Norman puts it[21]—Goethe's carnival piece is an instructive case of how serial forms can come to very different answers to the question of how antiquity persists into the present. Goethe and the *Modejournal* offer divergent types of knowledge about the effects of seriality upon the awareness of time, and they invite divergent interpretations of how print objects configure cultural forms as more or less permanent.

A First View of *The Roman Carnival*

"A Small, Interesting Work"

The short book titled *Das römische Carneval* appeared in the spring of 1789 with a print run of three hundred copies.[22] This was a joint undertaking, not just by Goethe, Bertuch, Schütz, and Kraus but also by two other publishers, Unger (Berlin) and Ettiger (Gotha), for Bertuch did not yet have the capacity to print the book himself. Bertuch's thematization of the book's production in an advertisement in the *Modejournal*—calling it "a small interesting work," "perhaps even the

---

20. Thorsten Valk, "Weimarer Klassik. Kultur des Sinnlichen," in Böhmer et al., *Weimarer Klassik*, 20.
21. "Simply put, every classicism (except perhaps the first in the series, generally assigned to Periclean Athens) is in reality a *neo*classicism." Norman, "Multiple Classicisms," 21.
22. Johann Wolfgang von Goethe, *Das römische Carneval* (Weimar and Gotha: Ettinger, 1789).

first and only of its kind in this well-known branch of newer luxury"[23]—represents a deliberate, self-promotional foray into the luxury book market.[24] Even if booklets depicting costumes or national dress were not uncommon in the broader European market, this volume is an important milestone in Germany, and it would turn out to be the most expensive single book of Goethe's entire career.[25] Offering proof of its superlative quality, the advertisement describes the coloring of the images and the "beauty" of the printing, paper, and typography, and calls it a "work" (*Werk*) five times in just three pages. This emphasis on production details is reminiscent of Bertuch's later discussions of typography and his praise of Göschen's 1794 Wieland edition. Antiqua is the typeface of choice for luxury editions, and, perhaps unexpectedly, this is one of the few books by Goethe that utilizes this font during his lifetime.[26] The advertisement also explicitly associates the book with antiquity, noting that the author makes use of the "form and taste of the ancients ... to make [carnival's] revelries all the more piquant."[27] In effect, Bertuch enlists Goethe in his project of setting the terms of a developing branch of the luxury print market and establishing the criteria for a classicizing print object. However, given this keen evocation of classical aesthetics, Bertuch's qualification of the book as "small" is peculiar at first glance, given the common association of the "work" with a certain grandeur and monumentality (as in Bertuch's vision of luxury editions as *National-Monumente*[28]). Perhaps this smallness refers more to the book's length (just over one hundred pages, including the images) and less to its size relative to the

---

23. F. J. Bertuch and G. M. Kraus, "Das Römische Carneval [advertisement]," *Intelligenzblatt des Journals des Luxus und der Moden* 2 (February 1789): xvii–xvix, xvii.
24. On this piece against the backdrop of this market, see Ludwig Uhlig, "Goethes *Römisches Carneval* im Wandel seines Kontexts," *Euphorion* 72, no. 1 (1978): 75; Erlin marks the 1794 works edition of Wieland as a key turning point in the production of luxury editions of prominent authors; see Erlin, *Necessary Luxuries*.
25. See Knorr, "Georg Melichor Kraus," 213.
26. Bertuch enlists the printer Unger in the project, who is the only printer in Germany at the time with the privilege of printing entire books in Antiqua type.
27. Bertuch and Kraus, "Das Römische Carneval [advertisement]," xvii.
28. F. J. Bertuch, "Ueber den Typographischen Luxus mit Hinsicht auf die neue Ausgabe von Wielands sämmtlichen Werken," *JLM* 8, no. 11 (November 1793): 599–609.

octavo *Modejournal* (and the duodecimo size of many illustrated pocketbooks). The book's quarto pages leave considerable blank space around the text and images—in a rather conspicuous consumption of expensive paper—allowing readers to appreciate the appearance of both. To be sure, it is a feature of certain branches of European book markets to produce smaller, more affordable versions of elaborate, multivolume antiquarian works.²⁹

The qualifier "small" also likely refers to the realm of more occasional cultural journalism and travel writing from which this piece emerged. In this same advertisement, Bertuch reveals Goethe as the book's author through a reference to writings appearing just months before in one of Bertuch's own journals: the author is "a man whom Germany holds to be among its finest art connoisseurs and its most favorite writers; [to reveal his name] we merely have to refer to his excellent *Auszüge aus einem Reise-Journal* [Excerpts from a travel journal] in the last installments of *Der Teutsche Merkur* of 1788."³⁰ In the late 1780s, Goethe published a variety of short pieces in Wieland's journal under this title; there, smallness is a function of these texts having been excerpted from a larger, ongoing travel diary. Cultural, fashion, and art historical journals share a particular thematic and structural affinity with travel writing, and journal publication is mutually beneficial for authors and publishers, with authors previewing longer works and prominent correspondents enhancing journals' reputations. Karl Philipp Moritz, whom Goethe befriends while in Rome, is also adept at publishing travel writing and art criticism, even founding his own journal *Italien und Deutschland in Rücksicht auf Sitten, Gebräuche, Litteratur, und Kunst* (1789–1792)— the first German art historical journal of the period to use Antiqua type—and publishing in it what would become his three-volume travelogue, *Reise eines Deutschen in Italien in den Jahren 1786 bis 1788* (Travels of a German in Italy in the years 1786 to 1788)

---

29. On the case of Sir William Hamilton in this regard, see Thora Brylowe, "Two Kinds of Collections: Sir William Hamilton's Vases, Real and Represented," *Eighteenth-Century Life* 32, no. 1 (2008): 49.

30. Bertuch and Kraus, "Das Römische Carneval [advertisement]," xvii.

(1792–1794).³¹ Moritz also republishes some articles in his 1793 single-author collection *Vorbegriffe zu einer Theorie der Ornamente* (Preliminary ideas toward a theory of the ornament) (1793), which adds to the flurried format migration of these writings.

Building on the work of J. J. Winckelmann, Moritz, Goethe, and others fuel renewed interest among German readers in the art and cultural life of antiquity as it is preserved in various ways in modern Italy. Central to these writings is the technique of visualizing the presence of the past, a mode of writing time, if you will, that straddles antiquity and modernity. Along with describing encounters with ancient art, journalistic travel writings include quasi-ethnographic observations of everyday life as manifested in clothing, dress, customs, public rituals, popular songs, and more. Moritz and Goethe place strong emphases on visual observation as a way to test out the continued relevance and exemplarity of antiquity. Like many contemporary travelers, they engage in ekphrastic descriptions of sculpture, painting, and architecture, and they guide readers through a sequence of urban and rural scenes.³² Goethe would later call the carnival piece a *tableau mouvant*, and in it he describes the challenge of representing carnival in terms of organizing a chaotic sequence of visual (and other sense) impressions into a coherent whole.³³ In turn, the carnival piece would leave a particular mark on Moritz, who declines to offer an original account of the festival in his own travelogue, instead directing readers to Goethe's depiction, which, as he puts it, represents "the whole as deceptively and truly as the images in a perspective viewbox."³⁴ The analogy of Goethe's piece to a viewbox (or zograscope) reveals a keen

---

31. See Heide Hollmer and Albert Meier, "Kunstzeitschriften," in *Von Almanach bis Zeitung. Ein Handbuch der Medien in Deutschland 1700–1800*, ed. Ernst Fischer, Wilhelm Haefs, and York-Gothart Mix (Munich: Beck, 1999), 169.

32. One example of this is an essay of Goethe's in *Der Teutsche Merkur* from 1789 that describes print reproductions of a cycle of paintings of Christ and the twelve apostles by Raphael.

33. See Graczyk, *Das literarische Tableau zwischen Kunst*, 248, note 231. See also Gibhardt, *Vorgriffe auf das schöne Leben*, 175–91, for further connections between the logic of the tableau and Goethe's piece.

34. "Das Ganze so täuschend und so wahr, wie die Bilder in einem optischen Kasten." Karl Philipp Moritz, *Reise eines Deutschen in Italien in den Jahren 1786 bis 1788* (Berlin: Maurer, 1792), 162.

awareness of the potential of serial viewing for creating a sense of phenomena as consistent wholes, a sense that is "true" because of, not despite, the "deceptive" manipulation brought about by specific media. Moritz and Goethe cast the process of education and self-formation (*Bildung*) as a personal drama of processing antiquity and its different traces in the present day through various media-based techniques. This occurs against the backdrop of the unruly flow of images characteristic of modernity; as Moritz puts it, the challenge is to orient oneself in "the flight of time, [where] it is all we can do just to capture the outlines of the images that rush pass us."[35] Writing time in this context entails finding stable points of orientation in the face of the transience and constant change of modern life.

Public festivals lend themselves especially well to this project of visualization, embedded as they are in the expectations of serial culture for the ongoing representation of new and recurring spectacles. The aspiration to represent various popular events functions as a testing ground both for the writing of contemporary history (*Zeitgeschichte*) and for different types of literary representation. The contemporary interest in festivals emerges amid shifting valuations of festivals in the Enlightenment and amid the desire to imagine national cultures as collective totalities. Echoing Jean-Jacques Rousseau's famous account on the popular *fête* as an alternative to theater spectatorship, Goethe describes carnival as an occasion for the collective self-experience of the Roman people: it is "not given for the people [*Volk*], but [a festival] that the people give themselves."[36] Carnival's yearly repetition shows how forms of popular expression can persist over millennia—the festival is a "modern Saturnalia"—but also how such forms can permeate daily life: as Goethe writes, in Rome, "it seems to be carnival all year long."[37] The temporal footprints of popular collectivities and their different forms of self-expression have the potential to reveal what persists and what changes over time.

Accounts of popular festivity also produce reflections about the present, not least at a time when new public rituals are being established

---

35. Moritz, *Anthousa*, 6.
36. MA, 3.2, 218.
37. MA, 3.2, 221.

in revolutionary France.³⁸ As the 1790s progress, readers grow accustomed to encountering multiple descriptions of the same revolutionary festival in different papers and to reading accounts of various events as they recur every year. As an article from the August 1790 *Modejournal* reads, "you will have read the more detailed description of the festivities in all the newspapers and will spare me the effort of regurgitating them for you."³⁹ Proliferating festival descriptions facilitate a comparative approach, with readers consuming multiple accounts of the same or different festivals. Critical commentary seeks analogies between different sites and styles of popular self-expression, something that can be seen in Goethe's and Moritz's invocations of the buzzwords of the French Revolution in their carnival descriptions. Though Goethe concluded his reflections on the festival in early 1789, he would later say that his work from this period captured a prerevolutionary atmosphere and expressed his "frightful premonitions" for what was to come.⁴⁰ The carnival piece does in fact reference the festival's transient "freedom" and "equality," where "the difference between upper and lower [classes] seems to disappear for a moment," though he concludes the piece by observing that "freedom and equality can be enjoyed only in the frenzy of madness."⁴¹ Moritz's *Anthousa, oder Roms Alterthümer: Ein Buch für die Menschheit* (Anthousa, or Rome's antiquities: a book for humanity), which details the religious festivities of ancient Rome, appears in 1791, and its evocation of egalitarian ideals is more unequivocal about the intersections between ancient republicanism and the cultural politics of the revolution, describing ceremonies where "the Roman Volk triumphantly

---

38. As Mona Ozouf puts it, with the festivals of the French Revolution, "an enormous ritual ensemble surges while another—the Catholic ritual—is swallowed up, or appears to be." Mona Ozouf, "Space and Time in the Festivals of the French Revolution," *Comparative Studies in Society and History* 17, no. 3 (1975): 372.

39. "Mode-Neuigkeiten," *JLM* 5, no. 8 (August 1790): 457.

40. As Goethe noted in 1792, he had these premonitions as early as 1785 and came to Italy with them in mind. See Unseld, *Goethe and His Publishers*, 85.

41. "Daß Freiheit und Gleichheit nur in dem Taumel des Wahnsinns genossen werden können." MA, 3.2, 250.

celebrated all the freedoms and rights that it had attained and that protected it from the oppressions of the more noble and the more powerful."[42] It is a general scholarly consensus that Goethe and Moritz alike use the visualization of carnival and of ancient Rome as aesthetic wholes as ways to contain and neutralize what they perceive to be the revolution's destructive and threatening elements, a conclusion that I will elaborate on later in this chapter. It is likewise notable that their oblique engagement with the revolution emerges from a print landscape in which readers are constantly encountering descriptions of public spectacles.

The cultural politics of the revolution relies heavily on various print formats. Revolutionaries depend on proliferating accounts of festivals and other public events in print to reinforce an aesthetics of patriotic unity, to aid public memory, and to create a sense that new and durable cultural forms are emerging. The documentation and amplification of public spectacle through serial print is an important example of how material objects can be given emphatic temporal indexes as commemorative devices, a more general feature of the temporalization characteristic of the 1790s. The memorialization of public festivities by various kinds of print objects runs parallel to other commemorative modes that mark time on a spectrum between ephemerality and permanence. Commentary on public spectacles lends itself to various modes of pro- and antirevolutionary journalism, including reflections on the classicizing bent of newly founded festivals and the tendency of revolutionaries to dress themselves up in the trappings of antiquity, a tendency which Karl Marx would so ironically diagnose some sixty years later.[43] This

---

42. Moritz, *Anthousa*, 217. As Yvonne Pauly notes in her excellent commentary on the book, Moritz wrote this in 1790; Yvonne Pauly, "Überblickskommentar," in Karl Philipp Moritz, *Anthousa oder Roms Alterthümer*, vol. 4.1 of *Sämtliche Werke*, ed. Yvonne Pauly (Berlin: De Gruyter, 2005), 339–418.

43. As Marx put it in 1852, bourgeois revolutionaries "borrow from [from the Romans] names, battle cries and costumes in order to present the new scene of world history in this time-honored disguise and this borrowed language." Karl Marx, "The Eighteenth Brumaire of Louis Bonaparte," in *Marx: Later Political Writings*, ed. Terrell Carver (Cambridge: Cambridge University Press, 1996), 31.

critical commentary extends to antirevolutionary treatments that liken the revolution to carnival in its status as a fashionable yet ephemeral masquerade.

Public spectacle is also a testing ground for aesthetic aspirations to work-like completion and wholeness analogous to the supposed totality of popular collectivity. The impulse to represent popular spectacle in an aesthetically cohesive form—rounding out the small, occasional tableaus of journalistic reportage and travel writing into a whole, if you will—can be found in book projects such as Moritz's *Anthousa*, which he premiered as a series of lectures at the Berlin Academy of Arts. Modeled on ancient chronological lists of religious events, or "fasti," Moritz's project describes the religious festivities of ancient Rome as they occurred across a single calendar year, aiming at visually engaging representation rather than scholarly abstraction: "We [are to] see [the Roman *Volk*] before us, acting and living in its homes and on its streets and public places of gathering."[44] For Moritz, it is the intertwining of the religious and the aesthetic that makes Roman public life a beautiful whole, the "the center of beauty" (*Mittelpunkt des Schönen*). The subject of *Anthousa*, titled after a Greek word meaning "in blossom," is the "the individual existence of a people" (*das individuelle Daseyn eines Volks*), which is to be observed "for its own sake and for the sake of its own existence."[45] The wholeness and autonomy attributed here to Roman life parallels Moritz's account of the work of art as a self-standing, non-instrumental totality in other aesthetic writings.[46] His vision of the Roman people as a collective whole (or of ancient mythology as a beautiful whole) aligns the book more with the literary artwork than with dry scholarly analysis.

Several design choices tied to serial form organize Moritz's book and position it both as a self-contained whole and as a modest prod-

---

44. Moritz, *Anthousa*, 3.

45. Karl Philipp Moritz, "Über die Würde des Studiums der Altertümer," in *Karl Philipp Moritz Werke*, vol. 2 (Frankfurt: Deutscher Klassiker Verlag, 1997), 1047, 1045.

46. As in Moritz's important essay, Karl Philipp Moritz, "Versuch einer Vereinigung aller schönen Künste und Wissenschaften unter dem Begriff des in sich selbst Vollendeten," in *Karl Philipp Moritz Werke*, vol. 2.

uct of "small" print luxury. For one, the inclusion of multiple plates of simple outline drawings based on Roman coins and gems aligns *Anthousa* with aesthetic observation—in figure 2.1, we see a positive valuation of the mere "outlines" of objects that, as Moritz puts it, we are able to grasp hold of in the "flight of time." Here we see an image of the Suovetaurilia procession that was presumedly produced by anonymous members of the Berlin Academy of Arts, of which Moritz was a member.[47] These images are copied from a well-known collection of reproductions by P. D. Lippert of antique gems, or dactyliotheca, a popular and successful antiquarian product in the second half of the eighteenth century, which Moritz also draws on for the *Götterlehre* (Doctrine of the gods).[48] In effect, Moritz's reproductions are modest, more functional, workaday copies of this elaborate product of print luxury. This modesty can be seen in the simple line work and the fact that the images are printed on pages with text on the reverse side rather than on a separate page. Such illustrations deliberately leave much to the imagination; as Reinhart Wegner has argued, the use of illustrations and vignettes to lead readers to self-reflective observation is a characteristic feature of Moritz's publications.[49] In the case of this religious procession, the image fuels a sense of movement through the city and of the festival and the calendar year passing readers by.

Furthermore, Moritz's choice to structure his book according to a single calendar year contributes to a sense of both completion and continued repetition. Similar to the revolutionary calendar in the *Modejournal* discussed in the previous chapter, Moritz includes a timeline of the Roman festival calendar at the end of *Anthousa*, positioning it in relative proximity to other themed literary annuals such

---

47. See Yvonne Pauly, "Stellenerläuterungen," in Moritz, *Anthousa oder Roms Alterthümer*, 451.
48. Moritz's 1791 *Götterlehre* likewise contains such images, and it also relies on the so-called *Lippertsche Daktyliothek*. See Pauly, "Überblickskommentar," 381–82.
49. See Reinhart Wegner, "Augenblicke. Autonomie und Selbstreferenzialität sprachlicher Formen beim Betrachten von Bildern," in *Europäische Romantik. Interdisziplinäre Perspektiven der Forschung*, ed. Helmut Hühn und Joachim Schiedermair (Berlin: De Gruyter, 2015), 83–97.

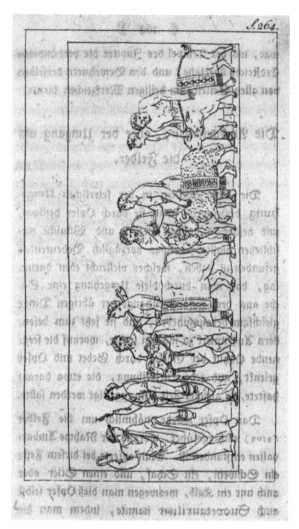

Figure 2.1. Anonymous, "Suovetaurilien-Prozession." *Anthousa, oder Roms Alterthümer. Ein Buch für die Menschheit* (Berlin: Maurer, 1791), 264. Bavarian State Library, Munich. Ant. 265. 6 ¾ inches × 4 inches.

as almanacs and *Taschenbücher*. There is a certain elegiac timelessness to this festival chronology, with the end of the book coinciding with the end of the year and the implication that the calendar will repeat anew, as a "beautiful cycle" (*schöner Kreislauf*) (in contrast to the more final temporal horizon of the fall of Rome, for example).[50] And yet Moritz's book also achieves an accumulative temporal effect by means of the repeated contemplation of antiquity, not least because the modern commemorative recollection and repetition of the religious calendar parallels the function of Roman festivities themselves, which memorialize important events in Roman history. Moritz is entirely clear about the unattainability of the true presence of antiquity, but, at the same time, he is interested less in a kind of mimetic ruin-gazing than in a humanistic *Bildung* enabled by imagining ancient Rome as a blossoming aesthetic totality.[51] The self-reflective viewing that Moritz seeks to catalyze in readers thus involves observing a classicizing shape of time based in cyclical repetition and recursive memorialization.

"The Whole of Carnival in a Coherent Form"

Moritz's *Anthousa* emerged from personal exchanges with Goethe first in Rome and then back in Weimar, where he composed parts of the book, but he also wrote it in dialogue with Goethe's carnival text, quoting extended sections from it (around ten pages in the original edition of *Anthousa*) in lieu of describing the ancient Saturnalia. As Moritz writes, Goethe brings "the ancient Saturnalia, as if in a new costume, before our eyes."[52] Goethe's text is also predicated on the idea of guiding readers through a sequence of images and on experiencing the festival and the Roman people as wholes or totalities. As he states, his goal is to present readers with an "overview and the enjoyment of an overly rushed and quickly passing

---

50. Moritz, *Anthousa*, 18.
51. On the aesthetics of Roman ruin gazing, see Julia Hell, *The Conquest of Ruins: The Third Reich and the Fall of Rome* (Chicago: University of Chicago Press, 2019).
52. Moritz, *Anthousa*, 241.

pleasure" (*Übersicht und Genuss einer überdrängten und vorbeirauschenden Freude*), and he deliberately foregrounds the role of artistic representation in visualizing the festival as a "whole."[53] The appeal to overview is evident at the end of the piece, where he claims to have presented to readers "the whole of [carnival] in a coherent form" (*das Ganze in seinem Zusammenhange*).[54] Throughout the piece, Goethe dramatizes the challenge of spatial and temporal orientation; as he writes, the festival culminates in a "crowding that transcends all concepts [*ein Gedränge, das alle Begriffe übersteigt*], indeed that cannot be recalled by even the most attentive memory."[55] *Das Gedränge*—"throng," "crowd," a "crowding," or a "rushing"—is Goethe's shorthand for the unruly visual and indeed physical experience of carnival, both for the crowds of people on the streets of Rome and for the sensory data confronting the observer who seeks to take it all in.[56]

Writing both for readers who have already experienced carnival and for "those who still [have] that trip ahead of them," Goethe seeks to reorganize the flow of information by presenting a series of short textual passages and images. Recounting his method of observation in the *Italienische Reise*, he writes, "I closely observed the progress of the follies, and how everything actually proceeded with a certain form and decorum. In so doing I noted the individual happenings in sequence [*Hierauf notierte ich mir die einzelnen Vorkommnisse der Reihe nach*]."[57] Sequential observation is the primary organizing conceit of the text's short, individually titled vignettes (twenty-eight in total). These pieces portray specific scenes

---

53. MA, 3.2, 219. This echoes the contemporaneous short essay of Goethe's where he suggests that the highest ideal of artistic form-giving (what he in the essay calls "style") entails attaining an overview of a series of possible forms through "exact and deep study of the objects themselves." MA, 3.2, 188.

54. MA, 3.2, 249.

55. MA, 3.2, 247.

56. On the motif of the "Gedränge" as the "Grundgerüst des beschriebenen Karnevalstreibens," see Elena Nährlich-Slatewa, "Das groteske Leben und seine edle Einfassung. 'Das Römische Karneval' Goethes und das Karnevalskonzept von Michail M. Bachtin," in *Goethe Jahrbuch* 106 (1989): 187.

57. MA, 15, 612.

and refer readers to corresponding images; some describe spatial locations ("The Corso," "The World of Beauty at the Ruspoli Palace," or "Side Streets"), while others address delimited frames of time ("The Early Period," "Evening," or "The Last Day") or are devoted to specific costumes ("Ecclesiastical Costumes," "Masks," or "King of Pulchinellas"). Moving diachronically through the week or so of carnival, these short pieces encourage a form of serial viewing that unfolds in and with time and enfolds the *Gedränge* into patterns of necessary movement.

To the end of creating an orderly sense of the whole, Goethe employs compositional techniques of selection and isolation, techniques that he dramatizes when noting the intermittent need of festival participants to withdraw from the chaos of the crowd and into quieter side streets.[58] The illustrations in particular play an isolating function by foregrounding individual figures against a blank background, with most plates featuring between two and five people. As with fashion plates, the reader's gaze is directed to specific costumes and gestures.[59] Here, again, we see the importance of blank space for facilitating imaginary viewing by leaving out the tumult of the street described by the text and thus breaking up the chaotic temporality of the instant into consumable segments. The text also includes indexical markers that recall the gestures of the travel guide or cicerone: "Here a pulcinella comes running... here comes another of his kind."[60] Directing the reader to consider specific plates creates a sense of movement, isolating but also enumerating the different masks and costumes. Footnotes direct the reader to the back of the book, and the reader must then find their way back to their previous place in the text. It is not uncommon for journals, illustrated books,

---

58. See MA, 3.2, 249.
59. Bakhtin's diagnosis of Romantic accounts of carnival and their displacement of the liberating potential of popular festivity from social life to the subjective imagination is helpful here to understand the abstraction and isolation involved in these images, though I would want to place more emphasis on the specific print formats that do this. See Mikhail Bakhtin, *Rabelais and His World*, trans. Hélène Isowlsky (Bloomington, IN: Indiana University Press, 1984), 36–38, 244–56.
60. MA, 3.2, 225.

pocketbooks, and calendars to situate their plates at the beginning or end of the volume, and readers would have been accustomed to navigating back and forth, but the effect of an unbroken flow of images is mitigated by the placement of the illustrations at the back of the book.

The entry "Masks" clusters a good number of the references to images. Though the images are intended to evoke a sense of individual momentary scenes as they pass by, they likewise access a variety of different temporal registers and historical times. Certain costumes represented in "Masks" lend color to contemporary fads in which Goethe himself partakes, as Romans dress up as the Northern European artists and writers who have flocked to Rome such as he and Moritz.[61] Other costumes reference decidedly contemporary fashions; Goethe describes, for example, how carriage drivers wear "feminine garb" (*Frauentracht*) and how "a broad, ugly fellow dressed up in the very latest fashion, with a high coiffure and feathers, becomes a great caricature."[62] Other costumes access a more expansive historical time, representing different "artistic epochs" or well-known statues in the city.[63] Traces of antiquity likewise inhere in the headgear of Pulcinella, which has its origins in the ancient Saturnalia (see figure 2.2). This image depicts by far the largest number of figures and conveys a bit more of the sensory chaos of the festival with its depiction of a procession containing musicians and people singing from songbooks. The Pulcinella costume is a particularly good example of serial proliferation, with multiple people dressed up as the same figure; as Goethe notes, "everyone seeks to reproduce this universal costume" (*jeder* [*sucht*] *diese Tracht zu vermannichfaltigen*).[64] Goethe exhibits no desire to arrange the disjunctive temporalities evoked by these costumes into any specific historical coherence (this would differ in some of the processions that he organized in Weimar and documented with text and images in the *Modejournal* [see figure 1.2],

---

61. MA, 3.2, 230.
62. MA, 3.2, 231.
63. MA, 3.2, 245.
64. MA, 3.2, 237.

Figure 2.2. Georg Melchior Kraus, after drawing by Christian Georg Schütz, "Aufzug des Pulcinellen-Königs." In Johann Wolfgang von Goethe, *Das Römische Carneval*, plate XIII. HAAB Weimar. 10 × 8 inches.

for some of these exhibit more of a historical, developmental logic[65]). The images allow readers to linger with single, static moments, but they also create a sense of bodies moving dynamically though space. Serial form thus allows Goethe to contain the crowd, *das Gedränge*, and to document the proliferation of costumes and bodies but also to slow such a proliferation down and parse it out into consumable parts.

Another key strategy of Goethe's is marking different kinds of beginnings and ends, a strategy that draws on the propensity of serial forms to dramatize endings and to express various modes of continuation, including repeated viewing and rereading. Marking beginnings and ends is a technique of writing time, including the beguiling temporality of carnival as both ephemeral and recurring. On the one hand, carnival's existence is all the more fleeting because daily life always restores the temporarily subverted status quo. On the other hand, as a "modern Saturnalia," the festival is "really just a continuation [*Fortsetzung*], or rather the culmination, of those customary Sunday and festival-day delights; it is nothing new, nothing unique, but, on the contrary, is just a natural extension of the Roman way of life."[66] This mixture of ephemerality and duration is also a reason why the festival calls out for repeated viewing. Furthermore, its yearly repetition helps to authenticate his account: "We would hardly dare to continue [our description] if so many people who have attended Roman carnival could not testify that we have stayed strictly with the truth, and if it were not a festival repeated annually and that will be viewed in the future by many an individual with this book in hand."[67] Goethe offers readers the perhaps ridiculous (but in his day and age increasingly familiar) sight of *bildungsbürgerlich* tourists walking the streets of Rome, guidebooks in hand. The proper treatment of carnival promises insight into how cultural forms are sustained across centuries.

---

65. See the review and images in the *JLM* 25, no. 3 (March 1810), on the processions dramatizing the migration of the Germanic tribes (*Völkerwanderung*) and Romantic poetry.
66. MA, 3.2, 220.
67. MA, 3.2, 232.

Along with demarcating the time span of the festival itself, Goethe also marks the beginnings and ends of its different parts. One particularly important moment he describes is the beloved carriage race in the Corso. In just a few short sentences, Goethe narrates the flurry of preparations, the instant the race begins, the procession of the horses and decorated carriages, and its end: "Thus does this festivity end with a violent, momentary impression, flashing by like lightning. Many thousands of people were eagerly anticipating it for a long time, but few can explain why they were waiting for this moment and why they enjoyed it so much."[68] By tracking a sequence of distinct, momentary occurrences, he creates a sense of the events of carnival as a linear procession, moving from instant to instant.[69] Clear framing gestures at the piece's beginning and end likewise create a sense of the whole of the carnival. The end of carnival is the beginning of Lent, and the final vignette is titled "Ash Wednesday," evoking the historical transition from polytheism to Christianity and from the ancient festival calendar to the Gregorian calendar. But, as with the conclusion of Moritz's *Anthousa*, the end of carnival season implies seasonal repetition. In this final section, Goethe shifts to a more serious, almost sermonizing tone, offering what he calls an "Ash Wednesday meditation":

> So then, an unrestrained [*ausschweifendes*] festival is over, like a dream, like a fairy tale, and perhaps less of it remains in the soul of the participant than of our readers, to whose imagination and understanding we have presented the whole of it in a coherent form [*das Ganze in seinem Zusammenhange*].[70]

For Goethe, his text and images are better able to achieve coherence than actual participation. As a material artifact and as a literary

---

68. MA, 3.2, 242.
69. On Goethe's exploration of the temporality of the instant, see Karol Berger, who explores Goethe's association of Faust with the kairotic moment: Karol Berger, *Bach's Cycle, Mozart's Arrow: An Essay on the Origins of Musical Modernity* (Berkeley: University of California Press, 2007), 266; see also Nicholas Rennie, *Speculating on the Moment: The Poetics of Time and Recurrence in Goethe, Leopardi, and Nietzsche* (Göttingen: Wallstein, 2005).
70. MA, 3.2, 246.

work, Goethe's text secures permanence through the promise of renewed viewing, either through readers' memory or rereading. Goethe's assertion of the permanence and artfulness of his account depends on the specific media ensembles that allow him and his readers to attain a position of being able to survey "the whole." In effect, Moritz's likening of Goethe's text to an optical viewbox addresses these literary and media-based techniques.

The title page's vignette likewise undergirds the assertion that the carnival book is an aesthetic whole and shores up its association with a classicist shape of time (figure 2.3). This image stems from a third artist involved in the project, Johann Heinrich Lips, a Swiss painter and engraver whom Goethe met in Italy and who taught at the drawing school in Weimar.[71] The image depicts a container amid several theater masks upon an abstract grid. The amphora-like vase is decorated with what appear to be satyr masks and a ram's skin evocative of the origins of antique drama. With their exaggerated expressions, two of the main masks are clearly from the theater of antiquity, and a third gazes at the masks on the vase rather than out at the reader. Scholars have conjectured that this face is a likeness of Goethe himself; at the very least, it is more realistic than the other two and evokes a sense of a modern viewer contemplating antiquity.[72] This image stages yet another scene of serial viewing, taking the viewer through a consideration of the larger masks and those on the vase. The winding of the masks around the vase evokes a certain cyclical movement, either of the vase as it turns around a fixed center, or of an observer moving around the object to view it from all sides; in both cases, such cyclical movement involves a process of serial viewing enabled by a classicizing form. Like Goethe's text, the vase and the figures winding around it promise that more views of the same are to come. The vase's isolated, symmetrical form and the implication of its cyclical rotation are

---

71. Goethe and Lips were in contact during the production of the book, and so Goethe likely had input into the image's composition. See Michael Schütterle, "*Untadeliche Schönheit." Kommentarband zum Rudolstädter Faksimile von Johann Wolfgang von Goethe: "Das Römische Carneval"* (Rudolstadt: Hain, 1993), 20.

72. Katja Gerhardt, "Goethe und 'das Römische Carneval.' Eine Betrachtung zu Text und Bild," *Weimarer Beiträge* 42, no. 2 (1996): 293–94.

DAS

RÖMISCHE CARNEVAL.

Berlin, gedruckt bey Johann Friedrich Unger.

Weimar und Gotha.
In Commission bey Carl Wilhelm Ettinger.
1789.

Figure 2.3. Johann Heinrich Lips, title page illustration. *Das römische Carneval* (Weimar and Gotha: Ettinger, 1789). HAAB Weimar. 10 × 8 inches.

evocative both of the seasonal recurrence of carnival and of the permanence and durability of Goethe's work.

Here we should return to the question of the revolution and the contemporary historical resonances of this text. Goethe's book presents an allegorical treatment of possibilities and limitations of popular energies—the dreamlike experience of "freedom" and "equality" brings with it a certain madness, intoxication, and confusion. The impulse to live out such freedom and equality recurs, but it is not permanent, for the return to the status quo always comes. The carnival piece casts the *Volk* as an aesthetic object without any genuine power of self-determination.[73] Serial form also plays a role in this depiction of popular energies, with the classicist shape of time suggested by carnival's yearly repetition precluding the interruption of the revolutionary new. The time span between the beginning and end allows for "freedom" (*Freiheit*) and "impudence" (*Frechheit*) but not for the emergence or institutionalization of the new.[74] Goethe does dramatize the revolution in terms of the trauma of the new in later works, and the carnival piece is by no means his last word on the revolution.[75] But, to the extent that his treatment of carnival's simultaneous transience and persistence does in fact obliquely engage with the possibility of revolution, Goethe remains skeptical about popular self-determination, and he enlists serial form to give this skepticism shape.

---

73. See Susanne Lüdemann, "Vom Römischen Karneval zur ökonomischen Automate. Massendarstellung bei Goethe und E.T.A. Hoffmann," in *Massenfassungen: Beiträge zur Diskurs- und Mediengeschichte der Menschenmenge*, ed. Susanne Lüdemann and Uwe Hebekus (Munich: Fink, 2010), 107–23; and Uwe Hebekus, "Goethes Feste. Allegorien der Geschichte," in *Goethes Feste*, ed. Uwe Hebekus (Frankfurt: Insel, 1993), 273–302.

74. As Goethe puts it, "the difference between high and low seems to be set aside for a moment; everyone draws closer to everyone else, everyone accepts whatever happens to him with ease, and reciprocal impudence (*Frechheit*) and freedom (*Freiheit*) are balanced by a general good humor." MA, 3.2, 246.

75. On this trauma, see Andreas Gailus, "Poetics of Containment: Goethe's Conversations of German Refugees and the Crisis of Representation," *Modern Philology* 100, no. 3 (2003): 436–74.

Second (and Third) Views of Carnival: Republication, Print Luxury, and Consumable Classicism

"What comes next?" is a perennial question for both serial entertainment and the news cycle in an age of revolution, and one that is certainly operative in the case of carnival's recurrence and subsequent viewings of Goethe's carnival writings. In fact, the publication of the piece in the January 1790 issue of the *Modejournal* at the time of carnival does indeed deliver on the second viewing. Republication forces us to recontextualize Goethe's piece and its status as material object because its text and images are placed in new environments. This suggests that an immanent reading of the perpetual return of carnival might not be the last word. Of course, perhaps the most striking feature of the piece's publication history is that the French Revolution has begun in the period since the book's publication, but its republication also brings the piece into proximity with additional reports in the *Modejournal*. Republication, a process that extends not merely to the journal version but also to subsequent authorized and unauthorized publications, also recasts the piece's status as a stand-alone work. And finally, the journal version presents readers with a print object altogether different from the book version. A second viewing of Goethe's piece necessarily complicates our discussion of its status as a material object, as the question of what comes next becomes relevant to additional texts and images in the orbit of the *Modejournal*. How these material objects generate shapes of time that potentially conflict with the book format and how they might open onto parallel and conflicting classicisms associated with the *Modejournal* are questions we can begin to address by lingering a bit more with the circumstances of republication.

"The Luxury Edition Is Completely out of Stock"

Given the ubiquitous association of periodicals with ephemerality, one might assume that a second view of *Das römische Carneval* would reinforce the standard dichotomy between lasting books and fleeting journals. As we've seen, Goethe associates the book version with permanence. His account is more lasting for readers than their in-person impressions of the celebration, and future travelers are guaranteed to hold the work in their hands. It is ironic, then, that, as Bertuch and Kraus state in a note explaining the necessity of the journal version, "many connoisseurs have not been able to obtain a copy of the beautiful edition [schöne Ausgabe] ... and many of our readers are not yet at all familiar" with it.[76] As the editors go on to note in the January 1790 issue's advertising supplement, "the luxury edition [prächtige Ausgabe] published at the last spring book fair is already completely out of stock" despite continuing "demand."[77] After a first run of three hundred copies, Bertuch and Kraus conclude that they cannot "make the decision to do a second of the same edition."[78] This was particularly frustrating to Goethe, who had given away his copies and was unable to obtain a personal copy.[79] In effect, just as the journal version was appearing, the luxury book version was disappearing before everyone's eyes. This curious episode brings the book and journal versions into the same orbit insofar as each comes to be associated with a perhaps all-too-fleeting fashionableness.

To be sure, there are ways in which journals are associated with duration and permanence. A contemporaneous defense of the merits of journals over "many exceptional artworks" put forth by J. H. Campe in his *Braunschweigisches Journal* (Braunschweig journal) (1788–1791) cites the wider circulation of journals and their ability to make information more accessible.[80] Out-of-date journals are

---

76. Johann Wolfgang von Goethe, "Das Römische Carneval," *JLM* 5, no. 1 (January 1790): 1–47, note 1.
77. "Die ... prächtige Ausgabe [ist] bereits gänzlich vergriffen." "Nachricht, das Römische Carneval betreffend," *Intelligenzblatt des Journal des Luxus und der Moden* 1 (1790): iii.
78. "Nachricht, das Römische Carneval betreffend," iii.
79. See Unseld, *Goethe and His Publishers*, 88.
80. Joachim Heinrich Campe, "Beantwortung dieses Einwurfs," *Braunschweigisches Journal* 1, no. 1 (1788): 34. On this episode see Richard B. Apgar, "Flooded: Periodicals and the Crisis of Information around 1780," in *Market Strategies and German Literature in the Long Nineteenth Century*, ed. Vance Byrd and Ervin Malakaj (Berlin: De Gruyter, 2020), 34–35.

always being saved and bound together (like many periodicals, the pages of the *Modejournal* are numerated according to yearly runs, taking on a certain archival function akin to Bertuch's original idea for publishing yearly fashion annals). Additionally, serial formats can be associated with the kinds of print luxury that Bertuch promotes. This applies in particular to the booklet that is to accompany the journal version of Goethe's piece and contain the twenty images etched by Kraus. This booklet did not have a large run (eighty-five copies were printed), and its appearance recalls key features of the book version, especially through its title vignette (figure 2.4).[81] However, for readers able to obtain a copy of this supplement, certain differences between book and journal versions would have been readily apparent, including between the book and pamphlet's Antiqua type and the journal's black letter Fraktur.[82] Connotations of "small" and "large" print commodities are likewise at stake: Bertuch called the book version "a small interesting work," but the octavo journal is smaller than the quarto book, and there is not nearly the same amount of white space on the journal page. Readers are tasked with collating the journal with the quarto pamphlet on the basis of footnotes in the journal version. At the same time, the journal version's section headings resemble other paratextual markings in the *Modejournal*, bringing the segmentation structuring Goethe's piece in line with the journal's appearance.

Journal publication also does the work of constellating the text and its images with other material. This January 1790 issue includes a title vignette commemorating the new year, an article detailing the accessories of a sixteenth-century aristocratic bride, miscellaneous theater reports from several German cities and Paris, and more. Along with the image of the French National Guard uniform discussed in the previous chapter, this issue's images include a depiction of a woman

---

81. On the booklet, see Schütterle, "*Untadeliche Schönheit*," 45.
82. Falk addresses the question of typography and typographical luxury in his comparison of book and journal versions; see Rainer Falk, "Sehende Lektüre. Zur Sichtbarkeit des Textes am Beispiel von Goethes *Römischem Carneval*," in *Ästhetische Erfahrung: Gegenstände, Konzepte, Geschichtlichkeit*, Freie Universität Berlin, 2006, http://www.sfb626.de/veroeffentlichungen/online/aesth_erfahrung/aufsaetze/falk.pdf.

Figure 2.4. Title page. *Masken des römischen Carnevals* (Weimar and Gotha: Ettinger, 1790). Leipzig University Library, Hirzel.A.291. 10×8 inches.

dressed for one of the carnival-season winter balls, which, as the "Fashion News from France" states, are still being held even though the masked processions of carnival had been greatly curtailed by Parisian authorities in 1790.[83] Taken on their own, the theatrical masks of the booklet's title vignette might seem benign enough, but would readers have been tempted to compare the masks with the bodiless heads on pikes depicted in contemporaneous almanacs and journals, as in the readily available late 1789 German almanacs?[84] Though the guillotine would not be implemented as a form of punishment until 1792, literal and symbolic decapitation is very much on the minds of contemporaries in early 1790. A "Theater Anecdote" in this same January issue takes the image of severed heads in different direction, relating a scene of two actors perched under a table with their heads sticking through it as if cut off and resting in bowls, disrupting the terrifying scene with a fit of sneezing.[85] Journal publication brings Goethe's piece back into the flow of information and imagery characteristic of the contemporary journal landscape and back into the orbit of the *Modejournal*'s distinctive project of chronicling this flow more or less directly. Furthermore, journal publication shifts questions of what repeats and what comes after into a register more closely aligned with cultural journalism. Goethe's piece might still be encounterable as a self-contained sequence of images, but it can also be experienced as a tableau predicated on being followed by other tableaus, a "piece" followed by other "counterpieces," its masks and heads followed by other masks and heads.

---

83. This is a feature of the Parisian social calendar that would repeat in the years to come and upon which the journal would frequently comment, for many revolutionaries were critical of carnival's perpetuation of certain prerevolutionary traditions. See for example the March 1790 issue, two issues after the Goethe piece, *JLM* 5, no. 3 (March 1790): 166; see also Bringemeier, *Ein Modejournalist*, 54. On the revolutionaries attempts to reshape and replace carnival, see Mona Ozouf, *Festivals and the French Revolution* (Cambridge, MA: Harvard University Press, 1991), 228–29.

84. As, for example, the *Historischer Almanach fürs Jahr 1790, enthaltend die Geschichte der Großen Revolution in Frankreich*, ed. Lorenz Westenrieder and J. C. F. Schulz (Braunschweig: Schulbuchhandlung, 1790), plate 14, unpaginated introductory materials. This work is published by the same publishing house as Campe's *Braunschweiges Journal*.

85. "Theater-Anekdoten," *JLM* 5, no. 1 (January 1790): 55–56.

It is therefore not merely an ironic literary-historical footnote that the book edition goes out of print so quickly. The format of the journal version accesses the promise of serial print to return in ways that diverge from the logic of the book version. Each version calls to mind a different shape of time and invites potentially conflicting literary-historical and media-historical interpretations. It is no accident that Bertuch and Kraus publish Goethe's piece in the first issue of the new year, in the season of both modern carnival and the ancient Saturnalia. The book version of Goethe's *Das römische Carneval* was published at the 1789 spring fair (*Ostermesse*), a little more than a year prior, but the time span between first and second publication is nonetheless somewhat evocative of the carnival's yearly recurrence. Putting the text at the beginning of the January issue also aligns Goethe's piece with the supplemental beginning-of-the-year articles and images offered by the *Modejournal* to its readers, that is, its "new year's presents of fashion." This convention brings the piece into resonance with the journal's yearly and monthly periodicities and its position in the broader print marketplace. Along with functioning as a form of print luxury, journal publication also taps into the proliferation of material on carnival and other festivals. Seen in this light, Goethe's text is both an instantiation of ongoing "fashion news" about carnival and a text that fuels future production, both in more self-contained projects such as Moritz's and across a variety of journalistic and literary undertakings.

Finally, journal reproduction can also be seen as a harbinger of the numerous republications of Goethe's piece in authorized and unauthorized versions. The journal version inaugurates a long, winding journey of reconstellation: it is reprinted in the 1792 *Goethe's Neue Schriften* (Goethe's new writings); in pocketbooks and unauthorized anthologies in 1793, 1796, 1799, and 1826; in a new 1801 edition of *Goethe's Neue Schriften*; seven times in works editions between 1808 and 1829; and in Swedish (1821) and English translations (1829).[86] All told, the piece is republished up to fifteen times before it reaches its place in the *Italienische Reise*, in the *Ausgabe letzter Hand* (Edition of

---

86. For a complete list of the various publications of the piece, see Schütterle, "*Untadeliche Schönheit*," 43–54.

the last hand) (1827–1830). In each case, the carnival text is part of an anthology-like collection, either multi- or single-author, and is placed in relation to other surrounding texts according to different logics. Republication therefore marks a dual drift toward merging with the broader flow of print matter and toward consolidation in an authorial oeuvre, a topic to which I return at the end of the chapter. Meanwhile, there is more to say about the *Modejournal*'s treatment of carnival and the journal's integral place in the business of print.

Böttiger's View of Carnival

Goethe's carnival piece enhances the historical scope of the *Modejournal* and boosts its reputation as a place to experience antiquity. Even if Goethe, Schiller, and others would later dispute the cultural-historical bona fides of the journal's editors, the carnival piece serves as a touchstone for the journal's classicizing approach, which Böttiger helps to amplify after becoming an unnamed coeditor in 1795 or 1796 (he also took over editing *Der Neue Teutsche Merkur* [The new German mercury] in 1794). Not least because of his partnerships with Bertuch, he developed a reputation for being ubiquitous in the journals of the day—"What is friend Böttiger not writing in?" wrote Schiller to Goethe in 1795.[87] He is also a scholar of antiquity, though unlike Winckelmann, Goethe, Moritz, and Herder, he never visited Rome; his furthest travel destination was Paris, where he developed close ties in scholarly and journalistic circles. Böttiger's articles in the 1790s bring to the *Modejournal* a focus on the daily life of antiquity, and he peppers such pieces with ostentatious scholarly gestures, satirical flair, fictional scenarios, and frequent tableau-like visualizations and image commentaries. As Angela Borchert puts it, an interest in the everyday life of Rome is the part of the "double view of antiquity" characteristic of the period, namely the consideration of

---

[87]. "Worin schreibt aber Freund Böttiger nicht!" Schiller to Goethe, December 29, 1795, MA, 8.1, 145. On Böttiger's nickname "Magister Ubique," see Julia A. Schmidt-Funke, *Karl August Böttiger (1760–1835). Weltmann und Gelehrter* (Heidelberg: Winter, 2006).

both the fine arts and the day-to-day habits of the ancients.[88] This can be seen in Böttiger's multipart article series about the complicated dressing rituals of a Roman lady that he republished in the influential Parisian journal *Magasin Encyclopédique*, edited by Böttiger's colleague and friend Aubin-Louis Millin.[89] Böttiger thus follows a path distinct both from Goethe and Schiller's literary classicism and from the institutionalization of classics (*Altertumswissenschaft*) as an academic discipline in the emerging research university of the nineteenth century. Instead, Böttiger fuses antiquarian scholarship and cultural journalism, treating writing in journals for more general audiences as both a method of distributing antiquarian knowledge and a mode of serialized entertainment that sells.[90]

Böttiger's two-part article titled "The Saturnalia Feast [*Der Saturnalienschmaus*]: A Carnival Scene of Ancient Rome" in the February/March 1797 issue of *Modejournal* brings us directly back to Goethe's carnival piece. These articles are continuations of sorts of his previous pieces on the dressing rituals of a wealthy Roman lady, but here he turns to the male members of the same household, focusing on a festive dinner shared by patricians and slaves. The articles detail the meal's course, seating order, silverware and tablecloths, food, and other festive practices, including the selection of the Saturnalia king. Böttiger follows familiar tropes about these festivities' perpetuation into the present—"for three thousand years, the names of the plays and the actors have always changed, but never the content of the piece and the view of the different scenes"—and he even begins the article with an extended quote of Goethe ("the artful depicter" [*der kunstreiche Schilderer*]) where

---

88. Angela Borchert, "Ein Seismograph des Zeitgeistes: Kultur, Kulturgeschichte und Kulturkritik im *Journal des Luxus und der Moden*," in *Das "Journal des Luxus und der Moden": Kultur um 1800*, ed. Angela Borchert and Ralf Dressel (Heidelberg: Winter, 2004), 97.

89. K. A. Böttiger, "Morgenbesuche im Ankleidezimmer einer alten Römerin," *JLM* 11, no. 7 (July 1796–December 1796). On this episode, see René Sternke, *Böttiger und der archäologische Diskurs* (Berlin: Akademie, 2008), 124.

90. On journalism as a "material facilitation [*Ermöglichungsbedinung*] and form of distribution of the archaeological discourse," see Sternke, *Böttiger und der archäologische Diskurs*, xvii.

Goethe comments on Christianity's inability to fully do away with carnival's traditions.[91]

In drawing readers' attention to present-day customs originating in antiquity, Böttiger touches on issues of contemporary-historical importance. Here he enlists Diderot and Mercier as proof of the festival's modern residues, in particular as they relate to the selection of the ephemeral Saturnalia/carnival king. He cites Diderot's satiric verses mocking the French king on the tradition of selecting a so-called bean king (*roi de la fève*) as a premonition of the revolution itself and then cites Mercier's "witty" (*launigt*) remarks on carnival in his prerevolutionary *Tableau de Paris*: "That festival, founded in gorging, will be immortal" (*cette fête fondèe sur la bâfre, sera immortelle*).[92] He then goes on to weaponize the ephemerality of carnival against the postrevolutionary directorial government (1795–1799), citing a present-day Parisian bakery's advertisement for *gateaux du directoire* (carnival cakes) that likens the current government to the carnival king. In effect, Böttiger mobilizes the convention of the carnival king to cast both pre- and postrevolutionary regimes as fleeting debauches. And yet, each of his sources' takes on this convention do not stray from the assumption at the heart of carnival that more will come and that the festival (and a carnivalesque politics characteristic of the postrevolutionary atmosphere) will continue in coming years. It is in this context that Böttiger returns once more to Goethe's piece, directing readers to his image of the contemporary garb of the modern "King of Pulchinellas" as an example of the styles of hats used to crown the ephemeral king of the Roman household. Böttiger musters the Goethe piece to show another side of the festival's "immortality." This is a form of satirical neo-Roman mimesis that weaponizes carnival against the revolution, even while embracing the festival as a

---

91. K. A. Böttiger, "Der Saturnalienschmaus. Eine Carnevalsszene des alten Roms. 1. Tafelkleid und Kapuze, Modekostüm der Saturnalien—Eintritt ins Tafelzimmer," *JLM* 12, no. 2 (February 1797): 55, 53.

92. K. A. Böttiger, "Der Saturnalienschmaus. Eine Carnevalsszene des alten Roms. 2. Tischordnunge. Serivietten, und die Königswahl," *JLM* 12, no. 3 (March 1797): note 109.

temporary yet recurring transport (and one from which adept journalists and editors can profit).[93]

"New Year's Presents of Fashion"

Along with bringing antiquarianism and a certain style of antirevolutionary *Zeitgeschichte* into resonance, Böttiger highlights the place of various kinds of material objects in ancient Roman life. Of particular relevance are the journal's "new year's presents of fashion," which Böttiger takes in an increasingly classicizing direction as editor. These images lend themselves very much to being considered as part of Moritz and Goethe's project of visualizing antiquity and of Bertuch's project of linking antiquarian topics to the dissemination of print products. A pair of articles in the January 1796 issue illustrates this. The first glosses the issue's supplemental new year's *Titelkupfer* titled "Venus and the Graces, with Good Wishes for the Year 1796" (see figure 1.4). The main image is based on an antique gem in the Museo Florentino, and Böttiger imagines the bathing scene depicted there, drawing on various ancient literary sources, including Homer and Ovid. In Böttiger's hands, this image of Venus regarding herself in the mirror allows contemporary readers a certain amount of self-reflection: as Borchert puts it, in Böttiger's hands, "Venus and the graces become a bathing scene that could just as well play out at the court in Gotha or Ludwigsburg as on Cyprus."[94]

Böttiger goes on to stress how the image exemplifies the journal's neoclassical commitments, leaving readers to decide whether it partakes of the more dignified side of the ancient Roman custom of giving new years' presents, or *strena*, or of its less honorable (and less costly) variant, namely the practice of gifting small tablets with the names of luxury items on it rather than the actual items themselves: a flask of wine, a "wild boar haunch," "a beautiful

---

93. On the channeling of carnival's subversive energies in restorative directions and back into the orbit of the prerevolutionary aristocratic fête through commercialization and depoliticization, see Matala de Mazza, *Der populäre Pakt*.

94. Borchert, "Ein Seismograph," 99.

overcoat of Gallician wool, a silver chalice, or a Corinthian candelabra."[95]

> Sympathetic male and female readers of this journal may decide for themselves whether its editors, who otherwise so gladly do the justice due to the taste of the model nations of the ancient Greeks and Romans in everything concerning the arts, costumes, and decoration, have followed their example even in this unseemly custom? The editors, too, now present the audience interested in this magazine the small and modest toll of a congratulatory new year's present.[96]

Böttiger's demonstrative gesture filters the trope of the persistence of antiquity through the question of large and small print luxury: it is not a monumental sculpture, architectural structure, or weighty book that confirms the duration of classical norms, but rather the "small and modest" page of a fashion journal. The continuity with ancient Rome plays out in terms of style and design and also in terms of attempts to profit from this custom of gift giving by making ever new products for this market, as an article in the previous year's January issue on the English manufacture of classicizing ceramics details.[97] In a self-deprecating twist, though, Böttiger does not shy away from concluding that the journal's new year's presents might disappoint readers looking for more valuable print objects.

He continues to link the various features of the *Modejournal* to Roman practices when he embeds his commentary on this new year's presents in a media-historical genealogy of sorts in which serial reproduction plays a vital role in keeping ancient styles and practices alive. As he writes, even though the representation of the antique gem is a copy, it is able to reach a broader audience through the art of etching (*Kupferstichkunst*) and print reproduction. Despite being a "mere copy and reproduction" (*Copey und Abzeichen*)

---

95. K. A. Böttiger, "Venus und die Grazien, zum Glückswunsche für das Jahr, 1796," *JLM* 11, no. 1 (January 1796): 5, 6.
96. Böttiger, "Venus und die Grazien," 5, 6.
97. The 1795 new year's article focuses on a vase and English manufacturing producing classically inspired Derbystone vases. K. A. Böttiger, "Glückwunsch-Vasen. Zur Erklärung des Titelkupfers," *JLM* 11, no. 1 (January 1796): 3–12.

the image "still speaks through form and outline."[98] Etching on the one hand continues the antique practice of proliferating small reproductions used as gifts, and on the other, it is a clearly a modern improvement. By being deprived of it, "antiquity missed out on thousands of aesthetic pleasures," but modern craftspeople are now able to make antiquity more accessible.[99] Böttiger thus filters the *Modejournal*'s own etched images such as "Venus and the Graces" through the trope that coins and gems are traces of ancient life. In both content and format, the journal is in the business of broadening reader exposure to antiquity and classicizing forms. Böttiger's article is thus not merely one more piece of literary entertainment whose topic is antiquity but rather an imitative copy of specific cultural practices, taking the kind of virtual, imaginary "participation" in ancient ritual as proposed by Moritz into the realm of material culture and the business of print.[100]

Xenia

The very next article in the January 1796 issue delves deeper into this media-historical genealogy. Böttiger's "Painted and Written New Year's Presents of the Ancient Romans" continues to linger with gift giving, addressing hospitality gifts, or *xenia*, in particular.[101] With roots in Roman harvest festivals, these presents played a part in Saturnalian festivities and later in carnival.[102] That said, Böttiger takes issue with the "pious interpretation" (*fromme Ausdeutung*) of the practice advanced by Moritz's "catalogue of festivals" (*Festverzeichniss*), noting that Moritz falsely traces such gift giving back to the Saturnalia's temporary transport of Romans into (quoting Moritz) an "innocent world where universal freedom and equality reigned

---

98. Böttiger, "Venus und die Grazien," 6.
99. Böttiger, "Venus und die Grazien," 6.
100. See Pabst's discussion of the "Nachahmung antiker Lebenspraxis" around 1800. Pabst, "Kultur der Kopie," 138.
101. K. A. Böttiger, "Gemahlte und geschriebene Neujahrsschenke der alten Römer," *JLM* 11, no. 1 (January 1796): 18–25.
102. See Manfred Fuhrmann, "Fasnacht als Utopie: Vom Saturnalienfest im alten Rom," *Narrenfreiheit: Beiträge zur Fasnachtsforschung* 51 (1980): 29–42.

along with reciprocal loyalty among humans."[103] Insisting on a different genealogy of this practice, Böttiger presents an image of ancient Rome that functions less as a model for the republican or even revolutionary potential of humanity and more as a site of commercial innovation where various artistic, fashion, and luxury items are in a constant process of development and differentiation. Böttiger outlines this strand of ancient gift giving and its various permutations, including the gifting of memorial coins and medallions, which then develops into the circulation of drawings and paintings of such coins, referencing the unseemly practices of providing reproductions rather than the actual objects he mentions above: "What was more natural . . . that, over time, people would send dainty reproductions and paintings [*zierliche Abbildungen und Gemälde*] of these items to each other?"[104] The proliferation of such representations also led to the growth of increasingly specialized artists and craftsmen, including so-called rhyparographers, genre and still life painters of sordid or distasteful subjects. Situating the work of these craftsmen in a genealogy of antique arts and crafts, he has more positive things to say about this art than other neoclassical aesthetic theorists of the period.[105] Indeed, Böttiger goes so far as to trace a direct line from ancient satire and genre painting to the political and social caricature of the present day, a topic explored in greater detail in the next chapter.

This lineage of practical and material culture includes the emergence of short satirical verses, likewise called *xenia*, and Böttiger closes the article by translating some Roman examples and even offering a few of his own. In effect, he provides another layer to the enactment of the very cultural practices he describes. The article ends with several verses "to test out this style" and as additional new year's presents, in the form of a "a poetic platter" (*eine dichterische Schlachtschüssel*). Titled "Wine and Ointment," one piece reads: "Leave your heir money, but ointments and wines, / I advise

---

103. Böttiger, "Gemahlte und geschriebene Neujahrsschenke," 18.
104. Böttiger, "Gemahlte und geschriebene Neujahrsschenke," 21.
105. On eighteenth-century debates about caricature, see Hans-Georg von Arburg, *Kunst-Wissenschaft um 1800. Studien zu Georg Christoph Lichtenbergs Hogarth-Kommentaren* (Göttingen: Wallstein, 1998), 64–76.

you, do not leave him: give them all to yourself."[106] Playing with the distinction between consumable or usable items and their medial representation—here, satirically falling much more on the (unseemly) side of giving small drawings of bottles rather than the wine itself—Böttiger playfully ends on a note of celebrating the pleasures of life (*Lebensgenuss*) as they cut across a variety of forms of luxury items. At the same time, though, the selfish gesture of "save the good stuff for yourself" is also a call for readers to enjoy the print products that they hold in their hands and to commemorate the new year with something nice that is sublimated into the form of literary and visual entertainment. Böttiger thus associates the varied contents of the journal—its articles, its images, its occasional poetry, and its cultural and historical journalism—with these small, consumable products of artistic and artisanal craft. In the process, he gives readers tools to map practices of literary and material gift giving across multiple temporal continuums.

This article by Böttiger in particular caught Goethe's eye, not least because he and Schiller were in the process of compiling *xenia* of their own in the form of polemical and satirical verses aimed at the contemporary literary landscape. In January of 1796, Goethe draws Schiller's attention to Böttiger's articles, even including a copy of this issue of the *Modejournal* in the letter. He takes swipes at both Böttiger's abilities as an antiquarian and the *Modejournal* itself: "The writer doesn't know that one is being prepared for him for the next year, these people are just so pitiful and untalented when it comes down to it. Offering only two of these little poems, and so poorly translated on top of it. It's as if everything spiritual had taken flight from this fire-red soft cover [*Es ist aber, als wenn alles Geistreiche diesen feuerfarbenen Einband flöhe*]."[107] The journal's lack of spirit (*Geist*) implies a certain deformation or formlessness. Goethe suggests, in contrast, that his and Schiller's *xenia* project is doing justice to the language, style, and formal innovations of the

---

106. "Laß dem Erben Geld nach. Aber Salben und Weine, Rath ich dir, gibe ihm nicht: alles dieß schenke dir selbst." Böttiger, "Gemahlte und geschriebene Neujahrsschenke," 25.

107. Goethe to Schiller, January 30, 1796, MA, 8.1, 157.

ancients. This extends to these modern poets' effortless ability to invent new verses in this style on a much more prodigious scale than Böttiger could. Goethe writes, "The distichs increase daily, they are now up to around two hundred." For Goethe and Schiller, the *xenia* are tools for polemical self-differentiation in a crowded literary market, while for Böttiger, they are aligned with satirical entertainment as a consumable literary commodity and with the passing pleasures of the festival week.[108]

Seen in light of Böttiger's genealogy of new year's gift giving and the editors' deliberate timing in positioning pieces on these festivals in the first issues of the new year, Goethe's carnival writings might retroactively come into view as not unlike one of the journal's "new year's presents of fashion." Bertuch and Böttiger are in the business of giving readers things that they like and want, and the new year's gifts are material objects that fuel readers' desires for more. A reading of the carnival piece as a type of print luxury promoted to readers cast new light on the relative "smallness" of the book mentioned by Bertuch in the advertisement for it, for this smallness links the book with other ephemeral print objects in the journal. In light of the business model of the *Modejournal*, such a reading of the carnival piece takes control of the piece out of the hands of the author and the literary politics that Goethe and Schiller pursue. The act of viewing the piece as part of the constellation of content on offer in the journal brings the piece's publication into alignment with certain cyclical patterns of recurrence mapped by Goethe himself, yet this series of associated texts—and the shapes of time that they catalyze—is also more thoroughly saturated with a sense of the commercial standing of print, fashion, and "small" luxury. Seen in this way, the visual culture of the *Modejournal* promote a form of self-reflective observation of time. Collector objects attune readers to the passing of time, to questions of what remains and what does not, and to the different shapes of time which these objects mark, whether it is the persistence of antiquity in the present, the patterns

---

108. On Borchert's reading of this encounter, Böttiger pursues "classicism without cultural criticism" rather than an exclusionary literary politics. Borchert, "Ein Seismograph des Zeitgeistes," 96–102.

of the print marketplace, the time of the seasons, the time of the revolution, and more. This is a mode of pleasure, enjoyment, and diversion befitting the realm of "small" print luxury, but it is also a commemorative mode that gives readers tools for observing time by demonstratively giving them an ongoing series of differently timed material objects. As scholars have noted in regard to practices of reproduction and copying in this period, proponents of reproduction such as Böttiger, Bertuch, and Kraus shift the question of originality from the work to the technology and the materiality of the copy.[109] The association of specific brands with specific new technologies (or the adept use of existing ones) help manufacturers and publishers such as Wedgwood, Klauer, Bertuch, and Böttiger develop recognizable brands. The question is not whether an art object is one of a kind but whether it is a Wedgwood or a Bertuch and Böttiger, if you will. This brings the larger commercial project of the Comptoir into view as a kind of marketing operation: what matters first and foremost is not that something in the *Modejournal* is extraordinarily original or *geistreich*, but that it is packaged in the journal's fire-colored packaging and readers know that more will follow in the coming months.

After Goethe's *Carnival*

Like the strikingly predictable repetition of carnival, Goethe's carnival piece lays the groundwork for more to come, but it is not always clear or certain what this more will be. The print object tells us something about how it is to be reencountered in the future, yet readers go on to make use of it in various unpredictable ways. Goethe's piece enables a certain amount of knowledge about future views of carnival and future views of both his text and literary and journalistic representations by other writers and artists. The association of carnival with year-end consumer and commemorative practices only reinforces this tendency. From a literary-historical perspective, tracking the afterlives of Goethe's piece allows us to en-

---

109. See Pabst, "Kultur der Kopie," 145.

vision temporal structures that go beyond the individual work and depend on patterns of temporal succession that are as characteristic of the broader print market as they are of logics of Goethe's development as an author or of the piece's narrative structure.[110] The fact that the carnival piece is republished fifteen times before Goethe's death is an initial sign that there are multiple texts related to the piece that call out for constellation. Exploring afterlives also entails exploring different inflections of classicism and ways in which Goethe's politics of his works, or *Werkpolitik*, both converge with and diverge from classicist conceptions of the work.

As I suggested in my discussion of *Das römische Carneval*, the book version encourages a *work-oriented reading with a classicizing inflection*. The after of such a project thus might well be considered in terms of other works that mimic the direct claim of Goethe's piece to a logic of coherence (*Zusammenhang*), organic unity, and totalizing representation. This is a logic of the work in line with the idealist and classicist aesthetics that Moritz and Goethe developed in this period, and I have suggested ways in which *Anthousa* articulates these aesthetics with its conception of the religious culture of ancient Rome as a beautiful totality. Moritz's work profits from the analogy between the unity of the Roman people and the unity of its artistic and scholarly representation, and it elegiacally articulates a particular classicizing shape of time predicated on the perpetual repetition of the ancient Roman religious calendar. The *Anthousa* material is an experiment of Moritz's in giving form to his experience of antiquity in a way that departs from his travelogue, which operates very much in the sentimental tradition familiar from his earlier British travel writing. The *Anthousa* project also stands out because Moritz so explicitly situates it in line with Goethe's carnival piece, adapting its logic of serial, "lively" representation and even ventriloquizing Goethe to envision the ancient Saturnalia.

---

110. These temporal structures point toward what Mattias Pirholt and others have described as the "heteronomy" of the work. See Mattias Pirholt, "Goethe's Exploratory Idealism," in *Beyond Autonomy in Eighteenth-Century British and German Aesthetics*, ed. Karl Axelsson, Camilla Flodin, and Mattias Pirholt (New York and London: Routledge, 2021), 217–38.

Moritz's text is also part of an ensemble of different writings and anthologies of previous published texts dealing with related topics, and this opens up a different interpretive and literary-historical horizon, namely that of *multiple works by a single author, and of author-based republication across different formats*. Goethe avidly published his writings in various anthologies and collections, and the carnival piece is republished across a variety of authorized and unauthorized anthologies.[111] Furthermore, he published multiple authorized editions of his collected works, with twenty-two volume works editions on the market before he started with his final, most ambitious *Ausgabe letzter Hand*.[112] As a "virtuoso of the completed works" (Martus) and as someone keenly in pursuit of the "poetics of reprinting" (Spoerhase), Goethe experiments with different placements of the carnival piece in his works editions, and this experimentation thus represents another answer to the question of what comes "after."[113] The second republication of the carnival piece is the first of a seven-volume edition of *Goethe's Neue Schriften* published in 1792 by Unger in Berlin. This 1792 volume contains other material obliquely responding to the lead-up to the French Revolution such as the drama *Der Groß-Cophta* (The Grand Kofta) and the essay *Des Joseph Balsamo, genannt Cagliostro, Stammbaum* (The family tree of Joseph Balsamo, a.k.a. Cagliostro).[114] It is significant that Goethe puts his carnival text in the very first volume of his *Neue Schriften*, thereby conveying a sense of its timeliness and responsiveness in connection with companion writings that also deal with the Revolution's causes and effects. In subsequent editions the carnival piece is clustered with the 1795 *Unterhaltungen deutscher Ausgewanderten*

---

111. See Wolfgang Bunzel, "Publizistische Poetik. Goethes Veröffentlichungen in Almanachen und Taschenbüchern," in *Almanach- und Taschenbuchkultur des 18. und 19. Jahr-hunderts*, ed. York-Gothart Mix (Wiesbaden: Harrassowitz, 1996), 63–76.

112. See Waltraud Hagen, *Die Drucke von Goethes Werken* (Berlin: Akademie, 1971), 1–94.

113. See Steffen Martus, *Werkpolitik. Zur Literaturgeschichte kritischer Kommunikation vom 17. bis ins 20. Jahrhundert mit Studien zu Klopstock, Tieck, Goethe und George* (Berlin: De Gruyter, 2007), 261; and Spoerhase, *Das Format der Literatur*, 459–624.

114. See Reiner Wild, "Einführung," in Goethe, MA, 4.1, 917.

Goethe's The Roman Carnival *and Its Afterlives* 137

(Conversations of German émigrés), another key text of Goethe's that reflects on the revolutionary times via serial form.[115] These pieces come into view as small or occasional works (the *Unterhaltungen* appeared in Schiller's *Horen* journal), but they also function to give shape to an unruly sight (whether of carnival or the revolution), a kind of aesthetic seeing and form-giving that cut across cultural and natural eventfulness. We might also identify a commemorative function at work in the placement of the carnival piece at the front of the *Neue Schriften*, for it and related writings mark Goethe's early engagement with the implications of the revolution and his preferred mode of addressing it obliquely via literary form. This moment of republication thus shows how the ordering of multiple works itself becomes a concrete literary act (as Martus puts it, "the order of the works become a legible text").[116] Collecting and republishing individual works also temporalizes them; it gives them a temporal marker. They are "new" in that they respond to recent events, but they are also new in the chronology of Goethe's development as an artist, following on the earlier successes of his *Sturm und Drang* dramas and *Werther*. The temporalization of works on the basis of a sense of the unfolding of the artist's life is a typical feature of collected works projects of the time, as with Lessing, Wieland, Klopstock, and others.

The anthology format presumes the coexistence of multiple works, and this comes to bear on associations of the work with "smallness" and "largeness." Landing in the *Neue Schriften* edition, the carnival piece is juxtaposed with other works that pursue different form and genre solutions, including dramas, novellas, essays, and even fairy tales. This genre repertoire is constitutive of Goethe's varied "literary experiments" in the 1790s that do not always take recourse to classical form.[117] As Koselleck has pointed out, Goethe's

---

115. This appears as volume 12 of thirteen in the 1806–1810 edition of Goethe's works published by Cotta; see Hagen, *Die Drucke von Goethes Werken*, 26–27. On questions of seriality in the *Unterhaltungen*, see Rüdiger Campe, "To Be Continued. Einige Beobachtungen zu Goethes *Unterhaltungen*," in *Noch einmal Anders. Zu einer Poetik des Seriellen*, ed. Elisabeth Bronfen, Christiane Frey, and David Martyn (Zurich and Berlin: Diaphanes, 2016), 119–36.
116. "Die Werkordnung wird zum Text." Martus, *Werkpolitik*, 477.
117. Wild, "Einführung," 920, 921.

idiosyncratic engagement with history writing and with the revolutionary era in particular is characterized by a multiplicity of approaches and modes of writing.[118] This multiplicity relativizes the classicizing form of the carnival piece, diminishing what was already a "small" work. Though Goethe is instrumental in reviving classical genres in poetry and drama in particular and in valuing neoclassicism in the fine arts, his literary experiments are never strictly constrained to classical form. In subsequent works editions, the carnival piece migrates further back in the volumes; in the 1810 to 1817 *Sämtliche Schriften* (Complete writings) edition published in Vienna by Anton Strauß, it appears in volume 13 of twenty-six alongside "Fragments from Italy," the Cagliostro essay, the *Unterhaltungen*, and "The Good Women."[119] This new placement marks a shift from commemorating the author's indirect engagement with an age of revolution to tracking the course of his development and maturation as an artist. With the piece's 1829 incorporation into the *Italienische Reise*, the rhetoric of finality associated with the *Ausgabe letzter Hand* applies to the carnival piece—it reaches its "final place" (*endgültiger Platz*).[120] The incorporation of the piece into Goethe's travel writings aligns it with diaristic life-writing.[121] Its location in the *Italienische Reise* preserves the piece's connection to the carnival season, for it falls between January and February of 1788. This location aligns the carnival piece with the new year, but with the year 1788, when Goethe experienced carnival a second time, rather than with 1789 or 1790, the years of the book and journal publication. This "backdating," if you will, places the experience of carnival more firmly in a prerevolutionary context, and it also inserts Goethe's experience more decidedly into a narrative of his personal and artistic development, a feature of the book and journal versions that is much

---

118. Koselleck, "Goethe's Untimely History."
119. See Hagen, *Die Drucke von Goethes Werken*, 35–38.
120. Schütterle, "*Untadeliche Schönheit*," 49.
121. It is at this point that Goethe's framing remarks in the *Italienische Reise*, where he notes the significance of his double viewing of carnival, that I mentioned at the beginning of the chapter are placed alongside the carnival piece. MA, 15, 611–12.

less pronounced.[122] The inclusion of this piece in the section "Zweiter Römischer Aufenthalt" (Second Roman stay) in particular places the text amid a mixture of diary entries and miscellaneous articles that Goethe wrote at the time. This is evocative in certain ways of Moritz's much earlier collection of diverse pieces in *Vorbegriffe zu einer Theorie der Ornamente* (Preliminary ideas toward a theory of ornaments) (1793), and Goethe even reproduces parts of Moritz's important aesthetic treatise "Über die bildende Nachahmung des Schönen" here in the 1829 text, a favor he likewise shows Moritz in 1789, commenting on the piece in *Der Teutsche Merkur*.[123]

It also stands out that the images are removed in every works edition publication, beginning with the 1792 *Neue Schriften* and continuing through to the *Ausgabe letzter Hand* in 1829. Footnotes and other references to the images are likewise removed; some scholars have suggested that this represents a "repression" of the images.[124] Do we read this excising of the images as a drift toward textual representation and away from the pictorial imagination? Or as an attempt on Goethe's part to downplay the association of the piece with Bertuch's fashion journalism? At any rate, it would seem that the choice to omit the images takes the material out of the orbit of the illustrated serial entertainment in which it emerged and places it more into a narrative of implied authorial development. The incorporation of the carnival piece into works editions is a sign that classicizing form is not the final word for Goethe, but rather one option among others, something that recent work on Goethe and the poetics and politics of his works confirms. Carlos Spoerhase and Andrew Piper have both tracked various textual networks constituted by republication strategies, while Kai Sina has focused on Goethe's awareness of the fragmentary structure of his works as a collective grouping and argues that they must be understood as

---

122. On the reconstellation of the text in the *Italienische Reise*, see Uhlig, "Goethes Römisches Carneval im Wandel."

123. Johann Wolfgang von Goethe, "Über die bildende Nachahmung des Schönen von Carl Philipp Moritz," *Der Teutsche Merkur* (July 1789): 105–11.

124. See Gerhardt, "Goethe und 'das Römische Carneval,'" 289.

a "varied, ununified work" (*vielgestaltiges, uneinheitliches Werk*).[125] Here Sina follows Ralph Waldo Emerson, who writes of Goethe's works: "A great deal refuses to incorporate: this he adds loosely as letters of the parties, leaves from their journals, or the like. A great deal still is left that will not find any place. This the bookbinder alone can give any cohesion to; and hence, notwithstanding the looseness of many of his works, we have volumes of detached paragraphs, aphorisms, Xenien, etc."[126] The carnival piece and the *xenia* come into view as a series of unconnected units, unified perhaps only by having being penned by Goethe.

Multiple works editions and Goethe's "virtuosity" in navigating the business of print bring us back to the question of the literary text as consumer good. A third important horizon in which the "after" of Goethe's carnival unfolds is that of *serial entertainment and cultural journalism*. As we have seen, carnival remains an important and recurring topic in the *Modejournal*. Here Goethe plays the role less of an inaugurator of a new form of literary observation and more of yet another writer who taps into and guides preexisting reader interest. Even though he is disdainful of the *Modejournal*, he continues to place articles and images from masked balls in Weimar there. Despite the laments about the steady stream of reports about festivals, readers' desire for representations of carnival remained unabated long into the nineteenth century, and the festival was a popular topic in journals, books, *Taschenbücher*, and other serial forms. On both practical and symbolic levels, carnival and festivals like it function as engines for viewing ever new costumes and new masks at the intersection of fashion, popular national culture, and current events. This association with a multiplicity of events and print organs brings Goethe's text more into the frame of the time of the world (*Weltzeit*) rather than that of authorial life (*Lebenszeit*), as his piece provides one model among many for tracking worthy recurring events and providing a template for marketable literary entertainment.

---

125. See Kai Sina, *Kollektivpoetik. Zu einer Literatur der offenen Gesellschaft in der Moderne mit Studien zu Goethe, Emerson, Whitman und Thomas Mann* (Berlin: De Gruyter, 2019), 53–60.

126. On Emerson's affinities to Goethe, see Sina, *Kollektivpoetik*, 118–25.

Along with being published in *Neue Schriften*, Goethe's piece is published in unauthorized anthologies in 1793, 1796, and 1799. These include *Taschenbuch für das Carneval* (Pocketbook for carnival) (Frankfurt and Leipzig, 1793); *Taschenbuch der alten und neuen Masken* (Pocketbook of old and new masks) (Frankfurt, 1793); *Die Nationalfeste, Feierlichkeiten, Ceremonie und Spiele aller Völker, Religionen und Stände* (The national festivals, ceremonies, and games of all peoples, religions, and estates) (Weisenfels, 1796); and *Beschreibung der vorzüglichsten Volksfeste, Unterhaltungen, Spiele und Tänze der meisten Nationen in Europa* (Descriptions of the most exquisite popular festivals, entertainments, games, and dances of most of the nations of Europe) (Vienna, 1799). Anthology publication reveals another side to the piece's connections to the middle- and highbrow literature of pocketbook and almanac collections, that is, the natural rivals of the *Modejournal*. Some of these publications are more middlebrow fare without illustrations, while others have high production values, such as the *Taschenbuch für Freunde und Freundinnen des Carnevals mit Illuminierten Kupfern* (Pocketbook for male and female friends of carnival with illuminated plates) (Leipzig, 1804), which is printed in German and French. This is the realm of "small" and "large" print luxury with which Bertuch and Böttiger are concerned. These projects confirm the marketability of carnival masks and costumes. Indeed, in the initial advertisement for Goethe's book, Bertuch also announced a future French version, though this version never materialized, most likely due to the outbreak of the revolution soon after the German version's March 1789 publication.

Carnival likewise continues to play an important role as a model for visual spectatorship, for tropes of the passing by of ever more scenes as facilitated by serial print. Satirical periodicals of the mid-nineteenth century are commonly personified as shape-shifting devils or charlatan figures, as in the satirical journal *Der hinkende Teufel zu Berlin* (1827) cited at the beginning of the chapter, which presents its contents "in a colorful series like a masked procession in carnival."[127] Carnival comes into view as a trope for periodical liter-

---

127. Koch, *Der Teufel in Berlin*, 31.

ature more generally, its "unruliness," and its expressly serial form. The scenes produced by the "lawful lawlessness" (*gesetzliche Gesetzlosigkeit*) of carnival (as the twentieth-century theorist Florens Christian Rang put it) are not unlike the scenes generated by the print landscape more generally, and the demand for fashion imagery, caricature, and art prints representing carnival scenes would only grow throughout the nineteenth century, such as in the virtuosic lithograph series by Garvani on Parisian carnival published throughout the 1830s and 1840s in the satirical journal *Le Charivari*.[128] And finally, the affinities shared by carnival and serial journalism help explain how carnival would remain a template for writing contemporary history into the nineteenth century, for evaluating the political crosscurrents of revolution and restoration, and for making sense of time and its disjointed flow. Heine, for example, uses carnival as a trope for the French government's farcical political masquerade in his articles for the Augsburg *Allgemeine Zeitung* in the early 1830s, suggesting that the season of carnivalesque politics lasts the whole year: "This larger carnival begins with the first of January and ends with the thirty-first of December."[129] Heine ironically adapts the carnivalesque shape of time as a template for making sense of the present and its likelihood of lasting into the future, in the process envisioning the unsettling convergence of the world time of carnival with the time of individual lived experience: If one experiences the entire year as a carnivalesque farce, who is to say when it will end? In light of all these experiments with temporal scale and patterning, Goethe's text comes into view as one in a series of different representations of carnival and also as one in a series of attempts to use carnival to write time. Carnival can function as a metaphor and template for serial entertainment, but it can also serve as a metaphor and template for self-reflective viewing, for seeing oneself seeing, and for writing time by finding order and disorder in the flow of time and of print artifacts.

---

128. Florens Christian Rang, *Historische Psychologie des Karnevals*, ed. Lorenz Jäger (Berlin: Brinkman and Bose, 1983), 13; on these series by Garvani (Guillaume-Suplice Chevallier, 1804–1866), see Nancy Olson, *Garvani: The Carnival Lithographs* (New Haven, CT: Yale University Art Gallery, 1979).

129. Heinrich Heine, *Französische Zustände* (Hamburg: Hoffmann and Campe, 1833), 113.

3

CARICATURE AND EPHEMERAL PRINT IN *LONDON UND PARIS*

For those living through the early and mid-1790s, finding a sense of equilibrium was challenging enough with the dizzying succession of governments, the introduction of the revolutionary calendar, and the emergence of new types of public memorials. Napoleon's rise to power in November of 1799 only intensified the feeling of disorientation that reverberated through France and Europe, a feeling of living through a historical and temporal reordering. At first Napoleon was seen by many observers as a stabilizing, decelerating force, but as his reign progressed, it, too, was viewed as a continuation of the upheaval of the past decade, further catalyzing broader discussions about time and "the times" in Germany and across Europe.[1] The government preceding Napoleon's rise to power, the

---

1. See Ernst Wolfgang Becker, *Zeit der Revolution!—Revolution der Zeit? Zeiterfahrungen in Deutschland in der Ära der Revolutionen 1789–1848/49* (Göttingen: Vandenhoeck und Ruprecht, 1999), 92–93, 130.

Directory (1795–1799), was seen by many as a rollback of democratic achievements, and from a certain perspective, Napoleon's rise reinscribed the break between pre- and postrevolutionary epochs. At the same time, the Directorial government continued certain political and cultural innovations of the revolution, and Napoleon would go on to be decried as an illegitimate, imperial tyrant. In the early 1790s, some late-century observers were inspired to apply the interpretive template of the long-standing Polybian doctrine of the cyclical rise and fall of political constitutions to the compressed and accelerated time frame of recent events,[2] while others found their predictive abilities thwarted in the face of "the restless iteration of the new."[3]

Throughout the decade, the desire for up-to-date journalistic reporting and topical entertainment that arose in the wake of the revolution remained unflagging. As Bertuch and Böttiger note in their announcement for their new journal *London und Paris* in 1798, "writing for newspapers [*Zeitungsschreiberey*] is a massive line of business in cultivated states, and it has become the sole notable form of literature in countries like France [in the postrevolutionary period].... The age of paper [*Das papierne Zeitalter*] nearly drowns [*erstickt*] under all the journals and newspapers."[4] Inundation, saturation, and flooding are all metaphors used to describe the print landscape, and the journals, newspapers, albums, almanacs, and other serial formats of the period pursue a host of different strategies to manage the flood and stay afloat.[5] Some influential literary projects turn away from the realm of journalism and the pervasive distraction (*Zerstreuung*) associated with serial print and instead direct readers to literary works that could help them find stable points of orienta-

---

2. See Reinhart Koselleck, "Does History Accelerate?" in *Sediments of Time: On Possible Histories*, trans. and ed. Sean Franzel and Stefan-Ludwig Hoffmann (Stanford, CA: Stanford University Press, 2018), 92.
3. Peter Fritzsche, *Stranded in the Present: Modern Time and the Melancholy of History* (Cambridge, MA: Harvard University Press, 2004), 5.
4. Bertuch and Böttiger, "Plan und Ankündigung," 3.
5. On the metaphor of print saturation, see Multigraph Collective, *Interacting with Print: Elements of Reading in the Era of Print Saturation* (Chicago: University of Chicago Press, 2018).

tion. This is the strategy of Schiller's influential literary journal *die Horen* (1795–1797), which sees the "all-pursuing demon of political critique" to be at work in all contemporary writings and discussions.[6] Schiller offers readers "a close, trusted circle for the muses and charites" and a productive, "cheerful" diversion from the "noise of war" and the "battle of political opinions and interests."[7] At the same time, this period witnesses the rise of new (and what would be long-running) newspapers reporting on world events from the intersection of politics and history.[8] Two examples are the publisher Cotta's *Europäische Annalen* (European annals) (1795–1820) and his *Neuste Weltkunde* (Newest world news), which was founded in 1798 and later became the *Allgemeine Zeitung* (1798–1929). Such serials are the sites of the "battle of political opinions" described by Schiller, and they also commonly mix cultural, political, and commercial news. Böttiger, we should remember, wrote frequently for the *Allgemeine Zeitung* and *Der Teutsche Merkur*, which he edited for a time. This is likewise a boom time for historical journals seeking to depict the distant and more recent past.[9] As Daniel Moran puts it, "history became the common language of politics during [this era], and no field was more profoundly affected by its rise than political journalism."[10] The project of writing the history of the present is central to the almanacs, travelogues, historical treatises, albums, and other print formats that seek to tell the story of and commemorate the good and bad sides of the revolution, something we caught a glimpse of in chapter 1 with the Janus-faced title plate in the *Modejournal* (figure 1.5). In this context, it is common to include a variety of print ephemera to document

---

6. Friedrich Schiller, "[Ankündigung]," *Die Horen, eine Monatsschrift* 1, no. 1 (1795): iii.

7. Schiller, "[Ankündigung]," iv, iii.

8. As Koselleck notes, "beginning with the French Revolution, we can witness a boom in journals and book series that were to inform the reader about current events." Koselleck, "Constancy and Change," 110.

9. See Horst Walter Blanke, "Historische Zeitschriften," in *Von Almanach bis Zeitung. Ein Handbuch der Medien in Deutschland 1700–1800*, ed. Ernst Fischer, Wilhelm Haefs, and York-Gothart Mix (Munich: Beck, 1999).

10. Daniel Moran, *Toward the Century of Words: Johann Cotta and the Politics of the Public Realm in Germany, 1795–1832* (Berkeley: University of California Press, 1990), 64.

current events in the form of reprinted images, speeches, public proclamations, festival advertisements, and the like, which add significantly to the flood of serial print that Bertuch and Böttiger refer to (and to which they shamelessly add). These multifaceted print objects are central to German observers' expressly media-driven experience of the French Revolution.[11]

Political caricature is an excellent inroad into examining this inundation of print matter. Caricature emerged as a visual genre in the seventeenth century; the term "caricature" has connotations of "overloaded" and "exaggerated" that come from the Latin *carricare*, referring to a loaded wagon on rolling wheels. Closely related to the portrait, caricature depicts persons and comic or grotesque types yet eschews the self-serious and often religious allegories of formal portraiture.[12] It began largely as a private genre, more for the personal sketchbook and artist's studio than for general consumption, but it became a popular public form of illustration in the eighteenth century. The 1790s in particular are a boom time for political caricatures, which function to visualize the events of the revolution and reflect the partisan back and forth about leading figures.[13] In this context, the term "caricature" has a broader meaning, denoting "not only visual satire but any characteristic graphic portrayal."[14] The British pro- and antirevolutionary caricatures of the period emerge amid a well-established market for print imagery pioneered by the likes of Hogarth and Thomas Rowlandson, and throughout the European press, caricature artists engage with the official iconography of the French Revolution and take advantage of the proximity of caricature and fashion journalism.[15] The basic techniques of caricature, namely exaggerated personal characterization, sim-

---

11. See Christoph Danelzik-Brüggemann, *Ereignisse und Bilder. Bildpublizistik und politische Kultur in Deutschland zur Zeit der Französischen Revolution* (Berlin: Akademie, 1996).
12. James Cuno, "Introduction," in *French Caricature and the French Revolution, 1789–1799* (Los Angeles: Grunwald Center for the Graphic Arts, 1988), 15.
13. See Reichardt and Kohle, *Visualizing the Revolution*.
14. Reichardt and Kohle, *Visualizing the Revolution*, 7.
15. "In the Revolutionary and Napoleonic period[s], dress featured as part of the textual joke in political caricature." McNeil, "Fashion and the Eighteenth-Century Satirical Print," 261.

plification, the subversion of high and low, and abrupt and unexpected juxtaposition, lend themselves well to the "picture journalism" of the period, which seeks to document the actions of political leaders and diagnose the national character of the European powers.[16] Furthermore, caricature's particular "vocabulary of scale," which makes figures larger or smaller than life and brings them into visual proximity with seemingly unrelated objects or people, has an essential affinity with the basic format and genre conditions of miscellaneous cultural journalism.[17]

The temporality of the caricature is likewise closely related to the standing of serial print, for modern caricatures are commonly associated with the ephemerality of current political and cultural debates.[18] Perceived as a quintessentially modern form of artistic expression and journalistic documentation, caricature is one important sign of a newfound interest in the present during this period and differs from earlier emblematic and allegorical representation by referencing historically unique situations rather than stock types or scenarios; as Koselleck has argued, caricature plays an essential role in the "historical individualization of events."[19] In this context, caricatures can also serve as a form of especially rich historical source material long after their initial publication. The temporal status of caricatures can also be seen in their standing as material objects, for they are often made for the moment and less costly than more elaborate images. At the same time, artists commonly situate their images in a continuum of recognizable visual points of reference, with Napoleonic era images by leading artists such

---

16. See Reichardt, "The French Revolution as a European Media Event."

17. On caricature's "vocabulary of scale," see Robert L. Patten, *George Cruikshank's Life, Times, and Art*, vol. 1 (New Brunswick, NJ: Rutgers University Press, 1992), 48.

18. See the famous comments on this topic in Charles Baudelaire, "The Painter of Modern Life," in *The Painter of Modern Life and Other Essays* (New York: Phaidon, 1964), 1–42. See also Angela Borchert, "Charles Baudelaire. Die Karikatur und die Genese einer Poetik des Flüchtigen," in *Flüchtigkeit der Moderne. Die Eigenzeiten des Ephemeren im langen 19. Jahrhundert*, ed. Sean Franzel, Michael Bies, and Dirk Oschmann (Hanover: Wehrhahn, 2017), 61–88.

19. See Reinhart Koselleck, "Daumier and Death," in *The Practice of Conceptual History: Timing History, Spacing Concepts*, trans. Todd Samuel Presner et al. (Stanford, CA: Stanford University Press, 2002), 267.

as Isaac Cruikshank or James Gillray citing famous prints from the mid-eighteenth century or other well-known historical paintings or portraits. Caricature is thus an essential serial form predicated on the continued production and circulation of ever more images that seek to capture the present in an entertaining and revealing visual satire.

Bertuch and Böttiger are quite prescient about caricature both as a newly effective medium of political communication and as a desirable print commodity, that is, as a form of "small" print luxury that could complement the fashion plates and commemorative illustrations considered in the preceding two chapters, and they make caricature and other satirical forms a central part of their new journal *London und Paris*. The new journal expands on the *Modejournal*'s repertoire of travel correspondence and cultural reportage, with the two coeditors initially planning to relocate the fashion journal's ever-growing material on England and France to this new publication. *London und Paris* likewise builds on the *Modejournal*'s practice of having multiple colored plates at the end of each issue (though the *Modejournal* would continue to be the primary home for fashion images in Bertuch's publishing empire).[20] Published eight times a year between 1798 and 1815, each eighty- to one-hundred-page issue of *London und Paris* consists of three to four sections, with the first two containing articles on each respective city and the third (and sometimes fourth) detailing English and French caricatures and other images. The journal's main correspondents Johann Christian Hüttner (London) and Friedrich Theophil Winckler (Paris) actively incorporate commentaries on images and other ephemeral print into their articles, and Böttiger firmly situates his glosses of British images in the tradition of Lichtenberg's Hogarth commentaries. Caricatures thus represent a central element of Bertuch's and Böttiger's pedagogy of the image.

Canalizing the Flow

Especially in its first six or seven years, prior to the escalation of the Napoleonic Wars in 1805–1807 and the onset of the continental

---

20. Bertuch and Böttiger, "Plan und Ankündigung," 9.

blockade, *London und Paris* is as successful as the *Modejournal* and known for the topicality of its hand-colored images. The journal tracks one of the key international rivalries shaping European politics and culture between France and England and fuels curiosity about the many sides of modern urban life.[21] The journal's topics include popular theater and vaudevilles; current festivities, spectacles, and exhibitions; street life, customs, fashion, and social habits; the shifting political winds prior to and under Napoleon; collections, shops, and the business of print; and the remaking of postrevolutionary Paris through new buildings, monuments, and museums. For the most part, Bertuch, Böttiger, and their correspondents are ideologically aligned with the more moderate commercialism of England and often take the side of the journal's anti-Napoleonic British caricature artists such as Gillray and Cruikshank. Images and their commentaries are central in establishing the journal's critical tone, and the journal lays the groundwork for the spread of satirical print and image-focused cultural journalism in the German-language literary market as the century progresses. Like the *Modejournal*, *London und Paris* is an important—yet often neglected—prototype for the *Unterhaltungsliteratur* of the subsequent century. The journal is part of an early wave of appreciation for the cultural significance of caricature that crested in the nineteenth and twentieth centuries.

One important way *London und Paris* builds on the *Modejournal*'s format and thematic ambit is through its cultural and political commentary that connects the present to antiquity. Throughout most of its seventeen-year run, the journal's cover features satirical epigrams in Latin, as in the first issue, which adapts lines from Juvenal: "Quicquid, quos Tamisis nutrit, quos Sequana rident / Gaudia, discursus nostri est farrago libelli" (Everything that enriches the Thames and that the Seine laughs at, / enjoyments, diversions are the mixed contents of our little book) (figure 3.1).[22] The epigram

---

21. On London and Paris as key points of orientation for Bertuch's commercial enterprises, see Purdy, *The Tyranny of Elegance*.

22. This is drawn from Juvenal's description of his collection of satirical poems: "Quicquid agunt homines, votum, timor, ira, voluptas, / Gaudia, discursus, nostri est farrago libelli" (Whatever men are engaged in, their wishes and fear, anger, / pleasures, joys, runnings to and fro, form the medley of my little book).

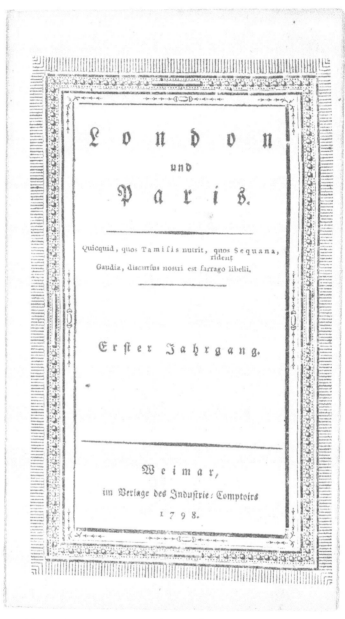

Figure 3.1. Cover. *London und Paris* 1, no. 1 (1798). HAAB Weimar. 7 ½ × 4 ½ inches.

introduces the journal as an entertaining cultural miscellany, a "little book of mixed contents" (*farrago libelli*), echoing the use of these lines from Juvenal by other eighteenth-century moral weeklies, including Steele's pioneering *Tatler*. The journal addresses an educated readership able to read Latin but also one in search of "enjoyments" and diversions.[23] The journal's reference to Roman satire is part of Böttiger's larger project of tracing certain forms of cultural entertainment back to antiquity, and *London und Paris* is quite clear about the ancient roots of contemporary satire and caricature.

Another striking feature of this title epigram is its evocation of the metaphor of temporal, spatial, and material flow through reference to the cities' rivers, signaling both the passage of time and a steady stream of new materials to be collected and disseminated to readers. The flow metaphor, which also applies to the aqueous origins of print and paper, is an important part of the journal's self-understanding, drowning, as it were, in the "age of paper." In their introduction for the journal in the first issue, Bertuch and Böttiger cite the British and French capitals as the "two main sources" from which "all this knowledge about the world and the times [*All diese Welt- und Zeitkunde*] flows, pouring out into so many larger and smaller canals."[24] Familiar tropes from the commercial realm, flow and canalization serve as metaphors for how periodicals manage the flood of printed matter, for, according to Bertuch and Böttiger, much of what readers encounter is misleading: "What is *seen* and *written* is often quite ambiguous; deceptions and mirages . . . even the most reliable reports of official daily papers rarely include . . . the actual *why* and *how*."[25] The conceit of canalization visualizes the journal's

---

23. *Discursus* can mean running or moving around but also conversation. Gerhard R. Kaiser aptly translates *discursus* as *Zerstreuungen*, linking it to the French semantics of "diversion" and "les divertissements." Gerhard R. Kaiser, "'Jede große Stadt ist eine Moral in Beispielen.' Bertuchs Zeitschrift 'London und Paris,'" in *Friedrich Justin Bertuch (1747–1822). Verleger, Schriftsteller und Unternehmer im klassischen Weimar*, ed. Gerhard R. Kaiser and Siegfried Seifert (Tübingen: Niemeyer, 2000), 558, note 41.
24. Bertuch and Böttiger, "Plan und Ankündigung," 3.
25. Bertuch and Böttiger, "Plan und Ankündigung," 4. On the flow metaphor and information management, see Markus Krajewski, *Paper Machines: About Cards and Catalogues, 1548–1929*, trans. Peter Krapp (Cambridge, MA: MIT

position in various communication networks, with the journal gathering time-specific contents—news, fashions, images, and more—from French and English sources and giving it to readers at predictable, periodic installments, while diverting less valuable information.[26] Canalization is also a technique of temporal orientation, for the diversion of information into canals sets various chronologies or measurements of time into motion—different kinds of *Zeitkunde* or knowledge about time or the times—chronologies that correspond to a variety of journals and other serial forms. Readers are asked to envision a network of multiple flows moving in different directions and at varied speeds, converging and diverging in space and time.

To be sure, there is a very material side to the "diversions" from these foreign capitals, and the ephemeral print artifacts produced by Bertuch's publishing house are essential elements of the flow. Along with their drafts, Parisian and French correspondents regularly send caricatures and other images and documents to Weimar, where they are reproduced, reprinted, and hand colored.[27] The journal builds on readers' desire for various sorts of ephemeral print, including the musical notation of popular ballads or theater tunes; images of bookshops and reading rooms; product catalogues, maps, images of monuments, artifacts, and public festivals; and advertisements for different events or products that might otherwise be discarded or recycled. The metaphor of canalization concretizes the conceit of the literary and journalistic tableau while at the same time reworking it in important ways. The notion of plural tableaus helps to illustrate the journal's

---

Press, 2011), 37. On the role of the flow metaphor in imagining economic life, see Joseph Vogl, *Kalkül und Leidenschaft. Poetik des ökonomischen Menschen* (Munich: Sequenzia, 2002), 223–25.

26. As Apgar nicely puts it, "Structured by well-defined rubrics, periodicals captured articles, reports, statistical information, texts, and travel accounts swept along by the current. Rubrics, continuing the metaphor a bit further, are the floodgates through which this material flows, organizing material and directing it into different streams." Apgar, "Flooded," 28.

27. On Hüttner, see Catherine W. Proescholdt, "Johahnn Christian Hüttner (1766–1847): A Link Between Weimar and London," in *Goethe and the English-Speaking World*, ed. Nicholas Boyle and John Guthrie (Rochester, NY: Camden House, 2001), 99–110.

innovative circulation of printed images, yet it falls short in capturing how these images and other print material make their way back to Weimar for reproduction. As much as the journal's correspondents are peripatetic "painters" of urban scenes *en plein air*, they are also collectors, archivists, sorters, and cataloguers—canalizers—of a wide range of printed matter. The journal thus comes into view as an ongoing instantiation of—but also self-reflective commentary on—the transfer of information across Europe. The "canals" of communication between these cities become particularly relevant in 1806, when the journal is forced to change its title and format after the French cut off continental trade with Britain for several years. The conceits of the tableau and of temporal and material flow help the editors package their cultural entertainment as an expressly serialized product.

Though *London und Paris* has not been addressed nearly as much in the scholarship as the *Horen*, the *Athenäum*, or the *Berliner Abendblätter*, it has been recognized as a high-water mark for the reception of political caricature in German letters. Karl Rosenkranz's 1853 *Ästhetik des Häßlichen* (Aesthetics of the ugly) cites the journal as a key propagator of caricatures even though nearly forty years of satirical print had added many more examples to this genre, and Eduard Fuchs's wide-ranging 1921 history of European caricature calls *London und Paris* "certainly the most well-regarded journal at the beginning of the nineteenth century."[28] More recent scholarship has continued to focus on the journal's pioneering role in exposing German audiences to British and French Napoleonic era political imagery and in paving the way for later nineteenth-century illustrated serial entertainment.[29] Building on this work, I am interested in how the journal prompts an understanding of caricature that applies not merely to images with clearly identifiable genre markings

---

28. Eduard Fuchs, *Die Karikatur der europäischen Völker. Teil 1. Vom Altertum bis zum Jahre 1848* (Munich: Langen, 1921), 183; Karl Rosenkranz, *Ästhetik des Häßlichen* (Stuttgart: Reclam, 1990), 361–400.

29. See especially Wolfgang Cilleßen, Rolf Reichardt, and Christian Deuling, ed., *Napoleons Neue Kleider. Pariser und Londoner Karikaturen im klassischen Weimar* (Berlin: G&H Verlag, 2006); and Frazer S. Clark, *Zeitgeist and Zerrbild. Word, Image, and Idea in German Satire, 1800–1848* (Bern: Peter Lang, 2006), 33–55.

but also to the styles of cultural reportage they engender and the commentaries that accompany them, down to the level of the layout of the journal itself. This expanded sense of caricature will help us to situate *London und Paris* as a pioneer in the realm of serialized cultural journalism and to appreciate how it processes the temporal reordering underway in the present day age of paper.

"Friends of the Art of Uglifying"

The status of caricature in the aesthetic debates of the day, particularly vis-à-vis debates about classicizing forms, makes a fitting backdrop for the discussion of the manner in which *London und Paris* presents its readers with ensembles of caricature-like articles and images. Contemporaries of Bertuch and Böttiger are all too aware of their keen interest in caricature, and in particular, Goethe and his circle—in a domestic literary feud that more or less weaponizes caricature—respond with antipathy to their successful promotion of the genre. Goethe dismisses Böttiger as "that constantly industrious distorter" (*der allzeit geschäftige Verzerrer*) and a hand-drawn caricature of Bertuch by Goethe's friend J. H. Meyer circulated in the author's circle in Weimar (figure 3.2).[30] Titled "Versuch in der Verhäßlichungskunst, dem großen Lobredner derselben gewidmet" (Attempt in the art of uglifying, dedicated to the great eulogist of it), the image references the Greek architect Dinocrates's failed project to build a monumental likeness of Alexander the Great into Mount Athos. Meyer depicts Bertuch fused into a mountainside, with Böttiger on his left as the messenger god Mercury with the publishers' multicolored journals under his arm and Kraus on the right as a devoted portraitist. While spoofing classicizing monumental form, this image also uses water (even the flood) as a pictorial trope for the rush of print products that flowed from Bertuch's publishing house, the Landes-Industrie-Comptoir, into foreign lands. Here, flow symbolizes a kind of bad seriality, an unremitting production of ugly things that leaves Weimar and Dessau (the two cities Bertuch holds

---

30. Goethe to Bertuch, January 12, 1802, WA, IV.16, 3.

Figure 3.2. Johann Heinrich Meyer, "Attempt in the Art of Uglifying, Dedicated to the Great Eulogist of It." HAAB Weimar. 8 ¼ × 11 ¼ inches.

in his hands) high and dry.³¹ Meyer uses distortion and disfiguration against the distorters, casting Bertuch's prominence in the publishing world as an empty, fleeting greatness.

This image and the cover epigrams of *London und Paris* give us an initial taste of the central role of caricature in debates about classicism and classicizing form in the period. The journal's intent in documenting various features of contemporary life frequently has an antiquarian tinge, and the editors' reliance on conventions of Menippean satire is evident, which, as Mikhail Bakhtin notes, is characterized by "a journalistic quality, the spirit of publicistic writing or of the feuilleton, and a pointed interest in the topics of the day."³² On the level of visual form, there are of course important affinities between classicism and satirical caricature, including the preference for outline drawing and minimalist backgrounds, and many classicizing artists of the period pursue caricature-like drawing and illustration.³³ At the same time, though, caricature's emphasis on distortion, exaggeration, and disfiguration stands in contrast to the ideal of beautiful, harmonious form. Winckelmann calls caricature "the complete other [to classicism], which must see it as its mortal enemy."³⁴ Goethe casts caricature artists as "friends of the art of uglifying" (*Freunde der Verhäßlichungskunst*), who propagate "a fragmentary and distorted form of entertainment" (*eine zerstückelte und verzerrte Unterhaltung*).³⁵ Despite being intrigued by caricature and even showing some interest in writing commentaries

---

31. This metaphor of water flow is also related to the story of Dinocrates not being able to realize the Alexander monument due to issues with water supply. See Cilleßen, Reichardt, and Deuling, *Napoleons Neue Kleider*, 159.

32. Mikhail Bakhtin, *Problems of Dostoevsky's Poetics*, trans. Caryl Emerson (Minneapolis: University of Minnesota Press, 1984), 119.

33. See especially Bernadette Collenberg-Plotnikov, *Klassizismus und Karikatur. Eine Konstellation der Kunst am Beginn der Moderne* (Berlin: Gebr. Mann Verlag, 1998).

34. Cited in Günter Oesterle and Ingrid Oesterle, "Karikatur," in *Historisches Wörterbuch der Philosophie*, ed. Joachim Ritter, vol. 4 (Basel: Schwabe, 1976), 696–701.

35. J. W. Goethe, "Die Guten Frauen, als Gegenbilder der Bösen Weiber, auf den Kupfern des diesjährigen Damenalmanchs," MA, 6.1, 842.

himself, Goethe never fully embraces the form.[36] Bertuch and Böttiger's journals, in contrast, straddle the beautiful and the ugly with more ease and commercially oriented pragmatism, circulating caricature even while continuing to hold up classical beauty as an ideal in the realm of fine arts and print luxury.

The embrace of caricature as an aesthetically valid form of cultural commentary corresponds to a key late eighteenth-century shift in aesthetic discourse from the distinction between the beautiful and ugly to one between the interesting and uninteresting.[37] That said, caricature likewise continues to work with an ideal of beautiful organic form as a negative point of contrast. Such an ideal is a common point of reference in satirical treatments of French cultural politics that castigate festival decorations or public monuments for not attaining the proper beauty, monumentality, or permanence. Such critiques only increase as Napoleon's imperial ambitions grow, and the journal satirizes the neo-Roman mimesis of his grand projects of commemorative monuments. Anti-Napoleonic cultural journalism weaponizes the ideal of classical form and puts it in the service of revealing official cultural forms as ugly, disfigured, or distorted. Despite the editors' allegiance to classical style in the arts and decorations, they and their correspondents adopt an anti-imperial, anti-Napoleonic stance.

Such criticism of French official culture is an important part of the style of journalism at work in *London und Paris*, which deploys caricature-like mockery in response to historical events and in opposition to the official cultural politics of postrevolutionary France. The Paris correspondent Winckler is highly critical of the Directorial

---

36. See the August 24, 1797, letter to Schiller, where he proposes writing caricature commentary for the *Horen* journal. Goethe, MA, 8.1, 400–401. Cilleßen and Reichardt describe a process of Goethe growing increasingly ill-disposed toward caricature in the early 1800s. Wolfgang Cilißen and Rolf Reichardt, "Nachgestochene Caricaturen. Ein Journal und sein bildgeschichtlicher Hintergrund," in Cilleßen, Reichardt, and Deuling, *Napoleons Neue Kleider*, 12–13. See also David Kunzle, "Goethe and Caricature: From Hogarth to Töpffer," *Journal of the Warburg and Courtauld Institutes* 48 (1985): 164–88.

37. See Niklas Luhmann, *Art as a Social System*, trans. Eva M. Knodt (Stanford, CA: Stanford University Press, 2000). On this shift in eighteenth-century art journals, see Hollmer and Meier, "Kunstzeitschriften," 157–75.

government, and he views Napoleon's early years with cautious hope before becoming increasingly critical of his rule. Winckler's reports, laced with political caricature and satire, readily mobilize a variety of related tropes questioning the permanence of the revolution and characterizing the French people: popular self-determination is a fleeting thing; French governments change so quickly one can hardly keep track; Parisians are a whimsical people who go from one divertissement to the next; and so on. The journal thereby deploys a repertoire of conceptual binaries—ancient and modern, pre- and postrevolutionary, fleeting and permanent, official and popular, fragmentary and whole, and repetitious and discontinuous—that explore the divergence between ideal and reality and reveal the jumbled temporalities of the present. Here the recourse to conventions of ancient satire represents less an attempt to make readers aware of certain cyclical patterns of politics and culture or of the unchanging transience and folly of life (even though this is a frequent refrain of the journal) and more one to shed light on an age of contrasts and contradictions. This mode of cultural journalism is skeptical of notions of historical progress per se and attunes readers to temporal complexity and manifestations of the contemporaneity of the noncontemporaneous.[38] It is characteristic of this journalism, then, to use caricatures to diagnose various kinds of serially recurring events such as festivals, public spectacles, museum exhibitions, popular theater, and more. Caricatures function as important tools for staging the encounter between patterns of natural and cultural time and the media times of print.

Les Cris de Paris

One way that cultural journals help readers orient themselves temporally and historically is by addressing events that recur across

---

38. On the departure of *London und Paris* from the philosophy of history in favor of the theorization of national character, see Jörn Garber, "Die Zivilisationsmetropole im Naturzustand: Das revolutionäre Volk von Paris als Regenerations- und Korruptionsfaktor der 'Geschichte der Menschheit,'" in *Rom-Paris-London: Erfahrung und Selbsterfahrung deutscher Schriftstellern in den fremden Metropolen*, ed. Conrad Wiedemann (Stuttgart: Metzler, 1988), 420–56.

various scales of time—years, months, and days—and tracking what persists and what changes over time. In the case of *London und Paris*, these events include popular theater and vaudevilles; festivities and exhibitions; street life, commerce, and fashion; popular songs and balladeering; scholarly lectures and public speeches; political ceremonies and rituals; the construction of new buildings, monuments, museums, and the arrival of plundered Italian and Egyptian art in Parisian museums.[39] Reports on recurrent events are frequently accompanied by a variety of different artifacts, including the texts of ballads, images of national uniforms and costumes, and lyrics and music from popular songs, as in the case of the *Modejournal*'s discussion of the text and music of "La Marseillaise," which as the article notes, "rings out now almost daily in all theaters and public meetings."[40] The popularity and serial repetition of this song make it worthy of preservation: "At certain points in time, and in certain political situations, universally popular folk songs sung with enthusiasm are the image and imprint of the spirit of the people, expression of its periodic feelings, and for that reason the most valuable archival objects for the history of the spirit of the nation."[41] Along with archiving this material for future historians, the journal also includes a plate with the song's lyrics and melody. This print artifact is a remedial undertaking, allowing German readers to sing, play, and even memorize the song, if they liked.

Depictions of the calls and fashions of peripatetic street merchants and news hawkers (*Neuigkeitsschreier* or *crieurs de journaux*) represent a prevalent (and less immediately political) part of this print material. The "cries" of London, Paris, Berlin, and more had long been beloved literary, visual, and musical subjects, ranging from their representations in children's books to fine art prints

---

39. A range of journal topics dealing with serial patterning will have to go unthematized in this chapter, including the book trade, vaudeville theater, the arrival of Roman art in Paris, and more. On the latter topic see Alice Goff, *The God Behind the Marble: Transcendence and the Art Object in the German Aesthetic State* (Chicago: University of Chicago Press, 2024).

40. Claude Joseph Rouget de Lisle, "Freyheits-Lied der Marseiller," *JLM* 8, no. 1 (January 1793): 21–22.

41. De Lisle, "Freyheits-Lied der Marseiller," 22.

and popular theater to classical art music. The calls of walking merchants could be heard in towns and cities throughout Europe long into the nineteenth century and in the literature and journalism of the later part of the century, their gradual disappearance would become an index of modernization.[42] In the late 1790s, representations of such cries are important for several reasons. They are a vehicle for comparing pre- and postrevolutionary epochs, as in Mercier's work; one could very well view the representation of these cries as a throwback to earlier modes of characterizing urban life, but I want to argue that they are used to diagnose the specific temporalities of the postrevolutionary era. They are also a key instance of how serial forms across text and image are deployed to represent chaotic urban media landscapes, streets where information and goods circulate and where the wandering observer is inundated by print merchandise. Street criers thus provide an occasion to comment on the daily news cycle, with tropes of time-specific news and the ephemerality of the voice growing intertwined. Finally, the low social standings of many of these vendors lend them to humorous, caricature-like treatments with an aspect of dissonance and ugliness.

The public circulation of the news is the topic of a short article in *London und Paris* from 1799 titled "Les Cris de Paris." As Winckler notes, "because every populous city has its own criers with special costumes and melodies, it has long since become a common speculation for image sellers to depict these and sell entire suites of them. One can find collections of figures from Vienna, Petersburg, or Leipzig that are very suitable for being caricatured."[43] To wit, the article then references a chapter from Mercier, citing the author's impression of these cries as a "une inexplicable cacophonie" and a "discordans" "ensemble" of sounds, reproducing an extended section of his piece in French.[44] In effect, Mercier's text is a kind of literary caricature that emphasizes these songs' dissonant ugliness.

---

42. See Aimée Boutin, *City of Noise: Sound and Nineteenth-Century Paris* (Champaign, IL: University of Illinois Press, 2015), 74–81.

43. "Les Cris de Paris," *London und Paris* 3, no. 2 (1799): 129–134, 129, note.

44. "Les Cris de Paris," 129–130, note.

Caricature and Ephemeral Print in London und Paris

In Winckler's hands, satirical depiction is a natural outgrowth of the literature and imagery of the urban tableau. The correspondent seeks to outdo Mercier, though, by providing yet another representation of the cries, this time via musical notation: "It will certainly be enjoyable for some readers to find these dissonances notated on this supplemental plate."[45] Mercier himself eschews the use of actual illustrations in his tableau collections (despite emphatically basing his literary sketches on visual observation), and this plate (*Tafel*) (figure 3.3) has the effect of adding a new medial layer to the representation of the cries in print.[46]

This plate is a curious artifact, inserted into the middle of the issue rather than placed at the end, as with the journal's more elaborate, hand-colored images. It captures the cries of a handful of sellers with musical notation, a rather whimsical attempt to preserve the fleeting sounds of the city for future re-vocalization, a sister convention to the one of including sheet music in journals, almanacs, and pocketbooks.[47] It is a bit unclear, though, how one is to actually use this score. Should a group of people sing the different parts? Should they be played on a piano forte or with several instruments? The fact that these short "songs" are in different keys and time signatures casts doubt on the plate's functionality as a score. While it was not uncommon for periodicals like *London und Paris* to include sheet music, this image seems more a silly diversion than any kind of parlor music that one would sit down to play. Along with being a favorite visual genre in the early modern period, the *cris de Paris* was a popular motif for sixteenth- and seventeenth-century composers, but it is clear that the rather rough plate in *London und Paris* aims at neither harmony nor beauty. In its ugliness or, rather, its figuration

---

45. "Les Cris de Paris," 130, note.

46. Mercier "considered painting an inferior art because it froze the ever-changing flux of life into a fixed form, whereas prose could suggest the constant succession of impressions that was the essence of the urban experience." Popkin, "Editor's Preface," 19.

47. See Heinrich W. Schwab, "Musikbeilagen in Almanachen und Taschenbüchern," in *Almanach- und Taschenbuchkultur des 18. Und 19. Jahrhunderts*, ed. York-Gothart Mix (Wiesbaden: Harrassowitz Verlag, 1996), 167–201.

Figure 3.3. "Les Cris de Paris." *London und Paris* 3, no. 2 (1799): plate B. HAAB Weimar. 7 ½ × 4 ½ inches.

of ugliness in tabular form, the printed page allows readers to imagine a layered multiplicity of fleeting sights and sounds as they occur across space and time.

The shape of time evoked by this small tableau is not merely that of a jarringly dissonant moment but also that of a predictable, intervallic recurrence:

> To satisfy incredulous readers who might suspect that I invented the above Cris de Paris for fun, I would like to announce that one can go and hear and see the original of these cries daily, between eleven and one o'clock, as they pass through the Rue de la Loi, formerly the Rue Richelieu, and that they pass through this street so exactly at this time that certain people treat this part of the city as a kind of clock, which takes the place of the ancient slaves who would announce the signs of the sundial out loud.[48]

The correspondent asks his readers to imagine the relationship between the single iteration of these overlapping cries and their daily repetition.[49] These criers help to measure multiple frames of time: the duration of the cries on a single day, day-to-day repetition, continuities between antiquity and modernity, the disjunction between pre- and postrevolutionary periods as referenced by the altered street names, and, more broadly, the disjunction between manual and mechanical modes of measuring time. These complex temporal coordinates align this scene more with modern caricature's interest in historically specific temporal frameworks and less with topoi of cyclically enduring popular life, despite the motifs being popular material for such depictions in earlier centuries. As a tableau cutting across both engraved plate and journalistic description, this article imagines the city via a complex, multilayered shape of time, situating momentary, fleeting occurrences as part of a structure of serialized and predictable recurrence. In contrast to Goethe's treatment of Roman carnival, Winckler treats popular culture and its quasi-cyclical patterns of

---

48. "Les Cris de Paris," 131.
49. Elsewhere the criers of Paris and London were called "living clocks"; see "Lebendige Uhren. Die Notwendigkeit der Zeiteintheilung in Paris," *London und Paris* 18, no. 6 (1806): 146–55.

repetition and recurrence more ambivalently, via satirical distortion rather than classicizing affirmation.

A topic closely related to merchant cries is that of the newspaper sellers who likewise engage in the performative street-level circulation of information and hawking of print ephemera in the form of newspapers, pamphlets, and chapbooks. With their penchant for promoting salacious crime stories, such singers are associated much more with the ugly yet perennially interesting features of urban life, and representations of them clearly tap into the European tradition of the "shocking ballad."[50] Several articles from a 1798 issue of *London und Paris* are revealing for how they explicitly thematize the "canalization" of print artifacts dating back to Weimar. These articles describe a gruesome murder that briefly caught Parisians' attention and discuss how news of this crime had since circulated, with the author equal parts dismayed and entertained by the many sources clamoring to report the story. The first article criticizes the newspaper criers for their rush to judgment and their prioritization of sales over truth and justice, and the second article gives a concrete example of this sensationalism, referring back to previous discussions of this phenomenon.[51] Titled "Supplement to the Previous Article: Murder story, as It Is First Called Out by the Crier According to Its Content, and Then Bellowed Out in a Miserable Ballad," this piece briefly details the murder in question, and then, "in order to visualize" (*als Versinnlichung*), includes a reproduction of a pamphlet that one specific *Neuigkeitsschreier* read and sang from.[52] Typesetters in Weimar reproduced the French text and layout of the original pamphlet, which contains a prose account of the crime and police interrogation followed by several pages of verse that retells the crime to the tune of a popular song. It is set in Antiqua typeface, a common feature of the journal's reproduction of foreign words and phrases.

The article calls upon the reader to imagine the *crieurs de journaux* as they sell their wares on the street, bringing further issues of

---

50. On this tradition see Tom Cheesman, *The Shocking Ballad Picture Show: German Popular Literature and Cultural History* (Oxford: Berg, 1994).

51. "Mordgeschichte, wie sie der Ausrufer erst dem Inhalte nach ausschreyet, und dann in einer kläglicher Ballade abheult," *London und Paris* 1, no. 3 (1798): 250.

52. "Mordgeschichte," 251.

reproduction and remediation into play: "Now imagine on the Pont Neuf or outside the Louvre several of these kinds of stentorian voices that bellow the headline in your ears and that direct people passing by to the beautiful woodcut, in order to attract customers: that way you have at least something of the beautiful image [of this scene]."[53] As with the "Cris de Paris" piece, at stake is an imagined auditory experience of layered, dissonant sounds coming from different sources. Winckler brings this chaotic image of competing sellers into the realm of caricature, sarcastically referring to the "beauty" of the pamphlet's image, which the editors take the liberty of not reproducing: "The original sent to us from Paris consists of a half folio page of dirty, yellow paper. Above, a woodcut prances along in the most tasteless uniform, which our readers will certainly allow us to skip over."[54] An ensemble of different print artifacts, some demonstratively withheld, creates the effect of an extended caricature. The crime is ugly, the voices are ugly, the paper and image are ugly, and even the public's interest in all of it is somewhat unseemly. The commentary on this local media ecology takes on the status of both social documentary and satirical entertainment.

Despite its ties to an all-too-temporary news sensation, this pamphlet is also associated with preservation: the subtitle of the ballad states that "deux exemplaires ont été déposées à la Bibliothèque Nationale" (two examples have been filed at the National Library). It might seem ridiculous that these pages would be preserved in the most permanent (though only recently refounded and renamed) of "national" archives, yet Winckler would know, working with and under the curator and professor of antiquities in the Bibliothèque Nationale, Aubin-Louis Millin.[55] Whether we take this peculiar paratext at face value or not, it establishes *London und Paris* and the Bibliothèque

---

53. "Mordgeschichte," 251.
54. "Das uns aus Paris mitgetheilte Original besteht aus einem halben Foliobogen von schmutziggelben Papier. Oben an paradiert ein Holzschnitt in der geschmacklosesten Uniform, die uns unsere Leser gewiß gern schenken werden" ("Mordgeschichte," 251, note).
55. Millin was an important connection of Böttiger's, and Winckler worked as Millin's amanuensis until his death in 1807; see Sternke, *Böttiger und der archäologische Diskurs*, 124.

Nationale as two different kinds of material archives: the journal holds one copy, and the library two; the journal "canalizes" the pamphlet in one direction, and the library in another. Indeed, the print run of the journal, with upward of 1,200 copies, amplifies the reach of the pamphlet considerably more than the library. And just like the visitor to the library, readers of the journal are called on to make their way through a heterogenous archive. But in contrast to the library, which preserves sources in their original form, the periodical deals in reproductions. Thus implicit in the circulation of ephemera is a sense that they have been preserved in different, potentially unrelated archives and that multiple copies (and copies of copies) are in circulation. The description and physical reproduction of these proliferating copies make visible and tactile the very undertaking of *London und Paris*.

Both scenes rely upon a clear notion of serialized repetition: "this song will recur at the same time again tomorrow; this performer first read, then sang the news story, then shoved a pamphlet that he was just reading into my hand (and we needn't even mention the image)," and so on.[56] These patterns extend into the past and present, and they presume recurrence and variation into the future: even if the same murder story has faded from public interest, another story will be bellowed out. The logic of the tableau thus organizes a flexible intermedial ensemble that can repeat the same scene in different ways. Here, too, this tableau caricatures the peripatetic merchants and news sellers as well as the gullible public that consumes it, and it also satirizes the canalization of print products, even while participating in it. This piece provides a different twist on the trope of the fashionableness of reading (and hearing) the news from what we encountered in chapters 1 and 2 and shows how a bit of self-deprecation from the journal's correspondents and editors—who, like the Parisian public, are to a certain extent intrigued by these print artifacts—makes the satirical ensemble of print artifacts all the more entertaining.

---

56. On the "episodic visual seriality" of headline, image, and text in ballad pamphlets, see Andrew Piper, "Transitional Figures: Image, Translation and the Ballad from Broadside to Photography," in *Book Illustration in the Long Eighteenth Century: Reconfiguring the Visual Periphery of the Text*, ed. Christina Ionescu (Cambridge: Cambridge Scholars Publishing, 2011), 161.

"Ephemeral Favorites"

In their introduction to the journal, Bertuch and Böttiger underline the important role periodicals have in tracking the fleeting fashions of the day: "[The journal] will name the daily pages and the writings, which, as ephemeral favorites [*ephemerische Lieblinge*], characterize the feeling of the public for this moment, but it will not deliver any actual excerpts or critical discussions of them."[57] Discussions of contemporary journals and the print marketplace in England and France are a topic close to Bertuch's heart and pocketbook, yet here the editors suggest that their journal is to function in this regard as something of a reference work that "names" the fashionable publications of the day but avoids the common practice of excerption and review. This peculiar statement presumes that the reader is perusing (or might want to peruse) multiple journals at the same time and that *London und Paris* is but one of several points of entry into the world of print. Simply documenting these "ephemeral favorites" plays a certain archival function in the service of informing readers about "the times"—a *Zeitkunde*—allowing readers to at least know of their existence in order to consult them at some point in time.

A specific episode from the seventh issue of 1799 delivers on this promise to reflect on and document the periodical landscape. Napoleon had just seized power with the coup of the Eighteenth Brumaire, and the French correspondent for *London und Paris* praises the lifting of the Directorial government's reign of censorship. Referencing Mercier's praise of robust press freedoms in the early days of the revolution, the correspondent hopes for renewal of this earlier liberal spirit through a free press: "The true freedom of the press is only now starting with the glorious palingenesis of the Eighteenth Brumaire, where a deplorable number of partisan journals soon will disappear on their own and thereby make room for the true freedom of the press."[58]

---

57. "Sie wird die Blätter des Tags und die Schriften nennen, die, als ephemerische Lieblinge, die Stimmung des Publicums für diesen Augenblick bezeichnen, aber sie wird keine eigentlichen Auszüge und Critiken liefern." Bertuch and Böttiger, "Plan und Ankündigung," 8.

58. "Die Freyheit der Presse," *London und Paris* 4, no. 7 (1799): 259.

Here, the ephemerality of the official journals of the Directory is cast in a positive light, for these journals are simply the biased mouthpieces of a repressive government. The Eighteenth Brumaire is a rebirth, a "palingenetic" recurrence of the revolution itself that leads to the dying off of the official press and the birth of new projects.

This article is situated in the section of the journal titled "French Caricatures" and is a gloss of sorts on a specific image (figure 3.4) attributed to the period directly after the coup: "The page you have in front of you represents quite accurately the moment when the journal criers disperse from the printer's as quickly as they can with the newspapers they have received there, in order to bring them out to the more remote quarters of the city."[59] The many journal sellers personify the new journals reentering the crowded print market; the many titles on view—in neat rows at the top of the image and in the hands of the sellers—and the multiple printing presses enlisted likewise dramatize this scene.[60] The jumbled, time-specific contents of the public sphere are represented both figurally and literally. Even though the Parisian correspondent is still relatively positive about Napoleon at this point, this caricature is more ambivalent about the periodical landscape, which appears active and industrious but also crowded and unruly.

The fact, though, that a change in censorship laws is configured as a repetition of previous events adds a degree of complexity to this scene, suggesting that the loosening and tightening of the laws recurs intermittently and that such changes indicate shifting political currents. Here we might note one further temporal complexity: the original French caricature on which this is modeled refers not to events of 1799 but to those of 1795, another period of relative liberalization.[61] Though readers would likely have not known that the original image did not apply to the aftermath of the Eighteenth Brumaire, a sense of recurrence, repetition, and layering of previ-

---

59. "Die Freyheit der Presse," 260.
60. This lends itself well to being read as an early version of nineteenth-century caricatures that enlist the "scene of printing," or *Druckszene*, as Borchert terms it; see Angela Borchert, "Die Produktion von Karikatur in der Karikatur: Zeichnungs-, Schreib- und Druckszenen in der französischen und deutschen illustrierten Satire-Journale (1830–1848)," *Colloquia Germanica* 49, nos. 2–3 (2016): 201–34.
61. See Cilleßen, Reichardt, and Deuling, *Napoleons neue Kleider*, 188–89.

Figure 3.4. "Liberté de la presse." *London und Paris* 4, no. 7 (1799): plate XXI. HAAB Weimar. 7 ¾ × 9 ½ inches.

ous events is nonetheless strongly present in this image and its commentary. The fact that the image can function interchangeably for different events would seem to suggest that the historical events under discussion might themselves be interchangeable or part of an identifiable pattern and thus registers uncertainty about the meaning and significance of the recent shift in government.

There then follows a "supplement" (*Beylage*) to this discussion that lists all of the journals published in Paris from September of 1797 until August of 1798:

> On this occasion it is perhaps not displeasing to certain readers of this journal to find all the daily papers and journals of all varieties that appeared

between the first Vendemiaire of year VI until the middle of Thermidor here next to each other in alphabetic order, as it was communicated to us by a connoisseur in Paris. Naturally some of these died directly after birth, or were resurrected three or four times in new form, according to the principle of Pythagorean metempsychosis. At the very least one will appreciate the inventiveness that gave rise to these new titles.[62]

This supplement references a frame of time that is neither the time ascribed to the caricature nor that to which the image had originally referred. Strangely, this period precedes the Eighteenth Brumaire by about a year, though it was in fact a time of strong freedom of the press following yet another coup carried out by the Directorial government. Given this discrepancy between the recent past and present, it is not entirely clear what the reader is supposed to get out of this alphabetic listing. Perhaps the list is meant to play a role as an archival reference work that documents the journals during a particular phase of the postrevolutionary, pre-Napoleonic period. At the same time, despite celebrating the freedom of the press, the correspondent speaks somewhat dismissively of these journals' brief lives—the freedom of journals to quickly die out is a somewhat unique take on the freedom of the press, to be sure. But there is also a sense that appreciating the inventiveness of journal names on an aesthetic level is itself a suitable response to this supplement—it is an add-on to the caricature section of *London und Paris*, after all. Editors of individual journals creatively devise clever new names for new journals while the editors of *London und Paris* pursue a different kind of creative naming, an inventory-like listing of multiple names.

Like the image, this supplemental text helps to evoke the metaphor of print's essential ephemerality, though here it is done via a list. Titles are placed "next to each other," including those that access temporal and spatial semantics (*nouvelles, magazins, bibliotheque, journal, feuilles*, and *chronique*) and slightly more unusual titles such as *le Don Quichotte des dames* or the *tachygraph*, the "speed writer" or writer of shorthand. Both the visual image and the list call attention to the "ephemeral favorites" referenced in the journal's introduction. This list helps to imagine the potential lifespans of these

---

62. "Beylage," *London und Paris* 4 (1799): 262–67, 262.

journals, and it once more positions *London und Paris* as an archive of fleeting frames of time, marking a yearlong period amid an especially turbulent time in recent history, but also marking the various microdurations suggested by the lives, rhythms of publication, deaths, and rebirths of these journals. It is likewise worth noting that the alphabetic list organizes the frames of time represented by these journals' lives synchronically, in contrast, say, to a table organized by the dates of these journals' publication history. This supplement is an excellent example of how the periodical juxtaposes frames of time without necessarily creating a narrativized, linear connection between them and how it draws on the tools of caricature to do so. In the same way that the correspondent praises the inventiveness of French journalists, this list, too, shows off an ability to call on different kinds of caricature-like representation to concretize the trope of the ephemerality of the press.

To the extent that this list turns *London und Paris* into something of a reference work, it is not one that provides an exhaustive catalogue of the print landscape of the decade after the revolution. Instead it is an incomplete archive that reflects something of the transience of what it seeks to document. Periodicals such as *London und Paris* are constantly marking and archiving things from the world around them, but lists such as these enable more general reflection upon the periodical landscape as a whole, or at least they give a brief temporal snapshot of that whole, a process of reflection that goes hand in hand with sending various kinds of print artifacts back to German readers.

Linen Monuments

London und Paris expands on the *Modejournal*'s focus on public festivals of various sorts, an all-important topic of the cultural journals of the period.[63] Viewed in tandem, these two journals have the

---

63. In founding the *Morgenblatt für gebildete Stände* in 1807, Cotta places popular festivities—"the characteristic features of nations, distinguished public festivals [*Volkscharacterzüge, öffentliche ausgezeichnete Feste*]"—near the top of his list of intended topics for the journal. Cited in Bernhard Fischer, "Einleitung," in *Morgenblatt für gebildete Stände/gebildete Leser (1807–1865): Register der*

advantage of tracking certain revolutionary festivals over multiple years, and public spectacles come up in the very first issue of *London und Paris*. Here, too, it is important to have a "tested observer on location."[64] The *Modejournal* lost its Parisian correspondent in 1793 and had no reports from Paris, fashion-related or otherwise, for over two years, while *London und Paris* began its run with a well-connected pair of correspondents on board.[65] News about the fate of revolutionary festivals into the Directorial and Napoleonic periods is part of the ever-surging flood of political and cultural reportage from Paris that would last in Germany until the beginnings of Napoleonic occupation. The periodical landscape is a key multiplier of representations of festivities, generating new accounts and recirculating previously published ones. Journals track festivals as they unfold over a given season or year, collate reports about the same celebration occurring at different places in France or in French-controlled neighboring territories, and follow such events over multiple years.[66] Festivals are also events that generate large amounts of paper. The journal's correspondents eagerly discuss the advertisements, newspaper reports, and more luxurious print artifacts tied to such events, and they send as much as possible to Weimar: caricatures of spectacles, colored drawings of fireworks, expansive tableaus of public gathering spots, carnival costumes, images of the elaborate thrones for Napoleon's coronation, and more. Not unlike accounts of the *cris de Paris*, these images work in a visual register of combining heterogeneous parts into co-

---

Honorarempfänger/Autoren und Kollationsprotokolle, ed. Bernhard Fischer (Munich: Saur, 2000), 14.

64. Bertuch and Böttiger, "Plan und Ankündigung," 5.

65. On the dearth of reports between April of 1793 and July of 1795, see Pia Schmid, "'. . . Das Rad der Kleider-Moden mauerfest und täglich neue überraschende Phänomene.' Die Französische Revolution im *Journal des Luxus und der Moden* 1789–1795," in *Französische Revolution und deutsche Öffentlichkeit. Wandlungen in Presse und Alltagskultur am Ende des 18. Jahrhunderts*, ed. Holger Böning (Munich: Saur, 1992), 419–38.

66. "We tend to speak of *the* Festival of the Federation, *the* Festival of the Supreme Being, forgetting that, duplicating and echoing the celebrations in Paris, there were thousands of festivals of the Federation, thousands of Festivals of the Supreme Being." Ozouf, *Festivals and the French Revolution*, 13.

herent wholes, an aesthetics that mirrors the symbolic function of the festivals themselves.[67] Such images complement verbal accounts of various processions, spectacles, performances, and the personalities, high and low, who attended them. At the same time as they draw on classicizing iconography in the service of constructing a sense of the unity of the French nation, many festival organizers likewise embrace the provisional and ephemeral qualities of such events and of the print matter that surround them; as Richard Taws has argued in the context of staging and documenting such festivals, "printed reproduction operates as an allegory of the reproduction of Revolution, and provisionality figures as a sign of things to come."[68] Ephemerality becomes a conceptual hinge for both the proponents and critics of official cultural politics.

In each of its first two years, London und Paris juxtaposes reports about a specific public event showcasing new spring fashions and reports of an official political festival. Again we find ourselves in the jumbled temporality of the weeks and months leading up to Easter, a focal point of the previous chapter. The "Promenade of Longchamp" is a public procession (*Lustfahrt*) of sorts along the Champs-Élysées to a rural area near the city, where high society shows off its carriages and the latest spring fashions. Mercier mentions this event in a prerevolutionary tableau, and we learn in the very first issue of London und Paris that the procession had ceased during the revolutionary period and is just starting up again in 1797.[69] Occurring on the Wednesday, Thursday, and Friday before Easter, this is the place to see and be seen, a "Corso in Paris," and the 1798 article comments on the personalities in attendance and fashions on display.[70] This procession was once based on a religious quasi-pilgrimage to an abbey in Longchamp, but its modern

---

67. See Günter Oesterle, "Suchbilder kollektiver Identitätsfindung. Die öffentliche Feste während der Französischen Revolution und ihre Wirkung auf die Deutschen," in *Vergangene Zukunft: Revolution und Künste 1789 bis 1989*, ed. Erhard Schütz und Klaus Siebenhaar (Bonn: Bouvier, 1992), 129–52.
68. Richard Taws, *The Politics of the Provisional*, 141.
69. Louis-Sébastien Mercier, *Tableau de Paris*, vol. 2 (Amsterdam: 1782), 53–55.
70. "Promenade von Longchamp," London und Paris 1, no. 1 (1798): 51–57.

form is wholly based on a "mutual desire to see and be seen" (*wechselseitige Schaulust*).[71]

Readers then encounter an article on the "Celebration of the Festival of the Sovereignty of the People," an event that occurs in the same week as the Longchamp procession.[72] The Directorial government inaugurated this festival in year six of the revolution (1797), and the event occurs prior to an important national voting day. The Directorial period is a time of bureaucratization and administrative consolidation and the limiting of direct democracy.[73] This festival is one of the *Fêtes décadaires* that is held on the *décades*, or the days of rest, that fall every ten days in the revolutionary calendar. Intended to encourage election participation and the generational transfer of civic virtues, this event stages ritualistic scenes of the young and old exchanging roles over the course of the festival.[74] Reflecting on the hypocrisy of celebrating the self-determination of the people at a time of decreased democratic participation, Winckler sprinkles in references to Easter and to other newly created festivals, including ones celebrating youth and old age, noting that the current event is when

> the (underage) French people plays and amuses itself a little bit with its sovereignty again for ten days (*sit superis placet!*), only to then put its sovereignty back into the closet for another year, just like holy Jesus, so that it stays new and lasts all the longer. For Aristophanes has already taught us that citizen *Demos* is quite the capricious old noggin; daily experience likewise teaches us that old men and children are unfortunately often all too similar, and the fact that children don't enjoy playing with the same toy for very long is something that we all know from the history of our own and others' youth.[75]

---

71. "Promenade von Longchamp," 52.
72. "Feyer des Festes der Volkssouverainetät," *London und Paris* 1, no. 1 (1798): 60–65.
73. See Jonathan Sperber, *Revolutionary Europe: 1780–1850* (Harlow, UK: Pearson, 2000), 105–7. On the difficulties faced by the directorial government to continue to implement and reshape revolutionary festivals, see Joseph F. Byrnes, *Catholic and French Forever: Religious and National Identity in Modern France* (University Park: Pennsylvania State University Press, 2005), 47–68.
74. See Ozouf, *Festivals and the French Revolution*, 194.
75. "Feyer des Festes der Volkssouverainetät," 61.

Winckler manipulates multiple temporal binaries, casting a disparaging eye at the political maturity of the French people and their religiosity, while also castigating the government for cynically celebrating something it does not entirely trust. Accessing the authority of ancient satire with its reference to Aristophanes, this passage relativizes the attempts to promote lasting civic virtue. An image emerges of a culture straddling an older Christian past (and the less distant galant past of the ancien regime) and a new quasisecular postrevolutionary era.

London und Paris returns to both events in the subsequent year with an article titled "Clothes for Watching Ice-Skating. Festival of the Sovereignty of the People in Linen Monuments. Procession to Longchamp. Bockay's. Overcoats with Eight Collars" serving as a continuation of sorts of the satirical treatment a year earlier, and this new treatment appears at a time of political turbulence, a half year prior to the coup of the Eighteenth Brumaire.[76] This time around, reports on the different events are bundled together in a single article, and the piece begins firmly in the register of fashion journalism. It has been an unusually cold winter, flooding has led to the Champs-Elysées being temporarily iced over, and the correspondent discusses the ridiculous marketing of clothing not merely to ice skaters but to the spectators (*Schrittschuhlaufzusehkleider*). The fleetingness of the frozen ice corresponds perfectly with the "ephemeral winter dress" (*ephemeres Winterkleid*) developed by Parisian designers for the occasion (Winckler also plays here on the term for an animal's winter coat), and ice skating had long been a familiar motif in the visual culture of preceding centuries as an epitome of the transience of all life.[77] The discussion of the world of fashion continues as the correspondent turns to the procession of Longchamp, noting readers' familiarity with the event and referring explicitly back to the previous year's article.[78] This year, there is some speculation that the festival would be canceled as an "appendage of the old calendar"

---

76. "Schrittschuhlaufzusehkleider. Fest der Volkssouverainität in leinwandenen Monumenten. Procession nach Langchamp. Bockay's. Ueberröcke mit acht Kragen," *London und Paris* 3, no. 4 (1799): 314–21.
77. See Koerner, *Bosch and Breugel*, 336–37.
78. "Schrittschuhlaufzusehkleider," 316–17.

(*Anhängsel des alten Kalendars*), that is, as a relic of the prerevolutionary past, but the livelihoods of too many people would be impacted.⁷⁹

As in the previous year's issue, the juxtaposition of different events lends a certain smallness and ephemerality to the festival, which is extended by the placement of the reports in the article, even down to the very appearance of the printed page. Though the discussion of this year's iteration of the festival ("Festival of Popular Sovereignty in Linen Monuments") precedes the Longchamp procession in the article title, the discussion of the official festival occurs entirely as a footnote, an afterthought, or appendage, if you will, to the extended account of the procession, which takes up most of the article. A glimpse at the layout of the page (figure 3.5) exhibits this plainly. This layout betrays a clear satirical intent and an ingenuity in using the printed page to enact the reversal of high and low and of civic virtue and the whimsy of a fashion show. The layered juxtaposition of the two different processions—two different frames of temporal unfolding and two different tableaus—operates much like the *cris de Paris* plate above. The page is a temporally complex visual ensemble that renders the contemporaneity of the noncontemporaneous visible.

The contents of this two-page footnote extend the satirical reach of this article, turning the fleetingness of the festival against itself. Giving a brief account of the festival's main monument (a column covered by shields and flags, topped with a liberty tree, and illuminated at night), the correspondent addresses the flimsiness of the decorations, which at first glance reflect poorly on their ostensible function in commemorating the French people's achievements: "One still has not yet abandoned the strange idea of erecting monuments made of cloth and paper, which can be blown away by the first wind and which give brave mockers opportunity, nay, leave them no choice but to make fun of them."⁸⁰ As Winckler notes, though, it

---

79. "Schrittschuhlaufzusehkleider," 316. As the correspondent notes, a certain sense of propriety led it to not be started on the day of rest (*décade*) on which the Festival of the Sovereignty of the People began, but this was not an important day for the fashion display anyway.

80. "Schrittschuhlaufzusehkleider," 317.

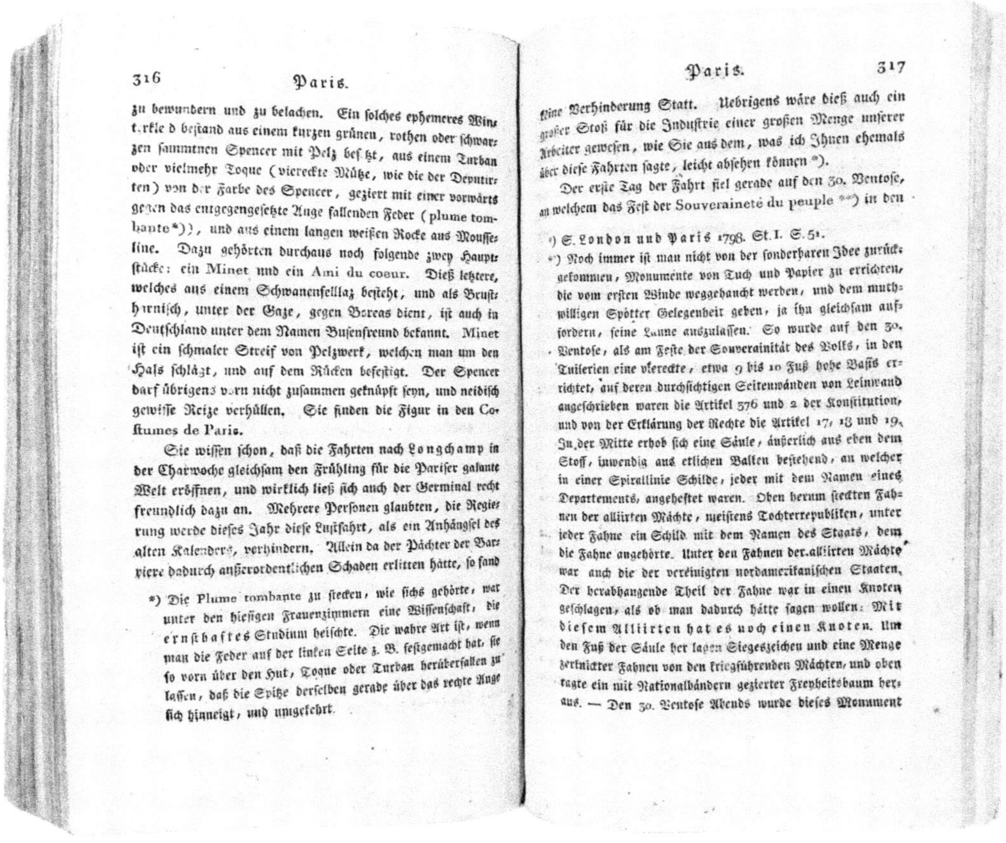

316 Paris.

zu bewundern und zu belachen. Ein solches ephemeres Winterkleid bestand aus einem kurzen grünen, rothen oder schwarzen sammtnen Spencer mit Pelz besetzt, aus einem Turban oder vielmehr Toque (viereckte Mütze, wie die der Deputirten) von der Farbe des Spencer, geziert mit einer vorwärts gegen das entgegengesetzte Auge fallenden Feder (plume tombante*)), und aus einem langen weißen Rocke aus Mousseline. Dazu gehörten durchaus noch folgende zwey Hauptstücke: ein Minet und ein Ami du coeur. Dieß letztere, welches aus einem Schwanenfelllaz besteht, und als Brustharnisch, unter der Gaze, gegen Boreas dient, ist auch in Deutschland unter dem Namen Busenfreund bekannt. Minet ist ein schmaler Streif von Pelzwerk, welchen man um den Hals schlägt, und auf dem Rücken befestigt. Der Spencer darf übrigens vorn nicht zusammen geknüpft seyn, und neidisch gewisse Reize verhüllen. Sie finden die Figur in den Costumes de Paris.

Sie wissen schon, daß die Fahrten nach Longchamp in der Charwoche gleichsam den Frühling für die Pariser galante Welt eröffnen, und wirklich ließ sich auch der Germinal recht freundlich dazu an. Mehrere Personen glaubten, die Regierung werde dieses Jahr diese Lustfahrt, als ein Anhängsel des alten Kalenders, verhindern. Allein da der Pächter der Barriere dadurch außerordentlichen Schaden erlitten hätte, so fand

*) Die Plume tombante zu stecken, wie sichs gehörte, war unter den hiesigen Frauenzimmern eine Wissenschaft, die ernsthaftes Studium heischte. Die wahre Art ist, wenn man die Feder auf der linken Seite z. B. festgemacht hat, sie so vorn über den Hut, Toque oder Turban herüberfallen zu lassen, daß die Spitze derselben gerade über das rechte Auge sich hinneigt, und umgekehrt.

Paris. 317

keine Verhinderung Statt. Uebrigens wäre dieß auch ein großer Stoß für die Industrie einer großen Menge unserer Arbeiter gewesen, wie Sie aus dem, was ich Ihnen ehemals über diese Fahrten sagte, leicht absehen können *).

Der erste Tag der Fahrt fiel gerade auf den 30. Ventose, an welchem das Fest der Souveraineté du peuple **) in den

*) S. London und Paris 1798. St. I. S. 51.

**) Noch immer ist man nicht von der sonderbaren Idee zurückgekommen, Monumente von Tuch und Papier zu errichten, die vom ersten Winde weggehaucht werden, und dem muthwilligen Spötter Gelegenheit geben, ja ihn gleichsam auffordern, seine Laune auszulassen. So wurde auf den 30. Ventose, als am Feste der Souverainität des Volks, in den Tuilerien eine viereckte, etwa 9 bis 10 Fuß hohe Basis errichtet, auf deren durchsichtigen Seitenwänden von Leinwand angeschrieben waren die Artikel 376 und 2 der Konstitution, und von der Erklärung der Rechte die Artikel 17, 18 und 19. In der Mitte erhob sich eine Säule, äußerlich aus eben dem Stoff, inwendig aus etlichen Balken bestehend, an welcher in einer Spirallinie Schilde, jeder mit dem Namen eines Departements, angeheftet waren. Oben herum steckten Fahnen der alliirten Mächte, meistens Tochterrepubliken, unter jeder Fahne ein Schild mit dem Namen des Staats, dem die Fahne angehörte. Unter den Fahnen der alliirten Mächte war auch die der vereinigten nordamerikanischen Staaten. Der herabhangende Theil der Fahne war in einen Knoten geschlagen, als ob man dadurch hätte sagen wollen: Mit diesem Alliirten hat es noch einen Knoten. Um den Fuß der Säule her lagen Siegeszeichen und eine Menge zerknickter Fahnen von den kriegführenden Mächten, und oben ragte ein mit Nationalbändern gezierter Freyheitsbaum heraus. — Den 30. Ventose Abends wurde dieses Monument

Figure 3.5. Page view. *London und Paris* 3, no. 4 (1799): 316–17. HAAB Weimar. 7 ½×4 ½ inches.

turns out that this flimsiness is a desired effect intended to allegorize the transition from the direct democracy of the revolutionary period to the elected representatives of the Directory.[81] Though ephemerality is built into the festival's design, Winckler cannot hold back from mocking its aspirations.[82] Quoting Horace's ode on immortality (*Exegi monumentum aere perennius*), the author closes sarcastically with the hope that the French will someday get their act together and produce more lasting monuments.[83]

These interrelated tableaus implicitly pose a question at the heart of serial form: what is and isn't to be continued? Will the fashion show have more staying power than the Directorial government? Will the next festival find a better aesthetic solution to the problem of projecting permanence through ephemeral constructions? Returning to the same spectacles across multiple issues has an entertaining effect, but it also gives a certain shape to time through repetition and variation. The processions of Longchamp and the sovereignty festival began at around the same point in 1797. Yet each hearkens back to different origins—to more or less distant prerevolutionary pasts and to the beginnings of popular self-determination in 1789. Winckler's satirical jabs at official culture are embedded in a larger set of temporal patterns that provide points of orientation—old and new Paris, and secular and Christian rituals—but do not offer any conclusive, predictive vision for the future, other than that there will be more attempts to mark the passing of time. Classical topoi are deployed to show where festivals depart from classical ideals, but this temporal effect is also achieved by the materiality of the printed page, which situates this material

---

81. "Schrittschuhlaufzusehkleider," 318.
82. On deliberately ephemeral monuments such as festival and theatrical preparations, see Michael Diers, "Ewig und drei Tage. Erkundungen des Ephemeren—zur Einführung," in *Mo(nu)mente: Formen und Funktionen ephemerer Denkmäler*, ed. Michael Diers (Berlin: Akademie, 1993), 2.
83. Horace, *Odes and Epodes*, ed. and trans. Niall Rudd (Cambridge, MA: Harvard University Press, 2004), 3.30.1–7. "May an impending peace soon allow Minister François de Neufchateau to have monuments erected to which the Horacian topos would apply!" ("Schrittschuhlaufzusehkleider," 318).

in a cultural hierarchy that casts both events in a ridiculous light through a series of ongoing, caricature-like vignettes.

The Monument as Caricature and as Ephemeral Event

Along with integrating classicizing iconography into public festivities, the French cultural politics of the two decades following the revolution is well-known for its imitation of antique sculpture and architecture. Like many contemporary journals, *London und Paris* eagerly track the construction of new monuments and buildings as an important form of history writing and of shaping temporal awareness more generally. Examining the journal's treatment of the famous victory column erected by Napoleon on the Place Vendôme, a monument that would remain a flashpoint in cultural and political debates throughout the nineteenth century, takes us deeper into the Napoleonic period and helps us to conceptualize the relationship of caricature to classical form and to the representation of historical personages. Monuments lend themselves to caricature because the conceit to wholeness, grandeur, and a unified artistic effect is prone to being distorted and disfigured—rendered ugly (*verhäßlicht*), to use Goethe's formulation. Napoleon is certainly the most depicted figure of the period; he cultivates a very deliberate public image across multiple media, and yet, of course, he is also a favorite target of political caricaturists. The Vendôme column, with its neo-Roman mimesis and larger-than-life representation of Napoleon in a toga at the top, is an irresistible target for Bertuch's journal, even after French occupation greatly curtails the ability of journalists to voice critical perspectives.

The Napoleonic occupation of German-speaking lands (1807–1813) is a difficult time for Bertuch's journals. Beginning in 1806, his journals are forced to reorient their offerings because continental blockades make it increasingly difficult to receive material from England. Bertuch's son, Carl, takes over editing the journal in 1804 and changes the name in 1811 to *Paris, Wien, und London—ein fortgehendes Panorama dieser drei Hauptstädte* (Paris, Vienna and London—a continuous panorama of these three capitals). As scholars have noted, the journals of the Landes-Industrie-Comptoir are subject in these years to a shift from the literature of the urban tableau to a "journal for the nobility" (*Adelsjournal*),[84] from trend setting to provincial middlebrow, from "political cultural reporting to pure cultural news."[85] In effect, *London und Paris* is a window onto the mixed fortunes of Bertuch's publishing house, with shifts in access and censorship over the years affecting the quality and relevance of his different journalistic enterprises. *London und Paris*'s modified title continues to emphasize the journal's status as an "ongoing panorama" of multiple cities, but at this time, the satirical epigrams fade from its front cover. Both *London und Paris* and the *Modejournal* continue to be interested in the arts. In 1813 the title of the *Modejournal* became *Journal für Luxus, Mode und Gegenstände der Kunst* (Journal for luxury, fashion, and objects of art) and then in 1814 *Journal für Literatur, Kunst, Luxus und Mode* (Journal for literature, art, luxury, and fashion). Despite this interest in the arts and the continued reliance on images, the number of caricatures and satirical commentaries declines markedly in both journals in the 1810s.

That said, the anti-Napoleonic sentiments of the elder Bertuch remain strong, and he is a key agent in the development of the nationalist press after the end of the Napoleonic occupation.[86] The cultural journals of his publishing house do not stop sending back reports on public spectacle and commemorative practices from Paris, Vienna, and London and continue to insert subtle mockery of Napoleon into their pages. In part from the perspective of the anti-Roman and anti-French "barbarian"[87] and in part as an oppositional neo-Roman mimesis that positions Germans as more capable than the French of imitating the artistic achievements of an-

---

84. Deuling describes the *Modejournal* this way; Christian Deuling, "Die Karikatur-Kommentare in der Zeitschrift *London und Paris* (1798–1815)," in Cilleßen, Reichardt, and Deuling, *Napoleons Neue Kleider*, 91.

85. Seifert, "Die Französische Revolution im Spiegel," 178.

86. He founded the journal *Nemesis. Zeitschrift für Politik und Geschichte* (Nemesis. Journal for politics and history) (1814–1818) with Heinrich Luden, which would be an important organ of contemporary history in the years prior to the Congress of Vienna.

87. See Hell, *The Conquest of Ruins*, 243–55.

tiquity, *Paris, Wien und London* pursues a style of cultural critique that bears important similarities to the more ostentatious satirical material in the early years of *London und Paris*.

The Columns of Austerlitz

London und Paris contains two different reports on the "Colonne de la grande Armée." The first was published in 1808 while the column was still being completed, and the second appeared following its dedication in 1811, just after the journal was retitled. This monument was modeled after the Column of Trajan in Rome and commemorated the defeat of the Austrian army at Austerlitz in 1805; the bronze for the bas-reliefs encircling the column was supposedly taken from Austrian cannons. For German-speaking lands, this column is a symbol of humiliation, and the 1808 article's title provocatively refers to it as the "Column of Austerlitz" and details a visit to the workshop where it is being made.[88] The symbolic regime under Napoleon is still very much a work in progress, and wondering where it might go and how it might end is a prime topic for contemporary history writing. As the anonymous correspondent notes (Winckler had by this time passed away), the viewer can learn things about unfinished monuments from "seeing something in the process of coming into being [*Entstehensehen*]." Presuming the work's completion and function as a whole, the correspondent nonetheless lingers with the merits of partial views and their procedural character: "I like to observe a large totality in parts, ... piece by piece" (*Ich betrachte gern ein großes Ganze theilweise ... Stück für Stück*).[89] Advance viewing of the parts prior to their final positioning is especially instructive in the case of the column's bas-reliefs depicting the history of Napoleon's victory. On installation, they wound their way up the column farther and farther from viewers on the ground and would not be visible as a continuous whole from any one location. This scene of viewing the bas-reliefs prior to their

---

88. "Die Säule von Austerlitz," *London und Paris* 22, no. 8 (1808): 265–71, 266.
89. "Die Säule von Austerlitz," 265–66.

final installation functions as yet another *tableau mouvant* based on shifting spatial and temporal perspectives.

If the journalistic disarticulation of the whole provides an initial hint that this article might be using the tools of caricature against the unfinished monument, the author's interest in elements of the structure that are distorted and disfigured leaves little doubt that this is the case.[90] As the correspondent notes, because manual laborers are doing the work rather than trained artists, "almost all of the figures have become caricatures" (*fast alle Gestalten sind Karikaturen geworden*).[91] Disfiguration also affects the workers assembling the columns, who appear to have become ill from all the metal and stone dust—there is "not a single healthy figure" among them.[92] Additionally, the soldiers depicted on the incomplete bas-reliefs stand unnaturally upright and lack heads. "To give the artist's taste the best possible interpretation, one could almost take them for satyrs, if all joking were not obscene in the face of such dreadful seriousness and the German blood shed so bravely."[93] These images are unbalanced and fragmented; so too is the body of Napoleon, who is to stand atop the column in the costume of a Roman emperor: though the head bears a striking resemblance to the leader, the body is "calculated for its elevation and should not be observed up close."[94]

Though censorship prevents the correspondent from saying it outright, this article's aim is to make this classicizing monstrosity seem as impermanent as the journal's caricatures and *tableaux mouvants*. Employing satire's characteristic reversals, the article undermines the sense of the monument as a stable, unified work. By focusing on procedural aspects—how it is being unskillfully built, or viewing it in parts—the article temporalizes and destabilizes the monument. In the context of more modern projects such as the art-

---

90. The column will function as an "enduring memorial of this martial time and its heroes" and that "after Rome only Paris can lay claim to such a triumphant monument." "Die Säule von Austerlitz," 271.
91. "Die Säule von Austerlitz," 269.
92. "Die Säule von Austerlitz," 266.
93. "Die Säule von Austerlitz," 267.
94. "Die Säule von Austerlitz," 268.

ist Christo's wrapping of the German Reichstag in the 1990s, the historian François Hartog has described methods of treating a building or monument as a point of reference in a dynamic process rather than as a stable, unified form with a fixed meaning. "One way of introducing something new is to play on the paradox of the durable and the ephemeral, by transforming a monument into an event."[95] This unassuming piece of Napoleonic era cultural journalism does just that, for it treats spectatorship of the monument as a process of deconstruction and disfigurement rather than as a process of constructing the object as a unified whole, as an affirmatively classicizing viewing might do. The lightly satirical yet devastating description of the monument as a work in progress rivals the commemorative temporality that the monument is intended to inaugurate. The column's completion will mark the beginning of its proper commemorative function, yet this account preemptively invests the monument with a different temporality, namely one that envisions its eventual irrelevance and destruction.

Though the second article on the column in the newly renamed *Paris, Wien und London* lacks any reference to the first article, it might be seen as something of a continuation of it (or as merely another instance in a steady stream of disparaging accounts of Napoleonic rule). This second view also pairs an account of the column with that of a second artwork unveiled on the same day, August 15, 1810. This is the monument built for the Place des Victoires to honor General Louis Desaix, a close confidant to Napoleon who accompanied him to Egypt and died in battle in 1800. Readers are presented with a sequence of discussions of two "products of contemporary art" (*Produkte der neuern Kunst*) that have attracted the attention of artists and friends of art and the "curiosity of spectacle-seeking public of all classes" (*gaffenden Publikums aller Klassen*).[96] In this issue (in contrast to the 1808 article), readers are provided with images of the monuments that bring them both down to fit the size of the printed page (figures 3.6 and 3.7).

---

95. Hartog, *Regimes of Historicity*, 159.
96. "Die Colonne des Place-Vendôme und die Statue des Generals Desais zu Paris," *Paris, Wien und London* 1, no. 3 (1811): 199.

Figure 3.6. "Die Colonne der grossen Armee auf dem Place Vendôme zu Paris." *Paris, Wien und London* 1, no. 3 (1811): plate VIII. HAAB Weimar. 9 ½ × 6 ¾ inches.

Figure 3.7. "Monument des Generals Desaix auf dem Place Victoire zu Paris." *Paris, Wien und London* 1, no. 3 (1811): plate IX. HAAB Weimar. 7 ½ × 4 ½ inches.

The column is no longer in pieces if the image is any guide, and soldiers seem to have already begun to use the Place Vêndome to commemorate the military's past successes. This article is more matter of fact than the earlier one, even issuing mild praise: it is understandable that this "imitation of the ancient masterpiece" makes a positive impression, for its proportions are taken from "one of the most beautiful monuments of antiquity."[97] The correspondent comments on the column's dimensions and the difficulty of making "continuous bas-reliefs" (*fortlaufende Basreliefs*) out of bronze.[98] This description continues to lightly evoke the semantics of progressive, forward movement suggested by the journal's title (*fortgehendes Panorama*). A tinge of criticism comes through at the end of the piece, though, with the correspondent noting the "strange contrast" of the soldiers' modern uniform and Napoleon's Roman costume: "Perhaps this all-too-conscientious faithfulness of imitation will, after many centuries, cause our descendants to believe that the statue was placed on top of the monument during a different age, and that under certain circumstances, our rulers occasionally made use of the costume of the Roman emperors."[99] The journal's tandem treatment of fashion and broader cultural and political affairs helps to envision a future long after the fall of the Napoleonic empire in which French attempts to find traces of antiquity in the present will border on the undecipherable. Here again, readers are invited to momentarily occupy the position of future historians (or archaeologists, to recall Börne's thought experiment with which we began this book), and here, too, the call to imagine the present as an ancient past gestures in a classicizing direction without fully affirming classical form.

The second part of the article turns to Desaix, who is depicted in a heroic style, almost naked, next to an Egyptian obelisk and a sphinx head. The monument was panned by the French press, presumably allowing the correspondent to be more forthcoming with his criticism. As in the discussion of the Place Vendôme column, this article addresses the question of historical dress and temporal disjunction.

---

97. "Die Colonne des Place-Vendôme," 200, 203.
98. "Die Colonne des Place-Vendôme," 202.
99. "Die Colonne des Place-Vendôme," 207.

The monument straddles antiquity and modernity and occident and orient (Desaix is pointing East), and the correspondent rehearses complaints about the appropriateness of depicting the general naked (why, for example, isn't he wearing the cloak he carries on his arm?). The disjunction of antique, heroic style and modern customs could, perhaps, be excused if the form of the body were well carried out, but this statue is little more than a massive caricature-like exaggeration: "Here, however, one views merely a gigantic, trivial statue, entirely common, purely exaggerated forms."[100] The correspondent has kinder words for the obelisk, but the lack of any correspondence or aesthetic coherence to the ensemble confuses the effect.[101] Intended as a fusion of the style of antiquity with the achievements of modernity, the monument manifests little more than the disjunctive coexistence of different temporal frames. A satirical reading of a classicizing statue unmasks the statue as (unwitting) self-caricature.

It is perhaps not an accident that the piece closes on a sartorial note: after being panned by the critics and disavowed by the artist who designed it, the Desaix statue has been covered back up: "It is said that they are in the process of clothing it, in order, if possible, to improve it."[102] Even as the monuments are being unveiled as completed, they are drawn back into a process of redesigning and reworking. The account of the process of unveiling, reception, and reveiling undercuts these commemorative representations of important leaders and their intended function, namely to manifest Napoleon and Desaix's lasting and unchanging presence in the public life of the nation. Instead, this report relegates such representations to a realm of temporal uncertainty and flux through caricature-like disfigurement.[103] Caricature brings down to size, if you will, the aspiration to historical greatness and the commemoration of a would-be

---

100. "Die Colonne des Place-Vendôme," 213.
101. "Die Colonne des Place-Vendôme," 213–14.
102. "Die Colonne des Place-Vendôme," 214.
103. The monumentalizing representation of historical personality is related to portraiture's aim of "representing the subject as actually present." Daniel Cooper, "Portraiture," in *Propaganda and Mass Persuasion: A Historical Encyclopedia, 1500 to the Present*, ed. Nicholas J. Cull, David Culbert, and David Welch (Santa Barbara CA: ABC-CLIO, 2003), 306.

permanent victory. The size of these printed images also contributes to this effect, with the plate of the Desaix monument the size of any other plate in the journal.

The consideration of the two monuments one after the other follows to a certain extent the course of official commemoration and its attempt to mark intelligible points in a heroic narrative of history—Napoleon's Egyptian campaign and the battle of Austerlitz function here as key moments in a series of French victories—yet the journal's sequence of images does not result in any kind of synthetic, comprehensible unity of ancient and modern or of past, present and future. Seen in the light of the journal's self-understanding as an "ongoing panorama," the subtle (and not so subtle) demonumentalization carried out by these pieces situates these monuments on par with other fleeting urban scenes instead of identifying a radically different temporality at work in the monuments that could fix historical memory. Rather than functioning as memorializing devices that one might preserve to remember Napoleon, they come to function as other caricatures in the journal do—as somewhat whimsical pieces that might or might not be preserved by readers as historically specific indicators of national folly. In line with the journal's aims since its inception, this ensemble of texts and images stresses the monument's status as an ephemeral process rather than as a commemorative structure that programs its own unchanging future reception into the act of viewing it. In the era when new cultures of monuments are in ascendance, the promise of permanence typical of such cultures is called into question.

Over the course of this chapter I have explored clusters of articles and images that caricature contemporary Parisian life and reflect on processes of collecting, reproducing, and disseminating various kinds of print products. An expanded concept of caricature is helpful in describing a specific style of ephemeral print that includes journalistic and editorial ploys across text and image and various kinds of print artifacts. Caricature is an inherently temporalized form, and in this period it is an indelible index of the current, the fleeting, the momentary, the fashionable, and the ridiculous, with humorous reversals playing leading roles in the journal's mise en page. The journal highlights the ephemerality of caricatures as print objects but nonetheless facilitates their preservation. Even while accessing topoi and motifs from early modern visual culture such as the *cris de Paris* or fashion processions, the journal's use of caricature, broadly understood to orient readers vis-à-vis the specific temporalities of the postrevolutionary era, confirms Koselleck's diagnosis of caricature as facilitating the individualization of historical events. In turn, caricature is a key part of a journalistic vocabulary that can be mobilized in different ideological directions; throughout this first part of the book, we have lingered with anti-revolutionary perspectives, while in subsequent chapters we will consider how caricature is mobilized in more pro-revolutionary ways in the works of writers such as Heine and Börne.

In chapters 1 and 2, I explored how Bertuch and his collaborators are keen to promote luxury print as beautiful, while in this chapter I have focused more on his journals' promotion of print products associated with the ugly. In both cases, though, smallness characterizes the print products that the journal canalizes for readers. Small print objects can be diverting and entertaining and they can commemorate people and events, but they can also be weaponized: sometimes an oblique, biting aside can be more effective than an extended serious treatise. Smallness is also a feature of serial form, with one small thing following another, and Bertuch and his collaborators prove adept at adapting existing strategies (and inventing new ones) of aligning different small forms accidentally and deliberately, even as these figures remain active in negotiating the criteria for canonical literary works and "larger" luxury editions. Bertuch and Böttiger's brand of cultural journalism is firmly grounded in the expectation that their journals present readers with an ongoing flow of certain print items—images, caricatures, new year's gifts, and more—and I have situated this brand in contrast to a literary aesthetics that privileges more lasting, stable works and that treats serial flow, ephemerality, and the satire of distasteful subjects as things to be avoided. In the next part of the book, I turn to the author Jean Paul, who treats the context of cultural journalism and ephemeral literary entertainment as a catalyzing and enabling force for his literary experiments.

Part II

Miscellanies of Time

To the extent that seriality is associated with continuation and the promise of more, Jean Paul—the pen name of Johann Paul Friedrich Richter (1763–1825)—is a quintessential author of serial forms. His writings, with their cascading allegories, indirect references to current events, and satirical and sentimental fantasias, give the impression that they could just go on and on: incomplete novels, miscellaneous aphorisms, aesthetic and pedagogical treatises with ample supplements and appended continuations, thematically connected occasional pieces on political and cultural topics, fragmentary autobiographical writings, and more. Jean Paul is a key figure in the development of literary *Unterhaltung* in the early nineteenth century, an association that contributes to his contested reputation as the "most read author of his age," even if his circuitous satires of the crowded landscape of journals, *Taschenbücher*, and anthologies make him difficult for modern readers.[1] To be sure, his works' propensity for continuation and digression leads to accusations that they lacked aesthetic coherence; Hegel, for example, claims that Jean Paul, "in his search for ever new material . . . superficially patches together the most heterogeneous things."[2] It must be said, though, that Jean Paul's preference for serial juxtaposition over classicizing unity and coherence emerges from participation in and satiric mimicry of the serial publications of the day, a mimicry, as we will see, that subverts the concept of the self-standing autonomous literary work. At a time when serial formats cut across book- and journal-based literature, Jean Paul places journal-based modes of writing at the heart of his authorial self-presentation. He thus comes into view as a catalyst for contemporary and subsequent writers of serial literature, both the politically active writers of *Vormärz* and more literary figures such as Adalbert Stifter.

A central concern of *Writing Time* is how serial forms shape the awareness of time. The promise of more tethers serial forms to both the past (the present installment continues the previous one) and the future (the next yet-unwritten installment will soon come). Writing speculatively into the future is an integral feature of Jean Paul's writings, which scholars recognize as being the "culmination of the processes of temporalization" of the period.[3] Among other things, he writes a "conjectural biography" detailing his future life, he announces the future demise of Napoleon, he imagines his own death, he writes the future history of the *Morgenblatt für gebildete Stände*, and he announces the coming publication of his collected works, envisioning the ongoing production of more and less ephemeral works and their potential for reencounter. Whereas scholars exploring Jean Paul's treatment of time have largely focused on the tem-

---

1. See Eduard Berend, "Jean Paul, der meistgelesene Schriftsteller seiner Zeit?" in *Jean Paul*, ed. Uwe Schweikert (Darmstadt: Wissenschaftliche Buchgesellschaft, 1974), 155–69.
2. G. W. F. Hegel, *Vorlesungen über die Ästhetik*, in *Werke in zwanzig Bänden*, vol. 13, ed. Eva Muldenhauer and Karl Markus Michel (Frankfurt: Suhrkamp, 1970), 382.
3. Dirk Göttsche, *Zeit im Roman. Literarische Zeitreflexion und die Geschichte des Zeitromans im späten 18. und im 19. Jahrhundert* (Munich: Fink, 2001), 119.

poral footprints of particular genres (including the novel, the idyll, and the digression),[4] I take a closer look in part II at the temporal and media-based specifics of his writings for journals in primarily the last roughly two decades of his life (1807–1825), a period when his writings for journals, *Taschenbücher*, and other anthologies increase in number and become a central part of his literary output.[5] In doing so, I suggest new perspectives on Jean Paul's significance both as a thinker of time and as an author of serial forms.

As Koselleck has argued, a fundamental feature of the early nineteenth-century temporalization of historical and cultural awareness is the turn away from the past to the future as a guiding temporal horizon. The future arises as a particularly acute concern in the tumultuous years of Napoleonic occupation and its aftermath: What is the proper vantage point from which to adequately understand the present? What will come of this revolutionary age or of Napoleon? What is this "new" time and what comes next? This is also a time of uncertainty about what is of lasting literary and cultural value: What formats secure an author's reception as part of a nascent, national literary canon? What will future readers value in an age of ever-growing literary diversion? What sites and styles of authorship are most successful across a variety of print formats? Chapters 4 and 5 address these issues from two different yet related angles. Chapter 4 explores Jean Paul's forays into political

---

4. Göttsche, Ralph Berhorst, and Helge Jordheim have all explored questions of time and the novel in Jean Paul; see Göttsche, *Zeit im Roman*; Ralf Berhorst, *Anamorphose der Zeit. Jean Pauls Romanästhetik und Geschichtsphilosophie* (Tübingen: Niemeyer, 2002); and Helge Jordheim, *Der Staatsroman im Werk Wielands und Jean Pauls. Gattungsverhandlungen zwischen Poetologie und Politik* (Tübingen: Niemeyer, 2007). On the temporality of the idyll and digression, see Ulrike Hagel, *Elliptische Zeiträume des Erzählens: Jean Paul und die Aporien der Idylle* (Würzburg: Königshausen und Neumann, 2003); and Magnus Wieland, *Vexierzüge: Jean Pauls Digressionspoetik* (Hanover: Wehrhahn, 2013).

5. Dorothea Böck designates these writings the "nucleus of his entire belletristic creative production in the period between 1807 up to his death, meaning both his journalistic and more narrow poetic production." Dorothea Böck, "Archäologie in der Wüste. Jean Paul und das ‚Biedermeier'–Eine Provokation für das Fach (ante portas)," in *Atta Troll tanzt noch Selbstbesichtigungen der literaturwissenschaftlichen Germanistik im 20. Jahrhundert*, ed. Petra Boden, Holger Dainat, and Ursula Menzel (Berlin: Akademie, 1997), 263.

commentary and contemporary history, as he seeks to come to terms with the present and envision the future in analogy to other kinds of historical and literary projects. In chapter 4, I turn to how he envisions his authorial oeuvre both up to and beyond the horizon of his own death. I am particularly interested in how Jean Paul envisions the afterlife of his writings across journal and book formats, using the promise of continuation to craft his literary legacy while satirizing tropes of authorial immortality. He engages with various serial formats and genre conventions to create the sense of a dynamic, growing body of work that changes as time moves forward and new readers (re)encounter it. Jean Paul thus brings together key strands of contemporary history writing and authorial self-assertion in the realm of journal literature that is at the heart of this book, filtering his temporal reflections all the while through the trope of the ephemerality of print. In this way, a detailed case study of his nontraditional authorial career proves instructive in a book that is concerned as much with serial formats as with individual authors.

A key part of Jean Paul's mimicking of the forms and formats of journal literature lies in his playful embrace of miscellaneity. The miscellany was a long-standing literary format convention with roots in early modern notions of the florilegium and eighteenth-century moral-satirical traditions of mixed writings, or *Vermischte Schriften*. The miscellany tradition flourished in the moral weeklies of the eighteenth century and related anthology genres, which presented readers with a deliberately varied mixture of edifying and entertaining materials.[6] The guiding principle of miscellaneity takes on new cultural authority around 1800, as expanded reading audiences grow more eager for mixed contents in cultural journals. Indeed, in a piece commissioned for the inaugural issue of the *Morgenblatt für gebildete Stände*, Jean Paul states that miscellaneity is the essence not merely of the *Morgenblatt* and all other periodicals but of the age itself.[7] Such programmatic statements are echoed by

---

6. On the miscellany tradition, see Barbara Benedict, *Making the Modern Reader: Cultural Mediation in Early Modern Literary Anthologies* (Princeton, NJ: Princeton University Press, 1996).

7. Jean Paul, "Abschiedsrede bey dem künftigen Schlusse des Morgenblatts," *Morgenblatt für gebildete Stände* 1, no. 1 (January 1, 1807): 3; II/3, 234. In cases

later definitions of nineteenth-century periodical literature in terms of the formal properties of seriality and miscellaneity.

Being an author in an age of the miscellany requires strategies for distinguishing oneself, a challenge that Jean Paul addresses in a series of aphorisms and other short pieces titled "My Miscellanies" (*Meine Miszellen*).[8] He notes that, like so many other writers for the periodical press, he actively contributes to an ever-accumulating flood of textual units on offer: "If there are Russian, English, French, etc. miscellanies, then why shouldn't there be German ones? And if there are German ones, why not mine?"[9] Part of Jean Paul's joke here is in referencing specific products on the literary market, with *Russian Miscellanies*, *French Miscellanies*, and *English Miscellanies* all titles of contemporary journals; indeed, Cotta created the *Morgenblatt* in 1807 by consolidating his two earlier journals, *Französische Miszellen* and *Englische Miszellen* (French miscellanies and English miscellanies) (1803–1806), which were modeled on the tremendous success of *London und Paris*.[10] In writing his "own" miscellanies, Jean Paul mimics the format and structure of periodicals and other anthologies (including the *Taschenbuch* in which it appears), but he stamps them with his own particular voice and style: they are "his." Authorship lends provisional order to heterogeneous print. The gesture of writing his "own" miscellanies is thus an ironic reflection on his authorial brand in an age abounding with literary entertainment.

---

where I deal in an extended fashion with a text by Jean Paul, I cite the text in its relevant journal, anthology, or works edition version as well as in the modern Hanser critical edition, *Sämtliche Werke in 10 Bänden* (henceforth cited in the footnotes with no abbreviation, with part and volume number followed by page number). See figure 4.1 for a diagram of publication history that foregrounds journal, anthology, and works edition publication patterns. In contrast to the table at the end of the Hanser edition showing the location of each of Jean Paul's publications across five nineteenth- and twentieth-century works editions, my figure seeks to visualize the patterns of republication beginning with the journal version of parts or the whole of given publications.

8. He first published this in 1807 in the multiauthor *Taschenbuch für Jahr 1807, der Freundschaft und Liebe gewidmet* (Frankfurt: Wilmans) and republished it in the 1810 *Herbst-Blumine* anthology.

9. "Wenn es russische, englische, französische, etc. Miszellen gibt, warum soll es nicht deutsche geben? Und wenn diese, warum nicht auch meine?" II/3, 129.

10. On the rise in titles, see Roman B. Kremer, "Miszellen," in *Historisches Wörterbuch der Rhetorik*, ed. Gert Ueding, vol. 10 (Berlin: De Gruyter, 2012), 714.

There is a strong logic of serial continuation in this piece. As Jean Paul notes, with mock resignation, "I don't know how one might bring this reading [of miscellanies] to an end" (*Ich weiß nicht, wie man diesem Lesen ein Ende machen soll*).[11] Like satire and digression, two of Jean Paul's favorite discursive modes, the principle of miscellaneity does not on its own contain a clear directive for how it might conclude or wrap up. A combined sense of ever-proliferating texts and of the lack of any decisive conclusion informs Jean Paul's choice to call his writings for periodicals *Werkchen*, "little works," associating them with the ephemeral, the topical, and the occasional, and ironizing the aspiration for stand-alone cohesion (*Zusammenhang*) and monumental completion (*Vollendung*). Scholars have recently explored how Jean Paul's embrace of the *Werkchen* challenges standard notions of the literary work.[12] Along with embracing provisionality and the promise of more, Jean Paul's journal-based writings are premised on being part of a collection of multiple *Werkchen*. Indeed, such collections—ranging from *Taschenbücher* to journals and various literary anthologies—are a defining feature of the age, and such anthologies build on the moral miscellany tradition while also capitalizing on the material and metaphorical potential of contemporary serial formats as archives of varied contents.[13] Jean Paul makes extensive use of such formats when repackaging his writings in single-author collections, including the three-volume *Herbst-Blumine, oder gesammelte Werkchen aus Zeitschriften* (Autumn flora, or collected little works from journals), the 1814 *Museum* (Museum), the 1817 *Politische Fastenpredigten während Deutschlands Marterwoche* (Political Lenten sermons during Germany's holy week), and an 1825 collection of his book reviews. Jean Paul constantly faces the challenge of having his writings excerpted,

---

11. II/3, 133.
12. See Nicolas Pethes, *Vermischte Schriften. Jean Pauls Roman-Anthologie "D. Katzenbergers Badereise" (1809)* (Hanover: Wehrhahn, 2022); and Bryan Klausmeyer, "Fragmenting Fragments: Jean Paul's Poetics of the Small in 'Meine Miszellen,'" *Monatshefte* 108, no. 4 (2016): 485–509.
13. On the importance of collections in this period, see Friedrich Sengle, *Biedermeierzeit. Deutsche Literatur im Spannungsfeld zwischen Restauration und Revolution 1815–1848*, vol. 2 (Stuttgart: Metzler, 1972), 1–82.

repackaged, and reprinted without authorization (*Raub-* or *Nachdruck*). This is another side of the age of the miscellany with which he contends. In a sense, Jean Paul's authorized anthologies represent additional versions of "his" miscellanies; as we will see, he also uses the anthology to ironize the hermeneutic coherence of the idea of collected works. Emphasizing plurality and open-endedness, Jean Paul presents readers with a network of plural, recirculating works that resist the norms of the book and of the works edition at a time of their ascendancy.

Jean Paul's keen awareness of print's ephemerality and its potential for preservation and recirculation is at the heart of his attempts to write the time of the present and the recent past (historical time) as well as the time of an authorial oeuvre at the end of his life and beyond. If chapter 4 asks about the time and timeliness of miscellanies, chapter 5 asks how a miscellaneous oeuvre might end. Jean Paul pursues a collected works edition at a time when this format was under consolidation in the world of German letters, with his and Goethe's *Ausgabe Letzter Hand* published at almost the same time. This was a time of ever-increasing interest in the literary legacies of important authors, but Jean Paul ironizes the tendency to include ever more material in his collected works. In the process, he repeatedly comes back to scenes where his own death and the realization of his works edition converge. On the one hand, these scenes subject the time of his own life to the dictates of literary form and medial format. On the other hand, imagining the end of his life and works also provides an occasion for imagining the continuation of both. Writing the end thus paradoxically is a way of writing the future and of imagining the open-ended futures that ephemeral writings might have.

4

Jean Paul's Paper Festivals

On October 27, 1806, the Prussian capital of Berlin was captured by French forces in the aftermath of the Battle of Jena–Auerstedt, beginning six years of occupation by Napoleon. Like many contemporary intellectuals, Jean Paul sought to respond to these and subsequent events through writings in journals, anthologies, and pamphlets, contributing to a boom in topical publications.[1] His contributions include *Friedens-Predigt an Deutschland gehalten von Jean Paul* (Peace sermon to Germany held by Jean Paul) (1808), *Dämmerungen für Deutschland* (Twilights for Germany) (1809), *Nachdämmerungen für Deutschland* (After twilights for Germany) (1810), and an anthology of previously published pieces titled *Politische*

---

1. "Such an intensive deployment of topical literature to mobilize for war had no precedent in German history." Karen Hagemann, *Revisiting Prussia's Wars against Napoleon: History, Culture, and Memory* (Cambridge: Cambridge University Press, 2015), 98.

Fastenpredigten während Deutschlands Marterwoche (Political Lenten sermons during Germany's holy week) (1817). Each contains essays of various sizes, fictional scenes of war and occupation, stoic musings, and more, and each tests the limits of French and German censorship regimes. Genre conventions of the political sermon and of the Janus-like gaze forward to the future and backward to history help make these pieces an identifiable series (a "war section" [*Kriegsabtheilung*] of his collected works, as Jean Paul put it[2]) characterized by miscellaneous cultural commentary and fictionalizations of the scene of occasional writing.

Reflections on time and the times are all too characteristic of this epoch. Contemporaries repeatedly register changes in the perception and experience of time: Johann Gottlieb Fichte, for example, feels that Napoleonic occupation has imposed a "foreign" time on German-speaking lands, and observers across the political spectrum would go on to welcome (at least initially) the post-Napoleon moment as an emancipatory, expressly "new" time.[3] Competing visions of the implications of the French Revolution for the past, present, and future are in constant circulation. Jean Paul's topical works attempt to lend shape and direction to this "new time." As he says in 1809, "the new time demands new powers."[4] Through the repeated invocation of the transience of all things, he seeks to console and inspire readers amid the German "culture of defeat."[5] In the wake of victory over Napoleon, he then seeks to memorialize the past and present for future generations; this includes recalling the writings and speeches of the revolutionary period—"freedom sermons," as he calls them—and their relevance in a time of censorship and occupation. At the same time, he gives voice to a sense of witnessing a "chaos of times working against each other,"[6] of living through an

---

2. Eduard Berend, *Prolegomena zur historisch-kritischen Gesamtausgabe von Jean Pauls Werken* (Berlin: Verlag der Akademie der Wissenschaften, 1927), 10.
3. See Becker, *Zeit der Revolution!*, 131.
4. Jean Paul, *Dämmerungen für Deutschland* (Tübingen: Cotta, 1809), v.
5. On the notion of the culture of defeat, see Wolfgang Schievelbusch, *Culture of Defeat: On National Trauma, Mourning, and Recovery* (New York: Picador, 2004).
6. "Ein Chaos wiedereinander arbeitender Zeiten." From a section of Jean Paul's pedagogical treatise *Levana* titled "Über den Geist der Zeit." I/5, 572.

age of political and cultural "fermentation" (*Gährung*), with Napoleon as the "brewmaster."[7] His evocation of the coexistence of multiple temporal frameworks—including worldly transience, hopeful orientation toward the future, the rediscovery of the past, and more—stands out not least because he recognizes the literary landscape's role in generating this sense of chaos and literature's potential to give the turbulent times provisional structure. In contrast to certain contemporaries skeptical of the press as an ideal form of politically relevant communication, Jean Paul embraces occasional writings for cultural journals and anthologies as formal points of departure for writing about current events.

Jean Paul has played a minor but not always entirely marginal role in histories of Napoleonic era "wars of the quill" (*Federkriege*).[8] The writers of the *Vormärz* celebrate his biting wit and his advocacy of press freedoms and adapt key features of his digressive style in the service of political critique. However, many of Jean Paul's own contemporaries doubt whether he is up to the task of intervening in political debates, finding his views more patriotic than nationalist and more moral than partisan—"undependable," as Hans Mayer summarized in a 1966 edition of *Dämmerungen für Deutschland*.[9] I will return to the question of political reception below, but I am ultimately less interested in Jean Paul's political ideology per se than in these writings as engagements with serial literature and as literary repurposings of genres of history writing and occasional public speech. As we will see, he embraces formats capable of communicating the interrelation of different times and the passing of time as serial flow. The historian Susan Crane aptly characterizes this era in German-speaking lands as a time when writers turned to print to configure "the

---

7. Jean Paul, "Nachdämmerungen für Deutschland," *Vaterländisches Museum*, no. 1 (1810): 13; I/5, 1081.
8. A recent monograph on literary authorship in Germany during the Napoleonic Wars, for example, does not cite his topical writings. Christoph Jürgensen, *Federkrieger: Autorschaft im Zeichen der Befreiungskriege* (Stuttgart: Metzler, 2018).
9. As Günter De Bruyn puts it, "nicht deutsch-romantisch-nationalistisch, sondern deutsch-aufgeklärt." Günter De Bruyn, "Dämmerungen. Jean Paul und die Politik," *Sinn und Form* 38, no. 6 (1986): 1150. Hans Mayer, "Der unzuverlässige Jean Paul," in *Politische Fastenpredigten während Deutschlands Marterwoche* (Frankfurt: Insel, 1966), 147.

ephemeral, fleeting sensation of historical perception ... as having solidity and depth."[10] Jean Paul's topical writings clearly engage with this dynamic, tapping into the temporality of short occasional pieces to both enact and ironize the drive to establish cultural continuity.

I begin this chapter by looking at several basic metaphors that orient Jean Paul's approach to time and these metaphors' role in his characterization of his topical writings as sermons and temporal thresholds, or "twilights." I then situate these writings amid other contemporary strategies of imagining present and future encounters with literary, historical, or journalistic texts, including political journalism and the writing of contemporary history (*Zeitgeschichte*), the philosophy of history, and literary entertainment, as well as older moralizing traditions from eighteenth-century moral weeklies. Jean Paul adapts various styles of authorship in preparing literary works and journalistic writing for future readers, suggesting how his texts might be continued or reencountered at different historical junctures. Republication is a particularly important technique for Jean Paul as he navigates the transition between writing for journals and for single-author books. He invests the usually pejorative semantics of the prepublication of a bookish work in a periodical (*Vorabdruck*) and of unauthorized reprinting (*Nachdruck*) with temporal and indeed historiographical significance.[11] His characterizations of miscellaneous writings as festivals and commemorative monuments function not only as ironic meditations on the repeated reencounters of works in the future but also as a deliberate attempt to craft a successful authorial brand. Though Jean Paul's miscellanies on time and the times might not have had the political afterlives he intended, they represent important reflections on the potential and peril of serial formats for modeling cultural permanence.

---

10. Susan A. Crane, *Collecting and Historical Consciousness in Early Nineteenth-Century Germany* (Ithaca, NY: Cornell University Press, 2000), 34.

11. Pirated versions of his writings are a recurring issue for Jean Paul, something that he fictionalizes to comic effect, as Nicola Kaminski and others have shown. See Nicola Kaminski, "'Nachdruck des Nachdrucks' als Werk(chen)organisation oder Wie D. Katzenberger die *Kleinen Schriften von Jean Paul Friedrich Richter* anatomiert," in *Jahrbuch der Jean Paul Gesellschaft* 52 (2017): 29–70. On the question of *Vorabdruck*, see Spoerhase, *Das Format der Literatur*, 528–50.

Figures of Time

Dirk Göttsche sums up well the centrality of reflections on time for Jean Paul's work: his "modern sense of critical time is at the very heart of his writing and of his critique of political and cultural history in the wake of the French Revolution."[12] Jean Paul straddles traditionalist and modern visions of time, engaging with the dialectic between the finite and the infinite, the world of transience and the eternity of the divine, cycling through "all levels of temporal reflection."[13] A central message of his topical writings is that reflecting on current events entails reflection on time more generally. This interest in time as literary and critical topic saturates the humorous mode of his work, for humor inverts the self-important claim of serious, high style to sublime permanence and lingers with the mundane, ridiculous, and transient.[14] The humorous mode is particularly compatible with literary periodicals and their embrace of fashionable *Unterhaltung*.

In this context, certain temporal figures play a recurring role in his writing. Perhaps the most basic of these temporal figures is that of temporal flow. To be aware of time unfolding as a linear sequence of singular moments is to be aware of the pervasive transience of worldly life, "this never-ending atomization into the shortest little particles of time—that we call life."[15] He repeatedly invokes the Christian-Stoic insight that we cannot resist time's passing, reminding readers both to live in the moment and to look to a future of immortal life in God with hope.[16] The figure of transient flow can bring into convergence the times of the world and of life. Jean Paul also applies the idea of linear temporal flow to language and writing more generally, such

---

12. Göttsche, "Challenging Time(s)," 238.
13. Göttsche, *Zeit im Roman*, 117–18.
14. See Paul Fleming, *The Pleasures of Abandonment: Jean Paul and the Life of Humor* (Würzburg: Königshausen und Neumann, 2006), 50.
15. "Dieses ewige Zerstäuben in die kürzesten Zeitteilchen—welches wir Leben nennen." Jean Paul, "Neujahrsbetrachtungen ohne Traum und Scherz, samt einer Legende," *Morgenblatt für gebildete Stände* 14, no. 1 (January 1, 1820): 2; II/3, 948.
16. On Stoic themes in Jean Paul, see most recently Jörg Kreienbock, *Malicious Objects, Anger Management, and the Question of Modern Literature* (New York: Fordham University Press, 2012).

that "[the] ceaseless perishing and coming into being in each minute, or the long procession of corpses of deceased moments" correspond to "the letters of this article that have already been read, [which] stand as little grave stones for the once alive moments of reading [*die Grabsteinchen der lebendig gewesenen Lesaugenblicke da*]."[17] Drawing on Lessing's account of writing as a temporal medium, Jean Paul configures the temporality of language, writing, and reading via a more general allegory of transience and also via the model of ongoing sequential unfolding. Here we catch a glimpse of how media shape the experience of worldly time. This concept of writing and print shares important features with the tableau considered in part I: the flow of time and the flow of language both roll forward into the future, grounded in the promise that more is coming.[18]

A counterpoint to temporal flow is the figure of rearranging diachronic temporal unfolding, of heterochronicity. Jean Paul has a keen sense of the storage potential of writing and of cultural artifacts more generally: "Only art, this transfiguring *retrieval* of all things [*diese verklärende* Wiederbringung *aller Dinge*], allows for the lively resurrection of old feelings from the past, by preparing times and spaces of rebirth for them."[19] As a particular subset of "art," writing revitalizes the past by reorganizing textual units into new temporal patterns. Invoking the eschatological notion of the restoration of all things at the end times (*apokatastasis*), Jean Paul's point here is nonetheless more general and secular, namely that art has the potential to allow

---

17. Jean Paul, "Saturnalien, den die Ende 1818 regierenden Hauptplaneten Saturn betreffend; in sieben Morgenblättern mitgeteilt von Dr. Jean Paul Fr. Richter," *Morgenblatt für gebildete Stände* 12, no. 1 (January 1, 1818): 1; II/3, 857–58.

18. As Ingrid Oesterle puts it, Jean Paul's "narration is not primarily oriented toward the past, but rather draws from the future and offers a flood of images instead of a narrative based in experience" (*[Sein] Erzählen [ist] nicht primär auf das Vergangene angewiesen, sondern [speist] sich aus Futurischem, [läßt] an die Stelle eines auf Erfahrung beruhenden Erzählzusammenhangs Bilderfluten treten*). Ingrid Oesterle, "'Es ist an der Zeit!' Zur kulturellen Konstruktionsveränderung von Zeit gegen 1800," in *Goethe und das Zeitalter der Romantik*, ed. Walter Hinderer (Würzburg: Königshausen und Neumann, 2002), 27.

19. Jean Paul, "Ausschweife für künftige Fortsetzungen von vier Werken," *Morgenblatt für gebildete Stände* 17, no. 309 (December 26, 1823): 1234; II/3, 1080.

the past to repeat and reemerge. The future is not just the linear rolling out of time but also the reemergence and repetition of the past in new constellations, in new plural "times"; art thus plays a role analogous to memory.[20] Here Jean Paul draws on Johann Gottfried von Herder's vision of a plurality of cultural and individual proper times (*Eigenzeiten*) that renders untenable the unified notion of absolute time characteristic of Kant's transcendental idealism.[21] As Jean Paul puts it, "time shatters into times, as the rainbow shatters into falling drops."[22] On the basis of the awareness of multiple times, he doubts whether it is possible to capture the single, overarching spirit of the age (*Geist der Zeit*), a conceit of Napoleonic era topical writings of contemporary authors such as Ernst Moritz Arndt and more generally of projects that present certain privileged locations—"London–Paris–Warsaw"—as ground zeros of the contemporary *Zeitgeist*.[23] Temporal complexity blocks our access to any unified sense of the time of the worldly present, a hindrance that literary writing, journalism, and more only exacerbate. This model of multiple times is ripe for literary adaptation: Jean Paul accesses the figure of reordering temporal flow in his autobiographical *Selberlebensbeschreibung*, where, in jumping between different childhood episodes, the narrator concedes that he must injure the unity of time "because the hero ... must always go from one time to another."[24] Digression, a beloved

---

20. On this structure, see Hagel, *Elliptische Zeiträume des Erzählens*, 90–99.
21. On the concept of aesthetic *Eigenzeiten*, see Michael Gamper and Helmut Hühn, "Einleitung," *Zeit der Darstellung. Ästhetische Eigenzeiten in Kunst, Literatur und Wissenschaft*, ed. Michael Gamper and Helmut Hühn (Hanover: Wehrhahn, 2014).
22. "Die Zeit [zerspringt] in Zeiten, wie der Regenbogen in fallende Tropfen." Jean Paul, "Über den Geist der Zeit," I/5, 567.
23. "Aber da dieselbe Zeit einen anderen Geiste heute entwickelt in Saturn—in seinen Trabanten—in seinen Ringen—auf allen zahllosen Welten der Gegenwart—und dann in London—Paris—Warschau;—und da folgt, daß dieselbe ausausmeßbare Jetzo-Zeit Millionen verschiedene Zeit-Geister haben muß: so frag' ich: wo erscheint euch den der zitierte Zeitgeist deutlich, in Deutschland, Frankreich oder wo?" Jean Paul, "Über den Geist der Zeit," I/5, 568.
24. "Weil der Held vom Antritt seines Lebens bis zum Antritt seiner Professur ja immer aus einer Zeit in die andere gehen muß." Jean Paul, "Selberlebensbeschreibung," I/6, 1049.

formal and stylistic principle of Jean Paul's, likewise serves to interrupt continuous narrative time.²⁵

A third key temporal figure is that of the threshold between before and after and beginning and end. The notion of temporal threshold is at work in the passage above ("the long procession of corpses of deceased moments"), where the present moment of reading straddles words and even letters. As Jean Paul puts it in an epigraph in the *Morgenblatt*, "every time consists of two parts, the end of the previous period and the beginning of the following one."²⁶ The threshold is a double-sided figure that suggests both continuation and finality and life and death. On the one hand, an end of whatever sort can always be taken as a reminder of death: "One feels the vanity of all human things most deeply when one ends something, it may be a book or a year or an affecting novel or the end of life itself."²⁷ On the other hand, the end of one thing is always the beginning of another: this thought is the point of departure for Jean Paul's many reflections on the year's end and for his Napoleonic era explorations of transitions between political regimes. The threshold figure also plays a central role in his myriad engagements with prefaces and postscripts and in his vision of his collected works edition, a topic I examine in greater detail in chapter 5.²⁸

Conceiving of moments in time as thresholds in temporal series is inherent to figures of both temporal flow and heterochronicity. On the one hand, temporal flow takes us from one instant, season, or generation to another cyclically and diachronically. Wherever we are in the Heraclitean flow, we can look forward and backward. On the

---

25. As Wieland puts it, "digression marks something of an untroubled asylum in the temporal progression of the stream of narrative." Wieland, *Vexierzüge*, 204.
26. "Jede Zeit besteht aus zwei Theilen, dem Schluß der vergangenen und dem Anfang der folgenden Periode." *Morgenblatt für gebildete Stände* 18, no. 1 (January 1, 1824): 1.
27. "Der Mensch fühlet die Eitelkeit aller menschlichen Dinge nicht tiefer ... als wenn er etwas endigt, es mag ein Buch oder ein Jahr oder ein anziehender Roman oder sein Leben selber sein." Jean Paul, "Entwurf zu Auswahl aus des Teufelspapieren," SW HKA I/19, 219.
28. On Jean Paul's engagement with the preface, see Séan M. Williams, *Pretexts for Writing: German Romantic Prefaces, Literature, and Philosophy* (Lewisburg, PA: Bucknell University Press, 2019).

other hand, the world of print media in particular can likewise manifest a plurality of differently timed, proximate temporal frames: again, an idea at work in the notion that reading and publication mark different threshold moments in different overlapping series. The intersections of these three concepts of time show how Jean Paul's oeuvre stages the confrontation between the theological postulate of the inescapable transience of life and a heterochronic, layered temporal awareness. From the perspective of the diachronic flow of never-ending transient moments, the gaze backward and forward from each and every temporal threshold is the same: the gaping eternity before one's birth and the gaping eternity after one's death. But the perspective of synchronous temporal layering reveals the coexistence of differently structured times—and "millions of different spirits of the times"—with multiple incongruent beginnings and ends.[29]

Preaching at Twilight

Jean Paul's Napoleonic era topical writings put these figures of time to work in multiple ways. In characterizing miscellaneous writings as plural "twilights," "political sermons," and "festivals," he models moral, political, and literary responses to the past, present, and future via specific conventions of serial (re)publication. *Dämmerungen für Deutschland* (1809) and its continuation, *Nachdämmerungen für Deutschland* (1810), are oriented by the metaphor of plural dusks and dawns, the so-called Hesperus motif. Twilight (*Dämmerung*) can refer both to dawn (*Morgendämmerung*) and dusk (*Abenddämmerung*) and evokes the symbolism of a solar eclipse making the morning and evening star (both names for Venus) visible at the same time: "When life darkens for us through pains that are too large, then youth and death appear quite clearly to us; morning star and evening star."[30] This duality captures the transitional nature of the present, and it carries a basic moral consolation: a new day dawns, and an old one recedes into the past. Characterizing the present epoch as especially transient

---
29. Jean Paul, "Über den Geist der Zeit," I/5, 568.
30. Jean Paul, *Dämmerungen für Deutschland*, 245; I/5, 1033.

in nature, Jean Paul applies this Christian-inflected moral message to a variety of current events, including the French occupation or the *Aktualität* of the latest reports about the state of the war. His overarching message is one of solace and hope: the hardship of war will pass and German-speaking lands will rise again. In a way, all one has is the present ("the present is your eternity and never leaves you"[31]), but this can be a consolation ("one can endure anything if it only lasts a moment"[32]). Scaling time in different directions can relativize suffering, and turning to the future makes the present seem all the briefer: again, this idea maps nicely onto notions of patriotic rejuvenation.

This notion of plural twilights also captures the essentially serial format of these collections, for *Dämmerungen für Deutschland* and *Nachdämmerungen für Deutschland* both contain multiple "twilights" of various sizes: larger essays, aphorisms bundled together as "small twilights" (*kleine Zwilichter*), and various medium-sized pieces. Conceiving of a collection of texts as a plurality of temporal thresholds gives the miscellany an expressly temporal register. This metaphor catalyzes a sense of time as both diachronic temporal flow (each day brings a new dawn and dusk) and a heterogeneous mixture of times, with each "little" twilight presenting different forward and backward gazes into disparate pasts and futures. *Nachdämmerungen* adds an additional temporal layer, for it continues serially and is published temporally later than *Dämmerungen*. *Nachdämmerungen* first appears in Perthes's *National Museum*, a monthly scholarly-patriotic journal, and is then republished in the 1817 anthology *Politische Fastenpredigten*. Furthermore, republication adds another layer to the serial unfolding of miscellaneous textual units. Jean Paul positions himself as a prophet of rebirth and renewal, though always with a healthy dose of self-irony, and anthology republication allows him to test out his predictive powers. As he retrospectively notes in the preface to the *Politische Fastenpredigten*, this anthology's contents are

---

31. "Die Gegenwart ist deine Ewigkeit und verläßt dich nie." From an aphorism titled "Trost gegen die ewige Flucht der Zeit" published in the *Damen-Kalendar auf 1818*. II/3, 853.

32. "Alles ist zu ertragen, was nur *einen* Augenblick dauert." From "Bruchstücke aus der 'Kunst, Stets Heiter zu Sein,'" published in Jean Paul's *Museum* (1814). II/2, 972.

remarkably consistent in their message of hope: "The one thing that runs through all my political articles, from the pressure [*Drucke*] of the first Consul to the pressure [*Drucke*] of the last Emperor, rather unbowed and upright, the thing I now prefer most to find there, is—hope."[33] Jean Paul documents the events that bookend these topical writings: the dual "pressure" exerted *by* Napoleon in his rise to the position of First Consul in 1799 and *upon* him, forcing him off his imperial throne. This dual *Druck* also riffs on the dual printing of these pieces first in journals and *Taschenbücher* and then in the *Politische Fastenpredigten* anthology. This is not *Vorabdruck* per se (which commonly applies to the pre-publication of novels in journals) but of authorized *Nachdruck*. The publication dates 1810, 1811, 1812, and 1817 each represent a different threshold between distinct pasts and futures.[34]

These topical writings interlink metaphors of twilights and sermonizing: indeed, the 1809 *Dämmerungen* serves as the "completion" (*Vollendung*) of his 1808 *Friedens-Predigt an Deutschland gehalten von Jean Paul.*[35] Occasional speeches and sermons are quite common in Jean Paul's works; like many German literati of this period, Jean Paul's father was a pastor, and he relates listening to his father's sermons as a child in his autobiographical *Selberlebensbeschreibung*. Jean Paul models the scene of topical address on the *Zeitpredigt*, the occasional sermon on current events, in which the homilist seeks to integrate morality and politics.[36] With the *Friedens-Predigt*

---

33. "Übrigens geht durch alle meine politischen Aufsätze von des ersten Konsuls Drucke bis zu des letzten Kaisers Drucke, etwas ungebeugt und aufrecht, was ich jetzo am liebsten darin stehen sehe—Die Hoffnung." Jean Paul, *Politische Fastenpredigten während Deutschlands Marterwoche* (Cotta: Stuttgart and Tübingen, 1817), vi–vii; I/5, 1072.

34. This preface is likewise dated "Baireuth, in der Herbst-Tag-und Nachtgleiche. 1816" (Baireuth, in the Fall Equinox. 1816), which represents yet another turning point straddling seasonal cycles as well as the temporal footprint of the fall book fair, when such anthologies hit the market. Jean Paul, *Politische Fastenpredigten*, xii; I/5, 1074.

35. Jean Paul, *Dämmerungen für Deutschland*, iv; I/5, 919.

36. As Ursula Naumann notes, "the message and problematic [of these occasional writings] are genre-specific: nowhere else did Jean Paul identify so much with the spiritual tradition." Ursula Naumann, *Predigende Poesie. Zur Bedeutung von Predigt, geistliche Rede und Predigertum für das Werk Jean Pauls* (Nürnberg:

and the later *Fastenpredigten,* Jean Paul likewise adapts the convention of printed lectures and sermons. Actual or fictive scenes of oral, occasional address are central to topical writings such as Fichte's *Reden an die deutsche Nation* (Addresses to the German nation) (1808) (which Jean Paul reviewed in 1808) and cultural journals of various stripes.³⁷ In such printed speeches, writers such as Fichte, Schleiermacher, and Arndt adapt the conceit of addressing the reading public as a stand-in for the entire nation, and Jean Paul too goes out of his way to title his *Friedens-Predigt* as "held to Germany."³⁸ The scene of oral address also lends his writing a sense of occasionality, of intervening at a particular historical moment, and of speaking with the authority of a specific moral, scholarly, or religious office. Though he is often quick to ironize the scene of embodied oral address, this invocation of the scene of address functions as a way of underlining authorial originality: it is no accident that the work's title includes the attributive "held by Jean Paul," signaling that this is his "own" original take on the *Zeitpredigt*.³⁹ That said, this express embrace of ostentatious rhetorical displays was not always received well; Theresa Huber, one of the later editors of the *Morgenblatt,* for example, dismisses the excesses of the *Dämmerungen*: "He writes like a woman, all of his ideas are filtered through fantasy in order to come into being.... It is impossible to endure such a long rhetorical effort. These kinds of people don't help us! What can help us? Steely adversity [*Die eiserne Not*]!"⁴⁰

Verlag Hans Carl, 1976), 55. On the genre of the literary sermon, see also Nicholas Saul, *Prediger aus der neuen romantischen Clique. Zur Interaktion von Romantik und Homiletik um 1800* (Würzburg: Königshausen and Neumann, 1999).

37. On this conceit, see the recent publication by Maike Oergel, *Zeitgeist—How Ideas Travel: Politics, Culture, and the Public in the Age of Revolution* (Berlin: De Gruyter, 2019), 86.

38. In its first journal publication, *Nachdämmerungen* appeared alongside a text titled "Several Lectures on the True Character of a Protestant Clergyman, by Professor Marheinecke of Heidelberg." *Vaterländisches Museum* 1, no. 1 (1810). On the role of the Protestant sermon in developing national consciousness in the period, see Heidemarie Bade, *Jean Pauls politische Schriften* (Tübingen: Niemeyer, 1974), 90.

39. As Wieland notes, Naumann's extended study of the sermon in Jean Paul (*Predigende Poesie*) fails to take this ironization into account. Wieland, *Vexierzüge*, 141.

40. SW HKA, I/14, l.

Despite their name, the "sermons," like the *Dämmerungen*, decidedly look like collections of miscellanies, and the conceit of the extended address often corresponds more to the message than to the form of the many shorter pieces gathered there. The *Friedens-Predigt* is a sixty-page pamphlet, while the *Dämmerungen* is longer, around 250 pages. These collections include longer pieces staged as addresses to captive audiences, but shorter aphoristic pieces are interspersed throughout. In Jean Paul's hands, "twilights" and "sermons" designate small texts addressing the times, the "new time," texts that can be scaled up or down in size and that can address temporal frameworks that are likewise open to modular scaling. If the philosophical-historical lecture used by the likes of Fichte and later Hegel profits from a sense of sequential, forward movement in the service of constructing a sense of the future, then the heterogeneous mixture of these pieces lends a sense of world-historical time as being characterized by multiple, coexisting, disjunctive temporal frames. Taking the sermon and the miscellany as rough equivalents sheds new light on the notion of the freedom sermon, which comes into view as a more general term encapsulating time- and context-specific texts published in "freedom"-minded journals and newspapers. In Jean Paul's hands, the sermon evokes both a sense of an occasional speech held at a specific time and the sense of a heterogeneous mixture of different times.

The sermon conceit marks the occasion and context of his political interventions, something that applies all the more with republication, as with the *Fastenpredigten*. Anthology republication rearranges occasional pieces and recontextualizes the events to which they refer at various kinds of historical remove. In writings from 1810, 1811, and 1812, Jean Paul adopts a predictive stance vis-à-vis the future end of Napoleonic occupation: in 1817, these same writings show readers what a provisional history of the recent past might look like. The conceit of Lenten sermons maps the worldly, political time of Napoleonic occupation onto the church calendar, equating the period of 1806 to 1815 with the week leading up to Easter, calling it the "true fasting time (or Quadragesima) of Germany."[41] The metaphor of

---

41. Jean Paul, *Politische Fastenpredigten*, ix.

twilight still applies here, with 1817, the present, being the bright new day predicted years earlier. Jean Paul taps into homiletic conventions of specific topics recurring at different times in the liturgical calendar as well as publication conventions of collecting different kinds of rhetorical speeches in anthologies. This anthology also plays with temporal scale, compressing the years of Napoleonic occupation (1807–1813) into the seven days of Christian Holy Week, contracting (the now past) suffering in the very way Jean Paul coached his readers to do several years before. Perhaps even more than the metaphor of twilight, the genre conceit of the sermon brings with it a range of different temporal models of repetition and recurrence, not least because the sermon is usually calibrated with the liturgical calendar and intended to recur on a yearly basis. Sermons were a key part of the more or less directly liturgical *Gebrauchsliteratur* of the previous century and were often intended to be reread intensively. This sense of (serialized) reencounter applies here, as Jean Paul stages the scene of rereading his sermons in a post-Napoleonic epoch, except that the new time equivalent to Easter is now the status quo. That said, Jean Paul's evocation of temporal unfolding, including patterns of yearly recurrence and diachronic movement, is more secular than liturgical.

Republishing and anthologizing likewise play an important role in representing multiple frames of time and giving sense to historical events, even allowing Jean Paul to configure his pieces as a form of history writing. By 1817, Napoleon's demise had of course entered into the history books, but the temporal remove from occupation also makes Jean Paul's writings from that period historical events in their own right, a thought experiment he pursues in the introduction to the *Politische Fastenpredigten*, which briefly relates the publication history of the four pieces collected, telling "the small history of these four sections of this little work, printed many years ago, in *one* minute."[42] Here Jean Paul repurposes Lessing's formulation that forewords should be histories of the publication and no more, but he places more emphasis on

---

42. Jean Paul, *Politische Fastenpredigten*, iii.

republication as a mode of history writing.[43] Jean Paul once more sets past events into a contracted temporal frame; in this case, the past events subjected to historicization are his own writings. Looking back at past historical events and looking back at a body of work come into view as interrelated undertakings. These writings already had a strong sense of their place in time when originally published, and republication casts this occasionality in a new light. Jean Paul thus reconstellates temporal indices of before and after and of prefaces and postscripts to the end of representing the historical past.

Anthologizing also serves a rhetorical and moral function, for these collected pieces give voice to paradigmatic sentiments such as consolation in defeat or the celebration of victory and rebirth. Taken as a kind of moral primer, this collection of topical writings may well retain its currency (*Aktualität*) in future political constellations, yet in a different way than it might if taken purely as an exercise in history writing. To the extent that Jean Paul's treatment of current events is general enough to be applicable to a variety of situations, his political writings share as much with moral miscellanies that model affective displays based around certain stable topoi, as they do with the historical documentation of unique events. Both the older tradition of the miscellany and the more modern topical writings that presuppose the historical individuality of events use textual practices and techniques of reading, writing, archiving, re-actualizing, and more to shape a sense of world-historical time. Straddling history writing, rhetorical imitation, and literary fantasy, Jean Paul writes in dialogue with various models for how texts might be repurposed at later historical moments. Consistent throughout is his authorial voice and the attempt to inscribe his own works into patterns of continuity and continuation and to lend a kind of permanence to ephemeral *Werkchen*.

---

43. Jean Paul, *Politische Fastenpredigten*, ix.

Writing the Present, Writing the Future

Jean Paul's writings lend themselves to contextualization in the broader literary and critical landscape for they commonly take this landscape as a point of departure for thought experiments of various sorts. Jean Paul shares with his contemporaries an orientation to the future that imagines the reencounter of material texts—journalistic reports, historical documents, literary sketches—at different historical junctures, and he reserves a positive role for serial, miscellaneous formats in repurposing various styles of history writing and literary entertainment. It is in this context that we can make sense of Jean Paul's tendency to filter questions of time through specific forms and formats of writing rather than through the dynamics of conceptual thought. His satiric reflection on the literary landscape is encyclopedic and even monstrous in scope,[44] but here I would like to focus on a just few key points of reference, including styles of authorship based in political journalism, the philosophy of history, cultural-historical scholarship, literary entertainment, and rhetorical-moral instruction.

For one, Jean Paul shares an interest in critically processing current events with journalistic proponents of *Zeitgeschichte*, which is firmly rooted in various serial formats across books, journals, and newspapers. The intersection of politics and history is the express focus of newspapers and journals founded in the late 1790s, such as Cotta's *Europäische Annalen*, edited by E. L. Posselt (1795–1820), or *Neuste Weltkunde/Allgemeine Zeitung* (1798–1929), both papers that represent the beginning of modern political journalism in Germany. Journals founded in the Napoleonic era such as *Die Zeiten, oder Archiv für die neueste Staatengeschichte und Politik* (The times, or archive for the newest state history and politics) (1805–1820) or *Nemesis, Zeitschrift für Politik und Geschichte* (Nemesis, journal for politics and history) (1814–1818) remain oriented to broader world-historical events while attending to the repercussions of French occupation and play a key role in shaping the temporal awareness of

---

44. See Armin Schäfer, "Jean Pauls monströses Schreiben," *Jahrbuch der Jean Paul Gesellschaft* 37 (2002): 216–34.

the period.[45] Serial anthologies of political and cultural criticism are also common, such as Arndt's *Geist der Zeit* (Spirit of the time), which spans four volumes from 1806 to 1818. These newspapers and anthology series approach the question of *Aktualitat* in different ways, depending on their goals.[46] On the one hand, these projects can model a sense of sequential temporal unfolding, with patterns of print going hand in hand with events as they occur; this is a sense of time that is particularly salient in war reporting.[47] Contemporary historical writing frequently also undertakes retrospective surveys of the recent past, as in early German histories of the French Revolution, and this is the task of Jean Paul's 1801/1809 piece on Charlotte Corday (the assassin of Jean-Paul Marat), which first appeared in a *Taschenbuch* that he coedited with Friedrich Gentz.[48] Despite being situated in a fictional frame narrative and republished in the miscellaneous novel *Dr. Katzenbergers Badereise* (Dr. Katzensberger's trip to the spa), Jean Paul's Corday portrait is a literary *Zeitgeschichte* of sorts, at times drawing verbatim on historical documents, including old issues of the *Moniteur* newspaper. Such writings disprove characterizations of Jean Paul as irredeemably provincial and distanced from current events—as a "disaster in a dressing gown," as Nietzsche put it.[49]

Projects of *Zeitgeschichte* likewise operate on a spectrum of more or less organization and overview. Writers and editors constantly face the challenge that the materials they are in the process of collecting are only ever provisionally ordered. Some writers of contemporary

---

45. See Nora Ramtke, "Zeitschrift und Zeitgeschichte. *Die Zeiten* (1805–1820) als chronopoetisches Archiv ihrer Gegenwart," *IASL* 45, no. 1 (2020): 112–34.

46. See Nicola Kaminski, "25.Oktober 1813 oder Journalliterarische Produktion von Gegenwart, mit einem Ausflug zum 6. Juli 1724," in *Aktualität: Zur Geschichte literarischer Gegenwartsbezüge vom 17. Bis zum 21. Jahrhundert*, ed. Stefan Geyer and Johannes F. Lehmann (Hanover: Wehrhahn, 2018), 241–70.

47. See Brehm et al., *Zeit/Schrift 1813–1815*.

48. Jean Paul first published this piece as "Der 17.Juli oder Charlotte Corday" in the *Taschenbuch für 1801* that he coedited with Friedrich Gentz, and he then reworked and republished it in his miscellaneous 1809 satire *Dr. Katzenbergers Badereise*. On the Katzenberger corpus, see Pethes, *Vermischte Schriften*; and Kaminski, "'Nachdruck des Nachdrucks.'"

49. "Verhängnis im Schlafrock." Quoted in Böck, "Archäologie in der Wüste," 267.

history eschewed all systematism, opting to create archives for "future historians" that are scattered across various book and periodical formats. The usefulness of semirandom collection is expressed in journal titles such as *Archiv* and in the notion of collected "pages," as in the *Deutsche Blätter* or *Friedensblätter*. Such an approach invariably comes under fire from philosophical approaches to history. Hegel, for example, dismisses journalistic history writing for "transforming all events into reports" and for lacking necessary overview, something that only statesmen (and philosophers) can attain with great effort: "Only when one looks down from above can one have a proper overview of things and see everything, not when one has looked up from below through a limited opening."[50] But even if it is common for journalists to defer to future historians, prediction and prognosis remain a central part of writing *Zeitgeschichte*: as Iwan D'Aprile writes, "it is common to all contemporary historians to claim that prognoses are possible and that they represent an essential and useful aspect of historical knowledge."[51] This propensity to predict the course of the future finds echoes in the literary scene, as writers experiment with modes of prophecy and prediction.[52] Jean Paul is keenly interested in such modes, writing a conjectural biography of his own life and constantly encouraging readers to imagine the time after Napoleon's fall. Jean Paul is thus quite interested in a position of future overview as well as in the prospect that archived materials might be fruitfully reencountered at some point to come.

The philosophy of history represents a second competing orientation to the past, present, and future, one that is more bullish about the possibility of overview and less rooted in the daily grind of journalistic publication. Various philosophers construct a future point in time that, whether as regulative idea, utopian horizon, or realizable

---

50. Hegel, *Vorlesungen über die Philosophie der Geschichte*, 14.

51. Ivan-Michelangelo D'Aprile, *Die Erfindung der Zeitgeschichte. Geschichtsschreibung und Journalismus zwischen Aufklärung und Vormärz* (Berlin: Akademie, 2013), 42.

52. "A timeframe—the future—is impressed upon literature and this requires new gestures of writing and oration. Future-oriented forms of oration such as announcement, promise, the prophetic and prognostic are introduced into poetry, literary theory, and criticism." Oesterle, "'Es ist an der Zeit!,'" 106.

telos, can make sense of and legitimate the present and past. The philosophy of history proposes a vision of time and of history as a singular, unified course of development, the laws of which can be determined by rational thought. Kant finds the observation of the French Revolution from afar to be conjectural proof that the human race is progressing toward a rational future; in his Berlin lectures, Fichte positions the current Napoleonic era as the third of five stages of world history, an epoch of pure egotism on the cusp of a more enlightened age; and Hegel lectures on the philosophy of history in the 1820s and tracks the "cunning of reason" in producing the philosophical-historical understanding of the present day on the basis of the historical developments of the past. The scholarly lecture plays an important role in creating a sense of forward movement through time with its regular installments.[53] Kant, Fichte, Hegel, and other academic figures publish in leading journals of the late eighteenth and early nineteenth centuries, but they also distance themselves from the back and forth of political journalism. Furthermore, the idealist philosophy of history commonly elides the material work of historical research upon which its conjectures are based.[54] Though scenes of reading and rereading are important structural features of this approach to history, as Peter Gilgen has pointed out, this textual work comes to occur primarily via writings belonging to the philosophical canon.[55] For the philosophy of history, the temporal unfolding of history is modeled on the development of the concept rather than the periodicity and seriality of print artifacts.

Jean Paul addresses the possibility of philosophical-historical prediction throughout his oeuvre, playfully engaging with contemporary models of "conjectural" history, and he repeatedly comes back to the question of historical and religious approaches to time, as in his piece in *Dämmerungen für Deutschland* titled "On God in History and in Life," which suggests that the Christian worldview

---

53. See Sean Franzel, "Constructions of the Present and the Philosophy of History in the Lecture Form," in *Performing Knowledge, 1750–1850*, ed. Mary Helen Dupree and Sean Franzel (Berlin: De Gruyter, 2015).

54. See Friedrich Kittler, *Die Nacht der Substanz* (Bern: Benteli, 1989), 15–24.

55. See Peter Gilgen, *Lektüren der Erinnerung: Lessing, Kant, Hegel* (Munich: Fink, 2012).

can bridge competing accounts of human history based either in the determinism of the physical world or in human freedom.[56] Despite admiring Herder's philosophical-historical writings, Jean Paul's stoic-moral reflections on transience and on the perspective of distant futures remain at a distance from the philosophical-historical optimism of the Enlightenment and the historical ethos of philosophical *Wissenschaft*.[57] By filtering his temporal reflections through medial format rather than the conceptual work of philosophy, Jean Paul is closer to journalistic and literary proponents of *Zeitgeschichte* than to the idealists, of whom he was often so critical. Following Koselleck, we might note that Jean Paul, like Goethe, is both untimely (*unzeitgemäß*) in diverging from the ascendant philosophy of history and very much of his time in shaping the pervasive temporalization of culture and thought around 1800.[58]

The impulse to collect and preserve various historical materials at work in Romantic cultural-historical journals represents a third orientation to historical time that would prove important to Jean Paul.[59] Jean Paul publishes some of his topical writings in Friedrich Schlegel's *Deutsches Museum* (German museum) (1812–1813) and Friedrich Perthes's *Vaterländisches Museum* (Patriotic museum) (1810–1811), associating the latter in particular with expressly nationalist political discourse.[60] These journals are modeled on the long-standing Enlightenment era journal *Deutsches Museum*, edited by H. C. Boie (1776–1791), though Perthes casts the project of "conserving" products of German culture for the future as much more urgent in the Napoleonic era.[61] Engaging in the scholarly reconstruction of and commentary on historical texts, antiquities,

---

56. See Jean Paul, *Dämmerungen für Deutschland*, 1–37; I/5, 921–36.
57. See Helmut Pfotenhauer, *Jean Paul: das Leben als Schreiben* (Munich: Hanser, 2013), 329.
58. See Koselleck, "Goethe's Untimely History," 60–78.
59. On this context, see Crane, *Collecting and Historical Consciousness*.
60. Jean Paul published the "Twilight Butterflies or Sphinxes" (*Dämmerungsschmetterlinge oder Sphinxe*) in Schlegel's journal and *After-Twilights for Germany* in Perthes's journal. Both were later collected in *Politische Fastenpredigten*. See figure 4.1.
61. See Friedrich Perthes, "Ankündigung," *Vaterländisches Museum* 1 (1810): n.p.

and monuments, these "museum" journals are committed both practically and symbolically to collecting products of national culture, even if their mixed scholarly, literary, and cultural contents are often indistinguishable from the contents of other magazines of the time. Jean Paul takes up discussions in these and similar journals when he addresses the possibility of founding new patriotic festivals and monuments.[62] The ideal of cultural preservation articulated in these journals reconsiders the past in order to build something new in a time of crisis, a model of historical time that goes beyond the mere recapitulation of the topological model of historical repetition and imitation, of "history as the teacher of life." Furthermore, in embracing the archival function of serial print these journals share a basic challenge with more journalistic *Zeitgeschichte*, namely that the material they collect might resist systematic ordering. Indeed, in his *Nachdämmerungen* (first published in Perthes's *Vaterländisches Museum*), Jean Paul doubts that future overview is possible, suggesting that contemporary cultural-critical activities share more with "fermenting tubs" than with well-curated collections.[63]

Jean Paul also publishes many of his shorter and more or less topical *Werkchen* in cultural journals more oriented to new trends and current fashions and explicitly based in the desire to present something for everyone—"allen etwas," as Cotta puts it in regard to the *Morgenblatt*. This includes excerpts of the Peace Sermon in the *Morgenblatt* and in the journal *Zeitung für Einsiedler* (Paper for hermits) edited by Achim von Arnim, Clemens Brentano, and Joseph Görres.[64]

---

62. On this new politics, see Hagemann, *Revisiting Prussia's Wars against Napoleon*; see also George L. Mosse, *The Nationalization of the Masses: Political Symbolism and Mass Movements in Germany from the Napoleonic Wars through the Third Reich* (New York: Fertig, 1975).

63. See Sean Franzel, "Von Magazinen, Gärbötticken und Bomben: Räumliche Speichermetaphern der medialen Selbstinszenierung von Zeitschriften," *in Archiv/Fiktionen. Verfahren des Archivierens in Kultur und Literatur des langen 19. Jahrhunderts*, ed. Daniela Gretz and Nicolas Pethes (Freiburg: Rombach, 2016), 207–30.

64. See the excerpt and review "Friedens-Predigt an Deutschland, gehalten von Jean Paul" *Morgenblatt für gebildete Stände* 2, nos. 157 and 159 (July 1 and 4, 1808); and the excerpt and commentary "Denksprüche aus einer Friedenspredigt an Deutschland von Jean Paul Fr. Richter," *Zeitung für Einsiedler* 3 (April 9, 1808).

Miscellaneity is the guiding principle of these and other smaller daily four-page organs such as *Der Freimüthige* (The candid one) (1803–1811), *Die Zeitung für die Elegante Welt* (1801–1859), or *Der Zuschauer* (The spectator) (1821–1823), as well as longer-format, less frequently published journals such as Kleist's and Adam Müller's journal *Phöbus* (1808).[65] In temporal terms, literary miscellaneity generates a multidirectional model of time based, on the one hand, on the co-presence of differently timed textual units written by a variety of authors and on the other, on the promise that the flow of serialized diversion will carry on uninterrupted into the future. As Jean Paul writes in his introduction to the first issue of the *Morgenblatt*: a journal is a "duodecimal or tertiary clock of time, it must move along with time, like every clock, and even fly along."[66] Here Jean Paul references the *Morgenblatt*'s near daily publication (Perthes's *Vaterländisches Museum*, for example, appeared monthly). Accelerated forward movement, *fortgehen* or even *fortfliegen*, also connotes transience and ephemerality, the *vergehen* of the mayflies (*Eintagsfliegen*). As a "clock of time," though, such journals track seasonally recurring occurrences such as carnival, fall and spring theaters, book fairs, and the end of the year, an occasion that Jean Paul would repeatedly commemorate in his contributions to the *Morgenblatt*. Cultural journals likewise tap into the periodical's archival function, assuming that readers will collect and bind together the year's issues: from its very first issue, the *Morgenblatt*, for example, was paginated as a yearly run. Journals thus prefigure future reencounters.

The prospect of repeated "intensive" reading in an age of "extensive" serial culture likewise opens up a perspective onto how Jean Paul taps into older models of moral, use-oriented literature (*Gebrauchsliteratur*).[67] Moral weeklies were a key part of mid-

---

65. On Kleist and Müller's approached to *Phöbus* as philosophical and critical miscellanies, see Heinrich Aretz, *Heinrich von Kleist als Journalist. Untersuchungen zum "Phöbus", zur "Germania" und den "Berliner Abendblättern"* (Stuttgart: Akademischer Verlag, 1984), 80–81.

66. Jean Paul, "Abschiedsrede bey dem künftigen Schlusse des Morgenblatts," *Morgenblatt für gebildete Stände* 1, no. 1 (January 1, 1807): 3.

67. On this connection see Dorothea Böck, "Satirische Raffinerien für Menschenkinder aus allen Ständen: Überlegungen zur Genesis von Jean Pauls Kunst-

eighteenth-century literary culture, with their heyday ending in the late 1760s.⁶⁸ Modeled on Addison's and Steele's *The Spectator*, these German-language journals commonly appeared weekly and offered a mixture of moral, religious, satirical contents organized around conceits of social observation (spectatorship), collecting, and fictional authorship. Jean Paul clearly adapts aspects of these organizing conceits by donning the mantle of the author as literary sermonizer and, as we will see in more detail in the next chapter, by structuring his final comic work as a fictional moral weekly modeled on *The Spectator*. It was common for early nineteenth-century journals to adapt certain features of their eighteenth-century predecessors to the context of the "multiauthor paratactical journalism" that would become increasingly prevalent in the nineteenth century.⁶⁹ These earlier journal forms straddled intensive and extensive reading, for they presented pedagogical and entertaining contents that could be reread and reapplied to different phases of life, but they also cultivated the anticipation of new material characteristic of serial culture. In both cases, an early modern model of reading that jumped around mixed content—florilegistic reading—is at play. The temporal orientation of these journals is compatible both with earlier Christian models of worldly time that coach against *vanitas* and with more contemporary models of fashion and cultural journalism; as Wolfgang Martens argues, "in being periodically published writings, moral weeklies segue from the regular, intensive reading of books of moral edification to the extensive reading of worldly literature based in the expectation of the new."⁷⁰ The fact that many leading moral weeklies (including Steele and Addison's *The Spectator*) are reprinted multiple times over the course of the eighteenth century brings this

---

modell," in *Greizer Studien*, ed. Harald Olbrich et al. (Greiz: Staatliche Museen Greiz, 1989), 149–208.

68. See Wolfgang Martens, *Die Botschaft der Tugend. Die Aufklärung im Spiegel der deutschen Moralischen Wochenschriften* (Stuttgart: Metzler, 1967).

69. On early nineteenth-century adaptations of moral weeklies, see Nicola Kaminski and Volker Mergenthaler, *Zuschauer im Eckfenster 1821/22 oder Selbstreflexion der Journalliteratur im Journal(text). Mit einem Faksimile des* Zuschauers *vom April/Mai 1822* (Hanover: Wehrhahn, 2015).

70. Martens, *Die Botschaft der Tugend*, 541.

potential for intensive reading into view and reveals some of the intersections between book and journal publication, with certain journals being collected and reprinted in larger volumes rather than being consumed as individual issues. The afterlives of use-oriented literary journals show how earlier models of intensive literature remain compatible with nineteenth-century reading practices; indeed, contemporaries would continue to read cultural journals intensively long into the nineteenth century and beyond.[71]

Though it might be counterintuitive, Jean Paul also explores how daily newspapers can lend themselves to "intensive" reencounters. In a short piece titled "Germanisms and Gallicisms and Catholicisms" in *Dämmerungen für Deutschland*, Jean Paul muses on Germany's and France's influence on each other and takes aim at the current reign of censorship under Napoleon. To this end, he undertakes a thought experiment with the French *Moniteur*, the daily paper that had been the leading organ of revolution and that is the official mouthpiece of the French government. Jean Paul notes the cognitive dissonance involved in readers still being able to acquire issues from the early 1790s while being prevented from encountering similarly liberal writings of the present:

> Even if the *Moniteur* cannot forbid its customers ... from entering its own beginning and heathen entrance hall, and even if its old impudent sermons [*Frechheits-Predigten*] can still be read without detrimental effect, ... I would like to know whether one such effect might nonetheless arise if the following words were placed atop the journal's page, as with old chapbooks [*Volksbücher*]: 'printed this year.'[72]

Punning on the term for pro-revolutionary writings as "freedom-sermons" (*Freiheitspredigten*), Jean Paul suggests that "impudent" (*frech*) occasional writings of old might retain their relevance long after being published.[73] To be sure, this suggestion flips on its head

---

71. See Stockinger, *An den Ursprüngen populärer Serialität*, 75–76.
72. Jean Paul, *Dämmerungen für Deutschland*, 62; I/5, 949.
73. In the 1827 *Sämmtliche Werke* publication of the *Dämmerungen*, this passage reads "Freiheitspredigten" (38), though subsequent issues return to "Frechheitspredigten" from the original 1808 publication.

the trope of newspapers' propensity to go out of date quickly (a trope that he does not hesitate to deploy elsewhere[74]). Certain calendars and almanacs of old were commonly predicated on yearly replacement, making excessive reference to the year to which they applied unnecessary: if readers held a calendar in their hands, it was always *this year's* calendar. However, imagining a modern newspaper typographically altered in this way would almost make the *Moniteur* issues in question all the more ephemeral: like chapbooks of old, wouldn't altering their dating make the issues much more likely to be thrown away at year's (or week's) end? Jean Paul makes precisely the opposite point, though, suggesting that the contents of past issues, archived over time, might still apply to situations that seem quite unrelated.[75]

In Jean Paul's hands, the tropes of print ephemerality, serial flow, and heterochronic, juxtapositional reencounter commingle. Yet this scene of reencounter is rather different from the use-oriented serial print of earlier centuries (and the propensity for entertaining parts of old calendars to be deemed worth saving from year to year). Here Jean Paul makes an historically specific point about a "new," post-revolutionary time, namely that out-of-date print matter can validate the permanence and durability of the revolution's basic ideals to the present day despite attempts of censors to suppress these ideals. Furthermore, Jean Paul's thought experiment directs our gaze into the future, calling out for future readers who might reactualize the freedom sermons of the past and the present. This sort of passage makes him appealing to liberal writers such as Börne and Heine, who return to this scene of reencountering discarded revolution era print matter. Though Jean Paul's patriotism might have

---

74. "Die meisten Leser interessiert, als Stadt-Weltklatschen, nicht die Begebenheit—noch ihr Einfluß—noch ihre Notwendigkeit—kaum ihre Wahrheit—sondern die Inschrift: daß sie in diesem Jahre gedruckt ist: alte Zeitungen und Obligationen verlieren gegen neue." *Jean Pauls Briefe und bevorstehender Lebenslauf* (Gera and Leipzig: Heinsius, 1799), 113; I/4, 967–68.

75. Going back to the French and German newspapers of the revolutionary period is a central conceit of Jean Paul's 1801/1809 piece on Charlotte Corday (who assassinated Jean-Paul Marat), which stages the scene of a narrator reading aloud from the *Moniteur*'s 1793 account of Corday's last days.

seemed untimely and outmoded to more chauvinistic nationalists, his long-standing commitment to press freedoms is one of the clearest political positions of a writer that later, compromised Nazi era editors would deem not properly political.[76]

Paper Monuments, Paper Festivals

Jean Paul's likening of literary works to festivals and monuments reflects another important side of his engagement with contemporary cultural-political debates. Jean Paul is obsessed with literary logics of incompletion and future production—he is always announcing new works, continuations of incomplete projects, abbreviated excerpts of fuller versions yet to be written—and he maps patterns of temporal recurrence and structures of cultural duration on the basis of these logics. Yet if it is characteristic of nineteenth-century German letters that emancipatory political ideals remain in the realm of the word (*Wort*) rather than the deed (*Tat*), then Jean Paul's expressly literary response to cultures of patriotic commemoration reveals certain limits to topical writing as political intervention. As we have seen in previous chapters, bemused curiosity and satirical treatment of the cultural politics of postrevolutionary France are characteristic of a certain strand of contemporary cultural journalism,

---

76. The historical-critical edition of Jean Paul's works begun in the late 1920s broke new ground in collecting his topical pieces for the first time under the heading "politische Schriften," even though the editor of the 1939 volume in question uses Carl Schmitt's definition of the political—the ability to distinguish between friend and enemy—to ground his claim that "Jean Paul was no political person and author" (*Jean Paul war kein politischer Mensch und Autor*). Wilhelm von Schramm, "Einleitung" and "Politische Schriften," SW HKA, I/14, vi. Jean Paul did in fact plan a "war section" (*Kriegsabtheilung*) of his collected writings, but calling his Napoleonic era topical writings political is a retrospective editorial decision that risks artificially distinguishing between political and nonpolitical projects. As Hans G. Helms puts it (with a pathos particular to the debates of the 1970s and 1980s), "it is a sublimely wearisome perfidy to sequester a certain section of Jean Paul's oeuvre under the rubric 'political writings' and to imply that everything else lacks any and all political implication." Hans G. Helms, "Jean Paul, ein politischer Autor," *Text + Kritik*, special volume (1983): 122.

and Jean Paul does not refrain from casting a satiric light on his own (self-)memorializing gestures.

Like many contemporaries, Jean Paul recognizes the need to organize cultural time anew and the danger of having it imposed from the outside, adding his voice to the calls for new monuments and festivals that memorialize German victories and defeats alike. As he puts it in a short piece in *Dämmerungen für Deutschland* titled "Proposal for Political Festivals of Mourning": "Formerly every century was concluded with days of penance, prayer and fasting. Rather than the religious feasts, which are now forbidden, fate called for political ones."[77] Jean Paul cites the revolutionary era's abolition of certain religious holidays and recent French celebrations of military victories across Europe, proposing that German-speaking lands would do well to follow the example of ancient Rome, where recurring public festivities commemorated important defeats along with victories. Jean Paul taps into his friend's Moritz's long-standing interest in the festival calendar of ancient Rome (as discussed in chapter 2), calling for "secular celebrations" modeled on both antiquity and more recent Christian traditions: in effect, France does not possess a monopoly on memorializing the Battle of Jena–Auerstedt.[78] Even though Napoleonic France is commonly associated with the overreaching and decadence of imperial Rome, Rome can also serve as a positive countermodel to French hegemony.

But Jean Paul is not merely concerned with memorializing German defeat. He closes the 1817 preface to the *Politische Fastenpredigten* by likening Germany's military resurrection to the resurrection of Christ: "We all hope to celebrate the feast of the resurrection continually" (*wir alle wünschen, das Fest der Auferstehung immerfort zu feiern*).[79] Celebrating the defeat of Napoleon as a yearly feast or festival accesses two different patterns of temporal unfolding; as a sign of a new political order, the victory persists throughout the year, but, like Easter, the celebration of political resurrection presumably does

---

77. Jean Paul, *Dämmerungen für Deutschland*, 135; I/5, 983.
78. "In short, do you not believe that there are states other than France who could celebrate the fourteenth of October, even if with a few tears?" Jean Paul, *Dämmerungen für Deutschland*, 130; I/5, 981.
79. Jean Paul, *Politische Fastenpredigten*, xii; I/5, 1074.

not occur more frequently than once a year or season. This analogy between political and religious resurrection is all too common at the time and is embraced by the restoration powers in characterizing the defeat of Napoleon as the advent of a "new" time.[80] Even though Jean Paul does not buy into this logic as much as the supporters of the restoration, he imagines the recurring memorialization of this historic moment of transition, anticipating the central place of the period of 1813 to 1815 in the national-political imaginary of the subsequent century. In a culture of memorialization in which literary texts are recirculated and reencountered as recurrent festivals are, Jean Paul's topical writings once again take on certain similarities to primers for rhetorical instruction in which repeated, "intensive" reading helps German audiences to reactivate certain moral-political emotions associated with victory over the French.[81]

Yet Jean Paul always tinges this analogy of literary writing and national political commemoration with ample doses of satire. Along with echoing calls for new festivals and physical monuments, Jean Paul also considers memorial cultures that remain entirely in the realm of print and paper. An aphoristic "small twilight" in *Dämmerungen für Deutschland* suggests that literary endeavors might be more lasting than edifices of wood and stone: "If we hand over two indestructible monuments to Germany to posterity through *echt*-German education and literature, it will be equal and no less than what the clergy contributes, who—according to the adage: *Nil Clerici relinquunt praeter libros liberosque*—leave behind books

---

80. The authors of *Zeit/Schrift* have shown how the discourse of a "new" time is paradigmatically articulated through the periodicity and anticipatory structures of periodical publication, with journals reporting on the return of the Austrian monarch to Vienna to construct an emphatic sense of the advent of the new and its continued commemoration into the future. See Brehm et al., *Zeit/Schrift 1813–1815*, 289–97.

81. Discussing Jean Paul's interest in monuments, paper and otherwise, Helmut J. Schneider comments that Jean Paul's commemorative texts "assume for [themselves] the character of a symbolic memorial space that is meant to draw in and unite readers." Helmut J. Schneider, "The European Machine God: The Image of Napoleon Bonaparte in the Political Writings of Jean Paul," in *Inspiration Bonaparte? German Culture and Napoleonic Occupation*, ed. Seán Allan and Jeffrey L. High (Rochester, NY: Camden House, 2021), 191.

and children."[82] Rehearsing tropes of print ephemerality and of the relative permanence of intellectual accomplishments over military ones, Jean Paul opens up a vista onto a future in which Germans commemorate the Napoleonic era through the literary production of the period (as well as through the vitality of new generations). Again, this was an altogether common view, with many leading authors and critics in the 1780s already calling for expressly literary monuments. Such appeals to the commemorative effects of literary culture likewise recall the *Modejournal*'s "New Year's Presents of Fashion" discussed in chapters 1 and 2. But likening books to monuments invites the question of the political and historical effects of a literary landscape in which, as Jean Paul himself admits, chaos and miscellaneous dispersal (*Zerstreuung*) run rampant. What are the chances that the print landscape—indeed, that Jean Paul's "own" miscellanies qua paper monuments—can be organized into patterns of repetition and recurrence around which modern political rituals might coalesce?

This, at least, is a question implicitly posed by the title of Jean Paul's 1809 "Programm der Feste oder Aufsätze, welche der Verfasser in jedem Monat des künftigen Morgenblattes 1810 den Lesern geben will" (Program of festivals or articles that the author intends to give to readers in each month of the coming 1810 *Morgenblatt*).[83] This piece was published in installments in the journal's last three issues of 1809, and it confronts the question of literary writing as a commemorative practice head-on. This end-of-the-year piece previews hypothetical works that are to be published in monthly cycles over the coming year, with the title serving as a kind of announcement of future works. At the end of each year, Jean Paul gives his readers excerpts or brief tastes—"foretastes" (*Vorschmäcke*), as he put it—of the full articles promised for the next year, even though these complete versions never actually materialize in the journal. This serialized piece is part and parcel of Jean Paul's authorial brand, foregrounding

---

82. Jean Paul, *Dämmerungen für Deutschland*, 203; I/5, 1014.

83. Jean Paul, "Programm der Feste oder Aufsätze, welche der Verfasser in jedem Monat des künftigen Morgenblattes 1810 den Lesern geben will," *Morgenblatt für gebildete Stände* 3, nos. 310, 311, and 312 (December 28, 29, and 30, 1809); II/2, 984–1003.

his role as author in personally presenting readers with a set of writings identifiable as his own.

This piece is very much in the miscellany tradition, with its contents including fictional speeches and sermons, letters, a discourse on marriage, a compendium of passages from other works cut by the censors, a discussion of a solar eclipse, and more. At first glance, this is a virtuosic display of journal authorship, underlining both the entertaining quality of the present pieces and their serial continuation across multiple journal issues. Again, naming texts "speeches" and "sermons" evokes structures of occasionality and periodic return, though his future pieces will come out monthly rather than daily, as the *Morgenblatt* does. Jean Paul calls these different pieces "festive sermons" (*Fest-Predigten*) and "proper sermon festivals" (*ordentliche Predigt-Feste*), suggesting both that his pieces are given on a particular occasion and that the "sermon" is itself a festive occasion meriting pomp and circumstance. For better or worse, though, these texts are merely previews of the real festivals. As Jean Paul puts it in a mock-apologetic aside, there is something unsatisfying about having to wait for the whole piece and for the festival proper—it is like printing summaries of the next day's homily on Saturday evening.[84]

Jean Paul engages with the project of writing contemporary history when he emphasizes the idea that he is inaugurating a process of serial recurrence (every month a new piece is to appear) and thus contributing to a growing archive for the benefit of future readers, though we might think of these future readers less as future historians and more as future cocelebrants. At the same time, though, the tongue-in-cheek nature of this piece's basic conceit—no monthly pieces actually follow—once more raises the question of whether monuments and memorials might only be transient constructs: the author claims to be inaugurating festivals, but isn't he in fact merely circulating more *Werkchen* that might not stand the test of time? We might read this as a kind of oblique commentary on the difficulty of creating new cultures of national commemoration that he advocates for elsewhere. There will be a future but an uncertain one, in which new festivals might or might not have taken hold. This is

---

84. Jean Paul, "Programm der Feste," *Morgenblatt*, 3, no. 310, 1237; II/2, 984.

a productive uncertainty, though, for it fuels readers' desire for more from Jean Paul, even if readers are already in on the joke that what will come will look rather different from what is promised.

At first glance, the topics of these pieces hardly resemble Jean Paul's more political interventions, but publication history sheds important light on the political undertone of these "festivals" or articles and the patterns of continuation they set in motion, both imaginary and actual. The original publication of the "Programm" in the *Morgenblatt* over the last three issues of the year only contained seven of the twelve articles, with the remaining pieces cut or abbreviated by the French censorship regime that Jean Paul took aim at the same year in *Dämmerungen für Deutschland* with his joke about rereading old issues of the *Moniteur*. The editors of the *Morgenblatt* are quite clear about the extensive cuts by the censors in a note at the end of the piece, apologizing that all twelve foretastes could not be provided and providing dashes in the body of the text to indicate to readers where these cuts were made.[85] It is up to the 1814 reprinted version to publish the piece in full; by this time, after all, the reign of French censors was over.[86] Jean Paul places the piece in his anthology *Museum*, invoking, on the one hand, other contemporary journals with "museum" in their title, thereby making the distinction between "written" and "built" museums, and, on the other hand, the scholarly society (founded in 1808) of the Frankfurt Museum, where Jean Paul had been invited to lecture (the basis of some of the pieces contained in this anthology).[87] Furthermore, the framing metaphor of museum performs a historicizing role, analogizing how the essay collects works from the past and preserves them in a more complete form (see figure 4.1 for a visualization of this publication history). Republication presents readers with these pieces a second time, if

---

85. As the editors of the *Morgenblatt* note at the end of Jean Paul's "Programm der Feste," "The Editors: We are sorry to have not been allowed to give our readers all twelve foretastes." *Morgenblatt* 3, no. 312, 1246.

86. On Jean Paul's use of books as places to print writings not accepted for journal publication by censors, see Wulf Koepke, "Jean Paul's Battles with the Censors and his *Freiheits-Büchlein*," in *Zensur und Kultur, Censorship and Culture*, ed. John A. McCarthy and Werner von der Ohe (Tübingen: Niemeyer, 1995), 107.

87. Jean Paul, *Museum*, 227–74.

"Peace Sermon to Germany held by Jean Paul" I/5	**1808** "Friedens-Predigt an Deutschland, gehalten von Jean Paul" (excerpt and review) *Morgenblatt für gebildete Stände*, nos. 157 and 159 (July 1 and 4, 1808). "Denksprüche aus einer Friedenspredigt an Deutschland von Jean Paul Fr. Richter," (excerpt and commentary) *Zeitung für Einsiedler*, no. 3 (April 9, 1808).
"Twilights for Germany" I/5	**1809** "Über den Gott in der Geschichte und im Leben," (excerpt) *Morgenblatt für gebildete Stände*, nos. 130, 131, 132 (June 1, 2, 3, 1809).
"After-Twilights for Germany" I/5	**1810** "Nachdämmerungen für Deutschland," *Vaterländisches Museum*, no. 1 (1810).
"Twilight Butterflies, or Sphinxes" I/5	**1812** "Dämmerungsschmetterlinge, oder Sphinxe," *Deutsches Museum*, no. 5 (1812).
"Program of Festivals or Articles that the Author intends to give to Readers in each Month of the coming 1810 *Morgenblatt*" II/2	**1809** "Programm der Feste oder Aufsätze, welche der Verfasser in jedem Monat des künftigen Morgenblattes 1810 den Lesern geben will," *Morgenblatt für gebildete Stände*, nos. 310, 311, and 312 (December 28, 29, 30, 1809).
"Farewell Speech on the Occasion of the Future End of the *Morgenblatt*" II/3	**1807** "Abschiedsrede bey dem künftigen Schlusse des Morgenblatts," *Morgenblatt für gebildete Stände*, no. 1 (January 1, 1807).
"Digressions for Future Continuations of four Works" II/3	

Figure 4.1. Jean Paul's *Werkchen* discussed in chapters 3 and 4 and their republication in anthology and works edition formats.

	Journal version
	Anthology or stand-alone book
	First Works edition

1808 *Friedens-Predigt an Deutschland, gehalten von Jean Paul* (Heidelberg: Mohr and Zimmer, 1808).		**1827** Reimer I, installment 7, no. 4 (vol. 34 of 65) (1827).
1809 *Dämmerungen für Deutschland* (Tübingen: Cotta, 1809).		**1827** Reimer I, installment 7, no. 4 (vol. 33 of 65) (1827).
	1817 In: *Politische Fastenpredigten während Deutschlands Marterwoche* (Stuttgart and Tübingen: Cotta, 1817).	**1827** Reimer I, installment 7, no. 4 (vol. 33 of 65) (1827).
	1817 In: *Politische Fastenpredigten während Deutschlands Marterwoche* (Stuttgart and Tübingen: Cotta, 1817).	**1827** Reimer I, installment 7, no. 4 (vol. 34 of 65) (1827).
	1814 In: *Museum* (Stuttgart and Tübingen: Cotta, 1814).	**1827** Reimer I, installment 7, no. 4 (vol. 34 of 65) (1827).
	1815 In: *Herbst-Blumine oder gesammelte Werkchen aus Zeitschriften* vol. 2 of 3 (Stuttgart and Tübingen: Cotta, 1815).	**1828** Reimer I, installment 12, no. 5 (vol. 60 of 65) (1828).
1824 "Ausschweife für künftige Fortsetzungen von vier Werken," Morgenblatt für gebildete Stände, vol. 17, nos. 304-307, 309-10, 313; vol. 18, no. 1 (December 20-31 1823; Jan. 1. 1824).		**1828** Reimer I, installment 12, no. 4 (vol. 59 of 65) (1828).

only as previews, but in certain cases, they are decidedly more complete in this republication than they were at initial publication. Indeed, anthology publication partially redeems the disingenuous claim that "full" versions of these excerpts would be published at a later date (though in the journal version, some of the censored pieces were not mentioned by title, and their existence was indicated only by dashes). The fact that we receive more complete versions of some pieces through republication nonetheless reveals a further temporal irony, for the supposed occasions on which these individual "festivals" were to have been published—once a month in 1810—have long passed by 1814.

These pieces do indeed map patterns of recurrence and variation, though the temporal parameters of monthly publication are replaced by those of the anthology. These pieces migrate from one textual environment to another, moving from the *Morgenblatt*, where they appeared alongside texts by other authors, to a miscellaneous single-author anthology. This migration across formats recalibrates the temporal indices of individual articles. The anthology introduces temporal displacements that recontextualize individual articles. The performative inauguration of a culture of printed "festivity" promises recurrence and return, but, as it turns out, at irregular, potentially tenuous intervals: there is a tomorrow, a *Morgen*, when these festivals will take place, but continuation is displaced from the *Morgen* of monthly issues to a later date. Jean Paul thereby echoes other satirical treatments of logics of commemoration and memorialization. He promises future works and commemorative festivities, but he does so by marking the print landscape's all-too-tenuous relationship to the calendar year and to natural time, as well as the rhythms of the world of publishing. Future works will come; we just can't be sure when.

Ends and Beginnings

My suggestion, then, is that, in memorializing a telling episode in his ongoing engagement with the censors, the "Programm der Feste" is part of the same textual universe as Jean Paul's other topical writings (despite the fact that he includes it in the *Museum* anthology rather than in the *Politische Fastenpredigten*).⁸⁸ In closing, we might consider additional ways that this text engages in the writing of time—writing about the times and about current events but also mapping patterns of temporal unfolding—at the intersection of *Zeitgeschichte* and satirical literary entertainment. I have already mentioned that this article appeared in installments at the very end of 1809, and it is as such very much of a piece with Jean Paul's new year's pieces. Reflections on the year's passing and calibrating expectations for the next are an all-too-common genre of periodical literature, dating back to the homiletic universe of earlier moral weeklies and forward to the family journals of the mid- and late nineteenth century.⁸⁹ New year's pieces help to imagine "the end," with all of its symbolic weight, but they also perform the absence (or at least deferral) of finality: a new year is starting. Jean Paul takes this genre to predictable extremes, developing it as part of his authorial brand, not least by anthologizing many of these pieces. Indeed, his very first piece for the very first January 1, 1807 issue of the *Morgenblatt* is an inaugural moment of sorts, preparing the ground for readers to come to eagerly await (or tire of⁹⁰) something from him in the December or January issues over the next fifteen years.⁹¹

---

88. In effect I subscribe to the point made in various ways by Helms, Göttsche, Jordheim, Hermand and others, that the distinction between Jean Paul's literary writings and his properly "political" pieces is a false one.
89. See Naumann, *Predigende Poesie*, 9.
90. Norbert Miller and Wilhelm Schmidt-Biggemann call this the "first in the long and occasionally tedious series of articles written for [the] new year." Norbert Miller and Wilhelm Schmidt-Biggemann, "Kommentar zu den Vermischten Schriften," in *Sämtliche Werke in 10 Bänden*, ed. Norbert Miller (Munich/Vienna: Hanser, 1974–1985), II/4, 570.
91. A prototype for this type of piece prior to the *Morgenblatt*'s founding is *The Marvelous Society on New Year's Eve* (1801), in which Jean Paul reflects not just on the end of the year but also on the much more momentous end of the century. For an extended reading of this piece in terms of the problematic of time, see Oesterle, "'Es ist an der Zeit!,'" 91–121. On the prevalence of moments addressing this "constellation of death and rebirth" in Jean Paul's writings, see Götz Müller, "'Ich vergesse den 15.November nie.' Intertextualität und Mehrfachbesetzung bei Jean

The final section of the "Programm der Feste" appears in the final December 30 issue of the *Morgenblatt* and is titled "December 31, 1810 presents: *My Awakening at the New Year's Ball in the Casino Hall*" (see figure 4.2 for page view of this issue).[92] This piece spoofs Jean Paul's own self-ascribed prophetic abilities but also has a serious takeaway, for it presents a vision of peace after a dream that morphs a high-society new year's ball into a scene of a battlefield, in effect allegorizing the war across Europe in the preceding year:

> In my sleep I had to watch the column of dancers hopping forward as a cavalry column trotting forward, the clapping hands of the Anglaise for the firing of pistols, and the entire dance for a war dance. . . . Then, all of a sudden, the dance and the music stopped and trumpet tones flared up out of the silence like skylarks batting their wings—it had rung midnight and the old year had passed.[93]

Recapitulating the conceit of the *Friedens-Predigt*, Jean Paul straddles the threshold between a future of peace and a past year of war (not unlike the Janus plate considered in chapter 1). In this final "festival"—which in this case does in fact correspond to an actual celebration, namely a new year's ball—he looks back on the old year and makes predictions for the new, though the piece is dated one full year in advance of when it was published. In effect, the piece marking the end of the coming year is published before author and readers have experienced the end of the current one. How, one might ask, could anyone know what will happen a year from now? As Jean Paul remarks, "not even the author himself knows, who, as usual, writes down everything prior to it being printed [*vor dem Abdrucke*]."[94] Jean Paul writes of an occasion that has not yet occurred and of a peace not yet realized; he writes into the future. As if to underline his

---

Paul," in *Jean Paul im Kontext. Gesammelte Aufsätze*, ed. Götz Müller (Würzburg: Königshausen und Neumann, 1996), 134.

92. "Der 31 December des Jahres 1810 gibt: "Mein Erwachen auf dem Sylvester-Balle im Casinosaale." Jean Paul, "Programm der Feste," *Morgenblatt* 3, no. 312, 1245; II/2, 1000.

93. Jean Paul, "Programm der Feste," *Morgenblatt* 3, no. 312, 1246; II/2, 1000.

94. Jean Paul, "Programm der Feste," *Morgenblatt* 3, no. 312, 1246; II/2, 1000.

Nro. 312.

Morgenblatt
für gebildete Stände.

Sonnabend, 30. December, 1809.

Wollt ihr, wie's Jean Paul ist, auch Bücherschreiber seyn,
Und Meister auch im Ernst und Scherz,
So habt nicht seinen Geist allein,
So habet auch sein Herz.

Gleim.

Programm der Feste oder Aufsätze, welche der Verfasser in jedem Monate des künftigen Morgenblattes 1810 den Lesern geben will. Von Jean Paul.

(Beschluß.)

Der 31 December des Jahres 1810 gibt: Mein Erwachen auf dem Sylvester-Balle im Casino-Saale.

„Obgleich — so fängt der Beytrag selbst an — die Todten- und Wiegenfeste der Zeit die jährlichen Erinnerungen an das irdische Hinunterleben ernster und mit anderer Vorbereitung gefeyert zu werden verdienen, als durch einen Vortanz in der letzten Jahresnacht und durch einen Nachtanz am ersten Neujahrs-Vormorgen und durch elende Abspannung am Neujahrstage: so mache ich es doch wie andere, ich gehe auch auf den Ball im hiesigen Casino-Saale, theils um das Fest mit einem Mitgliede mehr zu schmücken — theils um mich da niederzusetzen und in jenen künstlichen Schlaf zu fallen, welchen allein zweckmäßige Tanzmusiken beschreyen — theils um nach 12 Uhr von Trompetenstößen aufzufahren und mich ins allgemeine Küssen zu mischen und einer kurzen halbtrunkenen Liebeserklärung der Menschen zuzuschauen und beyzutreten. Dies that ich denn auch in der Sylvesternacht (1810); ich setzte meine Doppellorgnette auf, und versank bald hinter ihr (Musik und alles waren erwünscht) in meinem gewöhnlichen Schlaf;

ich thue gern hinter Brillen wie andere vor Nachtlichtern die Augen zu.

Ich mußte aber träumen, und zwar wie folgt: Ich sey — kam mir vor — niemand anders als der sizilische Prinz Januarius Karl Franz Joseph Johann Baptista Anton Ferdinand Kaspar Melchior Balthasar Franz de Paula Kajetan Agnello Raimund Pasqual Zeno Julius Johann von Nepomuk. Um mir aber noch mehr Namen zu machen und überhaupt einen langen, stell' ich mich an die Spitze meiner sizilischen Armee und kommandirte. —

In der linken Hand einen Sturmballen oder Sprengblock, in der rechten einen Partien in allen Taschen Taschenpuffer, an beyden Häften Hieber focht ich wie verzweifelt, und that sieben Wunder auf einmal; denn ich stand auf einem Telegraphen-Thurm und kommandirte und focht (die Telegraphen waren meine Adjutanten) so glücklich, daß ich (nach wenigen Generalstürmen auf Generale) den Feind in einer Entfernung von achtzig Meilen von mir mit dem Handgemenge meiner Leute schlug und verfolgte; in der That ein ganz anderer Sieg, als wenn man den Feind, den man niedermacht, schon vor der Nase hat. Indeß machte mich dieses Glück so verwegen, daß ich, sobald ich auf dem fünften Telegraphen erfuhr, mein Heer wende sich um, und auch das feindliche und jage meinem nach, daß ich mich sag' ich, ganz vermessen ohne mich an meine Prinzens-Pflicht gleich zu kehren, und wenig erwägend, wie fein ein Feldherr mit seiner Unersetzlichkeit zugleich ein ganzes Heer aussetzt und bloßstellt, vom Thurme herabbegab und mit

Figure 4.2. Page view. *Morgenblatt für gebildete Stände 3*, no. 312 (Sunday, December 30, 1809): 1245. HAAB Weimar. 8 ¾ × 7 ¼ inches.

certainty that the future will bring peace, Jean Paul makes a point of saying that this piece is presented in full, in contrast to the rest of the "Programm der Feste." In effect, readers are promised the very same text exactly one year later in the *Morgenblatt*'s final issue of 1810.

It is essential to the conceit of the "Programm der Feste" that these festivals and articles will be printed again, and this last piece was indeed reprinted, though in 1814 rather than in December of 1810. This might have disappointed those few naïve readers who might have wanted some orientation for 1811 in December of 1810, but in 1814, readers were that much more able to test out the prophetic claims made in 1809 for 1811, something that the announced reprinting in 1810 would not yet have been able to deliver on. Furthermore, the preface to the 1814 *Museum* is dated October 31, 1813, just weeks after the battle of Leipzig. A year of war has passed, and a year of peace is on the horizon: as a prediction from 1809, this proposition or prophecy is subject to verification, though now in a rather different political context. Both as an expression and a statement independent of authorial intention, Jean Paul's texts can be—indeed, call out to be—calibrated with a variety of real and imaginary events. This mixture of various fictional and real temporal frameworks marks patterns of recurrence—shapes of time, in Kubler's parlance—that are both regular and irregular, continuous and discontinuous, and linear and nonlinear. In mapping patterns of serial unfolding and temporal displacement, authors and readers play equal parts in this production of meaning, and both groups also have their blind spots. Jean Paul calls out for readers to map out the unfolding of time, including the prospect of future reencounters, on the basis of the formats and conventions of print, simultaneously keeping and breaking the promise that more is on its way.

Writing in a mode of *Zeitgeschichte*, Jean Paul intertwines the temporal footprints of media with those of historical events, showing how print can scale different frames of time up and down and reconstellate them. Again, this reveals a certain tenuousness in the logic of commemoration at the heart of the idea that articles are festivals: in staging how the future can be written via print in complementary and antagonistic relations with actually recurring calendar-specific events of popular culture, Jean Paul invites the conclusion that his contemporary histories "shatter" like raindrops into many miscellaneous texts rather than coalescing into structures of permanence associated with the nation.[95] Perhaps it is characteristic of Jean Paul's political positionality—his "undependability" (as Mayer describes it) as nationalist propagandizer—that his relativization of the power of topical writings occurs both via the contrast between eternity and historical time (the time of transient nations) and via a vision of the miscellaneity of the print landscape. Jean Paul wants his readers to find inspiration, consolation, and diversion equally in his diminutive *Werkchen* and in the assurance that more is coming, even if it is not exactly what was promised. In the process, he straddles journalistic and more literary modes of writing, with the former based in an ideal of responding in a timely fashion to current events and the latter based in the consolation that readers are content with simply receiving more from a favorite author's pen.

A related gesture toward preservation is thus at work in Jean Paul's fictionalization of the conceit to memorialize and commemorate: Isn't part of the joke of the "Programm der Feste" that future works are to coalesce as much around an author's personality as around political events? Following this line of thinking, the future reader would be less a future historian or a future cocelebrant of national political festivity and more a kindred reader seeking to reencounter Jean Paul's peculiar wit anew. These works, however miscellaneous and incomplete, call out to be read and reread as works by Jean Paul, the author. This gesture toward the kindred reader decouples his topical interventions from the patterns of continuation and repetition characteristic of historical time and the time of the nation (as manifest in temporal patterns of new festival cultures, for example) and shifts them into the time of the literary oeuvre, albeit one predicated on an unruly network of *Werkchen* rather than the self-standing, completed work. The idea of an authorial oeuvre that straddles different sites and styles of publication and mixes conventions of journal literature and authorial self-branding brings us to the topic of the next chapter, namely Jean Paul's (in)complete works.

---

95. "Die Zeit [zerspringt] in Zeiten, wie der Regenbogen in fallende Tropfen." Jean Paul, "Über den Geist der Zeit," *Levana*, I/5, 567.

5

JEAN PAUL'S INCOMPLETE WORKS

Writing with the end of life and the end of a body of work in mind is a typical feature of late style. Less than two years before his death, in what would end up being his last contribution to the *Morgenblatt*, Jean Paul states his aim to produce a "last work" "into which everything must be written—so that finally there will be an end of me and by me."[1] He takes this conceit directly from Steele and Addison's *The Spectator*, where the journal's fictional author-editor resolves "to Print my self out, if possible, before I Die" in the journal's very first issue.[2] For "the Spectator," and Jean Paul alike, writing, life, and death converge in scenes of almost frantic production. Jean Paul is perpetually announcing continuations that invariably

---

1. "Damit nur einmal ein Ende wird mit mir und von mir." Jean Paul, "Ausschweife für künftige Fortsetzungen von vier Werken," *Morgenblatt für gebildete Stände* 17, nos. 304–7, 309–10, 313; 18, no. 1 (December 20–31, 1823; January 1, 1824); here, 17, no. 304, 1214; II/3, 1065–91.

2. *Spectator* 1 (March 2, 1711).

run up against the transience of life. Whenever he writes an end, however, he always also writes a beginning of some sort. The end becomes an occasion to write the future, to write what comes after.

At first glance, Jean Paul's effort to put his life into lasting works seems like a classic strategy of authorial self-assertion in the face of death.[3] Death is an all-too-privileged topic across his career, and, along with being obsessed with notions of the afterlife and the immortality of the soul, he is prone to imagining life and death in tandem with print.[4] As he writes in an early satire, "death is not a period, but rather a dash, a hyphen that connects two worlds; likewise, the life to come is printed with the same, continuous call number as the present one."[5] Along with restating the Christian understanding of death as transition and not finality, this aperçu also articulates a vision of serially "continuous" writing and publication. Writing at the intersection of the journal and the book and in formats that straddle multiauthor miscellaneous publications and single-author works, Jean Paul's authorial self-presentation relies on a sense of an ongoing future production and of readers' future (re)encounters with his writing, satirizing tropes of the death of the author and his literary afterlives all the while. Jean Paul is a key figure in an epoch characterized by the turn from the past to the future as guiding temporal horizon and more specifically by the rise of strategies for curating the legacy (*Nachlass*) of canonical authors for future readers; as Christian Benne has put it, Jean Paul turns "the problematic of legacy into a question of future production."[6] Börne's well-known

---

3. On the relationship of writing and death and on narrative as the Scheherazade-like "effort to keep death outside the circle of life," see Michel Foucault, "What Is an Author," in *The Foucault Reader*, ed. Paul Rabinow (New York: Pantheon, 1984), 102.

4. See Berhorst, *Anamorphose der Zeit*, 25–38; and Sabine Eickenrodt, *Augenspiel: Jean Pauls optische Metaphorik der Unsterblichkeit* (Göttingen: Wallstein, 2006).

5. "Der Tod ist kein Punkt, sondern nur ein Abtheilungszeichen im menschlichen Dasein, ist ein Gedankenstrich, der zwo Welten verbindet: auch ist das künftige Leben mit *fortlaufender Signatur* des iezigen gedrukt." II/1, 1002.

6. "Jean Paul macht aus der Problematik des Erbes die Frage nach künftiger Produktion." Christian Benne, "'Kein Einfall sollte untergehen': Nachlassbewusst-

eulogy for Jean Paul bears witness to the author's future orientation: "A time will come when he will be born for everyone, and everyone will cry for him. But he is waiting patiently at the gateway to the twentieth century and waiting with a smile until his lagging people follow after him."[7] Yet Börne's earnest gesture of memorialization is a reader response that Jean Paul himself parodies. In envisioning the afterlives of his works, he is more prone to linger with the paradoxes of a miscellaneous oeuvre in an age of print saturation—how does a compulsively productive and digressive writer finish anything? What is the relationship of such an oeuvre to a broader network of print?— than with the ideal of canonizable authorial originality in emergence at the time.

Here, we are well advised to return to Jean Paul's playful term for his writings for journals. In his later career, Jean Paul's journal-based *Werkchen* are an increasingly important part of his literary output and authorial brand, a central part of which involves collecting these smaller pieces in serial formats such as the *Taschenbuch* and the literary journal as well as earlier florilegistic and eclectic anthologies that bordered on *Gebrauchsliteratur*.[8] By collecting and republishing his writings for journals, Jean Paul asserts control over them in a time of pirated reprinting, and he also draws on the logic of the collected works edition, a "typographical genre" in the process of emerging in its modern form in the nineteenth century. Like many authors of the period, Jean Paul is eager to have a works edition of his own—to "finally herd" his scattered works "onto a single bookshelf and into a single uniform,"[9] as he put it—and the posthumous edition *Jean*

---

sein und Nachlass-Selbstbewusstsein bei Jean Paul," in *Nachlassbewusstsein: Literatur, Archiv, Philologie, 1750–2000*, ed. Kai Sina and Carlos Spoerhase (Göttingen: Wallstein, 2017), 246.

7. Ludwig Börne, "Denkrede auf Jean Paul," *Morgenblatt für gebildete Stände* 19, no. 294–95 (December 9–10, 1825), here no. 294, 1173.

8. See Nora Ramtke and Séan Williams, "Approaching the German Anthology, 1700–1850," *German Life and Letters* 70, no. 1 (2017): 1–21.

9. "Nun ist es Zeit, das Bitten und Erwarten so vieler Leser durch die Herausgabe meiner sämtlichen Werke zu befriedigen, welche wegen ihrer Theurung, Zerstreuung, Unsichtbarkeit, endlich einmal auf Ein Bücherbret und in eine Uniform zusammen zu treiben sind." Jean Paul to Karl August Böttiger in Dresden, August 20, 1825. III/8, 286.

Paul's sämmtliche Werke (Jean Paul's complete works) (Berlin: G. Reimer, 1826–1838) wound up being published at the same time as Goethe's *Sämmtlichen Werke, vollständige Ausgabe letzter Hand* (Complete works, complete edition of the last hand) (Stuttgart, Tübingen: Cotta, 1827–1830). The works edition is one possible future for a miscellaneous oeuvre, and yet Jean Paul's characterization of his writings as subject to interruption and continuation stands in tension with the idea of a stable collection of standardized works. The emergent concept of authorial control over his or her works (*Werkherrschaft*) depends on a sense of an individual work's serial reproducibility, yet Jean Paul's embrace of interruption, deferred completion, and continuation troubles such control.[10] In envisioning "last" works in this manner, Jean Paul presents readers with a corpus that is contingent, topical, and mortal and that models experiences of serial and miscellaneous print more than the encounter with literary immortality.

Jean Paul thereby satirizes different authorial, editorial, and scholarly attempts to curate literary works and their afterlives. He spoofs the notion of the future reader as a kindred spirit to individual authors, something that Heine jokes about in an aside that "literary history is the great morgue where each seeks his dead, the one he loves or is related to. . . . How can I pass by without giving you all a quick kiss on your pale lips!"[11] This mode of reception envisions future literary encounters with the author's indelible "spirit." Jean Paul also spoofs the philological focus on the unpublished literary estate of canonical writers; his gesture to compulsively put as much as possible into print pokes fun at philologists, critics,

---

10. "The author's creative production is channeled into something repeatable, so that author and publisher produce serially, according to the same pattern" (*[Des Autors] Schaffen mündete nun in etwas Wiederholbares, so daß Autor und Verleger seriell, nach dem Gleichen Muster produzieren*). Heinrich Bosse, *Autorschaft ist Werkherrschaft. Über die Entstehung des Urheberrechts aus dem Geist der Goethezeit* (Paderborn: Fink, 2014 [1981]), 14. See also Matthias Schaffrick, "Ambiguität der Autor-Werk-Herrschaft (Bosse, Luhmann, Jean Paul)," in *Autor und Werk. Wechselwirkungen und Perspektiven*, special issue no. 3 of *Textpraxis*, edited by Svetlana Efimova, *Digitales Journal für Philologie* (2018), last accessed March 13, 2023, https://www.textpraxis.net/matthias-schaffrick-autor-werk-herrschaft.

11. Heinrich Heine, "Die Romantische Schule," DHA, 8/1, 135.

and unauthorized reprinters who comb through the scraps of paper handled by the great author. A third, related model of literary legacy is that of canonization and monumentalization—again, something that is associated with the works edition as a repository for self-standing museum-quality works.[12] The notion of the literary work as monument goes back to antiquity and the Horatian trope of a literary monument more lasting than bronze (*exegi monumentum aere perennius*). This trope witnessed a resurgence in the eighteenth century, as prose authors (rather than merely poets) sought lasting renown and as national literary canons started to be envisioned.[13] Even if the conceit of the literary work as an unchanging "national" monument—paradigmatically articulated via Goethe—is primarily a construct of the later nineteenth century,[14] Jean Paul's visions of the end of his own life and works warrant closer attention as a telling critique of this construct. If serial formats give us a sense of times beyond the horizon of an individual life, then Jean Paul's infusion of the unruly temporalities of miscellaneity and serial continuation into his body of work presents a model of literary afterlife poised perilously at the divide of authorial self-assertion and self-abnegation.

This chapter first turns to two episodes where Jean Paul writes the end of his life and works in tandem with serial print formats. In the first, he explores the productive tension between the book fair as medial dispositive and single-author literary production, while in the second, he envisions the conjunction of his life and works with the beginning and end of the *Morgenblatt*. These episodes encourage us to consider how his visions of future writing and reception trouble a notion of canonical authorial personas. Before closing with a return to Jean Paul's announcement of his "last work" and to the ways in which this late piece reflects on the past and

---

12. On Jean Paul's canonization as an "immortal" author directly after his death, see Böck, "Archäologie in der Wüste," 243.

13. See Jacob Sider Jost, *Prose Immortality: 1711–1819* (Charlottesville: University of Virginia Press, 2015).

14. See Andrew Piper, *Dreaming in Books: The Making of the Bibliographic Imagination in the Romantic Age* (Chicago: University of Chicago Press, 2009), 31–36.

future of a miscellaneous oeuvre, I consider Jean Paul's works edition, which he planned up to the point of his death, comparing his ideas for collecting the entirety of his writings with Goethe's *Ausgabe letzter Hand*. Across these various projects, Jean Paul sets into motion the unruly coexistence of multiple *Werkchen*, enabling multiple possible futures of ever more miscellaneous reading rather than the consolidation of a stable and unchanging body of work.

Before and after Death

"En Route"

In his mid-thirties, Jean Paul sets out to write a hypothetical biography of his own future life, which he titles his "Konjektural-Biographie" (Conjectural biography). He includes it in a 1799 miscellaneous collection of ostensibly autobiographical pieces titled *Jean Pauls Briefe und bevorstehender Lebenslauf* (Jean Paul's letters and impending course of life),[15] which he describes as a "historical novel of my I," yet it is a history of something that has not (yet) happened.[16] Parodying history writing and the philosophy of history through autobiography is also a feature of his later project, the posthumously published *Selberlebensbeschreibung*, which is staged as if the author were holding lectures in this history of his life.[17] While that later fragment is limited to an account of his childhood and adolescence, the "Konjektural-Biographie" sketches a future life of marriage, a successful writing career, an idyllic family life in a provincial setting, retirement, and death. Peculiarly, though,

---

15. Jean Paul, "Konjektural-Biographie," in *Jean Pauls Briefe und bevorstehender Lebenslauf* (Gera and Leipzig: Heinsius, 1799); I/4, 1027–82. Pfotenhauer calls this volume a "collection of the most heterogeneous texts solely united by the shared form of the letter" (*Sammelsurium verschiedenster Texte, nur durch die allen gemeinsame Briefform verbunden*). Pfotenhauer, *Jean Paul*, 196.
16. Jean Paul, *Briefe und bevorstehender Lebenslauf*, ix.
17. What Fleming calls a "series of lectures in Self-Studies." Paul Fleming, "The Promises of Childhood: Autobiography in Goethe and Jean Paul," *Goethe Yearbook* 14 (2007): 35.

the formal structure of the "Konjektural-Biographie" superimposes a key annual event of the publishing world, the Leipzig fall book fair, or *Michaelismesse*, onto the time of the author's life. The text is organized as seven "epistles," each corresponding both to different segments of his life to come and to different junctures of the weeks-long fair: the "barrel week" (*Böttigerwoche*), "the counting week" (*Zahlwoche*), and more. Jean Paul superimposes one narrated time on another: the time of the frame narrative, that is, the several weeks in the fall in which he tells his life story and the narrated time of his entire future life. Writing in tandem and competition with the book fair, the fall setting sets the stage for a series of allegorical explorations of the seasons as periods of life, with fall representing Jean Paul's own prodigious future production. The fall fair is also when almanacs and *Taschenbücher* appear, and it is not an accident that the miscellany is commonly symbolized by the harvest cornucopia. The concluding epistle bears the subtitle "Das Ende" (The end) and tells of the dual end of the fair and his life and is dated "Unter Wegs" (en route).[18] In the narrative frame, the author leaves Leipzig for Weimar, but in his future life, he departs for the afterlife.

The second-to-last epistle is a telling example of how Jean Paul shapes a sense of authorial oeuvre through reference to serial miscellaneous print. Jean Paul has reached the end of his writing career, his "Life-*Vendémiaire*" (the month of harvest and wine in the French revolutionary calendar), and he imagines holding his own retirement speech (*Jubelrede*). This is a farewell speech (*Abschiedsrede*), a preview of death, but it is also a celebration of culmination and completion, not least of his forthcoming "edition of his *opera omnia*," which he announces in the speech's opening remarks.[19] Yet Jean Paul's crafting of an authorial persona occurs decidedly under the sign of serial print: "Open up with me this fruit pantry [*Obstkammer*], and look at the small *Universal German Library* [*kleine allgemeine deutsche Bibliothek*] with all of its supplements that I have written up in this short life."[20] Likening authorial fecundity to an

---

18. Jean Paul, "Konjektural-Biographie," 434.
19. Jean Paul, "Konjektural-Biographie," 414.
20. Jean Paul, "Konjektural-Biographie," 402.

archived set of Nicolai's important Enlightenment era review journal the *Allgemeine deutsche Bibliothek* (1765–1806) depersonalizes his writings and suggests that they are produced according to the temporal and commercial dictates of serial print rather than the flash of genial inspiration. These are works in the "uniform" of a journal, aligned more with the ways a reader might peruse old issues of a multiauthor journal than with the sustained reading of a single author's life's work.[21]

The closing of the *Jubelrede* spoofs the promise of more implied by the medial dispositive of serial print and the "adieu, fair world" topos. There, Jean Paul envisions a future reader encountering his work "after many long, long years, after all has changed and I have flown away or sunk down for good,"[22] only to break off this reverie by shifting back to the present of his current life. Jean Paul's refractions of different temporal frameworks ironize the sentimental address to future readers. The *Jubelrede* also spoofs the scholarly treatment of literary afterlives: How does one stand out as an author, he muses, in a landscape full of authors who have a book each and every fair to send down the flow of the "German Lethe"?[23] The only thing to make an author's work less forgettable, he continues, is for the author to die: "The public will take brooms and comb through his museum as in the workroom of a goldsmith and sweep all the scattered paper clippings and compile a modest little volume, a posthumum."[24] Punning on "to imitate" (*Nachmachen*), "to follow" (*Nachkommen*), and the *Nach* (after) of illegal reprinting (*Nachdrucken*), he concludes that the only guarantor of inimitability is that no more works by an author follow.[25] Death guarantees

---

21. On the questions of books that look like journals and journals that look like books, see Kaminski, "'Nachdruck des Nachdrucks.'"
22. Jean Paul, "Konjektural-Biographie," 425–26.
23. Jean Paul, "Konjektural-Biographie," 403.
24. Jean Paul, "Konjektural-Biographie," 404.
25. "Because humans only honor (according to Jakobi) what is not imitable; with the first part of each and every original book, no one understands how a subsequent part is possible; the more additional parts appear, though, the more it seems possible to imagine its making and its imitation [*desto mehr leuchte uns die Möglichkeit des Machens und also des Nachmachens ein*]." Jean Paul, "Konjektural-Biographie," 404–5.

authorial originality,[26] but this is because the author is no longer generating new works, and it is left for scholars and critics (and illegal reprinters) to come up with subsequent writings in the author's name: this is a vision of the philological curation of the authorial oeuvre in an age of print oversaturation. The irony is that the death of the author always leads to something that comes "after." There is always some kind of posthumum.

An additional temporal framework suggesting both finality and continuation is likewise at work in the final epistle, titled "En Route" (*Unter Wegs*), in which the end of the book fair converges with impending death. Configuring life as a journey is a Christian trope, yet the piece's final words envision death as a secular destination: "The sun is going down—my journey is ending—and in a few minutes I will be with a beloved, dear heart—it is yours, immortal Wieland!"[27] The author's return to Weimar and his departure for the afterlife converge. In 1799, Wieland was still alive and living in Weimar, although the publication of his works edition (1794–1802) had already begun. But, described from the perspective of the future, Jean Paul's achievements in his "impending course of life" accord him a place of writerly immortality alongside Wieland. The end of the piece, the author's death, and the completion of his works all coincide. Nonetheless, the gap between the author's final words and his death—"in a few minutes"—becomes an important temporal hinge, for this gap straddles two different presents. In the present of the future, these few minutes are what remain before the author's actual death, but, in the present of the narrative frame (where the end is merely that of the book fair), these few minutes open up a space between now and the end of life when Jean Paul will actually write the works that he has looked back on in the *Jubelrede*—he still has to prove himself worthy of standing alongside Wieland! This scene of death simultaneously compresses this temporal frame down to just a few minutes and dilates it to many produc-

---

26. "The grave is the insulating stool for works [*Das Grab hingegen ist das Isolierschemel der Werke*]; they are enveloped by an isolating, holy magic aura for all eternity." Jean Paul, "Konjektural-Biographie," 405.

27. "Die Sonne geht hinab—meine Reise endigt—und in wenig Minuten bin ich an einem geliebten theuern Herzen—es ist deines, unsterblicher Wieland!" Jean Paul, "Konjektural-Biographie," 450.

tive years. The depiction of future life and fictionalized death alike serves to imagine a time in which he will make good on his promise that more in fact will follow. And again, it is the peculiarity of the "Konjektural-Biographie" that this future is punctuated as much by the periodicities of depersonalized serial print—of the fair's barrel and counting weeks—as it is by any naive notion of the organic development of an author's life. Along with suggesting the time it will take to consolidate his authorial standing, this media time suggests a time foreign to the life of the author that continues on independent of him. Jean Paul depersonalizes and ironizes the closing gesture to literary immortality even as he leaves readers eager for more.

"Ahead of Time"

Cotta was eager to secure Jean Paul as a contributor for the *Morgenblatt* and pressed him for a piece for the January 1, 1807, inaugural issue. However, instead of offering an introduction or prologue to the journal, Jean Paul proposed "an anticipated Epilogue (a Closing Speech [*Schlußrede*])."[28] This would become the "Abschiedsrede bey dem künftigen Schlusse des Morgenblatts" (Farewell speech on the occasion of the future end of the *Morgenblatt*), a three-page eulogy of the journal's illustrious past (see figure 5.1).[29] Here, too, he might well have drawn inspiration from Addison and Steele's *The Spectator*, which in issue 101 presents readers with an "Imaginary Historian" who chronicles the existence of the journal's essays three hundred years after their publication.[30] The "Abschiedsrede" serves as a programmatic introduction to the journal and to what would become Jean Paul's symbiotic relationship with it as a lead author.

The "Abschiedsrede" returns to the thought experiment that hypothetical conclusion leads to ongoing continuation. Like the

---

28. Jean Paul to Johann Friedrich Cotta von Cottendorf, December 11, 1806. SW HKA, III/5, 115–16.
29. Jean Paul, "Abschiedsrede bey dem künftigen Schlusse des Morgenblatts," *Morgenblatt für gebildete Stände* 1, no. 1 (January 1, 1807): 1–4.
30. See Jost, *Prose Immortality*, 33.

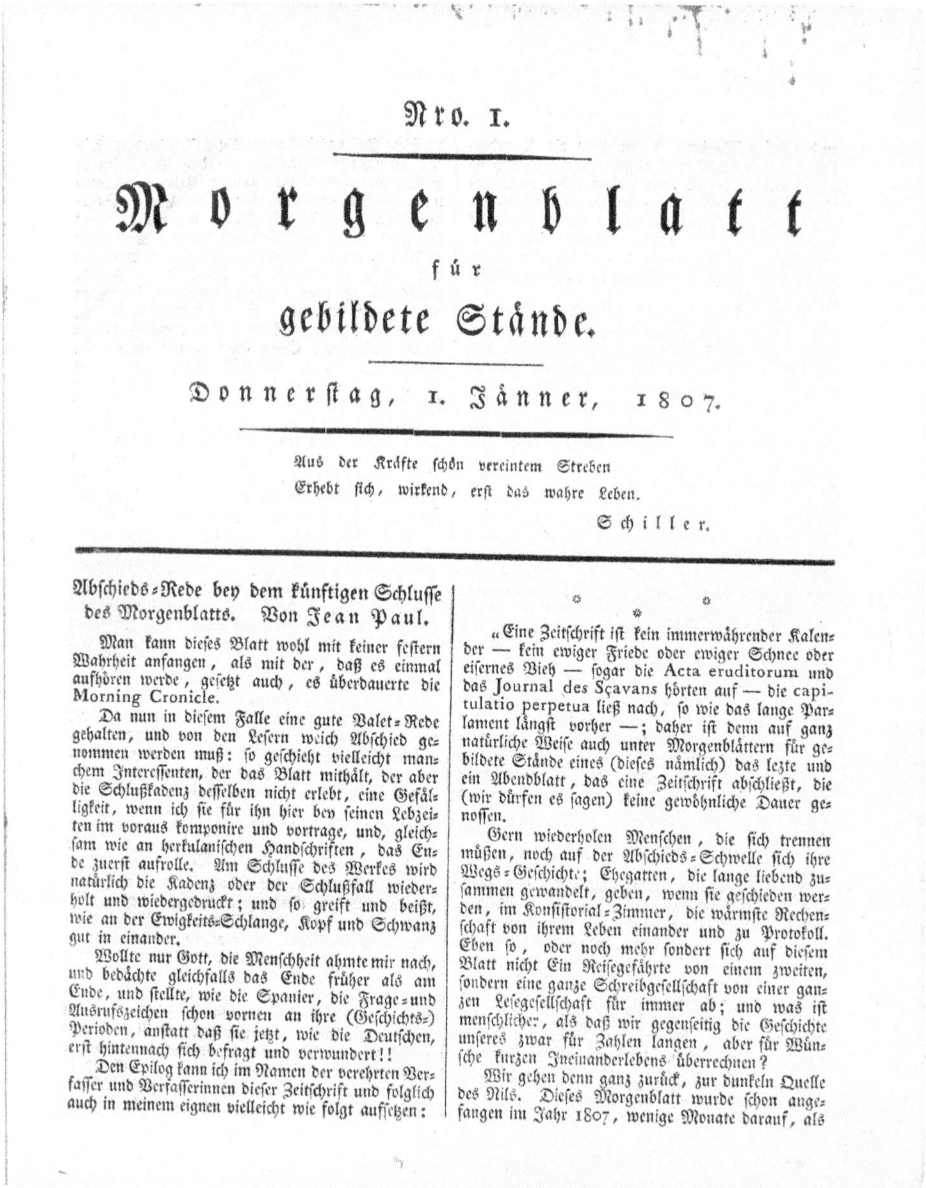

Nro. I.

Morgenblatt
für
gebildete Stände.

Donnerstag, 1. Jänner, 1807.

Aus der Kräfte schön vereintem Streben
Erhebt sich, wirkend, erst das wahre Leben.
Schiller.

Abschieds-Rede bey dem künftigen Schlusse des Morgenblatts. Von Jean Paul.

Man kann dieses Blatt wohl mit keiner festern Wahrheit anfangen, als mit der, daß es einmal aufhören werde, gesetzt auch, es überdauerte die Morning Cronicle.

Da nun in diesem Falle eine gute Valet-Rede gehalten, und von den Lesern weich Abschied genommen werden muß: so geschieht vielleicht manchem Interessenten, der das Blatt mithält, der aber die Schlußkadenz desselben nicht erlebt, eine Gefälligkeit, wenn ich sie für ihn hier bey seinen Lebzeiten im voraus komponire und vortrage, und, gleichsam wie an herkulanischen Handschriften, das Ende zuerst aufrolle. Am Schlusse des Werkes wird natürlich die Kadenz oder der Schlußfall wiederholt und wiedergedruckt; und so greift und beißt, wie an der Ewigkeits-Schlange, Kopf und Schwanz gut in einander.

Wollte nur Gott, die Menschheit ahmte mir nach, und bedächte gleichfalls das Ende früher als am Ende, und stellte, wie die Spanier, die Frage- und Ausrufszeichen schon vornen an ihre (Geschichts-) Perioden, anstatt daß sie jetzt, wie die Deutschen, erst hintennach sich befragt und verwundert!!

Den Epilog kann ich im Namen der verehrten Verfasser und Verfasserinnen dieser Zeitschrift und folglich auch in meinem eignen vielleicht wie folgt aufsetzen:

"Eine Zeitschrift ist kein immerwährender Kalender — kein ewiger Friede oder ewiger Schnee oder eisernes Vieh — sogar die Acta eruditorum und das Journal des Sçavans hörten auf — die capitulatio perpetua ließ nach, so wie das lange Parlament längst vorher —; daher ist denn auf ganz natürliche Weise auch unter Morgenblättern für gebildete Stände eines (dieses nämlich) das lezte und ein Abendblatt, das eine Zeitschrift abschließt, die (wir dürfen es sagen) keine gewöhnliche Dauer genoßen.

Gern wiederholen Menschen, die sich trennen müßen, noch auf der Abschieds-Schwelle sich ihre Wegs-Geschichte; Ehegatten, die lange liebend zusammen gewandelt, geben, wenn sie geschieden werden, im Konsistorial-Zimmer, die wärmste Rechenschaft von ihrem Leben einander und zu Protokoll. Eben so, oder noch mehr sondert sich auf diesem Blatt nicht Ein Reisegefährte von einem zweiten, sondern eine ganze Schreibgesellschaft von einer ganzen Lesegesellschaft für immer ab; und was ist menschlicher, als daß wir gegenseitig die Geschichte unseres zwar für Zahlen langen, aber für Wünsche kurzen Zneinanderlebens überrechnen?

Wir gehen denn ganz zurück, zur dunkeln Quelle des Nils. Dieses Morgenblatt wurde schon angefangen im Jahr 1807, wenige Monate darauf, als

Figure 5.1. Page view. *Morgenblatt für gebildete Stände* 1, no. 1 (Thursday, January 1, 1807): 1. HAAB Weimar. 8 ¾ × 7 ¼ inches.

"Konjektural-Biographie," the "Abschiedsrede" toggles between the present and a hypothetical future: for the reader of the first issue, a future moment is constructed in which the journal will have concluded, yet within the speech's fictive frame, the *Morgenblatt* is coming to an end, and the author is minutes away from death. To be sure, predicting the end of a journal just as it is starting is something of a heretical action, for it constructs an observer position usually closed off to readers, writers, and editors who are under the assumption that serial publication will ensure a periodical's ongoing life.[31] Jean Paul overlays the times of print and of a life of writing in the service of imagining a regimented, sequential production of works. Writing from the future allows Jean Paul to construct a kind of conjectural history both of the journal (which did not cease publication until 1865) and of Jean Paul's own literary career. Furthermore, it allows him to bring the temporal footprint of the journal—its almost daily periodicity, its orientation to the new, and its sequential accumulation—into resonance with his own life and works.

This piece is chock-full of reflection on time more generally, a stock component of Jean Paul's beginning- and end-of-year "speeches" in the *Morgenblatt* that this piece inaugurates. Jean Paul riffs on the temporal connotations of the journal's title: the *Morgenblatt* helps readers to begin the day, and each installment brings something new and represents a "daily youth in miniature, a rejuvenated rejuvenation."[32] *Morgen* means both "morning" and "tomorrow," with daily rejuvenation promising that tomorrow will bring another issue. As Jean Paul suggests, measuring the passing of time—"moving along, even flying along with time"—is a primary function of all periodicals and of the *Morgenblatt* in particular.[33] If the central allegory of the "Konjektural-Biographie" is autumnal literary production, then the allegorical thrust of the "Abschiedsrede" centers on the ephemerality of serial print, and Jean Paul does not pass up the opportunity to consider the transience of the political turmoil affecting central Europe. The

---

31. See James Mussell, "Repetition: Or, 'In Our Last,'" *Victorian Periodicals Review* 48, no. 3 (2015): 345; as well as my discussion of this article in the afterword.
32. Jean Paul, "Abschiedsrede," 2.
33. Jean Paul, "Abschiedsrede," 3.

"Abschiedsrede" is one of the first pieces that Jean Paul publishes after the Battle of Jena–Auerstedt; looking back from a conjectural future, Jean Paul mentions events that coincide with the journal's founding as they recede into "prehistory" (*Vorzeit*): "Let us go all the way back, to the dark source of the Nile."[34] In 1806, Napoleon broke up the Holy Roman Empire—this was the year "in which the newspaper the *Imperial Gazette* [*Der Reichsanzeiger*] rose up and became the *General Gazette* [*Der allgemeine Anzeiger*]," and 1806 witnessed the emergence of the eighth wonder of the world, the "surplus wonder" of the battle of "Jena."[35] Historical events unfold as a series of wonders (and as a series of changing journal titles) no longer contained by a completed set, but the reference to current events also relativizes the suffering of the present. Archived copies of the journal allow readers to register events as no longer current—as he states, the journal is "a valuable repository for miscellanies [*Miszellen*] [that] proffers everyone all kinds of things from everything."[36] In imagining the entire run of the *Morgenblatt*, Jean Paul invites readers to test whether the journal really does deliver on its promise to present something new each new day, to "open up the yearly volumes [of the journal], and for example, compare the articles of the year 1807...with those of the years 1810, 1817, 1825."[37] By encouraging readers to go back to old (and not yet written) articles, Jean Paul envisions scenes of future re-encounters made possible by the journal as archive and also by these texts' potential for migration to other formats. Here, too, he spoofs the hands-on paperwork of scholarly philological reconstruction.

The trope of transience also functions as a hinge by which to swivel back (or forth) from the contrasting temporality of the periodical and that of his own life and works: "The speaker will now lay down his pen, the not-infertile mother of one hundred and seventy-seven volumes, and depart; for the night frost of life is here, and the final yellow leaves fly down from the picked-over treetop."[38] As in the "Konjektural-Biographie," Jean Paul brings his readers to

---

34. Jean Paul, "Abschiedsrede," 1.
35. Jean Paul, "Abschiedsrede," 2.
36. Jean Paul, "Abschiedsrede," 3.
37. Jean Paul, "Abschiedsrede," 3.
38. Jean Paul, "Abschiedsrede," 4.

the onset of winter. Shortly afterward, though, he retracts the farewell gesture: "But I am truly writing myself into emotional states well ahead of time [*vor der Zeit*];—the *Morgenblatt* has hardly just begun, let alone concluded, and for my part, I am a forty-three-year-old with plenty of fruit still hanging from me."[39] Jean Paul shifts to a different, now "premature" time of writing. In writing from the present, he recalibrates the time of his life and works with the actual state of the new journal. Marking the end promises continuation.

Once again, Jean Paul juxtaposes the temporal frameworks of authorial production and the broader literary landscape. Indeed, the hypothetical one hundred and seventy-seven volumes of the future are almost more plausible as the proliferating issues of the *Morgenblatt* than as a notional works edition. As writing and periodical publication outpace the years of his life, media-based periodicities relativize "natural" time. And given that the periodicities of print outpace the cycles of individual life, isn't there something counterintuitive to Jean Paul's idea that the end of his life and the *Morgenblatt*'s will coincide? One might just as well conclude that the journal will continue into an indefinite future, dependent on patterns of literary production and reception independent of a single author. Imagining the complete set of all the issues of the *Morgenblatt* is an archival fiction that generates hypothetical scenes of future reencounter, and Jean Paul has a chance to make the scene slightly more actual by reprinting the "Abschiedsrede" in 1815 in the second installment of his anthology series *Herbst-Blumine oder gesammelte Werkchen aus Zeitschriften* (Autumn flora, or collected little works from journals).[40] Eight years later, the history of the journal belongs slightly less to the future, the *Morgenblatt* is the leading literary organ it was predestined to become, and readers can test out Jean Paul's predictions from the first issue. On the one hand, the anthology's title evokes the convention of the collected works edi-

---

39. Jean Paul, "Abschiedsrede," 4.
40. Jean Paul, *Herbst-Blumine oder gesammelte Werkchen aus Zeitschriften*, vol. 2 (Stuttgart and Tübingen: Cotta, 1815), 33–53. On the concept of archival fiction, see Daniela Gretz and Nicolas Pethes, ed., *Archiv/Fiktionen: Verfahren des Archivierens in Literatur und Kultur des langen 19. Jahrhunderts* (Freiburg: Rombach, 2016).

tion, with anthologizing potentially lending occasional pieces the permanence befitting an authorial "work." On the other hand, the title highlights the origin of its contents in florilegistic formats tied to the seasonal rhythms of *Taschenbücher* and other anthologies.⁴¹

The *Autumn Flora* curates the afterlives of his works in an ambivalent way. To a certain extent, he models the incorporation of scattered fragments into a more unified corpus, yet this corpus still appears under the sign of smallness and miscellaneity. Among other things, this anthology collects various new year's addresses that Jean Paul had written for the *Morgenblatt* since its founding. The anthology format decouples the addresses from the occasions for which they were ostensibly written, that is, the year-in, year-out passing of time. These texts mark the passing of the calendar years, yet they do so irregularly, interspersed with and interrupted by texts that perform other unrelated functions. This might suggest a mode of reencounter that allows readers to appreciate the texts as primarily literary experiments, as particularly original and humorous takes on established rhetorical genres that could be seamlessly integrated into the miscellaneous reading characteristic of the *Morgenblatt* and other journals like it. Yet the texts still bear traces of the temporality of the current events that they obliquely reference (such as the Battle of Jena–Auerstadt, which had been revenged by 1815). If the initial pieces write the present of the actual readers of the journal's first issues, then republication places this present into a sequence of past events, a sequence of past mornings and tomorrows accessible both in the archive of the journal's past issues and in Jean Paul's anthology. Jean Paul engages in something of an oblique and incomplete writing of *Zeitgeschichte* predicated on the open-ended temporalities and experiential contingencies of miscellaneous reading. Offering readers these reconstellated *Werkchen*, he underlines his works' status as archived journal literature with time-specific

---

41. Jean Paul's promise that each year would bring a new volume of his *Autumn Flora* likewise reinforces the similarity between the journal and anthology's serial formats (in fact, he would only publish three volumes, at five-year intervals). Jean Paul, *Herbst-Blumine*, vol. 1 (1810), xv.

relevance but also as expressly literary works with the potential for multiple future afterlives.

Opera Omnia

The 1820s was a boom time for works editions, as seen in an announcement of Jean Paul's works in the *Morgenblatt*, with his publisher G. A. Reimer offering readers collected works of modern (Tieck, Novalis, Kleist, and Lenz) and classic (Shakespeare) authors (see figure 5.2). Like other contemporary writers, Jean Paul undoubtedly approaches his literary output via the horizon of a unified body of work.[42] Over the course of the nineteenth century, works editions become one of the most "durable and effective vehicles for regulating, institutionalizing, and stabilizing the category of literature," ascribing "classical" timelessness to certain figures.[43] In Jean Paul's case, his works edition certainly makes good on the promise for more that we encountered in the "Konjektural-Biographie" and the "Abschiedsrede," and it stands under the sign of both the author's death and the impulse to collect and edit previously published writings. In Jean Paul's hands, though, the works edition comes to function as one element in a repertoire of serial formats that troubles the notion of the self-standing work and that prefigures afterlives for his *Werkchen* that depart from the conceit of naïve monumentalization. In particular, comparing Goethe's and Jean Paul's approaches to the works edition underscores Jean Paul's affinities to the world of serial literature and miscellaneous reading. To be sure, scholars have explored questions of formal open-endedness and serial modularity in Goethe's works, but Jean

---

42. "Jean Paul views all of his works, printed or unprinted, as part of a coherent body of works, as 'opera omnia.'" Benne, "'Kein Einfall sollte untergehen,'" 217.

43. Piper, *Dreaming in Books*, 54. On classicizing aspiration in Wieland's works edition, see Peter-Henning Haischer, *Historizität und Klassizität. Christoph Martin Wieland und die Werkausgabe im 18. Jahrhundert* (Heidelberg: Winter, 2011).

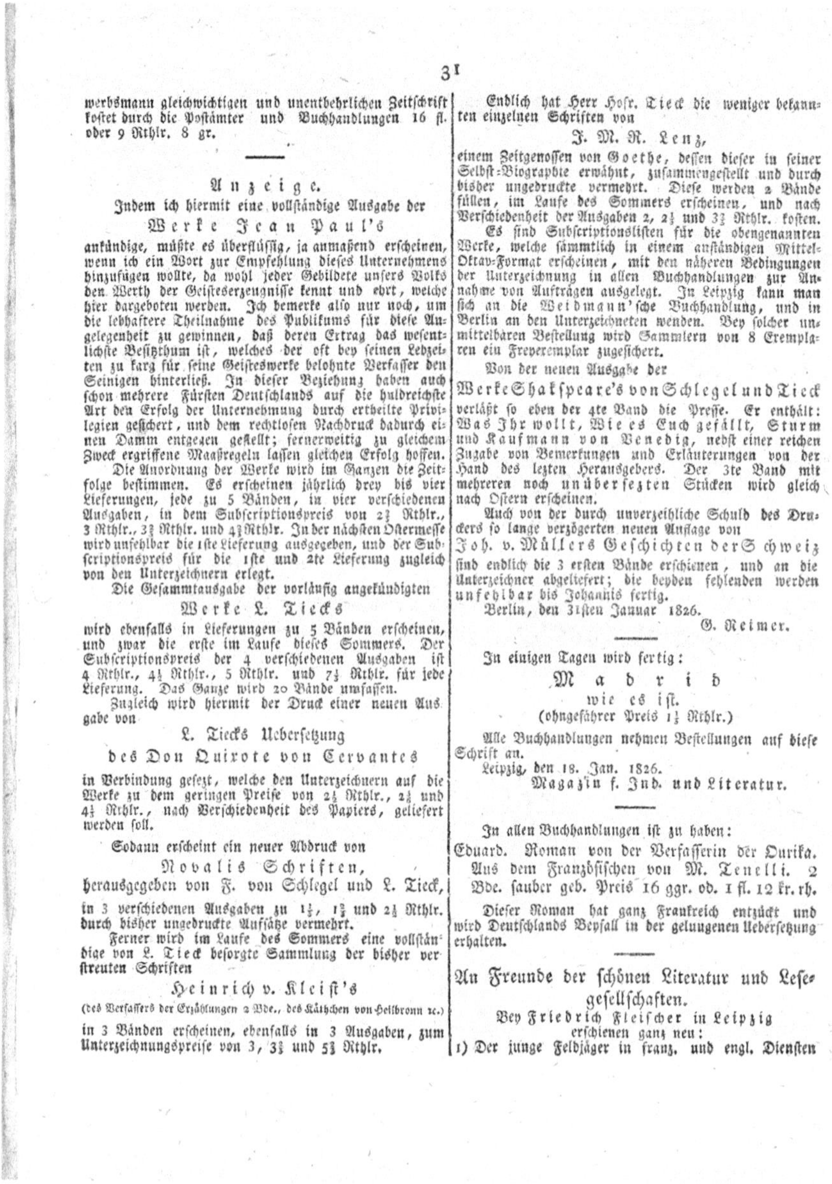

31

werbsmann gleichwichtigen und unentbehrlichen Zeitschrift kostet durch die Postämter und Buchhandlungen 16 fl. oder 9 Rthlr. 8 gr.

Anzeige.

Indem ich hiermit eine vollständige Ausgabe der

Werke Jean Paul's

ankündige, müßte es überflüssig, ja anmaßend erscheinen, wenn ich ein Wort zur Empfehlung dieses Unternehmens hinzufügen wollte, da wohl jeder Gebildete unsers Volks den Werth der Geisteserzeugnisse kennt und ehrt, welche hier dargeboten werden. Ich bemerke also nur noch, um die lebhaftere Theilnahme des Publikums für diese Angelegenheit zu gewinnen, daß deren Ertrag das wesentlichste Besitzthum ist, welches der oft bey seinen Lebzeiten zu karg für seine Geisteswerke belohnte Verfasser den Seinigen hinterließ. In dieser Beziehung haben auch schon mehrere Fürsten Deutschlands auf die huldreichste Art den Erfolg der Unternehmung durch ertheilte Privilegien gesichert, und dem rechtlosen Nachdruck dadurch einen Damm entgegen gestellt; fernerweitig zu gleichem Zweck ergriffene Maaßregeln lassen gleichen Erfolg hoffen.

Die Anordnung der Werke wird im Ganzen die Zeitfolge bestimmen. Es erscheinen jährlich drey bis vier Lieferungen, jede zu 5 Bänden, in vier verschiedenen Ausgaben, in dem Subscriptionspreis von $2\frac{2}{3}$ Rthlr., 3 Rthlr., $3\frac{2}{3}$ Rthlr. und $4\frac{2}{3}$ Rthlr. In der nächsten Ostermesse wird unfehlbar die 1ste Lieferung ausgegeben, und der Subscriptionspreis für die 1ste und 2te Lieferung zugleich von den Unterzeichnern erlegt.

Die Gesammtausgabe der vorläufig angekündigten

Werke L. Tiecks

wird ebenfalls in Lieferungen zu 5 Bänden erscheinen, und zwar die erste im Laufe dieses Sommers. Der Subscriptionspreis der 4 verschiedenen Ausgaben ist 4 Rthlr., $4\frac{1}{2}$ Rthlr., 5 Rthlr. und $7\frac{1}{2}$ Rthlr. für jede Lieferung. Das Ganze wird 20 Bände umfassen.

Zugleich wird hiermit der Druck einer neuen Ausgabe von

L. Tiecks Uebersetzung

des Don Quixote von Cervantes

in Verbindung gesezt, welche den Unterzeichnern auf die Werke zu dem geringen Preise von $2\frac{1}{2}$ Rthlr., $2\frac{5}{6}$ und $4\frac{1}{3}$ Rthlr., nach Verschiedenheit des Papiers, geliefert werden soll.

Sodann erscheint ein neuer Abdruck von

Novalis Schriften,

herausgegeben von F. von Schlegel und L. Tieck,

in 3 verschiedenen Ausgaben zu $1\frac{1}{3}$, $1\frac{2}{3}$ und $2\frac{1}{3}$ Rthlr. durch bisher ungedruckte Aufsätze vermehrt.

Ferner wird im Laufe des Sommers eine vollständige von L. Tieck besorgte Sammlung der bisher verstreuten Schriften

Heinrich v. Kleist's

(des Verfassers der Erzählungen 2 Bde., des Käthchen von Heilbronn rc.)

in 3 Bänden erscheinen, ebenfalls in 3 Ausgaben, zum Unterzeichnungspreise von 3, $3\frac{2}{3}$ und $5\frac{2}{3}$ Rthlr.

Endlich hat Herr Hofr. Tieck die weniger bekannten einzelnen Schriften von

J. M. R. Lenz,

einem Zeitgenossen von Goethe, dessen dieser in seiner Selbst-Biographie erwähnt, zusammengestellt und durch bisher ungedruckte vermehrt. Diese werden 2 Bände füllen, im Laufe des Sommers erscheinen, und nach Verschiedenheit der Ausgaben 2, $2\frac{1}{2}$ und $3\frac{2}{3}$ Rthlr. kosten.

Es sind Subscriptionslisten für die obengenannten Werke, welche sämmtlich in einem anständigen Mittel-Oktav-Format erscheinen, mit den näheren Bedingungen der Unterzeichnung in allen Buchhandlungen zur Annahme von Aufträgen ausgelegt. In Leipzig kann man sich an die Weidmann'sche Buchhandlung, und in Berlin an den Unterzeichneten wenden. Bey solcher unmittelbaren Bestellung wird Sammlern von 8 Exemplaren ein Freyexemplar zugesichert.

Von der neuen Ausgabe der

Werke Shakspeare's von Schlegel und Tieck

verläßt so eben der 4te Band die Presse. Er enthält: Was Ihr wollt, Wie es Euch gefällt, Sturm und Kaufmann von Venedig, nebst einer reichen Zugabe von Bemerkungen und Erläuterungen von der Hand des lezten Herausgebers. Der 3te Band mit mehreren noch unübersezten Stücken wird gleich nach Ostern erscheinen.

Auch von der durch unverzeihliche Schuld des Druckers so lange verzögerten neuen Auflage von

Joh. v. Müllers Geschichten der Schweiz

sind endlich die 3 ersten Bände erschienen, und an die Unterzeichner abgeliefert; die beyden fehlenden werden unfehlbar bis Johannis fertig.

Berlin, den 31sten Januar 1826.

G. Reimer.

In einigen Tagen wird fertig:

Madrid

wie es ist.

(ohngefährer Preis $1\frac{1}{3}$ Rthlr.)

Alle Buchhandlungen nehmen Bestellungen auf diese Schrift an.

Leipzig, den 18. Jan. 1826.

Magazin f. Ind. und Literatur.

In allen Buchhandlungen ist zu haben:

Eduard. Roman von der Verfasserin der Ourika. Aus dem Französischen von M. Tenelli. 2 Bde. sauber geb. Preis 16 ggr. od. 1 fl. 12 kr. rh.

Dieser Roman hat ganz Frankreich entzückt und wird Deutschlands Beyfall in der gelungenen Uebersetzung erhalten.

An Freunde der schönen Literatur und Lesegesellschaften.

Bey Friedrich Fleischer in Leipzig erschienen ganz neu:

1) Der junge Feldjäger in franz. und engl. Diensten

Figure 5.2. Page view. *Intelligenzblatt zum Morgenblatt für gebildete Stände* 8 (1826): 31. HAAB Weimar. 8 ¾ × 7 ¼ inches.

Paul represents an even more radical alignment of an oeuvre with principles of continuation, incompletion, and miscellaneity.⁴⁴

The posthumously published edition *Jean Paul's sämmtliche Werke* (Berlin: G. Reimer, 1826–1838) would come out in quarterly installments over the course of more than ten years. Working with this edition is difficult, because it is often hard to identify authorial or editorial intention; Eduard Berend, the early twentieth-century editor of the first critical edition of Jean Paul's works, called it "incomplete . . . organized without a plan, highly unreliable on a textual level" (*unvollständig . . . planlos angeordnet, textlich höchst unzuverlässig*).⁴⁵ Jean Paul did offer some input before his death, but some of his initial plans went unrealized in this and subsequent critical editions, which were predominantly oriented toward an ideal of bringing together the final versions of individual works.⁴⁶ He appears to have remained undecided about certain elements of the edition, and notes and letters detailing his plans were sometimes contradictory. In contrast to Goethe and his work overseeing and expanding *Ausgabe letzter Hand*, Jean Paul did not play a truly hands-on role. However, as with Goethe's approach and later scholarly editions, Jean Paul's tentative plans for this edition nonetheless do reveal certain important features of his approach to the editorial challenge of curating his works for posterity.

Works editions can reveal how authors understand the status of individual works and their interrelation,⁴⁷ for the author serves both as a creative catalyst and as a reader, an editor, and a rearranger of their own works.⁴⁸ The early nineteenth century witnesses

---

44. See Andrew Piper, "Rethinking the Print Object: Goethe and the Book of Everything," *PMLA* 121, no. 1 (2006): 124–38; and Geulen, "Serialization in Goethe's Morphology," 53.
45. Berend, *Prolegomena*, 12.
46. See Barbara Hunfeld, "Eine neue Jean-Paul-Werkausgabe," *Geschichte der Germanistik* 31/32 (2007): 111–16. The edition was overseen by Jean Paul's son-in-law Ernst Förster and the publisher Reimer. On the genesis of this edition, see Berend, *Prolegomena*, 6–10.
47. See Carlos Spoerhase, "Was ist ein Werk? Über philologische Werkfunktionen," *Scientia Poetica* 11 (2007): 276–344.
48. See Rüdiger Nutt-Kofoth, "Editionsphilologie als Mediengeschichte," *Editio* 20 (2006): 3; and Botho Plachta, "Goethe über das lästige Geschäft des

a perhaps surprising variety of approaches to the collection and organization of works editions. It is not uncommon to continue to rely on the genre hierarchies of old, as, for example, Goethe does in starting the *Ausgabe letzter Hand* with poetry, moving to different dramatic forms, and then to the novel.[49] This generic hierarchy presents readers with a sequence of individual works that successfully instantiate particular literary forms. In contrast, Jean Paul toyed with the idea of installment-based publication, in which each quarterly grouping of five volumes would present readers with a variety of genres: as he writes in a letter, "every installment [*Lieferung*] would simultaneously contain novels and stories and satirical essays or also didactic ones."[50] Here, the logical coherence of each installment stems from the varied arrangement of its contents rather than from the internal logics of the individual works themselves. Indeed, this vision of mixed installments evokes the structure of an open-ended serial anthology. Goethe specifically set aside certain volumes of his works edition for collecting entirely miscellaneous contents,[51] while Jean Paul envisions the entire edition as infused with miscellaneity. Though the Reimer edition only partially (and perhaps accidentally) realizes this deliberately miscellaneous approach to the installment structure, these initial plans reveal Jean Paul's lingering affinities to use-oriented *Gebrauchsliteratur* and its promise of regular, diverse content.

It was all too typical for works editions—and for novels, for that matter—to be published in multiple installments, so one might risk

---

Editors," in *Autor-Autorisation-Authentizität*, ed. Thomas Bein, Rüdiger Nutt-Kofoth, and Bodo Plachta (Tübingen: Niemeyer, 2004), 234.

49. On the *Werkchen* in relation to standard conceptions of the work, see Peter Horst Neumann, "Die Werkchen als Werk: Zur Form- und Wirkungsgeschichte des Katzenberger-Korpus von Jean Paul," *Jahrbuch der Jean Paul Gesellschaft* 10 (1970): 151–86, 169.

50. Jean Paul to Johann Friedrich Freiherr Cotta von Cottendorf, September 11, 1825. SW HKA, III/8, 288.

51. Goethe refers to the volumes 30 to 33 that are reserved for writings that exhibit "eine grosse Mannichfaltigkeit des Inhalts und der Form"; these volumes contain various autobiographical notes and book reviews that he wrote for various journals. Johann Wolfgang von Goethe, "Anzeige von Goethe's sämmtlichen Werken, vollständige Ausgabe letzter Hand," *Intelligenzblatt zum Morgenblatt für gebildete Stände* 25 (1826): 98.

placing too much importance on the serialized publication of a works edition. That said, Jean Paul does seem particularly attuned to their pace and scale, professing a desire for "quick installments" (*in schnellen Lieferungen*) in a letter to Böttiger.[52] For subscribers, the pace of receiving future installments would not be dissimilar to that of certain other serials. (I have included these organizing designators in my graphic showing republication in different formats [see figure 4.1].) Relatedly, Jean Paul does not shy away from breaking his novels up into parts, something that Berend takes issue with when applying a notion of the work as organic whole to Jean Paul's novels in particular.[53] The practice of consolidating multiple volumes of a given text into a single volume common in twentieth-century editions brings with it assumptions about the unity and totality of the work that stands in tension with the publication landscape of the early nineteenth century. Furthermore, Berend and other editors weighed trimming Jean Paul's many digressions, a common response to writers perceived to be overly digressive.[54] Partly through publication conventions that necessitate installment structures and partly through Jean Paul's embrace of protean continuation, his works seem to only partially conform to later editorial interventions that deemphasize serial and miscellaneous elements.

Another way that Jean Paul diverges from more classicizing conceptions of works editions is in his resistance to what Andrew Nash calls the "air of finality and completeness" that surrounds such editions.[55] Incompletion and interruption are inherent conditions of many of his works. In one of the only editorial statements he was

---

52. Jean Paul to Karl August Böttiger, August 20, 1825. SW HKA, III/8, 286.

53. Berend speculates that Jean Paul considered cutting out "the many inorganic 'extrapages' of his novels, which so frequently interrupt the flow of the narrative and annoy the reader," even though the author never carried this out. Berend, *Prolegomena*, 8.

54. Samuel Frederick has shown something similar in the case of Adalbert Stifter. See Samuel Frederick, *Narratives Unsettled: Digression in Robert Walser, Thomas Bernhard, and Adalbert Stifter* (Evanston, IL: Northwestern University Press, 2012), 160–61.

55. Andrew Nash, "The Culture of Collected Editions: Authorship, Reputation, and the Canon," in *The Culture of Collected Editions*, ed. Andrew Nash (New York: Palgrave Macmillan, 2003), 2.

able to include in the Reimer edition, Jean Paul addresses female readers in the edition's very first volume with the disclaimer that the *Invisible Lodge* is "born a ruin": "But what life in this world do we not see interrupted?"[56] Again, Jean Paul brings his (re)published work into resonance with his life and works, and it is almost as if the state of incompletion and interruption applies to his collected works.[57] In contrast to Berend's mid-twentieth-century edition and its status as a de facto *Ausgabe letzter Hand*, a new works edition project based in Würzburg, Germany, has sought to edit Jean Paul's works from a work-genetic perspective, collecting and annotating different versions of specific representative works on the basis of the *Nachlass*.[58] This new edition explores how works came into being and relies on digital formats to reproduce textual variants, in the process presenting readers with textual units that, as the editors put it, stand in decided tension with a stable notion of "the work."[59] Yet this is a project that is very clearly oriented to Jean Paul's unpublished writings and represents a different orientation to the authorial oeuvre than the republication of previously published works.

To be sure, the premise of "complete" works is usually merely aspirational, with the common distinction between "complete" (*sämtlich*) and ongoing, open-ended "collected" (*gesammelt*) works seldom holding up.[60] *Sämmtliche Werke* is the subtitle of Goethe's *Ausgabe letzter Hand*, for example, yet he would go on to add to this edition in the last years of his life. He also rejects the notion that works are complete in any absolute way: as published, they are in

---

56. "Welches Leben in der Welt sehen wir nicht unterbrochen?" Reimer I, installment 1, no. 1 (1826), ix.
57. Berhorst describes Jean Paul's novels as "non-teleological finitude[s] [*nichttelelogische Endlichkeit(en)*] that can break off and stop, but cannot be completed." Berhorst, *Anamorphose der Zeit*, 23.
58. On this new edition, see University of Würzburg, "Projektdetails," last accessed March 12, 2023, http://www.jean-paul-portal.uni-wuerzburg.de/neue-werkausgabe/pilotband-hesperus/projektdarstellung/projektdetails/.
59. See Hunfeld, "Eine neue Jean-Paul-Werkausgabe."
60. See Walther Morgenthaler, "Die Gesammelten und die Sämtlichen Werke: Anmerkungen zu zwei unterschätzten Werktypen," *Textkritische Beiträge* 10 (2005): 13–26.

their "last," rather than their truly finished, versions.[61] But as later nineteenth-century figures such as Börne, Heine, and Karl Gutzkow go on to anthologize writings first published in journals and newspapers in multivolume single-author collections, they align themselves more with Jean Paul's performative open-endedness and incompletion than with Goethe's careful curation of his self-development. Börne's announcement of his collected works edition—at the end of a republished collection of "Aphorisms and Miscellanies," no less—is a very Jean Paulian gesture: "I have not written any works. I have just tried my quill on this and that piece of paper; now the pages should be collected, laid on top of each other, and the book binder shall make them into books—this is all."[62] It is inherent to the poetics of miscellaneous *Werkchen* that they can be repackaged and repurposed in a variety of seemingly arbitrary ways and that readers' encounters with them are likewise organized by the felicitous and frustrating contingencies of miscellaneity.

Works editions also come to bear in important ways on the interrelated chronologies of life and works. Even while such editions tend to situate works in a dehistoricized, detemporalized pantheon alongside other edition-worthy authors, chronological organization likewise offers "an implicit biography of its author."[63] Such organization is a feature of later critical editions especially and was not yet standard practice in the early nineteenth century. Schiller's posthumous *Sämtliche Werke* (Complete works) (1812–1815) pursue such an ordering, for example, while Goethe's and many others' do not.[64] Goethe's reliance on genre hierarchy and his choice to add further volumes to the edition lend the *Ausgabe letzter Hand* a nonchronological structure. At the same time, though, Goethe states

---

61. "Wherever this term is used, it simply refers to the fact that the author has done his last and best, not that he is able to view his work as completed [*vollendet*]." Goethe "Anzeige," 98–99.
62. Ludwig Börne, "Gesammelte Schriften von Ludwig Börne," GS, 6, 205–10; SS, II, 330–34.
63. Michael Cahn, "*Opera Omnia*: The Production of Cultural Authority," in *History of Science, History of Text*, ed. Karine Chemla (Dordrecht: Springer, 2004), 92.
64. On this point see Plachta, "Goethe über das lästige Geschäft," 235.

that this edition is based on an organic model of the author's quasinatural self-development: it is to reveal "the author's nature, formation, progressing, and multifaceted striving in all directions" (*des Verfassers Naturell, Bildung, Fortschreiten und vielfaches Versuchen nach allen Seiten hin*), as he puts it in his 1826 advertisement for the edition in the *Morgenblatt*.[65] Jean Paul, in turn, is quite aware of the works edition's potential for self-historicization, which he spoofs on a small scale when prefacing anthologies with the "history" of the texts contained therein, that is, the details of their previous publication. The Reimer edition, rather than realizing Jean Paul's initial idea of journal-like mixed contents, hews rather close to the chronological survey of previously published works that Jean Paul presents at the end of his late novel *Der Komet* (The comet), but even this edition contains certain striking examples of temporal and generic heterogeneity.[66] In the seventh installment, for example, the first and second volumes contain the comic appendix to the novel from *Titan* (1800–1803); the third and fourth volumes contain the topical writings *Dämmerungen für Deutschland* (1809) and *Friedens-Predigt* (1808), respectively (the latter having been published prior to the former); and the fifth is *Jean Pauls Briefe und bevorstehender Lebenslauf*, published in 1799. This ordering might exhibit the lack of a plan mentioned by Berend, but it also bears the trace of a chronology more aligned with serial print than the author's biographical development. It would be up to the critical edition begun in the early twentieth century to provide a more coherent chronological organization of Jean Paul's works, but such editorial intervention entails a process of de-miscellanizing.

In a way, collected works editions are quintessentially serial forms that reveal the shared economy of journal and book publication characteristic of the nineteenth century, including the reliance on installment structure, the significance of advertisements and announcements in journals, the anthologizing of scattered journal pieces, and more.

---

65. Goethe, "Anzeige," 98.
66. See the "Ankündigung der Herausgabe meiner Sämtlichen Werke" at the end of Jean Paul, *Der Komet, oder Nikolaus Markgraf, eine komische Geschichte*, vol. 3 (Berlin: Reimer, 1820–1822).

But we have also seen how Jean Paul's works edition engages with serial structures under the sign of incomplete, plural *Werkchen*. To the extent that later editorial interventions seek to tamp down Jean Paul's initial embrace of miscellaneity, seriality, and self-interruption, these interventions give us a sense of the authorial and editorial control (*Werkherrschaft*) that Jean Paul deliberately flaunted. The Reimer edition thus represents a transitional moment in literary-historical terms; despite being tied to the contingencies of Jean Paul's death, it also betrays a certain amount of friction between his own authorial self-presentation and conventional notions of canonical authorship and literary bequest.

The *Papierdrache*

I'd now like to return to the *Werkchen* with which we began this chapter. Jean Paul's 1823–1824 "Ausschweife für künftige Fortsetzungen von vier Werken" (Digressions for future continuations of four works)[67] was one of the last, more substantive pieces published during his life, and it ended up being his last contribution to the *Morgenblatt*, though was not Jean Paul's actual "final word," as Berend's critical edition stylizes it.[68] In 1823, actual death was clearly more salient for him than it was almost twenty years earlier (he would die in November of 1825, at the age of sixty-two). Viewed in this light, this text represents an extended exploration of serial continuation as a response to the possibility of impending death. It appears in installments in the journal's last seven issues of 1823, concludes in the first issue of 1824, and is very much of a piece with

---

67. "Ausschweife für künftige Fortsetzungen von vier Werken," *Morgenblatt für gebildete Stände*, 17, nos. 304–7, 309–10, 313; 18, no. 1 (January 1, 1824); II/3, 1065–91.

68. In Berend's 1927 to 1964 edition, it is also presented as a concluding statement, and the editors even include a facsimile of Jean Paul's handwritten manuscript, presenting it as "das Letzte, was er in Druck gegeben hat," as his "last word," even though this is not accurate (!). SW HKA, I/18, xxxvii. In the Hanser edition edited by Miller, this piece is also placed at the end of *Vermischte Schriften*, the final volume of published writings of this edition.

Jean Paul's end-of-year discourses. It is presented as a set of continuations of four of his earlier novels, including *Der Komet*, or, more precisely, as a collection of digressions from continuations to come, following the format of *Der Komet*, in which Jean Paul seeks to give each individual chapter its own supplemental digression.[69] Like his novels, these digressions mix stock material from Jean Paul's oeuvre: fictionalized speeches, letters, scholarly and moral discourses, diaries, spoofs of pedantry, accounts of marital disputes, announcements for fictional and actual publications, aphorisms from fictional characters, and more, all in eight installments that add up to approximately twelve double-column pages of the *Morgenblatt*. Further complicating this piece's formal structure and temporal footprint is that these digressive continuations are themselves incomplete, introduced instead as excerpts of longer versions to come. Jean Paul demonstratively looks back to previous writings and forward to future ones, a gesture that creates a sense of continuity between past and present and also seeds future continuation. Furthermore, this gesture incorporates earlier novel projects into new structures of journal-based juxtaposition and proximity, doing the kind of work that a works edition organized in miscellaneous installments might do.

Elsewhere Jean Paul had made the same promise that he makes here—to present a last comic work "into which everything must be written—so that finally there will be an end of me and by me," including his last published novel, *Der Komet*, in which he also announces a cumulative "last work" titled the *Papierdrache*, or paper kite or dragon.[70] Indeed, the preface to the "Ausschweife" literally continues the novel's introduction, as Jean Paul reminds readers of

---

69. These are ostensibly continuations of uncompleted works, but, as Miller puts it, "these are self-standing contributions composed according to their own logics, though they resonate with each respective prototype in a refined way." Norbert Miller, in *Sämtliche Werke in 10 Bänden*, vol. II/4, ed. Norbert Miller (Stuttgart: Hanser, 1974–1985), 691.

70. The notion of a fantastical flying paper object profits off the near homonyms of *Drache* (dragon) and *Drachen* (kite) and the traditional association of comets with dragons. See Monika Schmitz-Emans, "*Der Komet* als ästhetische Programmschrift—poetologische Konzepte, Aporien, und ein Sündenbock," *Jahrbuch der Jean-Paul-Gesellschaft* 35/36 (2001): 76.

his announcement of the *Papierdrache* there and once more states his intention to publish a "last work" (*letztes Werk*) by this name.[71] This passage recapitulates the conceit from *The Spectator* "to Print my self out,"[72] and he goes on to further specify that, rather than operating as a single stand-alone volume, it should appear in octavo, "in the expansive form of a weekly periodical, like the English Spectator."[73] It was common for novels and works editions to be published in multiple volumes over several years, but this envisioned project takes this format to extremes.[74] Jean Paul did in fact work on this project in the last years of his life; posthumously published notes state that it is to have dual columns, like the *Morgenblatt*, and is to deal with the "newest," most current times.[75] And these notes are emphatic about this project's serial structure: it is to come out in "open-ended volumes" (*ungeschlossene Bände*); each article ideally refers both backward and forward in the hypothetical journal's run;[76] and "the continuation of a piece is always promised."[77] Jean Paul also intended to present himself as editor of this periodical work; the conceit of the author as editor of multiple fictional authors crops up in his earlier novels, in imitation of eighteenth-century moral weeklies. Indeed, an alternative name that Jean Paul considered was *Der Apotheker* (The apothecary), which was the title of an actual moral weekly and connoted the librarian-like collection of literary objects;[78] he likewise also conceptualized this as a baroque literary society, or "Fruit-Bearing Society."[79] As with the

---

71. Jean Paul, "Ausschweife," *Morgenblatt* 17, no. 304, 1214; II/3, 1066.
72. *Spectator* 1 (March 2, 1711).
73. Jean Paul, "Ausschweife," *Morgenblatt* 17, no. 304, 1214; II/3, 1067.
74. On this project see most recently Dennis Senzel, "Werkchen, die zum Werk werden. Zu Jean Pauls *Wochenschrift*," *Colloquia Germanica* 49, nos. 2–3 (2016): 119–36.
75. "Sie falle in die neuste Zeit"; "sie behandelt die neueste Zeit." SW HKA, II/6, 530.
76. "Die Aufsätze beziehen sich entweder auf das kommende oder auf das vergangene Kapitel." SW HKA, II/6, 523.
77. "Fortsetzung eines Stückes jedes mal vorausgesagt." SW HKA, II/6, 531.
78. "A library is the drugstore of the spirit; for this reason, here the apothecary is a librarian" (*Eine Bibliothek ist die Apotheke des Geistes; daher eben hier der Apotheker ein Bibliothekar ist*). SW HKA, II/6, 513.
79. SW HKA, II/6, 518.

collected works edition, the conceit of the author as (self-)editor is an important part of this project. Here, too, Jean Paul wants to get ahead of later philological curators of his literary bequest, preemptively spoofing the desire to print every last scrap of paper.

The emphatic seriality of this final work begs the question of the end: What exactly is the status of this "end of me and by me"? At first glance, Jean Paul seems to promise a definitive conclusion to his writing, and yet this finality becomes increasingly uncertain: as he puts it, the *Papierdrache* will be "a veritable overturned cornucopia, where all the windfall [*Fallobst*] still to come from writing and experiencing will be too much to be useful for anything, from which alone a length can be inferred, not to mention the final sheet [*Bogen*]."[80] Here Jean Paul interrupts himself at the thought of this future work's lack of conclusion and incompletion. Though it is his own work, he cannot presently predict how long it will become: the time the author has left to live could be so excessively productive that the writing that comes from it cannot be properly contained in any kind of conventional work. We are dealing once more with an end under the sign of continuation or continuation under the sign of the end. In a departure, though, from the "Abschiedsrede" and the "Konjektural-Biographie," which both stage an author late in life exhibiting retrospective control over his works, this piece envisions a scenario where the author's writings elude his control. This begs the question of the *Papierdrache*'s status as an emblem of permanent continuation.

The fourth and final segment of the "Ausschweife" brings the interrelationship of authorial life, death, and the time of literary production to an at least provisional conclusion. Reckoning with death and the relationship of writing to the unfolding of life is a pervasive topic in Jean Paul's late work, and the final segment of the "Ausschweife" is titled "Trostantwort auf Ottomars Klage über die Zeitlichkeit des Lebens (Extrablatt aus dem dritten Bande der unsichtbaren Loge)" (Consolation to Ottomar's lament about the temporality of life [Extra page from the third vol-

---

80. Jean Paul, "Ausschweife," *Morgenblatt* 17, no. 304, 1214; II/3, 1066.

ume of *The Invisible Lodge*]), and it is published on January 1, 1824.⁸¹ In effect, this is a "continuation" of the planned first work in the collected works edition, a perfect instantiation of Jean Paul's oeuvre as a network of interrelated texts. In the 1793 novel *Die unsichtbare Loge* (Jean Paul's first), the figure Ottomar is dramatically taken for dead and buried alive, again part of the protobaroque "constellation of death and rebirth"⁸² that is so central to his authorial brand. In *Die unsichtbare Loge*, this leads to an extended meditation on time, something which this "continuation" continues.

As the title states, this final piece has two parts: Ottomar's lament and a consoling response from an unnamed figure. Ottomar is unable to orient himself in the "flowing by of moments" (*Verfließen der Augenblicke*) and the corresponding "flowing by of people." The rejoining advice is rather simple: "Do something!"

> Make a campaign—[draft] a building plan—[write] an instructional book—[make] an artwork—even [take] a trip: the time of the present loses or hides its rolling away through your stride and your gaze toward a future that remains immobile; indeed, the fleetingness of time turns into the inertia of a non-time.⁸³

To distract oneself by having a clear goal in the future creates the impression of delaying time's passing. This solution is both secular and deeply Christian, for the orientation toward a temporalized future is grounded in the insight that a detemporalized future in God redeems worldly suffering. This also represents a moral technology of manipulating the experience of time, turning transience into sluggishness, slowing time down almost to the point of detemporalization. Paradoxically, Jean Paul proposes an orientation to pervasive ephemerality that seeks to decelerate the passing of the ephemeral. It is, of course, no accident that he once more invokes the process of writing: "[make] an artwork." He places the trope of authorial fecundity in the service

---

81. Jean Paul, "Ausschweife," *Morgenblatt* 18, no. 1, 2–4; II/3, 1086–91.
82. See Götz Müller, "'Ich vergesse den 15.November nie,'" 134.
83. Jean Paul, "Ausschweife," *Morgenblatt* 18, no. 1, 2–4; II/3, 1090.

of scaling time and of dilating the time of the present and near future as much as possible; we saw this gesture in both the "Konjektural-Biographie" and the "Abschiedsrede," in which the time between the present and death is configured simultaneously as an all-too-brief moment and as a more extended period that writing might stretch out indefinitely. Two different modes of writing determine the future, namely the conceptualization of a teleological work as point of orientation and a kind of ongoing writing that unfolds almost frantically over time. We are dealing here with the Scheherazade-like desire to stave off death through writing: working toward a "final work," continuing previously started individual works in the present, and promising more of them into the future are forms of writing into the future by serial means.[84]

This scene is both an extended spoof of the gesture of making a literary bequest to posterity and an all-too-pragmatic piece of moral-stoic advice, and these are the coordinates upon which Jean Paul operates as a writer of time and of the end. But what, then, if Jean Paul himself followed the advice of the unnamed respondent to Ottomar's despair? What would his response be to the call to "do something!" and "[make] an artwork"? Several possibilities come into view as points of future work–poetic orientation. On the one hand, the future work(s) might be the very continuations that the "Ausschweife" announces and prefigures. On the other hand, Jean Paul does describe the *Papierdrache* as a substantial and final opus. Are the "Ausschweife" foretastes of this later, more expansive work? Publication in the *Morgenblatt* certainly approximates the format conditions of a periodical-like work. As a last work, though, the *Papierdrache* also is the culmination of Jean Paul's life and works, and perhaps the collected works edition itself, with the *Papierdrache* as its capstone, is to serve as the unmoving future telos. Jean Paul is writing toward this edition, with the *Papierdrache* as its emblem, writing his own life as he goes. Each of these possible points of future orientation is both fixed and forever continuing. This imaginary network of future last

---

84. On digression as writing against death, see Wieland, *Vexierzüge*, 304.

works, each mirroring one another in different ways, encapsulates a vision of an oeuvre as ongoing miscellany.

Jean Paul's Literary Afterlives

The frame of time between the present of writing and future death must inevitably close, yet there are certain ways in which Jean Paul's works live on under the sign of ongoing generation and continuation. Like the paradox of a telos that is simultaneously fixed and unfixed, the finitude of individual life is a limiting condition that both does and does not apply to Jean Paul's oeuvre. Along with writing into the space of time before death, Jean Paul poses the question of the after: What comes after the author? What are the afterlives of a body of work, especially a body of miscellaneous *Werkchen*? When does his fictional "Fruit-Bearing Society" take over the *Papierdrache* and let him enjoy his retirement? Here we might explore several horizons in which literary afterlives unfold, horizons of future reception and production that Jean Paul himself anticipates and spoofs.

The first such vista is what we might call the *philological horizon*. Jean Paul was indeed unable to realize the *Papierdrache* in published form, and some of his draft material was published several decades after his death, in 1845. In contrast to the continuation of the *Morgenblatt* announced in 1807, the *Papierdrache* is never delivered. Writing with an end in sight becomes a way to forestall the end but only for so long; this, at least, is the vision of the incompletion of the *Papierdrache* as a "failure," as Helmut Pfotenhauer puts it.[85] But a failure in the hands of a dying author can be success in the hands of a philologist, with editors of the posthumous works taking over the task of reproducing and reprinting these works. Incomplete writings call out for the philological processing and critical revival of unfinished work, and this, too, is a kind of figural and literal continuation.

---

85. Helmut Pfotenhauer, "Das Leben Schreiben- das Schreiben Leben: Jean Paul als Klassiker der Zeitverfallenheit," *Jahrbuch der Jean- Paul- Gesellschaft* 35–56 (2000/2001): 58.

Indeed, new volumes of Berend's original critical edition are still being published up to this day, as are volumes of the new work–genetic edition. Ongoing critical editions become different kinds of literary monuments erected by those who come after Jean Paul. As the editors of the *Nachlass* argue, Jean Paul's unpublished manuscripts, letters, notebooks, and more allow for a fuller picture of Jean Paul's life and works, and it is philological work that enables continued encounters and reencounters with the author.[86] To be sure, with the *Papierdrache*, Jean Paul spoofed this desire to collect any- and everything from the author, preemptively putting as much into print as possible. This kind of philological work comes into view as a slightly less entertaining doppelgänger of the *Papierdrache*, a collection of the myriad ephemera that Jean Paul did not have the chance to put into print.

Considering Jean Paul's writings as ever oriented to continuation and revivification also catalyzes what we might call the *horizon of the kindred reader*, one well disposed to the author who rediscovers his myriad *Werkchen*. A sense of Jean Paul as a writer of the present and of unknown futures of course informs Börne's eulogy for Jean Paul and his conceit of Jean Paul waiting for "his people" at the gate to the twentieth century. Börne's is a vision of Jean Paul's works strongly oriented around the semantics of life and original authorial "spirit": "No hero, no poet has made known of his life so honestly as Jean Paul has done. The spirit has disappeared, the word has remained!"[87] For Börne, the rediscovery of his works is a kind of memorialization, a commemoration of individual works, but also of his life, a gesture the eulogistic speech performs. Such a scene of future reception is diametrically opposed to readings of Jean Paul as solely of his time and hence closed off to the present and inaccessible to modern readers or as culturally late. Though Börne eulogizes Jean Paul as a contemporary, as a writer of freedom in an age of repression, his person-oriented treatment nonetheless runs the

---

86. Indeed, Pfotenhauer writes that his new biography of Jean Paul was only possible on the basis of new material discovered in the *Nachlass*. Pfotenhauer, "Das Leben Schreiben-," 19.

87. Börne, "Denkrede auf Jean Paul," 1179.

risk of decontextualized monumentalization. The high style of Börne's eulogy performs certain functions similar to those of the classicizing works edition, lacking the ironic twists that we saw in the *Jubelrede*. Walter Benjamin would take Max Kommerell to task for literary-historical monumentalization in Kommerell's account of Jean Paul as a classical German poet (despite his anticlassical aesthetics) and as "Poet-Leader."[88] For Benjamin, Jean Paul's works express the intractable political contradictions of the Biedermeier period, and Kommerell's treatment of the author decontextualizes his work: "In Kommerell, the poet's head looms bare against the grey backdrop of eternity."[89] Here, too, the evocation of person and work go hand in hand.

One might take a different, less author-centered tack through what we can call the *"birth of serial literature from the death of the author" horizon*. The miscellanies stamped with Jean Paul's name peter out with his death, but they are followed by ever more textual units produced by the daily/weekly/monthly necessities of the business of serial print: this is the horizon of the periodic patterns of book fairs, periodicals, and multiauthor anthologies continuing on, as Helmut Müller-Sievers puts it, "like the world on the day after our death."[90] In the same way that time unfolds by one moment following another, there is no real end to miscellaneity as a motor of the print landscape. It is perhaps fitting that Jean Paul uses the scene of never-ending production by a fictional "Fruit-Bearing Society" as a way to imagine his own death as an author, merging back into an endless and endlessly miscellaneous ocean of print. From this perspective, the spirit of Jean Paul lives on as much in writings stamped with his name as in sites and styles of print characterized by

---

88. Walter Benjamin, "Wider ein Meisterwerk: Zu Max Kommerell, 'Der Dichter als Führer in der deutschen Klassik,'" in *Gesammelte Schriften*, vol. 3, ed. Rolf Tiedemann and Hermann Schweppenhäuser (Frankfurt: Suhrkamp, 1972), 253–54. On this episode in Jean Paul's reception, see also Böck, "Archäologie in der Wüste," 246–51.

89. Walter Benjamin, "Der Eingetunkte Zauberstab: Zu Max Kommerell's 'Jean Paul,'" in *Gesammelte Schriften*, vol. 3, 413.

90. Helmut Müller-Sievers, "Kinematik des Erzählens: Zum Stand der amerikanischen Fernsehserie," *Merkur* 64, no. 794 (2015): 29.

miscellaneity and seriality. In what ways do Jean Paul's writings open up a horizon onto subsequent serial modes of the nineteenth century? Perhaps this takes us back to the crucial impasse of "Jean Paul versus Goethe"[91]: to be sure, dominant strands of the nineteenth-century *Bildungspresse* (including the *Morgenblatt*) are oriented around an emphatic vision of Goethean *Bildung* and the project of lending life harmonic organic form through literary entertainment.[92] But what about the strands of the publication landscape that delve more playfully and self-reflectively into the ways that the self and life come to be refracted through ephemeral print and serial writing? Is it not in the multiple *Spectator* and *Zuschauer* journals, where the spirit of Jean Paul lives on; in the fools, devils, and charivaris that personify the periodical landscape of the nineteenth century; and in the many deliberately and provocatively contingent receptacles for miscellaneous contents?

Situating Jean Paul's body of work in analogy to the print landscape more generally puts the world of print (to the extent that it makes sense to create a notional idea of it) in the position of the *Papierdrache*. In effect, this entails viewing Jean Paul as programming a future history of miscellaneity, with the *Papierdrache* becoming a foil for imagining ongoing serialized production.[93] Jean Paul's promise of more to come is a promise of more by him and also by others. The series in which this "more"—this "after"—stands is a series not just of the ever new but also of continuations of older things as well, continued at different, heterogeneous paces: recall how the "Ausschweife" goes back to old pieces rather than simply producing new ones. The texts to which one returns through a kind of memorializing reading and through an ever-growing notional ar-

---

91. See Norbert Miller, "Jean Paul versus Goethe. Der Dichter und die Forderung des Tages. Jean Pauls Vermischte Schriften als Teil seiner Wirkungsgeschichte," in *Sämtliche Werke in 10 Bänden*, vol. II/4, 459–96.

92. See Maximilian Nutz, "Das Beispiel Goethe. Zur Konstituierung eines nationalen Klassikers," in *Wissenschaftsgeschichte der Germanistik im 19. Jahrhundert*, ed. Jürgen Fohrmann and Wilhelm Voßkamp (Stuttgart: Metzler, 1994), 605–37.

93. Pfotenhauer points to something similar when conjecturing about Jean Paul's interest in automated mechanisms of writing: "Jean Paul seeks writing mechanisms that never end, a sort of writing machine that can be automatized and can write onto into infinity by itself." Pfotenhauer, "Das Leben Schreiben-," 390.

chive constitute a heterogeneous textual network, not a detemporalized body of work, but rather works that can be rearranged into new serial formations, temporalized in new and different ways.

Yet this brings us to a final paradox, the paradox expressed in Jean Paul's assertion that "his" miscellanies are emphatically his— the paradox, too, at the level of literary-historical method, of looking for traces of a depersonalized media landscape in and through individual author figures, as I undeniably do in this book. It would be wrong to claim that Jean Paul isn't constantly underlining the fact that his works are just that: his. But he does take us up to the brink of this paradox, or, to shift the metaphor, he takes us to a horizon where the gaze back in time surveys the endless accumulation of ephemeral, miscellaneous writings and the gaze forward in time looks ahead to a never-ending, unruly, serial proliferation of more textual units.

Part III

Contemporary Histories (*Zeitgeschichten*)

Heine's 1840 book *Heinrich Heine über Ludwig Börne* (Heinrich Heine on Ludwig Börne), published three years after Börne's untimely death, provides an account of his two encounters with Börne, first in Frankfurt in the 1820s and again in Paris in the fall of 1831. More than a mere portrait of his friend and rival, Heine's memoir characterizes the turbulent times in which his generation came into its own. It includes an account of his initial enthusiastic response to the July Revolution of 1830 in the form of a series of letters dating from that summer. Supposedly written from the resort island of Heligoland off the northern coast of Germany, the letters show how Heine first learns of the events in France in early August, more than a week after the "three glorious days" of late July. Immersing himself in the history of late antiquity and the Bible, with "the holy prehistorical world roving like long caravan processions through [his] mind,"[1]

---

1. Heinrich Heine, *Ludwig Börne: A Memorial*, trans. Jeffrey L. Sammons (Rochester, NY: Camden House, 2006), 32. Translation altered.

Heine relates how the arrival of a packet of newspapers interrupts his studies: "I was reading this story ... when the fat packet of newspapers with warm, glowing hot news arrived from the mainland. They were sunbeams wrapped in printing paper, and they inflamed my soul into the wildest blaze."[2] This exposure to the latest news leads Heine to cut short his trip to the North Sea and set off to see the revolution with his own eyes. Ephemeral print converts him (at least initially) to a belief in progress and a commitment to the revolution.

This series of letters (fictionalized, as we now know[3]) captures the intensity of his initial enthusiasm for what became the defining political event for the many liberal thinkers of the day. The letters also stage the confrontation between different kinds of writing, different kinds of print, and different kinds of history writing, with the papers' accounts of the flow of revolutionaries on the streets of Paris supplanting biblical accounts of processions of ancient peoples. They capture the excitement of the moment, yet their belated publication relativizes the immediacy of Heine's enthusiasm. This episode also sets two medially conditioned delays in motion, including the delay in the papers reaching him, underlining Heine's remote location, and the delay in the letters' finally reaching the public nine years after their (supposed) initial composition. Delay characterizes the position of the German observer of the revolution and also the position of historical reflection, as he casts his thoughts and feelings from 1830 in new light. Heine writes himself into history, placing his own activities of reading and writing into a position of historical remove and entering into a historical relationship to himself. He writes a dual present, that of 1830 and of 1840, as he reflects on the events following 1830 in the remainder of his memoir.

Heine's stylized account of his awakening as a writer engaged with the present day reflects several key themes of this third part of the

---

2. Heine, *Ludwig Börne*, 40.
3. Jeffrey L. Sammons calls these texts a retrospectively written "phantom text" with no firm basis in actual letters. Jeffrey L. Sammons, "Introduction," in Heine, *Ludwig Börne*, xxxii.

book. The years leading up to and after the revolutions of 1830 and 1848 continue to be an era of temporal uncertainty, as the European old order seeks to stem the tide of the revolution, censorship regimes tighten, and partial revolutions reverberate in fits and starts across the continent. The 1830s see a blossoming of the periodical press and of cultural journalism, another key period after the 1790s.[4] Writing for journals and newspapers is one of the most important forms of expression and means of survival for liberal writers such as Börne and Heine: both attempt to found journals, and both are correspondents for the *Morgenblatt* and other publications, including Cotta's Augsburg-based *Allgemeine Zeitung*, the most important political newspaper of the time in Germany. With other means of institutional and political activity largely inaccessible due to their political commitments and Jewish family backgrounds, Börne and Heine choose journalism and cultural criticism as their primary mode of countering the repressive governments of German-speaking lands; as Heine puts it, "journals are our fortifications."[5] Both writers grapple with how to have a concrete effect on the world through journalistic writing. In asserting the ability of journals to shape the course of the present day, Börne programmatically self-identifies as a *Zeitschriftsteller*, a term that suggests a "writer" about "time," in the service of the "times," as well as a writer for periodicals.[6]

Heine's demonstrative gesture of setting off to the French capital in his Heligoland letters is based in biographical fact, but the gesture also carries broader symbolic weight. Heine and Börne both come into their own as exiles writing from Paris, sending their reports back to Germany along the same distribution routes by which the news of July 1830 originally reached Heine. Paris is by all accounts the center of Europe at the time: "Trips to Paris are trips to the historical present,"

---

4. Schmid calls the *Vormärz* "the true *Gründerzeit*" of the German press. Ulrich Schmid, "Buchmarkt und Literaturvermittlung," in *Zwischen Restauration und Revolution 1815–1848, Hanser Sozialgeschichte der deutschen Literatur*, vol. 5, ed. Gert Sautermeister and Ulrich Schmid (Munich: Hanser, 1998), 70.

5. Heinrich Heine to Gustav Kolb, November 11, 1828. HSA, 20, 350.

6. The term was already in use in the late eighteenth century, though Börne is often erroneously credited with coining it. D'Aprile, *Die Erfindung der Zeitgeschichte*.

as Oesterle puts it, and the period prompts newly urgent reflections on the temporal category of the present.[7] Like other German exiles, Heine and Börne mediate between Germany and France, using commentary on French affairs as a way to educate German readers about the political and cultural trends underway since 1789 and exposing French readers to German letters and society. Both writers are frequently translated into French and attempt to found journals in French. In addition to being an epicenter for world-historical events, Paris is also a hotbed of the most up-to-date historical studies, academic or otherwise, and Heine and Börne comment on and review the latest histories as they come out. They entertain the idea of writing a conventional history of the revolution yet end up rejecting forms and conventions of academic history writing—including the scene of the lectures and large, comprehensive histories of specific epochs—and embrace more journalistic modes. In contrast to Prussian historians such as Ranke, who adopt positions of quasi-official state historians, or French liberal historians such as Thiers, Michelet, and Mignet, who play leading roles in political and academic offices, Heine and Börne adopt the position of cosmopolitan observers addressing broader publics.

In studying their experiments in serial writing, I build on longstanding scholarly discussions about the role of journalistic publication (*Publizistik*) in the *Vormärz*.[8] But why do these figures warrant reconsideration now? For one, it is important to pay closer attention to their deliberate use of specific print formats, something often overlooked by more traditional intellectual-historical scholarship. Both figures' writings are characterized by a high level of self-awareness about the implications of different serial formats, and their writings shape their authorial self-understandings accordingly. I also consider anew how Börne and Heine are involved in various kinds of history writing based specifically in serial form. Both engage in projects of

---

7. Ingrid Oesterle, "Der 'Führungswechsel der Zeithorizonte' in der deutschen Literatur. Korrespondenzen aus Paris, der Hauptstadt der Menschheitsgeschichte, und die Ausbildung der geschichtlichen Zeit 'Gegenwart,'" in *Studien zur Ästhetik und Literatur der Kunstperiode*, ed. Dirk Grathoff (Frankfurt: Peter Lang, 1985), 15.

8. See Wolfgang Preisendanz, "Der Funktionsübergang von Dichtung und Publizistik bei Heine," in *Die nicht mehr schönen Künste: Grenzphänomene des Ästhetischen*, ed. Hans Robert Jauss (Munich: Fink, 1968), 343–74.

contemporary history writing, or what Heine calls "writing the history of the present" (*Geschichtsschreibung der Gegenwart*). Writing both in dialogue with and in opposition to academic historians and philosophers such as Ranke or Hegel, Heine and Börne chart new paths for the writing of history at the intersections of cultural journalism, literary fiction, and philosophical reflection. Though the question of Heine's relationship to the idealist philosophy of history has been well explored in the secondary literature, reframing these discussions via the question of serial form sheds new light on the historiographical accomplishments of both figures.

Both figures follow the lead of Jean Paul in embracing miscellaneous modes of writing at the intersection of fiction, satire, and journalism. Börne models his writing on contemporary Parisian journals: "That would be entirely my genre. Everything short, jumping from one thing to the other."[9] Heine likewise adopts long-standing and, at first glance, pejorative designations of journalism when he deems his correspondence reports for the *Allgemeine Zeitung* "fleeting pages" (*flüchtige Blätter*).[10] Both embrace modes of writing based in the serial succession of small forms, including the letter, the review, the sketch, the tableau, and more. These mixed forms are tied to the format of the periodical, but they also parallel the structure and temporality of the revolution itself: as Heine puts it in his memoir on Börne, "that political earthquake, the July Revolution, exploded relationships in all spheres of life to such an extent and threw together the most dissimilar phenomena, that the Parisian correspondent of the revolution only needed to report faithfully what he saw and heard to automatically achieve the highest level of humor."[11] The realization that the revolution is structured serially and brings forth a proliferation of serial forms is thus at the heart of Heine's and Börne's literary and historiographical project.[12]

---

9. "Das wäre so ganz mein Genre. Alles kurz, von einem zum andern springend." Börne, *Briefe aus Paris*. GS, IV, 637.

10. Heine, *Fränzösische Zustände*, vi.

11. Heine, *Ludwig Börne*, 88.

12. The serial structure of the 1848 revolutions in particular is the topic of Clare Pettitt, *Serial Revolutions 1848: Writing, Politics, Form* (Oxford: Oxford University Press, 2022).

The witty juxtapositional style that these figures inherit from Jean Paul likewise draws explicitly on visual logics, with the titles of Börne's 1822 to 1824 *Schilderungen aus Paris* (Scenes from Paris) and Heine's *Reisebilder* (Travel pictures) (1826–1831) effectively setting new standards for the already quite popular German literature of the urban tableau and travelogue.[13] Börne and Heine position the serial modes of the urban tableau, portrait, and caricature against older media such as historical books, rhetoric, and portraiture, embracing small forms as windows onto the present and its multiple historical refractions. Of course, criticisms of the literary merits of cultural journalism are all too common in the period; Georg Büchner, an important contemporary, rejects the conviction that writing for journals (*die Tagesliteratur*) might directly lead to restructuring societal relations.[14] Writing in periodicals is commonly dismissed for its frivolous miscellaneity; a contemporary critic called Börne's *Briefe Aus Paris* (Letters from Paris) "empty, boring coffeehouse- and newspaper-chatter, observations gathered from the surface, just like those that thousands of impudent reasoning 'critics' make on a daily basis."[15] Later in the twentieth century, Karl Kraus (himself a journal editor) would lay the blame for journals' and newspapers' banalization of language at Heine's feet, dismissing anthology collections such as the *Reisebilder* as "making bread out of bread crumbs."[16] We are well served to remind ourselves of the precarious status of Heine's and Börne's conscious embrace of small occasional forms, both in the contemporary literary scene and at later historical junctures.

Both figures also embrace the literary-aesthetic (and financial) potential of republishing works in single-author serial anthology edi-

---

13. The French title of the *Reisebilder* is *Tableaux de voyage*.

14. "*For my own part* I do not in any way belong to the so-called *Junges Deutschland*, the literary faction of Gutzkow and Heine. Only a complete misrecognition of our social conditions [*Nur ein völliges Mißkennen unserer gesellschaftlichen Verhältnisse*] could make people believe that the daily writing for journals could make possible the complete transformation of our religious and social ideas." Georg Büchner, *Werke und Briefe* (Munich: Hanser, 1980), 279.

15. Börne cites this critique by Eduard Meyer in his *Letters from Paris*. SS, III, 362.

16. Jonathan Franzen, *The Kraus Project: Essays by Karl Kraus* (New York: Farrar, Straus and Giroux, 2013), 55.

tions. The transition to book form establishes a stronger authorial voice, preempts unauthorized anthologizing, and places articles into new textual relationships, including via new transitions, beginnings, and ends. Republication also serves as a form of reverse remediation that incorporates the logic of the periodical into the collected works edition, as we have already seen in the case of Jean Paul. As we will see, Heine's and Börne's republication experiments work with temporal structures of historical delay and anticipation that are materialized through the details and format conditions of print publication. Both authors stage the scene of revisiting older materials, emphasizing the potential for reappraisal of the past as a basic feature of temporal and historical awareness. Heine calls his writings "historical files" on which future historians will rely, but he himself treats them in this very manner. Attending to the publication details of these works allows us new insight into how material formats shape temporal awareness, a feature of their work that subsequent critical editions often overlook.

This brings us to the historiographical stakes of their writings. Like Jean Paul, both write time according to the unruly temporalities of the periodical, yet they are more invested in explicitly historical discourse than Jean Paul. Part of this is simply because a wide range of new sites and styles of history writings emerge in the 1820s and 1830s in tandem with a wide range of new historical developments. For the generation of figures following on Goethe and Jean Paul, the July Revolution gives new meaning to the idea that the revolution is ongoing and can be reactualized. The prospect of the revolution repeating itself (whether as tragedy or farce, in Marx's famous misquote of Hegel) and continuing into the present and future lends new urgency to the question of the history of the revolution, as new models for the progression and "scripting" of revolution emerge.[17] The academic discipline of history is also still in formation in the first half of the nineteenth century. Prior to the

---

17. See Keith Michael Baker and Dan Edelstein, "Introduction," in *Scripting Revolution: A Historical Approach to the Comparative Study of Revolutions*, ed. Keith Michael Baker and Dan Edelstein (Stanford, CA: Stanford University Press, 2015), 1–24, 4.

nineteenth century, the term *Zeitgeschichte* had been understood as applying to all history writing, but in the early nineteenth century it increasingly comes to be associated with the present and very recent past.[18] As Koselleck and Oesterle have shown, writing ongoing, open-ended contemporary histories increasingly falls out of the standard professional practice of the historical sciences, while writing the present increasingly becomes the purview of literary writing and criticism, as historians opt to describe historical events in the past that are "finished" from the perspective of historical overview.[19] Serial forms—the lecture, journal, and book and anthology series—are both timely and untimely: they propel developments in the processing of the recent past, and yet they are disparaged and rejected by the gatekeepers of historical knowledge production.

In contrast to the commonplace that history progresses linearly and necessarily on the basis of the movement of the concept (as in Hegel's idealism), the material conditions of economic production (as Marx would later elaborate), or the Heraclitan flow from one internally coherent historical epoch to another (as nineteenth-century historicism teaches), Börne and Heine explore deliberately provisional modes of history writing, showing both how present-day constellations cast an ever-shifting light on the past and how the past comes to be revalued and reappropriated in new situations.[20] They ask readers to understand historical time as an unruly mixture of old and new, to consider how different aspects of the past can continue to have effects in the present, and to understand the revolution as a continuing process, one that is unpredictable and based in multiple contingencies rather than "a historico-philosophical concept based on a perspective which displayed a constant and steady direction toward the future," as Koselleck puts it in regard to the philosophy of history.[21] Even if both figures are ever oriented to the

---

18. See Koselleck, "Constancy and Change," 100–17, 110–11.
19. Oesterle, "Der 'Führungswechsel der Zeithorizonte,'" 20.
20. "The historicist is the Heraclitean of the human world: everything is in flux; no one steps twice into the river of history." Frederick C. Beiser, *The German Historicist Tradition* (Oxford: Oxford University Press, 2011), 2.
21. Reinhart Koselleck, "Historical Criteria of the Modern Concept of Revolution," in *Futures Past: On the Semantics of Historical Time*, trans. Keith Tribe

possibility of future revolution, both are ambivalent about shapes of monodirectional historical time, and both engage with serial form in order to undercut naive notions of progress and of the unprecedented newness of the present. Their contemporary histories are not "completed" historical narratives that deliver the final word about a given historical period. Rather, they give indeterminacy and contingency provisional shape via specific constellations of text and image.

(New York: Columbia University Press, 2004), 51. An irony of Koselleck's treatment of nineteenth-century figures is that, even while writing against the modern philosophy of history that emerges in the period, Koselleck lumps liberal authors such as Heine and Börne into a larger perspective of a linear vision of history and historical progress toward the revolution. For example, he situates Heine among other democrats of the 1830s and 1840s who shared a vision of an ongoing, permanent progressive revolution. See Reinhart Koselleck et al., "Revolution, Rebellion, Aufruhr, Bürgerkrieg," in *Geschichtliche Grundbegriffe. Historisches Lexikon zur politisch-sozialen Sprache in Deutschland*, vol. 5 (Stuttgart: Klett-Cotta, 1972), 762.

6

WAITING FOR THE REVOLUTION
(LUDWIG BÖRNE)

Ludwig Börne was born in 1786 as Löb or Louis Baruch in Frankfurt, a city with a historically large Jewish community. As a young man, Börne studied in Berlin with Markus Herz, a well-known Jewish student of Kant's and an accomplished doctor and scholar, and took part in the influential Romantic era salon presided over by Herz's wife, Henriette. Börne attained a doctorate in law in Giessen, converted to Christianity in 1818, and became a writer and editor of various journals, making a name for himself for his biting drama criticism addressing broader societal issues. As the 1820s progressed, he was a liberal critic of restoration powers and an inspirational voice for the Young Germany movement and its struggle against Restoration era censorship. He was acquaintances with Heine and then broke with him over what he perceived to be Heine's deficient political commitment, as Börne became increasingly radical in the 1830s. Börne lived and wrote in Paris from the early 1830s until his untimely death in 1837 and sought to enlist cultural entertainment and literary criticism in the effort to politicize a quickly growing reading public. His friend and confidant Jeanette Wohl played an important role in his life as a steady interlocutor, including as the implied addressee of his *Briefe aus Paris* (Letters from Paris), Börne's most influential work.

Börne is a compelling case as a journalist, critic, and historical thinker, for he confronts the temporal complexities of the Restoration and the July Revolution head-on, describing how traces of the past, both of the *ancient régime* and of the 1789 Revolution, haunt the present and how new democratic ideas promising future transformation arise even as repressive censorship regimes limit access to them. Scholarship on the *Vormärz* has explored Börne's role in debates about German identity, the influence of *Briefe aus Paris* on younger generations, and his role in "classic German Paris literature," as Karlheinz Stierle puts it.[1] In this chapter, I take a closer look at his specific uses of print formats to write time, including periodicals and books that take on the shape of periodicals.[2] Examining Börne's experiments with serial forms offers a helpful counterbalance to accounts of his supposed deficiencies as a historical thinker. In his memoir about Börne, Heine suggested that he was solely focused on the present day: in contrast to Jean Paul, who "rummaged about in the lumber rooms of all ages and ranged around through all parts of the world with seven-league boots, Börne had his eye only on the present day, and the objects that occupied him all lay within his immediate horizon."[3] Subsequent scholars have reiterated this conclusion as part of the post–World War II reevaluation of the legacies of the *Vormärz*.[4] In contrast to

---

1. See Karlheinz Stierle, *Der Mythos von Paris. Zeichen und Bewußtsein der Stadt* (Munich: Hanser, 1993), 205.
2. What Andreas Beck and Volker Mergenthaler call "journal-shaped books" (*journalförmige Bücher*). Andreas Beck and Volker Mergenthaler, ed., *Journalförmige Bücher—buchförmige Journale, Pfennig-Magazin zur Journalliteratur*, vol. 8 (Hanover: Wehrhahn, 2022).
3. Heine, *Ludwig Börne*, 8.
4. Norbert Oellers's judgment on this front is representative: "Börne was equally unphilosophical and unhistorical." Norbert Oellers, "Ludwig Börne," in *Deutsche Dichter des 19. Jahrhunderts. Ihr Leben und Werk*, ed. Benno von Wiese (Berlin: Erich Schmidt, 1969), 132.

both contemporary and retrospective dismissals of Börne as a historical thinker, I propose we reconsider his work as an intervention in the writing of *Zeitgeschichte*.

In this chapter I turn first to Börne's reflections on several different writing and editing projects he is involved in, including his journals and his collected works edition; in both cases, he programmatically suggests that the ephemerality of the periodical tells us something essential about the times. Even while embracing the periodical format, he does not rely on notions of regular periodicity, choosing instead to publish in irregular installments, or *zwanglose Hefte*. This extends to his volumes of *Gesammelte Schriften* (Collected writings) (1829–1837), which start coming out in 1829 and to which he adds newly generated material over the course of the 1830s. Like his idol Jean Paul, Börne positions his collected works edition in proximity or analogy to periodical publication, thereby engaging with the potential of republication to reactualize works from the past. The remainder of the chapter concerns Börne's 1832 to 1834 *Briefe aus Paris*, which appeared in six volumes as part of his *Gesammelte Schriften*. Here Börne tries his hand at the conventions of the letter format, long a popular mode of open-ended journalistic and literary correspondence. His *Briefe aus Paris* volumes are an innovative engagement with serial literature, and they mimic the format of the periodical in several important ways. In them, Börne foregrounds themes of delay and waiting. Waiting is a crucial part of serial forms, for the present installment always promises the next one, yet the break between installments prompts us to experience time in new ways.[5] Börne orients himself and his readers vis-à-vis the future through notions of waiting and delay that are shaped by the irregular seriality of print.

---

5. As Mark W. Turner puts it, "Built into the notion of seriality is necessarily some conception of waiting. The pause is a constitutive feature of periodical-ness, of all periodicities—there must be a break in time. What is important about this break is that it is the space that allows us to communicate." Mark W. Turner, "Periodical Time in the Nineteenth Century," *Media History* 8, no. 2 (2002): 183–96, 193.

Diaries of the Times

Can Sugar Beets Fly?

In July of 1819, Börne announces that he is taking over the editorship of the journal *Die Zeitschwingen* (The wings of time). In this first issue as editor, he demonstratively excises the subtitle "flying pages of the German people" (*des deutschen Volkes fliegende Blätter*) from the journal's title page. Since their inception in the seventeenth century, newspapers have been associated with flight and impermanence; the term "flyer" (*Flugblatt*) or "flying pages" (*fliegende Blätter*) is taken from the French *feuille volante*, which refers more to occasional print products—leaflets, flyers—than to recurring journals, though this connection became more common in the late eighteenth century.[6] In deleting this subtitle, Börne highlights the Germans' lack of freedom, their inability to "fly": in the wake of the French Revolution, they were briefly lifted into the air but have since fallen back down to earth.[7] This prefatory "Announcement" also references the current lack of political and social freedom via a bookish metaphor: the restoration is an age of parchment, not paper, and "the beautiful pigskin era [*schweinslederne Zeit*] of folio volumes returns with heavy steps."[8] Ironically, the imagined throwback to vellum pages and pigskin binding—and thus to the slowness and heft of handwritten manuscripts and large premodern printed books—is characterized by a periodicity analogous to (but much slower than) that of the periodical. This is a conservative form of reverse remediation, in which restoration forces are metaphorized through the idea of trying to contain the potential of new serial forms. Just like certain kinds of repressive governments, certain media keep marching back, in heavy steps (*Schritte*) that seem the opposite of any progressive forward movement (*Fortschritt*).

Die Zeitschwingen is published twice a week in Offenbach, near Frankfurt, and is a four-page, two-column cultural journal somewhat

---

6. See Hedwig Pompe, *Famas Medium: Zur Theorie der Zeitung in Deutschland zwischen dem 17. und 19. Jahrhundert* (Berlin: De Gruyter, 2012), 75.
7. Ludwig Börne, "Ankündigung," *Zeitschwingen, oder Des deutschen Volkes fliegende Blätter*, no. 53 (July 3, 1819): 210.
8. Börne, "Ankündigung," 211.

similar in size and appearance to the quarto *Morgenblatt*. Articles in the journal's short three-month run under Börne's editorship address press freedom and censorship, the role of Jews in German society, and antiliberal conspiracy theories, as well as other topics in politics, literature, and art. We might translate the title as "The Vibrations" or "Wings of Time," and it also connotes rising into the air in flight (in noting the journal's existence, French newspapers translated the title as *Essor* or "flight"). Börne's editorship of the journal coincides with the repressive Carlsbad congress (in August of 1819), whose decrees bring an abrupt end to his editorship and those of many other liberal writers. Short-lived journal projects such as this one are typical at the time, due not least to constant financial and political pressures. Just three months after the opening announcement, Börne is prompted to eulogize the journal in a piece that he would later retitle the "Last Will and Testament of the *Zeitschwingen*" in his *Gesammelte Schriften*.[9] This deeply ironic yet also quite serious short piece returns to flight as a metaphor for freedom: due to the crackdown by the censors, the *Zeitschwingen* "will lower its wings and adopt the name *Sugarbeet Pages* [*Runkelrübenblätter*]."[10] Just like the German people, the journal has experienced a brief period of freedom, only to be grounded once again and relegated to covering unpolitical, mercantile topics such as sugar beets. The journal's short life parallels the German people's brief flight into the heights of freedom; with every passing day and every passing issue of the journal under censorship as "sugarbeet pages," the brief duration of freedom recedes into the past.

At the same time, though, Börne looks to have the last laugh with the censors, taking up Jean Paul's joke about the accessibility of revolutionary periodicals in an age of censorship that we encountered in chapter 4:

> Strict oversight, censorship, common standards! And I should hold back from laughing? The *Moniteur* is spread out in front of me, these giant pages, this book of the kings of the nineties, the Napoleonic era, and the

---

9. Börne edited the journal from July 3, 1819, to October 9 of the same year.
10. The first version of this is titled "Unsere Arme Seele." Ludwig Börne, "Unsere Arme Seele," *Zeitschwingen*, no. 74 (September 15, 1819): 297–99; Ludwig Börne, "Testament der *Zeitschwingen*." SS, I, 786–87.

era of the Cossacks in Berlin. A book dealer recently gave me a big pile of them—and this kind of thing people are just *giving away*! Princes should pay millions for it . . .[11]

The *Moniteur* was the leading French newspaper of the French Revolution, later became Napoleon's official mouthpiece, and continued as an official organ of the French government into the 1810s and beyond. For Börne, it is highly ironic that censors shut down his own modest journal while past issues of this initially much more radical and long-lived publication are so readily accessible. For Börne, as for Jean Paul, the material existence of these seemingly worthless back issues ironically demonstrates the permanence of the ideals of freedom. It is print's very loss of value that points to the sustained worth of the ideas expressed therein. This ascription of value to ephemera extends to Börne's own failed journal project. Writing its last will and testament counteracts its short duration, as Börne positions his own work in a continuum of historical periodicals in the service of freedom. And by recalling the *Moniteur*'s outsize importance, Börne opens up a space between the present and the future, imagining a similar scene of retroactively reading the *Zeitschwingen*. The ephemerality of journals is not simply tied to the shifting present but also encourages future reception and reactualization, and this future horizon gives the activity of lingering with the present a predictive and even prophetic function. His repeated reference to journals' orientation to the present thus establishes a broader temporal continuum in which the preservation of past and present ephemera for future readers bears fruit, paradoxically both affirming and conditioning the periodical's orientation toward the present.

Ten years later, Börne explores a similar technique of writing for the future in the context of republishing his writings from journals in a collected works edition. As we have seen in the previous chapter, the early and mid-nineteenth century is a perennial age of works editions, and many of these are purely retrospective or "complete"— coming at the end of an author's career or even after his death. The collected works edition is organized around the author figure rather

---

11. Börne, "Unsere Arme Seele," 297.

than notions of currentness, periodicity, and seriality and lays the groundwork for writers' canonization in a pantheon of "national" authors.[12] However, it was also common to have ongoing, open-ended editions, with writers contracted to produce new material for new volumes, and this is the case with Börne's *Gesammelte Schriften*. Though he is undoubtedly proud to have such an edition, he dodges the aesthetics of completed, self-standing works, stating in an announcement for subsequent volumes of his *Gesammelte Schriften* published in 1829 in volume 6 of that edition that "I have not written any works. I have just tried my quill on this and that piece of paper; now the pages should be collected, laid on top of each other, and the book binder shall make them into books—this is all."[13] Here, again, we see the association of the sheet, page, or leaflet with miscellaneous writing and its positioning against the logic of the autonomous work; indeed, this announcement comes at the end of a collection of miscellanies first published in journals. This image of layered sheets of paper metaphorizes the occasional status of much of Börne's writing, as well as the serial unfolding of pieces such as *Schilderungen aus Paris*. In effect, Börne uses the format of the collected works edition to recast his writings' occasionality and ephemerality rather than expunging them through reformatting. This is an example of reverse remediation (of a journal into a book) that has a more progressive outcome, with the book taking on the features of the more up-to-date medium. Börne's practice of collecting his individual writings bears certain similarities to the process by which works editions gather self-standing works, but it also draws on his editorial activities in excerpting, commenting on, and collating different kinds of articles culled from the broader sea of periodical literature. Here again we have a journal-like book.

Börne also highlights this occasional quality of his pieces in an 1829 foreword to an earlier volume of his *Gesammelte Schriften*, where he draws attention to the fact that this and other volumes

---

12. As Piper puts it, collected editions argue "for a fundamental homogeneity of its contents through the overwhelming promotion of the author as the single organizing figure behind the collection." Piper, *Dreaming in Books*, 54.

13. Ludwig Börne, "[Announcement of Collected Works]." GS, 6, 205–10; SS, II, 330–34.

include the years of publication of certain articles, including framing remarks for his different journal projects such as the announcement and "Testament" for the *Zeitschwingen* (see the table of contents, figure 6.1). By referencing the duration between initial publication and republication, Börne once more evokes the tension between success and failure, value and worthlessness, and youth and old age:

> In this and the subsequent parts of my collected writings, readers will find articles with political contents, and I have noted the year in which they were written. I did this in order to denote their virtue rather than their age. They remain just as bare and shiny as if they just came from the thought mint yesterday. For political truth does not circulate in Germany from hand to hand, like money, it is not made grubby or misplaced—no, it lies quietly and cleanly in a trunk, unused, untouched. What a beautiful country, where one is born old and where one dies young! We come into the world with the wisdom of our grandfathers and we leave behind the wisdom of our grandfathers without adding to it. We are stubborn cattle who pay for the past as well as for the present, and who must hand the present down to the future in the manner that we have received it.[14]

Despite these texts' relative old age (though none are older than ten years old), they have remained youthful, fresh, and current because they have never been truly circulated and debated and because the conditions they critique have not been improved. Change occurs so seldomly and slowly in the restoration era, and new, "virtuous" political ideas preserve their freshness, even if they are several years old, in contrast to the genuinely backward-looking ideas and practices kept in circulation by the authorities. Republication might help Börne's texts to be reencountered, but it also reintroduces the prospect of being properly encountered after earlier missed opportunities for initial publication. Ideas both friendly and antagonistic to the conservative political order depend on structures of repetition, of handing things down, and of collecting and recirculating. Both subversive and conservative modes likewise assume that certain things of more or less old age stay current and new.

---

14. Ludwig Börne, "Vorwort." GS, 3, vii–viii.

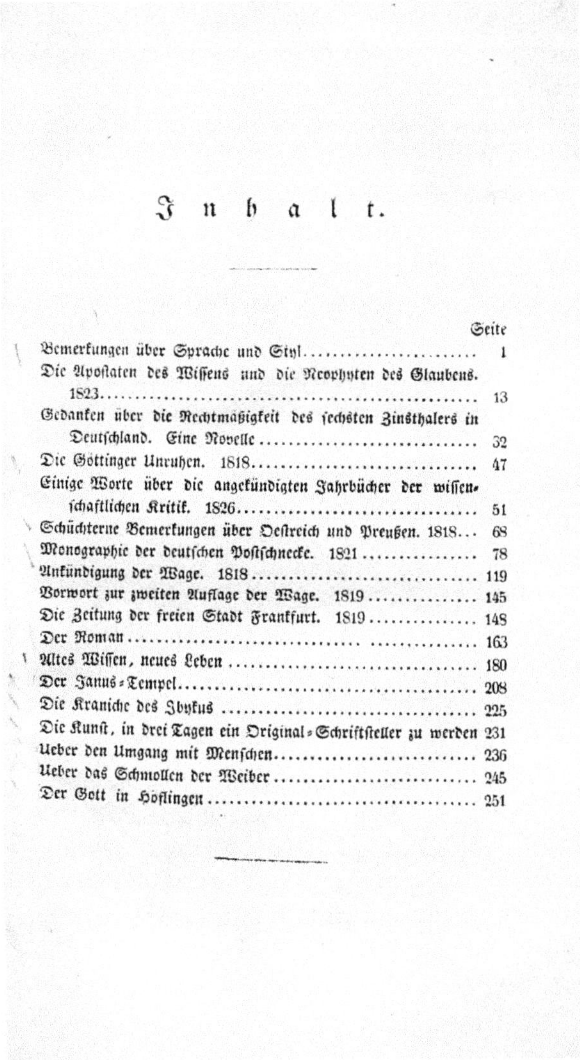

Inhalt.

	Seite
Bemerkungen über Sprache und Styl	1
Die Apostaten des Wissens und die Neophyten des Glaubens. 1823	13
Gedanken über die Rechtmäßigkeit des sechsten Zinsthalers in Deutschland. Eine Novelle	32
Die Göttinger Unruhen. 1818	47
Einige Worte über die angekündigten Jahrbücher der wissenschaftlichen Kritik. 1826	51
Schüchterne Bemerkungen über Oestreich und Preußen. 1818	68
Monographie der deutschen Postschnecke. 1821	78
Ankündigung der Wage. 1818	119
Vorwort zur zweiten Auflage der Wage. 1819	145
Die Zeitung der freien Stadt Frankfurt. 1819	148
Der Roman	163
Altes Wissen, neues Leben	180
Der Janus-Tempel	208
Die Kraniche des Ibykus	225
Die Kunst, in drei Tagen ein Original-Schriftsteller zu werden	231
Ueber den Umgang mit Menschen	236
Ueber das Schmollen der Weiber	245
Der Gott in Höflingen	251

Figure 6.1. Title page. Ludwig Börne, *Gesammelte Schriften*, vol. 3 (Hamburg: Hoffmann and Campe, 1829). Berlin State Library, Prussian Cultural Heritage Foundation. 6 ½ × 4 ¾ inches.

That said, it is unnatural for the young to be born old and the old to die young and for the past to serve as the exclusive model for the present and the future alike. Börne mobilizes this trope as part of a publicational politics that attaches a temporal marker to publications in anticipation of their future reception. Even though he would later come to be associated with the Young Germany movement, here he puts forth a more complicated idea of youth by filtering it through the practice of reprinting writings originally published in journals. These texts were born and have stayed "young," even as they have "aged." Youth is tied to a certain understanding of print materials in which coming into being in certain time-specific, potentially short-lived contexts is both a virtue and a limitation. By recirculating these texts and marking their original publication dates, Börne suggests that their moment will come and that we need to wait for the time when they become truly of the present or contemporary. The original date of publication and subsequent date of republication both point to an indeterminate future date where genuine reception is possible.

The technique of marking the original date of publication and collating these writings into a single book establishes a sense that his writings constitute a sequential series, both of different versions and different texts. But, as we can see from the title page, many of the texts are not in chronological order. These different writings each stand in a slightly different relationship to their potential future actualization, but they also create the sense of an author writing with political "virtue" and conviction over time, a writer dedicated to writing about such topics into the future. Here Börne's mention of the "subsequent parts" of his collected writings stands out; again, the collected edition is premised on the promise that more writings will be added. Two different types of waiting thus come into view: waiting for the future realization of these writings and waiting for the author to reapply himself to the topics at hand. The present volume held by the reader delimits an interval of time that marks both forms of waiting, providing an instance of the continued activity of the author while also recognizing the lack of proper reception of his ideas, with the current reader modeling a form of future reception. Börne folds an experience of time and history into the logic of serial publication, but this seriality is characterized by an irregular, uncertain periodicity—we know neither when the next volume will appear nor when old writings will take on new relevance. More will come, and the past will recur, but in unpredictable ways.

Die Wage (1818–1821)

Prior to and in the midst of Börne's brief editorship of the *Zeitschwingen*, he was also involved in a more substantial journal project called *Die Wage, Eine Zeitschrift für Bürgerleben, Wissenschaft und Kunst* (The scale, a journal for public life, science, and art), which was published in Frankfurt and ran from 1818 to 1821. This is a longer-form journal with individual issues of around fifty pages containing essays, largely written by Börne, that mix political topics with theater and literary criticism.[15] Indeed, it is this journal and his fiery theater criticism that establish his literary reputation at this early point in his career. In the 1818 "Announcement" (*Ankündigung*) for the journal, he undertakes an extended defense of writing in and for periodicals, in the process articulating a compelling and complex vision of the temporality of serial publication more generally. Here, again, Börne identifies the potential of the periodical to map irregular temporalities via multivalent metaphors of ephemerality and the present. Though a scale is not a temporal metaphor, Börne calls it a "diary of the time" (*ein Tagebuch der Zeit*), and it is here where Börne programmatically embraces the term *Zeitschriftsteller*.[16] As he puts it, the writer must diagnose and "write down" the current times, "listen" for "its utterances" and "interpret its expressions":

> To listen in on the statements of the time, to interpret its pantomime and write down both, this would be an honorable service, even if it were not dangerous. The fact that it is dangerous increases its allure.... People

---

15. For an excellent recent study of this theater criticism, see Michael Swellander, "Understanding the Present: The Representation of Contemporary History in Ludwig Börne, Heinrich Heine, and Georg Büchner" (PhD diss., Columbia University, 2019), 9.
16. Börne, "Einleitung." SS, I, 671.

are frightened, as if they were creatures of mere momentary duration. For this reason, so much good is left undone, both in word and deed.[17]

In a repressive era, people do not speak out for fear of risking their material survival, and, paradoxically, it is the task of the *Zeitschriftsteller* to risk publishing news and criticism that responds to the ever-changing present day specifically to stave off readers' fears of being merely ephemeral creatures. As in the *Zeitschwingen* announcement, lingering with time-sensitive, current topics is an indication of freedom and that there is something more lasting and true than day-to-day survival. The time of freedom and revolutionary change is not limited to the moment of revolution but instead entails using the present as a lens onto multiple shapes of time.

Börne calls *Die Wage* a diary of the times, but such chronicling does not simply pursue the fleeting present for its own sake, seeking instead to discern more permanent social and political structures by taking the pulse of the present moment. He thereby offers a rough outline of an approach to writing the history both of the present and of longer-term events. The image of the human species—the privileged subject of history since the rise of secular historiography—as a living body helps Börne to characterize this historiographical undertaking.

> The developmental stage that humanity is now passing through brings forth something concealed that is quickly covered up again as soon as this stage has been reached, and that will only reappear when the human species once more takes another step after centuries of standstill. As when life's secrets spring forth when it is in danger, or to when the laws of health reveal themselves in the phenomena of sickness, we must learn to identify the rules of this time's perfection in its defects, and, in order to study the inner structure of civil society, we must be able to see quickly through its open wounds before they close again.[18]

Börne evokes aspects of Enlightenment and Romantic era stadial philosophies of history, yet he also foregrounds a notion of quick-

---

17. Börne, "Einleitung." SS, I, 670.
18. Börne, "Einleitung." SS, I, 671.

ness characteristic of social and political events as well as of critical observation and its media-based filiations: the writer attuned to deeper structures must be timely in his examination of "open wounds" that point to a larger sickness. Despite this emphasis on quickness, Börne does not embrace a notion of the monolithic acceleration of all human affairs, a common view in the nineteenth century. Instead Börne envisions quick changes that are followed by long periods of "standstill" (*Stillstand*). The metaphor of sickness likewise runs counter to the notion of historical progress (*Fortschritt*): humanity takes "steps" (*Schritte*), yet their progressive movement is up for debate. Börne articulates a vision of the "inner structure of civil society" across historical time in which various processes of long and short duration coexist and certain symptoms appear and "reappear." By writing about the present, the *Zeitschriftsteller* creates a critical horizon for comparing these structures.

Börne also casts lingering with the transient present as a cultural achievement that only some historical nations have achieved. In contrast to ancient Greece, contemporary Christian society is unable to enjoy the "fleeting blossom" of the present for it works only for the future of the afterlife. Here too, the periodical press is an index for the extent to which different nations are able to take pleasure in the present, and Börne finds direct inspiration in the French press: "The happiest of all peoples, in whom the bleak view of life least dominates and who are most similar to the ancient Greeks, is the *French*. Whoever reads their newspapers [notices] how [F. J.] Talma's play on stage and the play of the ministers in the chambers are both discussed with the same seriousness and the same amusement."[19] Getting equally caught up in the "play" of the theater and of politics is modern, French, and deeply intertwined with cultural journals' characteristic mixture of seriousness and humor. As in the *Zeitschwingen*, serial print serves as a metaphor for engagement with a multivalent present, and the format of the newspaper, which integrates different realms of social and cultural life, helps to realize this.

It is remarkable, though, that Börne does not go on to link the transient present with any kind of regulated unfolding across time,

---

19. Börne, "Einleitung." SS, I, 672.

rejecting the embrace of regular periodicity that can be quite common in defenses of the periodical. As Börne states, the journal is to be published in irregular installments, only when the events of the present day warrant commentary:

> It is a wonderful arrangement that a periodical departs, like a mail coach, on certain days and at certain hours, no matter whether it is full or empty; death and marriage at least ensure that there is never any lack of stowaways [*blinde Passagiere*]. But the fact that there are so many of these institutions makes an additional one unnecessary. *The Scale* will start moving as soon as history or science has filled it with cargo, and its publication can therefore not be bound to any specific time.[20]

It is striking here that he casts the irregularity of the journal as an indication of its being up to date, on pace with the latest, most historically important developments.[21] Building off of connotations of "free," "unforced," or "uncoerced" that resonate with the term *zwanglos*, Börne aligns the development of media with the social progress that surged with the explosion of the French Revolution and continues in unpredictable fits and starts. This brings the journal closer to the occasionality of specific events—and thus closer to the metaphor of the pamphlet or *fliegende Blätter*—but this also maps the project of *Die Wage* onto Börne's conception of historical symptoms that open and close like wounds. History moves irregularly and unpredictably, and journals that track it must do the same. The journal is akin to a diary, as Börne suggests, but one tied less to the diurnal notation of commercial or professional practices (one early form of the modern diary) and more to a form of personal journal writing where the entries are only composed at important life junctures.[22] *Zwanglose Hefte*: the freedom and the lack of compulsion of these serial installments is decoupled from the rhythms of the calendar as well as of more regulated print projects that are cali-

---

20. Börne, "Einleitung." SS, I, 682–83.
21. See Wolfgang Labuhn, *Literatur und Öffentlichkeit im Vormärz. Das Beispiel Ludwig Börne* (Königstein: Forum Academicum, 1980), 136.
22. On the chronopoetics of the diary, see Stuart Sherman, *Telling Time: Clocks, Diaries, and English Diurnal Form, 1660–1785* (Chicago: University of Chicago Press, 1996).

brated with modes of production, circulation (the mail coach, as he mentions here), or distribution (via seasonal trade fairs). Instead, the serial unfolding of the periodical—the promise that future issues are coming—is tied to a process of waiting. The *Zeitschriftsteller* must wait as he listens and reads the "utterances" and "gestures of the time," seeking to spot the open wounds before they close, and the reader must likewise wait for the next installment, not necessarily sure if it will appear again in a month or half of a year. The relative indeterminacy of the journal's future carries with it a certain promise and generates a certain desire for more, and it creates a certain awareness of time on the basis of what is to come.

Letters from Paris

Like Heine, Börne rushed to Paris after hearing the news of the revolution, arriving in mid-September of 1831, and his *Briefe aus Paris* (1832–1834) form the cornerstone of his reputation as a political writer. For many observers, the July Revolution confirms the belief or hope that the revolution might repeat, continue, or complete itself, and the similarities of the 1830 revolution to the 1789 one lead to renewed questions about what is new and what has repeated in the popular energies of the revolution. There was a strong precedent for revolutionary correspondence from Paris dating back to the 1790s and the writings of J. H. Campe, Georg Forster, and others. The letter form allows writers to track ongoing events, a key conceit of various projects of serial *Zeitgeschichte* as well as of political writers aiming to channel the dynamism of current events into specific political movements. Correspondence reports about the July Revolution for various journals and newspapers are common at this time, including Heine's articles for Cotta's *Augsburger Allgemeine Zeitung*, which he would later republish under the title *Französische Zustände* (Conditions in France).[23]

---

23. This includes J. H. Schnitzler, F. A. Gathy, F. von Raumer, J. C. Held, and others. See Rutger Booß, *Ansichten der Revolution. Paris-Berichte deutscher Schriftsteller nach der Juli-Revolution 1830: Heine, Börne, u.a.* (Cologne: Pahl-Rugenstein, 1977).

Unlike Börne's *Schilderungen von Paris*, the texts in *Briefe aus Paris* are addressed to a specific unnamed female reader; as we know, they are reworked personal letters to his friend and confidante Jeanette Wohl. Given his interest in the brief and the quick, it is no surprise that Börne turns to the genre of collected letters. Here he follows Wohl's advice, who writes in a November 1830 letter,

> Is it not possible to achieve a much fresher, more lively, appealing, and engaging presentation in letters rather than articles? ... These letters would not only be placed alongside the best memoirs from the most memorable times, [but] they would also possess historical value. And you could be so useful, so effective as a result! Everyone reads letters, you could spread your principles through them as you would through newspapers.[24]

Wohl explicitly associates published letters with writing for newspapers, situating them as a natural extension of correspondence reports; indeed, as we saw in part I of this book, foreign correspondence reports around 1800 commonly take the form of an excerpted letter or travel journal, as in Goethe's "Excerpts from a Travel Journal" in *Der Teutsche Merkur*. Not only does a similar audience read newspapers and longer-form travel writing, but letters and journal issues alike are both structured as series of shorter, episodic pieces unfolding over time.[25] As Wohl suggests, letters are well suited to take the pulse of the present day, but they also allow Börne the chance to write something that stands up to later historical scrutiny, both as subjective recollections akin to the diary or memoir and as more objective, journalistic documentation of the times. Letters cut across book and journal formats, with one of the more influential German travelogues of the day being Pückler-Muskau's *Briefe eines Verstorbenen* (Letters of a dead man) (1830–1831). Furthermore, personal memoirs represent an important segment of contemporary

---

24. Jeanette Wohl to Ludwig Börne, November 1830. SS, V, 846. On the letters' genesis and Wohl's role in suggesting the letter form, see Christa Walz, *Jeanette Wohl und Ludwig Börne: Dokumentation und Analyse des Briefwechsels* (Frankfurt: Campus, 2001), 123–28, 187–91.

25. Both are forms of "temporalized perception," as Oesterle puts it. Ingrid Oesterle, "Der 'Führungswechsel der Zeithorizonte,'" 23.

reports about the 1789 revolution and remain so through the Napoleonic period and the 1830s.[26]

The letters open with Börne's third trip to Paris in September of 1830, almost exactly two months after the revolution, and they end in 1833 with the prospect of his leaving the city once more. His third visit (the first two were in 1819 and 1822) is something of a homecoming, and it also represents the beginning of his on-again, off-again exile from Germany (he lived in Paris from 1830 until his death in 1837). Here one might find echoes of Goethe's return to Rome and the second experience of Roman carnival discussed in chapter 2, though Börne would likely have none of the comparison, remaining a vehement critic of Goethe throughout his life. Börne is quick to note that this return to Paris finds him at a more mature stage in life, and the difference between youth and middle or old age remains a theme throughout the letters. They contain a remarkable range of topics, as Börne describes his experiences of the city and his responses to public political and cultural debates, explicitly mimicking the style of French newspapers. Theater reviews abound, as do discussions of the literary and periodical landscape of the time and the ways in which various public organs process the ever-shifting political landscape in postrevolutionary France, as conflicts crop up across Europe and as crises such as the cholera epidemic break out. Börne's detailed accounts of public spectacles—vaudeville theater, public demonstrations, festivities, monuments, and more—likewise stand out as yet another level of representation of the events of the past forty years. Such representations are in constant circulation, and Börne responds to and recirculates them.

Briefe aus Paris is published in six volumes over the course of three years (1832–1834) as part of his *Gesammelte Schriften*. The sequential publication is thus not dissimilar to that of a biannual periodical, and the location of the letters in the *Gesammelte Schriften* situates the work as a kind of continuation of the earlier *Schilderungen aus Paris*, which are in volume 5. The letters are dated between September of 1830 and March of 1833 and make up

---

26. See Anna Karla, *Revolution als Zeitgeschichte. Memoiren der Französischen Revolution in der Restaurationszeit* (Göttingen: Vandenhoeck & Ruprecht, 2014).

volumes 9 to 14 of the *Gesammelte Schriften*. The first four volumes are around 320 pages or twenty *Bogen* (proof sheets), the lower limit for avoiding precensorship.²⁷ The need to reach a certain page count is an important feature of what Carlos Spoerhase has discussed in other contexts as a "poetics of the *Druckbogen*."²⁸ But Börne has to go further than just the minimum Bogen limit to evade the censors, printing volumes 11 and 12 with a fictive title and publication information so as to deceive the censors. Indeed, this fictive title, "Notices from the Field of Geography and Ethnography" (*Mitteilungen aus dem Gebiet der Länder und Völkerkunde*) is evocative of a recurring, periodical-like format, and contemporary readers found it to be a highly successful satirical ploy.²⁹ As documents of current events, though, the *Briefe* has a somewhat peculiar publication history, for many letters first reach print up to two years after they are dated (the letters written in the fall and winter of 1830, for example, are not published until 1832). This is not unlike other similarly published letters or travel reports, but, again, the delay does stand out because the texts are positioned as a direct response to the July Revolution. Here, again, we see how Börne engages with frames of time that intervene between writing and these writings' reception, a delay that parallels the belatedness with which German readers heard about the revolution that Heine would thematize in his Heligoland letters.

The formatting of the *Briefe* likewise takes on certain important structural similarities to that of the cultural journal. The letter form inherently depends on breaking up the flow of text into discretely written chunks, something that applies both on the macro- and microlevel. In terms of the more general organization of the six volumes

---

27. See Katy Heady, *Literature and Censorship in Restoration Germany: Repression and Rhetoric* (Rochester, NY: Camden House, 2009), 11; see also Labuhn, *Literatur und Öffentlichkeit im Vormärz*, 236.

28. "The basic unit of literary culture around 1800 is not the single page or the side of the page, but rather the *Bogen*." Spoerhase, *Das Format der Literatur*, 576.

29. See the contents of Börne, *Briefe aus Paris*, GS, 13/14. As Heinrich Laube puts it regarding this volume of the *Letters*, "Börne is not merely a journalist (*Publizist*), he is a humorist, he is our best satirical author." Quoted in Inge Rippman and Peter Rippmann, "Lebensdaten." SS, III, 1037.

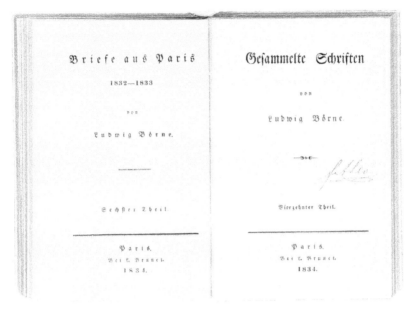

Figures 6.2. Title page. Ludwig Börne, *Briefe aus Paris*, part 6, vol. 14 of Ludwig Börne, *Gesammelte Schriften* (Paris: Brunet, 1834). Berlin State Library, Prussian Cultural Heritage Foundation. 6 ½ × 9 ½ inches.

of letters, they are broken up into three two-part sections, with the numeration of the letters starting anew in each new two-part section, lending the volumes the appearance of a biannual periodical, with *Briefe aus Paris* serving as a recurring title heading for changing contents, not unlike the function of a journal title (figure 6.2). Here we see a dual title page of sorts, with the title page of *Briefe aus Paris* followed by the *Gesammelte Schriften* title page; both designations present the book that readers are holding in their hands as a repository for contents that are being serially generated. The analogy between the *Briefe* and a periodical is not far-fetched: memoirs pertaining to specific historical events are intended to be read in tandem with other memoirs, like the common practice of reading different newspapers' perspectives on the same topic. As the historian Anna Karla observes, "memoirs, as commonly noted in advertisements for their collections, had to be read as part of a series so as not to remain stuck in the partisan perspective of an individual memoirist."[30] This segmentation and numeration of separate volumes is elided by the critical edition of Börne's writings published in the 1970s (*Sämtliche Schriften*, edited by Inge Rippmann and Peter Rippmann), which numerates the entirety of the letters sequentially.

The individual letters are also segmented into different pieces, with a single letter sometimes containing five or six discretely dated texts. Of course, this segmentation corresponds to the conventions of letter writing, in which individual letters might bundle multiple missives, yet it is also somewhat evocative of the rubrics common in cultural journals, with natural breaks between individual letters facilitating the shift from topic to topic, from day to day. Individual letters often contain a large amount of heterogeneous material, which is broken into discrete segments through dashes and other diacritical remarks (figure 6.3). The dashes that Börne uses to break up apparently unrelated textual units are likewise borrowed from the journals and newspapers of the time. Additionally, in a departure from the appearance of the pages of newspapers or journals, there is often significant blank space between letters, which can be read as a way of both filling space and managing the particular temporality of waiting for the next letter or the next piece of news.[31] This is not the blank space of the luxury book that we saw in Goethe's *Carneval*; instead, the blank space here points to a pause in the writer's and reader's experiences or a pause between the writing and reading of individual letters. From the macro- to the microlevel, then, these different techniques of segmenting the letters help Börne to give shape to his experiences of and attempts to write the complex temporalities of a post-1830 France.

Along with importing certain format conditions of the periodical press into his letters, the work functions as a kind of ongoing com-

---

30. Anna Karla, "Die verschlafene Revolution von 1789. Französisch-Deutsches Revolutionserzählen im Modus der Zeitgenossenschaft," in *Sattelzeit: Historiographische Revisionen*, ed. Elisabeth Découltot and Daniel Fulda (Berlin: De Gruyter, 2016), 212.

31. See Multigraph Collective, "Spacing," in *Interacting with Print: Elements of Reading in the Era of Print Saturation* (Chicago: University of Chicago Press, 2018), 260, 273.

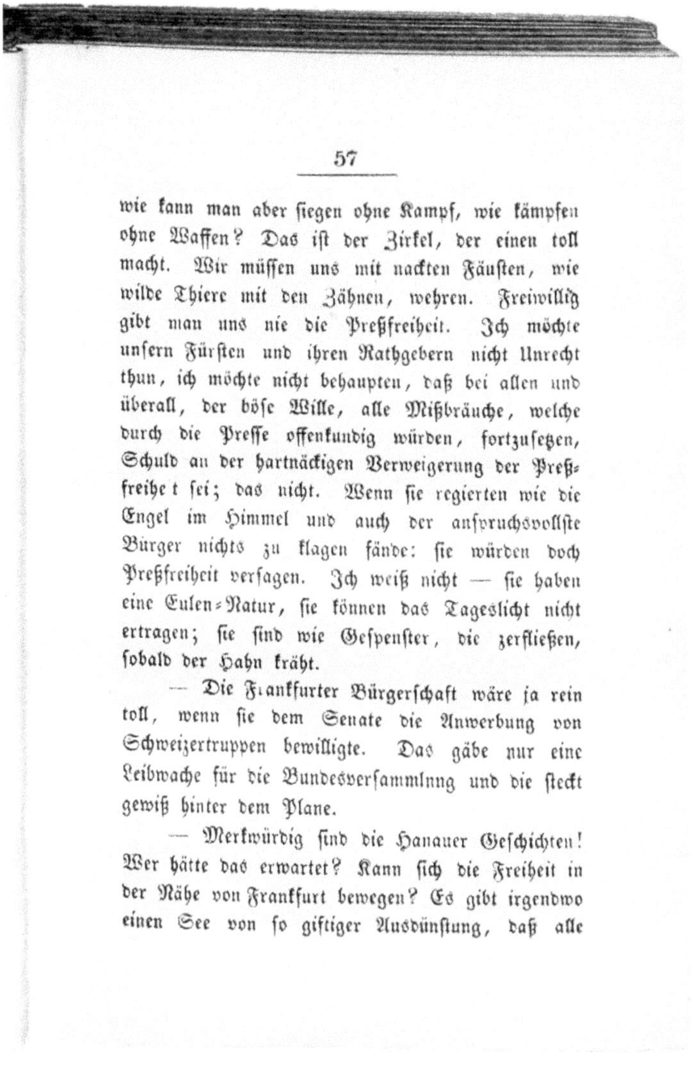

wie kann man aber siegen ohne Kampf, wie kämpfen ohne Waffen? Das ist der Zirkel, der einen toll macht. Wir müssen uns mit nackten Fäusten, wie wilde Thiere mit den Zähnen, wehren. Freiwillig gibt man uns nie die Preßfreiheit. Ich möchte unsern Fürsten und ihren Rathgebern nicht Unrecht thun, ich möchte nicht behaupten, daß bei allen und überall, der böse Wille, alle Mißbräuche, welche durch die Presse offenkundig würden, fortzusetzen, Schuld an der hartnäckigen Verweigerung der Preßfreihet sei; das nicht. Wenn sie regierten wie die Engel im Himmel und auch der anspruchsvollste Bürger nichts zu klagen fände: sie würden doch Preßfreiheit versagen. Ich weiß nicht — sie haben eine Eulen-Natur, sie können das Tageslicht nicht ertragen; sie sind wie Gespenster, die zerfließen, sobald der Hahn kräht.

— Die Frankfurter Bürgerschaft wäre ja rein toll, wenn sie dem Senate die Anwerbung von Schweizertruppen bewilligte. Das gäbe nur eine Leibwache für die Bundesversammlung und die steckt gewiß hinter dem Plane.

— Merkwürdig sind die Hanauer Geschichten! Wer hätte das erwartet? Kann sich die Freiheit in der Nähe von Frankfurt bewegen? Es gibt irgendwo einen See von so giftiger Ausdünstung, daß alle

Figure 6.3. Page view. Ludwig Börne, *Briefe aus Paris*, part 1, vol. 9 of *Gesammelte Schriften* (Hamburg: Hoffmann and Campe, 1832), 57. Berlin State Library, Prussian Cultural Heritage Foundation. 6 ½ × 4 ¾ inches.

mentary on the print landscape, unfolding at a pace that runs both parallel to and divergent from other periodically occurring print objects. Börne frequently directs readers to specific journals or books: he is constantly speculating about the veracity of different reports, constantly waiting for the latest reports about specific conflicts, constantly attending to what in the introduction to *Die Wage* he called the "open wounds of the time," and constantly trying to discern what is eventful and portentous from the mass of printed matter that surrounds him. Seen in this light, the letters take on a kind of digest quality (a feature of Heine's Parisian writings as well), yet in light of this status as digests of the daily news, the delay in publication stands out all the more—readers might have read what Börne is discussing, but it might have been more than a year since they did so.

Especially at the beginning of the *Briefe*, Börne establishes continuity with his previous writings, touching on urban sites and activities from his *Schilderungen aus Paris*—reading rooms, eating ice cream, social events with prominent literati, visiting monuments, and more—as well as mentioning other well-known writings of his. This self-citation shores up the uniqueness of Börne's authorial voice, and it also makes the letters a site where the author reflects on the reception of his own work, something that only grows over the course of the letters as they are reviewed and discussed increasingly frequently. Börne spends more and more time responding to criticism of the *Briefe*: "My letters are being discussed in all the papers, even in English ones."[32] Such self-reflexivity is characteristic of serial forms that thematize the media environment of which they are a part. Readers are presented with the often dizzying spectacle of letters discussing newspapers that comment on and sometimes even excerpt earlier volumes of his letters. The *Briefe* remediate the broader sea of print in which they are situated in an impartial, incomplete, yet ongoing manner. This reverse remediation serves to enhance and amplify the progressive impulse generated by the flow of periodicals and newspapers to a fast-growing reading public. Börne's *Briefe* are inherently intertwined with the journals and papers then in circulation, mimicking and reproducing them while at

---

32. Börne, *Briefe aus Paris*, December 8, 1831. SS, III, 387.

the same time selectively setting in motion alternative periodicities and alternate eddies and currents.

"Adieu until the Next Revolution"

We have seen the importance of delay and deferral for Börne's self-conception as *Zeitschriftsteller* in the 1820s, and the *Briefe*, too, are permeated by anticipation and impatience. Börne is never lacking in things to anticipate or things that lose their currency in the process of being communicated, yet, in the intervals of time opened up by delays and interruptions, structures of time become visible. One of Börne's more telling reflections on the delayed or expired actuality of his writing comes as he thematizes the form of the personal letter in letter 17 in the first volume:

> Nine days normally pass before one of us responds to the letter of the other, so that we both often don't know what the answer is referring to.... Diderot is often bothered by this in his letters and says: "I feel like the traveler who remarks to the person sitting next to him in the coach: 'That is a very lovely meadow.' An hour later this person replies, 'Yes, it is very lovely.'"[33]

Delays in transmission impinge on the actuality of the occasions under discussion. Communicating about fleeting events runs the risk of potentially missing them. The sense that something will happen in the interim between each individual communiqué is characteristic of Börne's own situation as a correspondent trying to digest conflicting information about ongoing political conflicts (indeed, this interim finds material form as the blank lower quarter of the page that signals the break between letters). Börne deliberately situates himself in a communicative network in which news and rumors are always coming in and being sent out at different times, a network in which newspapers, letters, pamphlets, and books all play analogous yet differently timed functions. He is constantly waiting for new information to arrive, but he always suspects that it will be

---

33. Börne, *Briefe aus Paris*, December 11, 1830. SS, III, 81.

outdated by the time it gets there. Waiting is a frustrating yet productive activity, for it entails the active perception of frames of time that one might have to endure in the process.

This kind of delayed or expired actuality is also an integral part of the larger political and historical stakes of his writing, which takes place under the sign of the coming revolution. In something of a continuation of Diderot's thought experiment, Börne closes this same letter in the following manner: "I am curious—which new revolutions will occur between this letter and my next one.—A new theater is being built on the Place de la Bastille. Adieu until the next revolution."[34] The joke here is that the revolution will occur in the interim between the letter's composition and its arrival, but this bon mot also allows Börne to set up the idea that the revolution will occur in an indeterminate future. The time between this letter and the next (and the time between these letters' composition and their arrival with their addressee[s]) opens up a space in which possible revolutions might occur. This is the space of waiting between serial iterations of a periodical form, and this seriality is itself broken up into even shorter segments of time and communication via the dashes he employs. A dash disarticulates curiosity about the next revolutions from the news that a new theater is being built on the Place de la Bastille, and yet the news about the theater is reintegrated into political speculation through the overdetermined location of this new theater as well as through a sense of Paris as the "stage" for political upheaval. This concomitant disarticulation and reintegration of these textual snippets of information models on a rhetorical level the serial structure of the letters themselves, both as individual installments of aggregated letters and as distinct volumes.

Occurring within this extended reflection about letters and the reporting of the ever-shifting present, the statement "Adieu until the next revolution" situates the revolution in a peculiar temporal posi-

---

34. "—Ich bin begierig—welche neue Revolutionen zwischen diesem und meinem nächsten Briefe vorfallen werden.—Auf dem Bastillenplatz wird ein neues Theater gebaut. Adieu bis zur nächsten Revolution." Börne, *Briefe aus Paris*, December 11, 1830. SS III, 84.

tion: it is less that the next letter will allow the addressee to experience the revolution in any sort of immediacy and more that any news of the revolution will once more be at some kind of temporal remove: "Goodbye until my next report about the next revolution." The onset of the revolution is situated in the future, yet any reporting of it necessarily relegates its events to the past. This is a complex temporal structure of anticipation and waiting and of retrospective processing and interpreting. Lingering with the ephemeral—in this case, lingering with the expired actuality of the ephemeral present—serves as a way of marking time, of opening up space for a certain kind of waiting for the new, and for the coming event of the revolution. The letter then comes into focus as an archive that enables the experience of certain actualities that have expired or been delayed, or potentially both. And the publication situation of these letters—that they appear almost two years after their composition—introduces yet another level of remove from the imminent revolutions that Börne references, creating ever more temporal complexities that coalesce around a sense of coming revolution.

In my reading, then, Börne's captivation with ephemeral occurrences is a technique of cultivating an anticipatory sense of an indeterminate future. He delves into the present in order to imagine the relationship between past, present, and future. We saw some of this in the introduction to the *Zeitschwingen*, where he stages the rereading of the *Moniteur* in order to imagine the hypothetical situation of future readers encountering his failed journal. The loss of fleeting actuality turns out to not be as serious a problem as one might think for, in the realm of archived print objects, ephemerality does not necessarily connote actual death. Instead, such ephemerality indexes possible structures of historical time and eventfulness. Börne is both ironic and serious when he suggests that the very mediality of his letters carries with it a certain kind of predictive, prophetic potential. Staging the loss of actuality thus comes into focus as an important part of his lingering with the present. In becoming uncurrent but persisting nonetheless, the significance of the ephemeral is transformed; at the very least, expired actuality raises the possibility that it might come to represent something other than itself. The tension between the sense that events are changing so rapidly, on the one hand, and that communication about these events is delayed, on the other, opens up a space for a mode of diagnostic writing. Börne creates something of a map of different moments in time, some of which are linked and others of which are not, a temporal topography upon which various histories can be located and upon which various anticipated, imagined, or hoped for futures can be mapped out. This is a model of history writing different from that of the idealist philosophy of history, which maps out historical eventfulness on the basis of the movement of the concept (Hegel), material forces (Marx), or of "universal" history that seeks a systematic overview of distinct historical epochs (Ranke and F. C. Schlosser).[35]

The seriality of the letters also contributes to this effect of plural, overlapping temporal frameworks. "Adieu until the next revolution" can also be glossed as "Adieu until the next letter." As in the introduction to *Die Wage*, Börne seems especially interested in irregular periodicities that can come to terms with (or at least mark) a variety of contingent delays, disruptions, and misinformation that characterize the topics of his letters. Börne overlays this medial structure onto the turmoil-laden era in history in which he finds himself, allowing him to track the ongoing struggle for freedom across Europe (which will certainly continue after he breaks off the *Briefe*); a slice of his own life in Paris; snapshots of the world of the arts, public performance and spectacle, and more. The fact that these letters are part of the *Gesammelte Schriften* from the get-go adds another historical and temporal layer, for the letters are added to an ongoing collection of previous writings, entering into new relationships with them. In each case, the seriality of the letters—the promise that more will come—assures the arrival of something more or less indeterminate in a more or less indeterminate future.

---

35. On the linear (and serial) model of Ranke's writings, see Mario Wimmer, "World History in Six Installments: Epistemic Seriality and the Epistemology of Series," in *Truth in Serial Form: Serial Formats and the Form of the Series (1850–1930)*, ed. Malika Maskarenic (New York: De Gruyter, 2023).

The History of the Coming Revolution

Heine's critique of Börne's writing as being negatively influenced by his incessant consumption of the periodical press is more complicated than it looks, not least because this is the very kind of criticism that is leveled at his own work. "His skipping from one topic to another no longer arose from a mad mood but from a moody madness, and was probably to be ascribed to the variety of newspapers with which Börne at the time occupied himself day and night."[36] Heine accuses Börne of only being a man of the present and a writer too involved with the daily press to gain a proper historical overview, yet, as scholars have repeatedly determined, Heine's portrait of Börne (to the extent that it can be understood as such) contains a good deal of indirect, often ironic self-portraiture. Rather than accept at face value Heine's criticism of Börne as an unhistorical creature of the present, I instead propose that Börne's writings offer up a mode of historical awareness that allows for the rediscovery of the past in the future—such rediscovery is, after all, a key feature of the very historiographical project pursued by Heine's Parisian writings, as we will see in the next chapter.

Like many contemporary commentators, Börne is attuned to Paris as a site of proliferating historical representations and spectacles and to the effects of these historical representations on his own history writing. This includes his admiration of the French vaudeville theater and its ability to incorporate the most current of current events into its performances. As Börne notes in the theater commentaries that pepper his *Briefe*, it is typical for these plays to depict more or less recent historical events ranging from the early 1790s to the period leading up to 1830. Börne intersperses his accounts of vaudeville with reports on other historically themed public events, including public lectures, panoramas, commemorative festivals, and more. He thereby taps into long-standing modes of cultural journalism and their association with public spectacle and fashion, while at the same time lending the material his particular authorial voice and a sense of historical urgency. This, then, is the

---

36. Heine, *Ludwig Börne*, 53.

context for his reflections on his own unconventional historical method in December of 1832.

> Today's papers are praising this new opera highly. I submit quite eagerly to all of this, because I profit from it. For two years now the boulevard theaters have guided my historical studies. As soon as I saw a historical play, the next day I went and got all the history books, memoirs, and chronicles that deal with the time period and the history that were presented on stage, and I read them. Of course, I would not recommend this way of studying history to young people, but for children and the comfortable [*bequeme Leute*] this is the proper way; even if I would be hard pressed to pass an examination by Schlosser, in the *Ambigu Comique* I am the most systematic historian.[37]

Börne conceives of historical awareness as a multidirectional, multimedial undertaking, with theater criticism in the papers directing him to the theater and the theater leading him back to history writing. Börne's remark that he gets most of his history from the vaudeville theaters is more than just a cheeky aside. Instead, this insight helps him to diagnose the particular media environment and historical situation in which he finds himself.

Börne writes this letter at the same time he contemplates writing an expressly popular history of the French Revolution, and the language he uses to conceptualize this project is strikingly similar to this passage: "How necessary and useful it would be," he writes in November of the same year, "to present the atrocities and insanities of the monarchical governments in a comprehensible language accessible to children, women, and childish, womanly men."[38] In characterizing a popular mode of history writing (with clear misogynistic overtones, it should be said), he firmly positions his writing against a more systematic, academic mode and instead addresses youth and adults and men and women alike. This is a time when

---

37. Börne, *Briefe aus Paris*, December 16, 1832. SS, III, 656–57.
38. Börne, *Briefe aus Paris*, November 26, 1832. SS, III, 616–17. On this project see Inge Rippmann, "'Die Zeit läuft wie ein Reh vor uns her.' Der Zeitschriftsteller als Geschichtsschreiber," in *"Die Kunst—eine Tochter der Zeit". Neue Studien zu Ludwig Börne*, ed. Inge Rippmann and Wolfgang Labuhn (Bielefeld: Aisthesis, 1998), 130–69.

French histories of the revolutionary period and its aftermath are proliferating and when many German writers seek to do the same. In the end, both Heine and Börne opt for more open-ended formats that incorporate aspects of the modern media landscape (the boulevard theater is a particularly serialized form of performance: Börne remarks that he has been attending them regularly, "for years now"). Börne doesn't seem repentant about his unscholarly approach to the past: even though he would fail an exam with the Heidelberg historian Schlosser, and even though his work does not share an ideal of systematic universality with Schlossser's, it has the potential to reach a broader public. To be sure, the letters are filled with Börne's self-doubt as a historian of the French Revolution, suggesting at one point that the *Briefe*'s affect-laden mode might be ill-suited to the task of "objective" history and that it has too much "heart" (*Herz*).[39] But there is a performative quality as well as a need for reassurance in such statements, and Börne did in fact make considerable headway toward an initial draft of a revolutionary history at this time.[40] The ordering of this material is telling, as we can see with notes compiled by Börne organizing literature on the French Revolution, in which he places journals at the top of a list of six items largely composed of serial print ("I. Journeaux. II Mémoires. III. Pamphlets. IV. Histoire. V. Théatre. VI. Pièces officielles.").[41]

The *Briefe* thus comes into view as perhaps the most important of Börne's attempts to process the current moment in expressly historiographical terms, probing the potential and limitations of a kind of "history writing of the present," to borrow Heine's phrase. The following passage from a letter of January 30, 1831, sheds important light on this attempt:

> You write that Heine speaks of the French Revolution in his fourth volume [of the *Reisebilder*]. I think that he only tried to speak, but didn't carry it out. What form of speech would be strong enough to contain this wildly fermenting time? One would have to place an iron yoke upon

---

39. See Börne, *Briefe aus Paris*, November 12, 1832. SS, III, 596–97.
40. This material is collected in Börne, "Studen über Geschichte und Menschen der französischen Revolution," SS, II, 1053–154.
41. See Börne, "Studen über Geschichte und Menschen," SS, II, 1121.

every word, and to do this one needs an iron heart. Heine is too timid [*mild*]. Campe [Börne's publisher] also wrote me; he expects me to write something *current* [*Zeitgemäßes*] in the eighth volume [of the *Gesammelte Schriften*]. This eighth volume that I am to write, here in Paris, fifteen minutes from the Tuileries, a half-hour from the Gendarmerie—nothing could be more comical! What, where, on what, with what should I write? The ground is shaking, the table is shaking, the lectern, hand, and heart are shaking, and history, moved by the storm, is itself shaking. I cannot chew over what I have devoured with such pleasure; I am not enough of an ox for that. I wanted to be a prophet for him, throughout all twelve volumes. And can the German be anything but a prophet? We are not writers of history [*Geschichtsschreiber*], but rather beaters of history [*Geschichtstreiber*]. Time runs out ahead of us like a deer; we, the dogs run behind it. It will run a long time before we catch up to it; it will be a long time before we become writers of history. But—I want to go now and listen to Beethoven. . . . The concert starts at 2 p.m. This is better than in the evening. The ear and the heart are more pure prior to eating. Perhaps I will visit the masked ball this evening. Not the one in the grand opera; I know that one from before; it makes you fall asleep; no, the one in the theater at the Porte-Saint-Martin. There I will find my good jacket-wearing people [*mein gutes Volk in der Jacke*] who fought so bravely in July. Pleasure and life is there. Long coats, boring times [*Lange Röcke, lange Weile*]—I always found these things together.[42]

Here we find ourselves back at the criticism leveled at Mercier's new *Tableau* of Paris by the editors of *London und Paris* that it cannot keep up with the changing times; a similar perspective colors Börne's positive self-identification as a prophet, for, if in his previous volumes of the *Gesammelte Schriften*, he wanted to be a prophet, his inability to predict or "yoke" the present was a limitation. Yet writing about the present is also by necessity writing about the revolution, a historical event that is still in the process of being completed—history is itself shaking from this storm. The challenge, then, is to prophetically write the "wildly fermenting" time of the revolution, including its past, present, and future. Hence the hunting metaphor of the "beater" or driver of history: Börne feels like he is behind the present and behind the future, yet, by writing, he is in some way also pushing it forward. We have encountered the notion of future-directed, quasi-prophetic writing in the preface to volume 3 of the

---

42. Börne, *Briefe aus Paris*, January 30, 1831, SS, III, 156.

Gesammelte Schriften, and here Börne casts prophecy both as potential and limitation characteristic of the German observer: because nothing is happening or has happened in Germany in terms of progress toward revolution, there is nothing to write about. This places the German observer in a subservient position, driving the game out into the clearing for noble hunters—perhaps the French historians are able to both participate in and theorize about revolutionary actions? To write the time of the revolution, one must become a future-oriented *Geschichtstreiber* rather than a past-oriented *Geschichtsschreiber*; one must attempt to catalyze historical events rather than merely reflect on what has already happened. On this line of thinking, becoming historical is equated with realizing the ideals of the revolution. For the German writer and for Germans, the eventfulness of history is something to come, it is something "out in front of us." Recognizing that any historical eventfulness in Germany is delayed thereby also entails marking the span of time that reaches back from the past, straddles the present, and projects into the future; it remains uncertain when "we" will catch up with time and be able to write about it as history (yet another marking of a span of time whose duration is indeterminate). Such prophecy anticipates the completion (or repetition) of the revolution but does not specify the duration between now and then.

To linger just a bit more with this passage: "But [Doch]—" Börne inserts another dash into his train of thought, digressing from philosophical-historical reflections to consider his afternoon and evening plans. Again, we have a kind of media-driven confrontation, with the slowness and weightiness of the volumes of his and Heine's collected writings standing in marked contrast to the fleeting realm of public spectacle. At first glance it might seem that the dash shifts the register and topic of the letter, but this digression involves more continuity than one might think, for a strong trace of revolutionary politics and of the recent historical past emerges at the end, as Börne reports his decision to attend the boulevard theater preferred by the working class, by "my good jacket wearing people, who fought so bravely in July." Ending on a note of solidarity with those who fought in the July Revolution (and a sartorial note at that), Börne lends the very temporal scales and durations at stake at the end of this passage—long ones and short ones, boredom and entertainment—a political valence. Long duration, *lange Weile*, and long coattails remind the reader of the persistence of the repressive powers of restoration, while the embrace of diversion, *divertissement* or *Kurzweil*, if you will, is associated with revolutionary partisanship and solidarity. Börne thereby shifts his identification from the German people to the French (*mein gutes Volk*), turning his allegiances away from those for whom the revolution is still to come to those whose steps toward revolution lie in the recent past. He thus ends on a note of implicit hope, namely that the short jackets might portend a shorter duration between the advent of the revolution than what he envisioned in his more historical reflections just prior. This is the hope, in other words, of catching up with time and of closing the distance between the beater and writer of history.

Once again, this scene stages a kind of waiting for the revolution, playfully suggesting a turn away from historical reflections to more fleeting diversions, but doing so exactly to create a temporal topography upon which the recurrence or completion of the revolution can be imagined. The in-between moment, the time of waiting, is not wasted, even if it is spent in masked diversions, for snapshots of fleeting moments in the past and present help to model a prophetic relationship to the future. Börne collects these snapshots, assembling them into a mode of writing time that looks for traces of the future in the experience of heterochronic modernity. This is a mode of writing history that is predicated on the belief that the revolution is not first and foremost a bygone, purely historical event but rather something that is still underway, vibrating, and "shaking" in the present. Like Hegel, Börne equates the process of becoming truly historical with realizing the revolution's ideal of freedom, yet he seeks to set this process in motion via the vibrations of the contingent and the ephemeral rather than through the teleologically driven necessity of the philosophical concept.

The very last letter of *Briefe aus Paris* brings the collection to an abrupt close with a similar gesture. The work ends in 1833, the day before March 20, "when, in the morning, at eight sixteen, spring begins." It also ends on a note of uncertainty and indeterminacy, with the prospect of Börne leaving Paris after his money and heating fuel run out:

> I can't be sure yet about the day of my departure; its dependent upon my wood. Yes, truly on my firewood; this is my tally stick [*Kerbholz*], my calendar. I have sworn not to have any more wood delivered and to get into the coach as soon as the last log sits in the fireplace.[43]

Maybe Börne will end up staying in Paris an entire additional spring, summer, and fall if his wood lasts until the warm weather. Or maybe he will be forced to leave. Börne marks the sequential unfolding of time through the few remaining pieces of wood that are his "calendar," for they represent a series of specific actions (heating his apartment) whose exact duration is unclear. Throughout the *Briefe*, questions of household economy (and the high cost of heating in particular) are intimately intertwined with Börne's identity as a writer—like Heine, Börne bitterly relishes his life as an impoverished exile. The pieces of wood (rather than a single tally stick [*Kerbholz*] that one leaves marks on) index a frame of time but in an indeterminate way that leaves the future open-ended. Once more Börne stages his own waiting; he stages the breaking up of time into discernable durations. But once more he does not mark a determinate point in time when these durations come to an end. That said, while the projected end point in question, whether of Börne's wood supply, his departure from Paris, or the end of his *Briefe*, is impending, this end point also marks the beginning of something new (indeed, by the time that readers encounter this letter, he will have left and returned to Paris). Börne will continue on the path of life, political and cultural developments will continue to unfold, and he will write about them in different ways, even if the *Briefe* comes to an end. In keeping with the propensity of serial forms to defer endings and envision continuation, Börne promises more to come. This performative marking of time through serial form promises the continuation of life, time, history, and maybe even also revolution.

---

43. Börne, *Briefe aus Paris*, March 17, 1833, SS, III, 863.

7

HEINE'S SERIAL HISTORIES OF THE REVOLUTION

Though I have argued that criticisms of Börne as an unhistorical thinker miss crucial features of his engagement as a writer of contemporary histories, Heine does ultimately bring many more expressly historical projects to fruition than Börne. These include his intellectual histories of German religious and philosophical thought and of the Romantic school and his extensive explorations of historical topics in his poetry. Heine's writings on the July Monarchy are infused with one of his central historical concerns, namely the past, present, and future of the revolution. His article collections *Französische Zustände* (1833) and *Lutezia* (1854) straddle the immediacy of tableau-like reportage and the remove of historical reflection, and they engage in complex refractions of historical time, placing reports from one to two years prior (as with *Französische Zustände*) and up to thirteen years prior in *Lutezia* into relation with events that have intervened since their initial publication. The formats of *Französische Zustände* and *Lute-*

zia are of particular interest because Heine pursued both collections at a time when he strongly considered writing a larger work on the history of the French Revolution, a project that, as with Börne, remained uncompleted.[1] Like Börne's *Briefe aus Paris*, these publications represent alternatives to more conventional histories of the revolution by Heine's European contemporaries such Adolphe Thiers, Jules Michelet, B. G. Niebuhr, and Thomas Carlyle. Heine thereby engages with a range of modern media to specific historiographical ends, contrasting different formats (newspaper, book, and historical lecture) and different styles of visual representation, favoring subversive genres such as caricature over traditional history painting. In this chapter, I explore how these Parisian writings create knowledge about time through the effects of serial print. Heine asks readers to understand historical time as an unruly mixture of the old and new to consider how different aspects of the past remain at work in the present and into the future. A particular feature of this temporal knowledge consists in anticipating the continuation of the revolution in the future. Heine calls Hegel "his great teacher," but he constantly relativizes and ironizes any systematic vision of linear, teleological progress. Heine's writings do not pursue the Hegelian pedagogy of sharing how reason comes to itself; instead they model uncertain, unpredictable futures and juxtapose alternative models of history rather than seeking any kind of philosophical resolution. Heine thereby relies on tropes of before and after, of prediction and retrospection, and of serial continuation to place the present into shifting relationship to multiple pasts and futures.

Positioning his articles and their republication as historical undertakings, Heine faces two key challenges. The first relates to form, for he embraces the myriad ironic and satirical modes from cultural journals, calling his articles "fleeting pages" (*flüchtige Blätter*).[2] Heine

---

1. On this project, see the editorial apparatus to *Französische Zustände* by Jean René Derré and Christiane Giessen. DHA, 12/2, 840.
2. "Superficial readers" might well find his articles on French affairs a "collection of petty anecdotes and the notes of a gullible fool." Heinrich Heine, "Preface to the French Edition of Lutezia," in *The Romantic School and Other Essays*, ed. Jost Hermand and Robert C. Holub (New York: Continuum, 1985), 298.

thereby eschews traditional history writing based on narrative conventions of closure and generic principles of the epic, in which one event necessarily follows the other, instead anticipating later techniques of montage.³ As Peter Uwe Hohendahl puts it, Heine "transports the viewpoint of the feuilleton, its wit and subjectivity, into historiographical representation itself."⁴ Yet the book versions of these articles also lay claim to deliberate "artistic arrangement" (*künstlerische Zusammenstellung*). The notion that history writing should synthesize disparate items into a whole goes back to the idealist thought of Schiller, Kant, and Wilhelm von Humboldt, who relegate the task of collecting fragmentary particulars to mechanical memory and task aesthetic judgment and speculative thought with philosophical overview, or *Zusammenhang*.⁵ Heine taps into this vision when asserting that both his initial authorial vision and his retroactive activity organize these pieces into a unified whole, in book form, that will retain its value into the future.⁶ On the one hand, he asserts that this unity stems from his commitment to the cause of the revolution: his "unwavering love for the cause of humanity and a perseverance in [his] democratic principles" is the "spirit" moving through the entirety of his writings.⁷ On the other hand, asserting such a unity through anthologized collections is a gesture of authorial control, as he signs anonymously published articles with his name. Heine's first

---

3. See Andras Sandor, "The Oak Tree and the Ax: Delaroche's Painting and Heine's Montage," in *Painting on the Move: Heinrich Heine and Visual Arts*, ed. Susanne Zantop (Lincoln, NE: University of Nebraska Press, 1989), 72.

4. Peter Uwe Hohendahl, "Literary Criticism in the Epoch of Liberalism," in *A History of German Literary Criticism, 1730–1980*, ed. Peter Uwe Hohendahl (Lincoln, NE: University of Nebraska Press, 1988), 228.

5. See Laurence Dickey, "Philosophizing about History in the Nineteenth Century: Zusammenhang and the 'Progressive Method' in German Historical Scholarship," in *The Cambridge History of Philosophy in the Nineteenth Century (1790–1870)*, ed. Allen W. Wood and Songuk Susan Hahn (Cambridge: Cambridge University Press, 2012), 793–816.

6. In a letter to his publisher, Heine states that *Lutezia* has a "closed unity" (*geschlossene Einheit*), "despite the hectic change in topics," and is "book of history [*Geschichtsbuch*] that speaks to the present day and that will live on in the future [*das den heutigen Tag anspricht und in der Zukunft fortleben wird*]." Heinrich Heine to Campe, April 18, 1854. HSA, 23, 320.

7. Heine, "Preface to the French Edition," 298.

challenge is thus to maintain ostensible authorial control even while eschewing historical narratives based on the generic dictates of the epic.[8]

Heine's second key challenge is writing at a time of tremendous uncertainty, with many observers concluding that the revolution is still ongoing. After having arrived in Paris in May of 1831 and beginning his work on the articles that he would later compile as *Französische Zustände,* Heine calls these writings "preliminary studies for the history of the present" (*Vorstudien zur Geschichtschreibung der Gegenwart*). They are provisional accounts of the present, but a present that is always disappearing into the past before the full-fledged writing of its history can be attained. In multiple turbulent presents ranging from the early 1830s to the mid-1850s, Heine attempts to articulate the experience that every new moment can potentially recast our understanding of the past. Here, he singles out institutionalized, academic historians for naively treating the revolution solely as a past event and for believing that

> the records of the history of the revolution were closed and that they had uttered their last judgment on people and things: all at once, though, the cannons of the great week [of the July Revolution] thundered, and the faculty of Göttingen observed . . . that not only was the French special revolution not finished, but that the far more comprehensive universal revolution had just begun.[9]

Unlike academic historians who prefer to deal with events that are completed and static in their meaning, Heine seeks a mode of writing that reveals the shifting status of both present and past, and, like Börne, he places anticipatory weight on present and future moments when the past is valued anew.[10] To this end he mines the

---

8. See Susanne Zantop, *Zeitbilder. Geschichte und Literatur bei Heinrich Heine und Mariano José de Larra* (Bonn: Bouvier, 1988), 107–8.

9. Heine, *Französische Zustände,* 146. Historians later in the nineteenth century would continue to confirm the sense that the history of the revolution is ongoing and not yet complete; see Anna Karla, "Die verschlafene Revolution von 1789," 212.

10. As Anthony Phelan puts it, Heine recognizes that "historical or cultural moments are not fixed functions in the representation of social or political formations. Rather, they are constantly appropriated, reappropriated, and revalued." An-

modern media landscape—ephemeral print, visual culture, popular theater, dance, and more—rather than the more staid source material of state archives that would figure prominently in the self-legitimation of academic historiography in Prussia.[11] His second challenge is thus to write open-ended histories that can reengage the past, present, and future at various points of temporal remove.

Heine takes up modes of serial writing and publication in response to both challenges, putting his own writings into proximity with momentous events of the past and situating them as eventful occasions in their own right. In *Lutezia*, Heine states his affinity with Scheherazade's serial storytelling in *A Thousand and One Nights*, as he endlessly interrupts himself and defers any final conclusions. His articles always bear the caveat that they are "to be continued," thereby adopting the conventions of serialized, periodical publications, while also reserving the leeway of open-ended perpetuation. In addition to the original periodical publications, republication in book form likewise represents a kind of serial continuation, for it places the articles in new textual environments and creates a new site at which to exercise authorial control and artistic ambitions; it doubles the previously published texts as historical artifacts that have participated in the past and adds new material originally published elsewhere or cut by censors. Republication in book form thereby makes it possible to place texts into new constellations and to present them as a unified whole reflective of author's aesthetic intentions. Intervening at the intersection of periodical and book publication (two complementary practices of serialized publishing), Heine uses republication to stage multiple positions from which to encounter time, "the times," and possible moments of provisional ending, continuation, anticipation, and delay.[12] Heine writes himself into the past through republication,

---

thony Phelan, *Reading Heinrich Heine* (Cambridge: Cambridge University Press, 2007), 182–83.

11. On state archives as historical sources, see Cornelia Vismann, *Akten. Medientechnik und Recht* (Frankfurt: Fischer, 2000), 226–66.

12. As Michael Gamper puts it, his historical projects pursue the "overt proleptically or analeptically oriented correspondence of different moments of historical eventfulness and literary creativity." Michael Gamper, "Gegenwärtige Politik des Vergangenen. Politische Nachträglichkeit bei Heinrich Heine," in *Gleichzeitigkeit*

situating his own pieces—and the scene of composing them and sending them off to the publisher—as part of historical events. Like the personalities or societal forces whose standings might have changed in the years since original publication, Heine's writings come into view both as relics of bygone moments and as interventions that lend themselves to mediated reactualization.

In this chapter, I first explore Heine's more general approach to history and his dual critique of academic historians and of the philosophy of history before turning to several specific episodes in his contemporary historical writings. The first deals with Heine's juxtaposition of significantly different modes of journalism and history writing and his placement of these modes into varying relations of before and after. Heine profits from the sense that his pieces function both as journalistic responses to specific moments and as historical reflections that place disjunctive presents into relation with each other. Like Börne, Heine explores how republication models open-ended structures of before and after, of looking out into the future and back into the past. Heine's critical take on historical portraiture is a second side to his engagement with serial forms. Conceits of the literary image, sketch, and caricature are a key part of his histories of the present, both those of the 1830s and 1840s, which he undertakes at a time of proliferating imagery in print, popular theater, and more. The portraiture of past and present figures is a popular mode of nineteenth-century history writing and literary entertainment more broadly and is itself an inherently serial mode. Heine's statement that *Lutezia* is a "daguerreotypic history book" (*daguerreotypisches Geschichtsbuch*) in part references this tradition. His sketches of figures in culture and politics become a crucial part of Heine's journalistic history writing, relying on the conceit of presenting readers with a series of images. Like Börne, Heine plays off different styles of history writing and cultural politics against each other by staging the confrontation between different media.

Though one could explore issues of caricature and characterization via a variety of episodes in both texts, I turn especially to *Lutezia*, not

---

des Ungleichzeitigen. Formen und Funktionen von Pluralität in der ästhetischen Moderne, ed. Sabine Schneider and Heinz Brüggemann (Munich: Fink, 2010), 89.

least because it is there that Heine registers his proximity to the new technology of photography. *Lutezia* is also the place where Heine engages in serialized accounts of academic historians. These accounts stand out because his ironic characterization of these scholars and their historical method help him to profile his own alternative historiographical vision. Heine frequently tells of how he listens in on lectures on history, staging his spatial and temporal convergence with these speakers, an experience that is by most accounts (including his own) an archetypal scene for him—it is Hegel, after all, whom Heine heard lecture in Berlin and with and against whom he argues throughout his writings. Heine sets apart his own historical character description from other modes of history writing through ironic mirroring and mimicry, a kind of anti-portraiture. In contrast to the conventional emphasis on historical personality—in Thomas Carlyle's 1841 *On Heroes, Hero-Worship, and the Heroic in History*, Karl Gutzkow's 1835 *Öffentliche Charaktere* (Public figures), or Franz Kugler's *Geschichte Friedrich des Großen* (History of Friedrich the Great) (1840), to name several contemporary examples—Heine uses caricature-like portraits to create knowledge about time rather than to reify and glorify historical personality. As I argue, the integrity of the individual as historical subject disintegrates and depersonalized historical forces shine through in Heine's contemporary histories. I close the chapter with the French and German prefaces to the book publication of *Lutezia*, exploring how these retrospective texts address the question of literary afterlives. His introductory preface dedicated to his friend Prince Hermann von Pückler-Muskau is an ambivalent, elusive portrait that highlights Heine's mode of writing time on the basis of texts written both for the turbulent present and for uncertain futures, texts that import the logic of ephemeral journalism into an important, legacy-defining late work.[13] In a medialized modernity characterized by "the ever-reconfigured constellation of the present at the interface of past and future," as Willi Goetschel puts it, the afterlives of serial journalistic endeavors model how the past can reemerge and be revalued in the future.[14]

---

13. See Phelan, *Reading Heinrich Heine*, 182.
14. Willi Goetschel, *Heine and Critical Theory* (London: Bloomsbury, 2019), 21.

Various Conceptions of History

Scholars have repeatedly drawn attention to the interrelation of Heine's mode of writing and his concept of history: his "performative" approach to history writing generates a "plurality of narratives" and constellates multiple competing conceptions of history, favoring ironic juxtaposition over unambiguous resolution.[15] Rather than developing a single, unified historiographical narrative, he pursues a variety of inroads to historical representation, constantly interrupting himself and redirecting readers. The French Revolution is a particularly salient subject for this form of history writing because of its multivalent temporal filiations across past, present, and future. The writer of history seeks to understand the effects of past events on the present, but he or she also seeks to understand how the concerns of the present and the anticipation of the future alike shape the view of the past. Heine dramatizes these kinds of temporal vectors in article VI in *Französische Zustände*. At first, he demonstratively turns his sights to the past, construing the noise and chatter of the present as a potential distraction but also as a riddle to be deciphered: "I wish to contribute as much as possible . . . to the understanding of the present and look for the key to the noisy enigma of today in the past. The salons lie and the graves are true."[16] This is one of several pithy, protodialectical formulations that Heine uses to parse the ambiguous status of the past in the present.[17] In stating that the salons lie and the graves are true, Heine asks how the 1789 revolution continues to influence events forty years later. However, he then goes on to state his desire to reveal "how the past first becomes understandable through the

---

15. Goetschel, *Heine and Critical Theory*, 160. See also Gerhard Höhn, "Eternal Return or Indiscernible Progress? Heine's Conception of History after 1848," in *A Companion to the Works of Heinrich Heine*, ed. Roger Cook (Rochester, NY: Camden House, 2002), 169–200.
16. Heine, article VI, *Französische Zustände*, 139–40.
17. On Heine's manipulation of Hegelian categories and his "clinical description" of the "decomposition" of the philosophy of history, see Stathis Kouvelakis, *Philosophy and Revolution: From Kant to Marx*, trans. G. M. Goshgarian (London: Verso, 2003), 46–47, 53.

present, and how every new day sheds new light upon the past, something of which our previous writers of historical handbooks had no idea."[18] This second statement shifts attention to how present concerns alter our understanding of the past, a feature of historical understanding that historians commonly seek to neutralize.

Here Heine straddles two models of engaging with the past. Reinhart Koselleck has shown how the late eighteenth-century understanding of history breaks with the traditional topos of history as the teacher of life (*historia magistra vitae*), which assumes that past events repeat themselves and serve as normative models for understanding the present and future.[19] Traditional history writing is a mimetic mode based in the classicizing concept of imitating great men and their deeds.[20] It is above all the French Revolution that undermines the idea that the past instructs the present, for the revolution is perceived to be unprecedentedly new. As Koselleck argues, postrevolutionary historical consciousness comes to assume a teleological notion of progress, justifying past and present actions from the perspective of a future goal rather than a repeatable past. Heine approaches this tension between differing approaches to the past in an unpublished fragment titled "Verschiedenartige Geschichtsauffassung" (Various conceptions of history) written at about the same time as his 1831–1832 articles for the *Allgemeine Zeitung*. For Heine, the traditional approach amounts to an "indifferent" outlook that sees history as a realm of bleak cyclical repetition (*trostlosen Kreislauf*).[21] Ranke and other conservative academic historians exemplify this model as they remain indifferent to the future because they see it as in no way diverging from the past and present.[22] The

---

18. Heine, article VI, *Französische Zustände*, 145.
19. Reinhart Koselleck, "Historia Magistra Vitae: The Dissolution of the Topos into the Perspective of a Modernized Historical Process," in *Futures Past: On the Semantics of Historical Time*, trans. Keith Tribe (New York: Columbia University Press, 2004), 26–42.
20. See Hell, *The Conquest of Ruins*, 112.
21. Heine, "Verschiedartige Geschichtsauffassung." DHA, 10, 301. See also Fritz Mende, *Heinrich Heine, Studien zu seinem Leben und Werk* (Berlin: Akademie, 1983), 208–18.
22. On Heine's engagement with Ranke, see Susanne Zantop, "Verschiedenartige Geschichtsschreibung: Heine und Ranke," *Heine Jahrbuch* 23 (1984): 42–68.

second, "providential" model is expressed most fully by the "philosophical school," that is, Hegel and his followers, which sees a future of rational progress and the betterment of the human condition. Heine views this model more positively, but he remains skeptical of the "fanaticism of those promising future happiness" (*Schwärmerei der Zukunftbeglücker*), for the progressive philosophy of history justifies the present as a means to the end of realizing the future: "We also demand that the living present be valued as it deserves, and not serve merely as a means to an end in the service of the future."[23]

This fragment is an often-cited example of Heine's particular combination of rejecting nonteleological views of history while remaining committed to the ideals of the revolution.[24] For Heine, the present is justified in its own right via the principle of life rather than that of a progressive, rational future: "Life is neither [a] means nor [an] end. Life is a right. Life desires to validate this right against the claims of petrifying death, against the past, and this act of validating life is the revolution ... 'le pain est le droit du peuple,' said Saint-Just, and this is the greatest word spoken in the entire revolution."[25] In being equated with "petrifying death," the past seems as far removed from instructing life as possible, yet Heine does not bestow this pedagogical function on the future either. He attempts to do justice to the suffering and struggles of the present on its own terms;

This cyclical view is also characteristic of certain strands of premodern Jewish conceptions of history that Heine was familiar with; see Christhard Hoffmann, "History versus Memory: Heinrich Heine and the Jewish Past," in *Heinrich Heine's Contested Identities: Politics, Religion, and Nationalism in Nineteenth-Century Germany*, ed. Jost Hermand and Robert Holub (New York: Peter Lang, 1999), 25–48.

23. Heine, "Verschiedartige Geschichtsauffassung," DHA, 10, 302; Heinrich Heine, "Various Conceptions of History," in Hermand and Holub, *The Romantic School*, 259–60.

24. "Heine did not banish the hope for emancipation from his thought, but he did however reject the goddess 'necessity,' the idea of *necessary* progress in history." Ortwin Lämke, *Heines Begriff der Geschichte. Der Journalist Heinrich Heine und die Julimonarchie* (Stuttgart: Metzler, 1997), 139. See also Jeffrey Grossman, "Fractured Histories: Heinrich Heine's Responses to Violence and Revolution," in *Contemplating Violence: Critical Studies in Modern German Culture*, ed. Carl Niekerk and Stefani Engelstein (Amsterdam: Rodopi, 2010), 67–87.

25. Heine, "Verschiedartige Geschichtsauffassung," DHA, 10, 302; Heine, "Various Conceptions of History," 260.

indeed, linking life and the present in this way was common in the liberal writings of the *Vormärz*.[26] It would almost seem that here Heine reverses his own pithy statement that "the salons lie, the graves are true": truth as well as moral and historical "greatness" are on the side of life's self-assertion over and against the past.

In "Verschiedenartige Geschichtsauffassung," Heine uses life as a conceptual lever to open up the problem of treating historical situations, constellations, or actors as autonomous entities in their own right. He writes with polemical, almost activist conviction, from the perspective of "our liveliest feelings of life" (*unseren lebendigsten Lebensgefühlen*), and yet in this fragment he never returns to the problem of an overarching historical *Zusammenhang* or to the problem of identifying connections between different self-standing historical entities: What links the self-assertion of life at one historical moment to that of a previous or future moment? Indeed, we might conjecture that the difficulty of placing different actions into historically coherent relationships to one another—an epistemological as well as historiographical difficulty—prevented Heine from finishing these reflections or led him to attempt to solve it through other conceptual or textual means. In *Französische Zustände*, Heine comes to a somewhat different conclusion as to the specifically historical manifestations of the present. There Heine shifts questions of life and death, of before and after, onto the publication conditions of print. Both in topic and format, Heine explores notions of before and after that go beyond a simple equation of the present with life.

Interrupting the History of the Revolution

Französische Zustände is one of many contemporaneous texts reporting to German readers about the aftermath of the July Revo-

---

26. "For Young Germany, the concept of the present is bound up with the concept of life. . . . Life appears as the basis for a progressive process in whose course conservative political and social forces are overcome." Hohendahl, "Literary Criticism," 202. On the semantics of life see also Wulf Wülfing, *Schlagworte des Jungen Deutschland. Mit einer Einführung in die Schlagwortforschung* (Berlin: Erich Schmidt, 1982), 159–67.

lution, texts which also include Börne's *Briefe aus Paris* (1832–1834). Heine wrote for Cotta's *Morgenblatt für gebildete Stände* in the 1820s and began working in 1831 as a Parisian correspondent for Cotta's more news-oriented Augsburg-based *Allgemeine Zeitung*, which was the most important German-language daily newspaper in the period. Almost every issue of the *Allgemeine Zeitung* in the early 1830s contained reports from Paris, and Cotta had six correspondents there at the time.[27] Heine's articles from the early 1830s and early 1840s mixed commentary on current events with historical reflection, and they presumed readers' acquaintance with important news items, parliamentary speeches, and more from elsewhere in the paper or from other sources.[28] This dynamic is reflected in the articles' placement in the "Außerordentliche Beylage zur Allgemeinen Zeitung" (Extraordinary supplement to the *Allgemeine Zeitung*), a section of the paper that is a further, additional supplement to the "regular" "Beylage." Though the *Allgemeine Zeitung* did not have a feuilleton section per se, these supplements serve a similar function, combining cultural commentary and theater and literary reviews and operating as a counterpart to more factual journalistic reporting through both content and format.[29]

The book version of *Französische Zustände* contains nine longer numbered and dated articles first published from December of 1831 to June of 1832, "Daily Reports" about the failed June Rebellion of 1832 (the first major public insurrection that Heine witnessed firsthand and an event immortalized in Victor Hugo's *Les Miserables*), and a short series of pieces titled "From Normandy" (*Aus der Normandie*). *Französische Zustände* is a companion, and even a rival piece, to Börne's *Briefe aus Paris* (1832–1834).[30] Heine viewed the article anthology as a somewhat unconventional,

---

27. Booß, *Ansichten der Revolution*, 80.
28. On the importance for Heine of newspaper reading as he was composing these articles, see Volkmar Hansen, *Heinrich Heines politische Journalistik in der Augsburger "Allgemeinen Zeitung"* (Augsburg: Stadt Augsburg, 1994), 10.
29. Hansen, *Heinrich Heines politische Journalistik*, 44.
30. Editorial apparatus to *Fränzösische Zustände*, DHA, 12/2, 674–75.

"rarely used form"³¹ of contemporary history, though it bears certain similarities in form and approach to contemporary travel writing and foreign reporting. Heine's longer articles in the *Allgemeine Zeitung*, titled "Französische Zustände," appear in serialized installments over several issues of the *Allgemeine Zeitung*, and are signed, while the shorter articles are often published anonymously. The book version is organized by the formal conceit of collecting varied articles by a familiar author, with Heine describing the project in the following manner:

> I am offering here a series of articles and daily reports that I wrote for the AZ [*Allgemeine Zeitung*] according to the desires of the moment, in stormy relations of all different sorts. I will now publish these anonymous, fleeting pages under my name as a solid book, so that no one else will arrange [*zusammenstellt*] them according to their own whims.³²

Republication preempts unauthorized reprinting and rearrangement, and it also allows Heine to reintegrate material cut by the censors; books longer than twenty sheets or *Bogen* were not subject to the same prepublication censorship as newspapers and journals, though this didn't stop Heine's preface—a text with its own complex publication and reception history—from being heavily censored.³³ He would have been quite familiar with the conventions of republication, for many of his articles were excerpted in other German papers and journals soon after appearing in the *Allgemeine Zeitung*; in such cases, book republication would have been the third or fourth printing of a given article.³⁴ Of course, there were financial advantages to republication, with Heine getting paid both from Cotta and Campe for journal and book versions respectively.³⁵

---

31. He calls publishing of articles in this way "eine wenig gebrauchte Form" in a letter to Varnhagen; cited in editorial apparatus to *Fränzösische Zustände*. DHA, 12/2, 649.
32. Heine, *Französische Zustände*, v–vi.
33. On the publication history see the extensive editorial apparatus to *Französische Zustände*. DHA, 12/2.
34. Editorial apparatus to *Französische Zustände*, DHA, 12/2, 669.
35. "For Heine, the constellation Campe/Cotta represented an attractive business model. Cotta would pay him for his journal contributions, and Campe a sec-

One might also conclude that Heine includes the additional material over and above the main nine articles simply to reach the page threshold necessary to avoid pre-censorship, though, as we will see, he uses the juxtaposition of longer and shorter articles in the book version as an important compositional effect.[36] Through a series of supplements, notes, and addenda, Heine performatively opens his editorial workshop up to readers, signaling where he has reintegrated censored passages and unpublished or incomplete material.[37] In the process, the book version presents readers with a complex series of texts which in their temporal pacing and documentary conceit both correspond to and diverge from the pacing of the newspaper in which these articles first appeared.

Article VI of *Französische Zustände* is a key testing ground for Heine's "preparatory studies for the history of the present." He begins both newspaper and book versions with the promise of an extended series of articles about the relationship between past and present, presenting the general historical remarks sketched above ("the salons lie . . .") as their first installment. His initial goal is to define the time of the revolution and its status as ongoing as a way to ascertain the continuity of historical events, actions, and agents (again, a question not positively addressed by "Verschiedenartige Geschichtsauffassung"). In the midst of these historiographical and indeed philosophical-historical remarks, Heine performatively interrupts himself with an extended report of the cholera outbreak. He thereby relegates these historical reflections to the status of an all-too-preliminary preview (*Bevorwortung*) of a future article: this is a "preview of an article, which seeks to deal with reflections on the past. But in this moment the present is the more important, and the topic that it presents to me for discussion is of a sort that all

---

ond time for the book versions." Rolf Hosfeld, *Heinrich Heine. Die Erfindung des europäischen Intellektuellen* (Munich: Siedler, 2014), 187.

36. Scholars speak in this context of the "censorship style" (*Zensurstil*) of Heine and his contemporaries; see Heady, *Literature and Censorship in Restoration Germany*, 19.

37. Michael Swellander's 2019 dissertation has an excellent discussion of these different articles and supplements as "mediating notes." Swellander, "Understanding the Present," 9.

continued writing depends upon it."[38] Heine highlights his own inability to continue to write anything at all (including reflective history), but he does in fact present readers with writing of a different kind. Heine positions reflections about the past, what came "before," in advance of his intervening subarticle about cholera, yet, in its entirety, this reflection is deferred to a later point in time. In effect, Heine enacts his own historiographical dictum that the present alters our awareness of the past and that any continued historical reflection remains dependent on the shifting present.

By inserting the account of the cholera outbreak, Heine stages a scene in which rapid-response reportage breaks into historical metanarrative. "The following communication has perhaps the benefit of being something of a bulletin written on—and during—the battlefield itself, and thus bears the color of the moment in an undistorted way [*unverfälscht*]."[39] To the extent that interruption shapes the awareness and representation of time and history, it is a central feature of the revolution and the newspaper alike, which both break in on the old and bring the new (a central idea in Heine's Heligoland letters). The advent of the latest news is also a feature of military reporting, a realm that Heine clearly associates his articles with as "bulletins" written "during the battle." As a textual effect, interruption can be disorientating, but such juxtaposition is also one of the basic format conditions of newspapers and other serial print products, and Heine asks readers to recreate the experience of orientating themselves to a rapidly shifting state of affairs. Heine treats the cholera outbreak as an echo of the street-level violence and uncertainty of the revolutionary break with the past—a less directly political echo, perhaps, yet one equally disruptive of the status quo.[40]

Yet readers expecting a continuation of Heine's historical retrospective in the subsequent article might have ended up disappointed, as he postpones it yet again: "The historical retrospectives announced by the previous article have to be postponed. The present

---

38. Heine, article VI, *Französische Zustände*, 147.
39. Heine, article VI, *Französische Zustände*, 149–50.
40. On Heine's treatment of the cholera outbreak, see Olaf Briese, "'Schutzmittel 'für' die Cholera': Geschichtsphilosophische und politische Cholera-Kompensation bei Heine und seinen Zeitgenossen," *Heine Jahrbuch* 32 (1993): 9–26.

made itself so harshly relevant that one is hardly able to contemplate the past."[41] At first glance, Heine's history writing seems to stage the inability to write history, making the idea that it is historically necessary to consider the present in light of the past a literal afterthought. But perhaps republication allows Heine to attain proper historical distance. The book version of *Französische Zustände* does in fact include the more extensive historical remarks promised in the articles, situating these remarks as supplemental material near the end of the book, in effect migrating his historical reflections from the "Extraordinary Supplement" of the paper to the appendix of the book. However, despite finding a home for this material in the format of collected articles, he is obliged to put off a full exploration of these historical questions to his next hypothetical book: "I want to present a fragment of the article that is announced here in the supplement. In a subsequent book the added material that I wrote later will follow. I was frequently disturbed during this work, mostly through the gruesome cries of my neighbor who died of cholera."[42] The cries of his neighbor serve as a figure for the transitory present, for the ever-present possibility that the life (and the death) of the moment might disrupt more general historical retrospection. The documentation of these cries of a dying man is perhaps also a tragic echo of the passage in "Verschiedenartige Geschichtsauffassung" where Heine justifies the present moment through life's self-assertion. Postponing the piece to the next article, then to the next book: in both cases, Heine works with a serial logic of before and after and of preview and postscript. This format relies on performative gestures of self-interruptions and continuations and on the (re)arrangement of various kinds of text into different sequences. If there is a homology between the continuation of historical time—the continuation of the revolution—and writing about it, it must be in terms of structures of stops and starts, and interruptions and disturbances. Seriality promises that more is

---

41. "Die geschichtlichen Rückblicke, die der vorige Artikel angekündigt, müssen vertagt werden. Die Gegenwart hat sich unterdessen so herbe geltend gemacht, daß man sich wenig mit der Vergangenheit beschäftigen konnte." Heine, article VII, *Französische Zustände*, 176.

42. Heine, article VI, *Französische Zustände*, 147.

to come, but what if more comes in a different way than initially promised?

It is instructive here to take a closer look at the specific location of this mere "Fragment" in the book version, for its placement raises as many questions as it answers. Curiously, Heine does not place it in the chronologically arranged nine articles comprising the bulk of the book. He instead nestles it into the "Daily Reports" (*Tagesberichte*) section following them, which comprises shorter reports dealing with the failed June Rebellion of 1832 published in the *Allgemeine Zeitung*. Heine introduces them in the following manner:

> The following daily reports, written in light of the events, in the din of the partisan battle, and always right before the departure of the mail, as quickly as possible so that the correspondents of the victorious Juste-Milieu would not gain the advantage—these fleeting pages I am communicating here, unaltered, to the extent that they have any bearing on the insurrection of June 5th. The history writer [*der Geschichtsschreiber*] may all the more conscionably be able to make use of them, for he is at least able to be certain that they were not composed on the basis of later interests.[43]

These are *flüchtige Blätter*, passed on "unaltered" (*unverändert*), except that the fragmentary *Beylage* is inserted after this editorial introduction and before the first *Tagesbericht*. Again, the auditory realm and the accelerated pace of these pieces are metaphors for the fleeting present and its revolutionary potential; these *Tagesberichte* are intended for future historians (a prediction borne out by the fact that historians of the period continue to rely on them[44]). And yet these reports are the textual environment for the historiographical supplement, which is far removed from the article that it ostensibly continues.[45] Furthermore, the placement of this "Fragment" in the original book version runs counter to his own editorial assertion that what follows is entirely characterized by the media time of journalistic

---

43. Heine, *Französische Zustände*, 193.
44. See Klaus Deinet, "Heinrich Heine und Frankreich—eine Neueinordnung," *Internationales Archiv für Sozialgeschichte der deutschen Literatur* 32, no. 1 (2007): 112–52, 141.
45. See Zantop, *Zeitbilder*, 101.

snapshots of the present. Heine's introductory remarks thematize his lack of time for extended historical reflection, yet he curiously goes on to insert precisely such reflections in advance of the daily reports, reversing from the cholera episode the order of what kind of text does the interrupting.

The anthology format of *Französische Zustände* underlines Heine's point that the present and historical awareness are always breaking into and recasting one another. His framing work foregrounds the external factors that force him into certain editorial decisions and that limit the potential for deliberate authorial composition. In a way, Heine performatively affirms the proposition that an understanding of the present must pass through the understanding of the past, yet he stages this proposition through a stance of coming after, both coming after as a stance toward the historical past and to a set of texts written at a different present moment. One might well be inspired to deconstruct Heine's various dichotomies—past/present, fleeting/permanent, journalistic/philosophical, impartial/partisan, and so on—but it seems clear that Heine uses the anthology format to destabilize these categories. That said, in subsequent twentieth-century critical editions of *Französische Zustände*, we can find a countervailing impulse to impose narrative continuity onto these articles and to soften the compositional effects of self-interruption and delay. In a perhaps minor yet nonetheless remarkable editorial overreach, the editors of the authoritative Düsseldorf *Heineausgabe* put the fragmentary *Beylage* in between articles VI and VII, stating that it was "senselessly" (*unsinnigerweise*) placed amid the *Tagesberichte*.[46] The editor of the 1961 Aufbau edition places it directly after Article IX rather than after the prefatory remarks introducing the daily reports, doing so "in the interest of the clearness and readability of the texts" (*im Interesse der Übersichtlichkeit und Lesbarkeit der Texte*).[47] While seemingly benign, such interventions distort the problem of coming after and of the afterlife of given articles and introduce

---

46. "In der Buchfassung ist diese Ergänzung unsinnigerweise zwischen die *Tagesberichte* und die zugehörige *Vorbemerkung* geraten. Sie wurde daher an den Artikel selbst herangezogen." Editorial apparatus to *Fränzösische Zustände*. DHA 12/2, 860.

47. Heinrich Heine, *Werke und Briefe*, ed. Hans Kaufmann and Gotthard Erler, vol. 4 (Berlin: Aufbau, 1961), 638–39.

ideals of "overview" and "readability" that Heine performatively undermines.

Heine writes the history of the revolution and its aftermath through an ensemble of more or less dissimilar texts. This constructive approach to the writing of historical time is articulated primarily through media-based effects rather than through the work of the philosophical concept or through the sense that history has an organic logic akin to biological life cycles or the lives of imitable, great actors. Heine models the time of the revolution on the basis of serialized textual operations that depart from the narrative logic of a cohesive, linear, epic plot. His serial histories proceed fitfully, in stops and starts, promising all the while that more is to come, both more disruption of the status quo and more opportunity for fragmented critical reflection.

Heine's Anti-Portraiture

I'd like to turn to a second feature of Heine's engagement with serial forms, namely his representation of historical figures, an important subgenre of his overall presentation of his writings as a series of images. He made a name for himself as a prose author with his four-volume *Reisebilder* anthology (1826–1831) containing texts originally published in periodicals; his four-volume anthology titled *Der Salon* (1834–1840) similarly gathers disparate writings for journals. In both anthology series, Heine uses the conceit of a collection of multiple images to play off different representational media against one another, including academic painting (as in his reviews of the Paris Academy exhibitions for the *Morgenblatt* collected in *Der Salon*), caricature, public oratory and scholarly lecturing, and early photography.[48] Building on the conventions of travel writing

---

48. On Heine's representation of historical figures as a kind of medial competition, see Petra McGillen, "Andauernder Effekt: Medienkonkurrenz und Rhetorik in Heinrich Heines Napoleon-Schriften," in *Zwischen Gattungsdisziplin und Gesamtkunstwerk: Literarische Intermedialität 1815–1848*, ed. Stefan Keppler-Tasaki and Wolf G. Schmidt (Berlin: De Gruyter, 2015), 203–22.

and the late eighteenth- and early nineteenth-century urban tableau tradition (the title of the French translation of the *Reisebilder* is *Tableaux de voyage*), Heine also engages with the multiple genres tasked with representing specific historical persons. It was quite common to present histories of the present and recent past as portrait galleries, characteristics, physiognomies, or character sketches, and Heine himself promised his editor that "many portraits" would be mixed into *Lutezia*.[49] Seen in terms of his entire oeuvre, Heine's writings take on a certain recursive quality, as he returns in multiple texts to previous personalities (Napoleon, Lafayette, and Robespierre), artists, or even specific caricatures or paintings such as Delacroix's *Liberty Leading the People*. The layering of these references generates a cumulative archive of images, metaphors, and scenes that readers come to associate with his authorial voice.

In the hands of a perennially ironic writer such as Heine, though, the more serious, official side of portraiture quickly comes under scrutiny, as he casts doubt on the value of writing history solely through the representation of individual actors. As he states in *Französische Zustände*: "In these pages ... [readers] may find many contradictory assertions, but they never concern things, only persons. Our judgment must stand firm on the first, while it may change daily on the latter."[50] Heine argues that history is shaped by "things"—*Dinge*, or *les choses*—rather than people, with things here understood as structures, forces, institutions, or transnational processes and constellations: "conditions," as in the title. This is part of Heine's broader conviction that in a post-heroic age, writing history must focus on collectives (parties, the people, the masses) as heroes of the modern age rather than individual persons.[51] In addition to the challenges Heine faces of writing history in fragmentary

---

49. Heinrich Heine to Campe, March 7, 1854. HSA, 23, 307.
50. Heine, *Französische Zustände*, 290.
51. On Heine's relativization of greatness, see Ethel Matala de Mazza, "Die fehlende Hauptsache. Exekutionen der Julimonarchie in Heines *Lutezia*," in *Heinrich Heine. Ein Wegbereiter der Moderne*, ed. Paolo Chiarini and Walter Hinderer (Würzburg: Königshausen and Neumann, 2009), 309–28; and Michael Gamper, *Der große Mann: Geschichte eines politischen Phantasmas* (Göttingen: Wallstein, 2016).

serial forms, of depicting ongoing events such as the revolution, I would add a third: he sets out to write the history of impersonal transnational political and cultural structures in part through personal portraits.[52] Portraiture allows him to envision the cumulative effect of multiple, conflicting images of historical actors. Rather than becoming absorbed in a single image, Heine's portraits of the same figures allow him to track the ongoing unfolding of time through compositional effects of before and after.

The full title of *Lutezia* is *Lutezia: Berichte Über Politik, Kunst und Volksleben* (Lutezia: Reports about politics, art, and popular life), and it anthologizes a series of articles he wrote for the *Allgemeine Zeitung* in the 1840s. Like *Französische Zustände*, the book version (published in German in 1854 and in French in 1855) contains a group of numbered main articles of various lengths followed by an appendix containing other tangential articles written about the same time and published in various other papers. They are published as part of a three-part series of "Mixed Writings" (*Vermischte Schriften*) (1854) that includes his late autobiographical *Geständnisse* (Confessions). At first glance, there is something Hegelian about Heine's project, as he tracks the conflicts between different societal and ideological forces, including the liberal elites, the conservative aristocracy, and the more radical socialist and communist movement, a conflict that Heine describes as the central topic of *Lutezia* in his 1854 introduction; this was characteristic of a certain protosociological strand of journalistic *Zeitgeschichte* at the time.[53] That said, Heine is also interested in the interplay—the "artistic arrangement" (*künstlerische Zusammenstellung*) as he put

---

52. Even in the case of his 1840 book on Börne, with Börne's name in the title and the many explicitly portrait-like sketches throughout, Heine states that the book is "not actually a writing about Börne, but about the epoch in which he operated [*über den Zeitkreis worinn er sich zunächst bewegte*]." Heine to Campe, July 24, 1840. HSA, 371. See also Jacques Voisine, "Heine als Porträtist in der *Lutezia*," in *Internationaler Heine-Kongreß*, ed. Manfred Windfuhr (Hamburg: Hoffmann and Campe, 1972), 220–21.

53. Heinrich Heine, "Zuneigungsbrief," in *Lutezia* (Hamburg: Hoffmann und Campe, 1854), I, x–xi.

it in the German dedicatory preface—of different textual units as a compositional and conceptual matrix that move in tandem with historical developments, as well as with the ebb and flow of the media landscape. As in *Französische Zustände,* Heine is interested in representing the revolution's persistence and potential for repetition, this time in the tumultuous era of the 1840s and refracted through the remove of the 1850s. In the process, he revises and reorganizes more pieces than in *Französische Zustände* and tends to make his reports more satirical and critical.

Heine positively associates his articles in *Lutezia* with modern media, in particular with caricature and early photography. Caricature is a subversive alternative to historical portraiture.[54] Caricatures often distort the appearance of important contemporaries (in *Französische Zustände,* for example, Heine discusses the famous satirical images of the French king as a pear), but they also shed light on broader social and political trends by not accepting self-serious representation at face value. Heine's work with caricature is part of his broader engagement with small forms such as physiognomies, urban sketches, and political chansons that engage in the partisan skirmishes of the day and that are closely linked to the rhythms of serial formats, including the illustrated press, which rose to prominence in the 1830s. Caricature depends on the witty, disjointed succession of images, it favors recursive mutation over iconic representation, and it is permanently banished to the base of the hierarchy of academic art forms, atop which historical portraiture continued to stand tall at this time.[55] Heine's commitment to caricature as serial form is on display in what is perhaps the most well-known

---

54. On Heine's engagement with history panting, see Zantop, *Zeitbilder,* 63. On caricature, see Günter Oesterle and Ingrid Oesterle, "'Gegenfüßler des Ideals'—Prozessgestalt der Kunst—'Mémoire processive' der Geschichte: Zur ästhetischen Fragwürdigkeit von Karikatur seit dem 18. Jahrhundert," in *"Nervöse Auffangsorgane des inneren und äußeren Lebens": Karikaturen,* ed. Klaus Herding and Günter Otto (Giessen: Anabas, 1980), 87–130.

55. "The lithographically reproduced sequence of images makes sensible, in a sequential way, the poetic procedure of metamorphosis that is at the heart of caricature." Helmut Schanze, "Heines Medien," in Keppler-Tasaki and Schmidt, *Zwischen Gattungsdisziplin und Gesamtkunstwerk,* 387.

and enigmatic section of the German dedicatory preface to *Lutezia*, where he casts the book as a gallery of photographic images, taking up once more the tension between people and things:

> To lighten up the doleful reports I wove in sketches from the realms of art and science, from the dance halls of good and bad society, and if I . . . sometimes drew all-too-foolish caricatures of *virtuosi* [*Virtuosenfratze*], it was done . . . to give a picture of the time in its most minute nuances. A truthful daguerreotype must truly reproduce a fly as accurately as the proudest horse, and my reports are a daguerreotypic history book, in which every day depicts itself [literally "counterfeits itself"], and through the arrangement of these pictures together [*durch die Zusammenstellung der Bilder*], the order-giving spirit of the artist has contributed a work in which what is represented authentically documents its fidelity through itself.[56]

On the one hand, Heine suggests that his caricature-like sketches of figures from the arts and sciences are to provide a diversion from his more serious political prognoses, yet these "all-too-foolish caricatures of virtuosi" have a serious core, delivering a "picture of the time in its most minute nuances." If in *Französische Zustände* the auditory realm—the "noise of the partisan struggle" or the cries of his dying neighbor—served as a figure for the present moment in all its transience, then here Heine invokes the newly invented daguerreotype to authenticate the snapshots of the present that he seeks to capture. Human portraiture is one of early photography's most important and lucrative functions, but Heine states here that his own articles depict individual "days" rather than individual persons: it is each day that depicts itself or copies itself: *sich abconterfeit*.[57] As a noun, *Konterfei* means portrait and has retained this meaning in contemporary usage, but, as in the English, *Konterfeien* suggests both an authentic and a false ("counterfeit") image, both portrait and caricature passing as portraiture. Heine's articles collect images of the times or of "days" into a gallery of sorts or an "arrangement of such pictures"—in effect, a gallery of distorted

---

56. Heine, "Zuneigungsbrief," *Lutezia*, I, xiii.
57. Siegbert S. Prawer, "Heine and the Photographers," in Zantop, *Paintings on the Move*, 75–90.

portraits where the day, the time, and the times shine through. In Heine's (anti-)portraiture, the person depicted is never fully there. There is no relic of the representative function of portraiture where the portrait was vicariously used to "represent the subject as actually present."[58]

Heine has conflicting things to say about photography. For example, he criticizes early photography for its deficient, overly mimetic realism along the lines of early nineteenth-century critiques of naturalism, yet he also associates photography more positively with artful caricature.[59] If we grant Heine a commitment to truthful representation and caricature alike, one initial takeaway from this passage might be that the caricature of a person reveals the truth of (the) time and even of time itself. Paradoxically, these images attain their documentary "fidelity" and force by being placed into relation with other images. It is the effect of snapshots of the day following each other—and the "order-giving spirit of the artist"—that lends individual images their authenticity, not their stand-alone simulation (or distortion) of presence or of the presence of the present moment. Time and the times cannot be adequately depicted through a stand-alone image.

Rhetoric after the Revolution

Heine's accounts of the lectures of leading French historians serve as a foil for his own mode of history writing. He depicts the lecturers as engaged in historical characterization, and he pits his writings for newspapers and journals against the scene of oral speech and its privileging of embodied presence. Even though he is more favorably disposed to French academic historians than to German ones, he still criticizes the French in terms of their approach to the artificial resolution of the historical past and their choice of rhetorical and publication modes that elide the complexity of the present.

---

58. Cooper, "Portraiture," 306.
59. See Sander L. Gilman, "Heine's Photographs," in Zantop, *Paintings on the Move*, 92–116.

Heine's interest in these figures is therefore also allied with his concern for the proper mode of historical representation, an interest he shares with Marx, who likewise addresses French liberal historians in his reckoning with the 1848 revolution in *Der achtzehnte Brumaire von Louis Bonaparte*. In particular, Heine is all too aware that lectures are a key site where the cultural politics of the day are enacted. In a sense, his accounts of lecturing historians are a form of second-order observation, as he writes about historical actors discussing revolution era historical actors. Reporting on political and scholarly speeches was a standard feature of contemporary cultural journalism and a staple of Heine's writings from the start of his career.[60] His commentaries tap into the all-too-standard mode of history writing through the portraiture of great orators (e.g., Thucydides on Pericles). His Parisian writings discuss parliamentary and academic addresses by leading politicians such as Adolphe Thiers and François Guizot; both wrote and lectured on the history of the revolution, as did other historians such as Jules Michelet, François Mignet, and Victor Cousin. These figures represented a liberal power block between the aristocracy and clergy on the right and the social movement on the left, and they were more or less kindred spirits to Heine: he admired and corresponded with them, he drew on their work (especially that of Thiers and Mignet), and, for a while, Thiers and Heine overlapped as correspondents for the *Allgemeine Zeitung*.[61] However, even people to whom Heine was well disposed had trouble evading his satirical gaze.

Over the course of *Lutezia*, Heine attended three different ceremonial speeches at the Académie Française by Mignet, the head of the academy at the time and the secretary for life, or *secrétaire perpetuel*; Heine knew him well and corresponded with him, even sending him first versions of the articles about these addresses in the 1840s. Like Thiers, Mignet was both a statesman and historian, and he rose to public prominence as both a journalist and the author of

---

60. See Helen Ferstenberg, "Heinrich Heine und George Canning," *Heine-Jahrbuch* 35 (1996): 113–27.

61. Deinet calls Thiers and Mignet Heine's "comrades in arms" and Thiers, "the greatest treasure trove for all friends of the revolution." Deinet, "Heinrich Heine und Frankreich," 130–31.

an important history of the revolution.[62] Heine reported positively on these meetings in various articles and drafts in the 1840s: in Mignet's voice, one hears the "voice of the history writer, the true head [*Chef*] of Clio's archives,"[63] and he has command of the topic of the revolution,[64] but Heine also suggests that Mignet remains very much the academic.[65] The final article in the book version's main article series is a reworked version of several of these earlier pieces, and it is a culminating moment, both of Heine's reports from the Académie Française and of the main body of the book. As in Mignet's previous speeches reported on by Heine, the topic of this lecture is a recently deceased revolutionary era statesman and historian, in this case, a figure named Pierre Daunou. In the reworked book version, Heine is quick to pounce on Mignet's title, suggesting parallels between his youthful appearance and the permanence of his position. As he remarks in a passage added to the book version, Mignet shares the "eternity" of his office with King Louis Philippe.[66] Mignet's office is perhaps a relic of an earlier pre-revolutionary epoch, but, in contrast to the king, who is "unfortunately already very advanced in age," Mignet

> is still young, or what is better, he is the epitome of youth itself, he is spared by the hand of Time, who paints the rest of our hair white if he does not pull it out altogether, and wrinkles up our brows in many a hateful fold; the beautiful Mignet still bears his gold-locked *frisur* as he did twelve years ago, and his face is always as fresh as that of the Olympians. . . . In these moments he looks to me like a shepherd who reviews

---

62. In the final installment Heine signals that this has been a recurring topic in his reports. "Each year I regularly attend the festive meeting in the rotunda of the Palais Mazarin." Heine, article LXI, *Lutezia*, II, 197. On the convoluted genesis of this article, see DHA, 14/2, 932–33.

63. Heine, article XXXV, *Lutezia*, I, 263.

64. Heinrich Heine, "Kampf und Kämpfer," *Zeitung für die Elegante Welt* 43, no. 36 (September 6, 1843): 876.

65. "The academic's traditional obligation to praise is only ever occasionally visible in Mignet's choice of expressions and moderating intonation." Heine, article XXXV, *Lutezia*, I, 263. For background on this article, see Hansen, *Heinrich Heines politische Journalistik*, 75.

66. "Whose office is an eternal one, like the monarchy." Heine, article LXI, *Lutezia*, II, 198.

his sheep. They all belong to him, to him, the perpetual one [*der Perpetuelle*]—who will outlive them all and dissect and embalm them all in his *Précis Historiques*.[67]

Mignet's hair is a sign that he will outlive and eulogize his contemporaries as he does Daunou and perhaps even that he will outlive the king, who would die in 1850. Heine retroactively inserts the 1848 collapse of the July Monarchy—its eventual lack of "eternal" permanence—and the subsequent death of the king into the reworked account of this scene from 1843. The trope of eternal youthfulness is decidedly ambivalent, associated with the perpetuation of the ideals of the revolution and of pre-revolutionary institutions such as the Académie Française. Heine uses the sketch of Mignet to juxtapose temporal tropes that access broader historical developments and that pertain to the "things" and conditions of French society more than to specific individuals.

Relatedly, Heine finds traces of rhetorical conventions from the pre-revolutionary era in Mignet's historical discourse: "Even though Mignet calls his speeches *précis historiques*, they are still just the same old éloges, and they are still the same compliments from the time of Louis XIV, except that now they are not set in full-bottomed wigs but instead have modern haircuts."[68] Mignet's historical method creates the effect of the past becoming present through the evocation of past personalities, drawing on earlier genres of scholarly commemoration based in the mimetic ideal of history as the teacher of life.[69] The continuity of scholarly self-valorization across historical epochs—a continuity bordering on the timelessness aspired to by the humanistic ideal of the eloquent scholar—almost becomes a limitation, for it neutralizes the disruptive power of the revolution, despite the very topic of the lecture.

---

67. Heine, article LXI, *Lutezia*, II, 196–97.
68. Heine, article LXI, *Lutezia*, II, 198.
69. On the eighteenth century éloge as model of scholarly commemoration that does not separate the "scholar" and "man," see Georges Canguilhem, "Fontenelle, philosophe et historien des sciences," in *Études d'histoire et de philosophie des sciences* (Paris: Libraire philosophique J. Vrin, 1968), 51–58.

Heine continues his riff on wigs and hairstyles and on youth and age as he construes the eulogy as a way of preserving influential historical persons for posterity, both by figurally bringing them back to life and embalming them:

> The current *secrétaire perpetuel* of the Academy is one of the greatest *friseurs* of our time and has the right *chicque* for this noble trade. Even when there is not a good hair on a man, he knows how to curl a few locks of praise on to him and how to hide his bald head under a toupee of phrases. How happy are these French Academicians! There they sit in the sweetest peace of soul on their safe benches, and they can die in peace, for they know that however dubious their deeds may have been in life, the good Mignet will laud and praise them after death. Under the palm trees of his words, which are evergreen as his uniform, lulled by the plashing of his oratorical antitheses, they rest in the Academy as in a cool oasis. The caravan of humanity passes by them ever and anon, without their noting it, or anything save the ringing of the camels' bells.[70]

Heine casts historical characterization as a kind of work on the appearance of the face and head: once more we are in striking distance of the portrait, profile, and daguerreotype. But the metaphor then shifts from hairdresser to undertaker, as the historian prepares the bodies of the dead. Heine imagines the audience members (of which he is a part) almost dead, emerging back from the grave through the historian's words. This passage encapsulates both Heine's slightly envious fascination with academic historians and his antipathy toward them. The revival of the rhetoric of the ancien regime and the traditionalist timelessness of reliving the deeds of the past becomes a strike against Mignet and stands in contrast to the world outside. Whether the members of the academy perceive it or not, the events outside on the boulevards explode the rhetoricians' self-satisfied self-embalming as a viable historical model. Perpetuity flips into its opposite: by seeking immortality, the scholarly eulogy takes on a fleeting quality; it is a historiographical activity with no real staying power; it is the sign of a particular historical constellation that will end in death, that will be *aufgehoben* (sublated), to speak, with Hegel. Heine does the historical work of understanding the ephemerality of this scene, work that Mignet cannot do.

---

70. Heine, article LXI, *Lutezia*, II, 202.

Heine thereby positions himself at the threshold between inside and outside, between timelessness and eventfulness. While Mignet's "orational antitheses" simply lull his listeners to sleep or even into a sweet, dreamlike death, the antitheses created by Heine's serial, temporal modes of writing have the opposite effect, creating an awareness of time that can help readers resist the temptation to reduce the present moment and world history alike to the repetitive, empty tinkling of bells. Heine's commentary on personal presence explores how multiple temporalities are refracted through given events rather than how such temporalities construct any notion of charismatic personality. And yet he faces the paradoxical challenge of telling history through individual persons who are not themselves the primary subjects of history. This is where his ironic critiques of historical portraiture and of the rhetorical model of the embodied speaker converge. Just as the rhetorical model of recurrent, repeatable historical topoi dissolved in the wake of the French Revolution, so, too, does Heine here dissolve the rhetorical model of embodied personality, not least by investing certain tropes—life and death, and dynamism and stasis—with contradictory meanings. Nonetheless, the scene of rhetorical performance remains instructive as a site both to register broader historical forces and to model varied encounters with multiple historical temporalities.

This brings us back to the question of format and republication: this article's placement is significant, for it functions both as a conclusion and a transition onto a subsequent set of texts. In a collection so concerned with ends and beginnings, this is the final article in the main section of *Lutezia*. Following this final passage culminating in the "ringing of the camels' bells" is an extensive appendix containing other articles not included in the main article series for the *Allgemeine Zeitung*. This appendix opens with a longer article titled "Communism, Philosophy, and Clergy" (*Communismus, Philosophie, und Clerisey*), which distills the main political ideologies of the day, including the radical social movement, the bourgeois liberalism of the academy, and the conservative religious reaction. This latter article is largely based on a piece that was first published in installments in *Die Zeitung für die elegante Welt* after having been turned down by the editors of the *Allgemeine Zeitung* as being too political, and in its original form it included some of the material on Mignet's eulogy of Daunou incorporated into the book version of article LXI. In the original article for the *Zeitung für die elegante Welt* as well as in the book version, Heine considers communism as a central societal force. As he notes in his prefaces to the German and French book versions, he was forced to remain oblique about the social movement in the original articles for the *Allgemeine Zeitung*, even though his conviction that the future belongs above all to the "socialists, or to give the monster its correct name, the communists" runs as a red thread throughout the articles.[71] In effect, Heine's inclusion of this piece at this key moment of transition, after the reworked account of Mignet, is an implicit provocation: What are the academicians missing when they mistake the din outside the lecture hall for tinkling bells? The very first word of the supplemental article's title gives the answer: "communism." Book publication allows Heine to stage the continuation of the article series that breaks off with the portrait of Mignet. The very format of the book constructs an outside to the lecture hall. Heine writes the after that Mignet cannot see; he writes a future of possible communist revolution in the form of a prophetic prediction but also in the form of a textual effect that once more conditions the media-based logics of portraiture and of oral eulogy. In 1854, Heine offers readers a continuation of his sketch of the Académie Française that departs from the institutional logic of the lecture and that presents an altogether different historical takeaway regarding the past, present, and future of the revolution.

Seriality functions as a central formal condition of these pieces both in their original article format and under the new medial and historical circumstances of the book version. The project of republishing these previous articles is in its own right a "historiographically ambitious undertaking," as Ethel Matala de Mazza rightly puts it, and it also is an intervention with strong medial implications, as Heine embraces the constraints as well as the potential of serial formats to model how the revolution can break into and interrupt the present.[72]

---

71. Heine, "Preface to the French Edition," 299.
72. Matala de Mazza, "Die fehlende Hauptsache," 310.

Through serial form, Heine models the abstract truth and logic of seriality that unexpected things come "after," and he uses print media to model this coming after rather than solely tracking the necessary movement of the concept or by engaging in a materialist analysis of social conflict. Even if Heine might share a certain belief in the necessity of a coming revolution with the likes of Marx, he writes the revolution's future through media times of before and after and through an ever-shifting series of events, actors, and medial representations.

After 1848: Literary Afterlives and the Death of the Author

I'd like to close this chapter by continuing to think about what comes after, both in terms of coming revolution and of the afterlives of Heine's writings. We have seen how Börne and Heine use remediation—putting journal articles into book form—to envision historical writings' potential for continuation and revaluation. Heine's propensity to curate his works and configure afterlives of earlier, ephemeral writings finds particular expression in *Lutezia*, not least because it is a late work from the end of his life after years of infirmity.[73] Heine uses German and French versions of *Lutezia* (1854 and 1855 respectively) to ironically deploy tropes of authorial immortality and future reception. Questions of format migration, recirculation, and textual (and historical) befores and afters are all pertinent to how Heine distinguishes his work from a reductive view of historical time in which past events are complete and have a stable, unchanging meaning. In the same way that the juxtaposition of articles can have a predictive, productive character, Heine uses the preface of both the German and French versions to open up new horizons of meaning and reception. Here we return to questions of literary afterlives that we addressed in chapter 4 via Jean Paul. Of course, Heine is concerned with getting his works in order so as to prevent misuse after his death, but he also reflects ironi-

---

73. On Heine's late style, see Roger Cook, *By the Rivers of Babylon: Heinrich Heine's Late Songs and Reflections* (Detroit: Wayne State University Press, 1998).

cally on this future reception with different French and German audiences. As with Jean Paul, the trope of the author's death helps Heine imagine future reencounters and reactualizations in a broader media environment saturated with serial forms and ephemeral interventions.

The most notable "after" to Heine's articles from the early 1840s was of course the violent end of the July Monarchy in 1848. We get a retroactive intimation of this in the juxtaposition of Louis-Philippe and Mignet added in 1854 as well as in the complex interplay of main articles and later addenda. In the German dedicatory preface, Heine addresses the fact that he does not include articles that directly thematize the 1848 revolution, "the catastrophe of February 24," although he certainly could have, having written articles in various papers about the event as it was unfolding at the time. However, as Heine jokes, his book was like the *Iliad* in this respect: like the sacking of Troy, 1848 is not depicted in the book proper, but it remains omnipresent, both anticipatorily in the 1840s and retrospectively, from the present.[74] But Heine also uses the prefaces to preview scenes of more distant future reception. The French language preface is more explicit about Heine's premonitions of the revolution and the rise of the socialist and communist movements, a feature of his crafting of the end of the book version considered earlier. He assures his French-language readers that this conviction remains a red thread, even in the articles' original form. Heine does not make this "confession" (*Bekenntnis*) lightly, as he envisions a future "when these dark iconoclasts will rise to power: with their crude hands they will then utterly shatter all the marble statues of my beloved world of art; they will smash all of those fantastic knickknacks that were so dear to the poet's heart."[75] Donning for a moment the hat of the Romantic poet, Heine expresses concern for the preservation of a life based in aesthetic appreciation, a life based in "the entire old Romantic world order" (*der ganzen alten romantischen Weltordnung*). At first glance, it would seem that Heine

---

74. Heine, "Zuneigungsbrief," *Lutezia*, I, xii.
75. Heine, "Preface to the French Edition," 299.

stakes out an aesthetic position not far from the one that Börne and others accused him of, that is, of not being politically committed enough in his art.[76]

Heine's vision of an iconoclastic future goes hand in hand with the prophecy of the decomposition his own oeuvre and of his books in material form: "Alas! The grocer will use my *Book of Songs* as little paper bags in which to pour coffee or snuff for the little old ladies of the future. Alas! I can foresee it all."[77] In the time to come, the cornerstone of Heine's reputation as a poet would be torn asunder, with individual pages being used as scrap paper. It is striking here that Heine takes the occasion of collecting scattered articles to envision the disarticulation, or even obliteration, of his works. The integrative force of authorial *Geist* at work in collecting previously anonymous pieces meets its match in peoples' basic daily needs. There is a certain tinge of false modesty here, but Heine also articulates a vision of the end of art, the future end and hence the ultimate transience of a literary aesthetics that misguidedly aspires to permanence. Part of Heine laments this coming demise, though another part of him affirms it; as he writes, he is haunted by and cannot dispute the logic of the proposition "that all humans have the right to eat," concluding, "Blessed be the grocer who will someday make little paper bags from my poems."[78] Playing dread and anticipation for a more comprehensive revolutionary moment off each other, Heine gives one further ironic twist to the question of how his histories of the present might be received at different historical junctures: if his prophetic history of the present is right—if the future belongs to communism—then the rending of his books will be decisive proof of his status as a historical visionary. The multivalent association of his pieces with ephemerality once more guarantees the truthfulness of the history of the present.

---

76. This is a good example of the "double voiced mode" from the Börne memoir, "where the words and the ideas of the two writers often overlap or become difficult to distinguish from one another," as Seyhan puts it. For a recent discussion see Azade Seyhan, *Heinrich Heine and the World Literary Map: Redressing the Canon* (New York: Palgrave Macmillan, 2019), 135.
77. Heine, "Preface to the French Edition," 300.
78. Heine, "Preface to the French Edition," 300.

The German version of 1854 pursues a rather different framing gesture, presented as a "Dedicatory Letter" (*Zueignungsbrief*) to Prince Hermann von Pückler-Muskau (1785–1871), a popular German-language travel writer of the 1830s and 1840s.[79] As in his Börne memoir, Heine uses the characterization of the prince as a form of self-reflection and even of ironic self-characterization, and we should regard this dedication as one more exercise in (anti-)portraiture that Heine adds to his series of contemporaries from the 1840s, many of whom have now since faded from public memory. In dedicating the anthology to the prince, Heine evokes the traditional form of the dedication to an aristocratic patron, though this particular dedication occurs more under the sign of the travelogue and contemporary-historical reportage than of the rhetorical conventions of praise with which Heine was so familiar.[80] He had in fact just met Pückler-Muskau for the first time in person in 1854 when he visited Heine at his Paris home where he had been bedridden for almost six years; Heine's resulting feelings of warmth and gratefulness to him seem genuine.[81]

Pückler-Muskau was the author of anonymously published popular travel writings on England, Wales, and Ireland, the *Briefe eines Verstorbenen* (Letters of a dead man) (1830–1831), which Heine mentions in the *Reisebilder*.[82] Pückler-Muskau also wrote

---

79. The 1855 French version does contain the German dedicatory preface directly after the new French preface. The French preface is dated "Paris, March 30, 1855," and the German dedication is dated "Paris, August 23, 1854."

80. Heine is careful to instruct his publisher not to set the dedicatory preface in a larger font, as was conventional in previous centuries, a formatting choice that would have framed the piece as a "devoted letter to a patron" rather than as the intended "friendly, whimsical letter" (*Brief kameradschaftlicher Laune*). See Volkmar Hansen's editorial apparatus to *Lutezia* I. DHA, 13/1, 615.

81. This visit occurred shortly before the publication of *Lutezia*; see Heinrich Heine's letter to Prince Hermann von Pückler-Muskau, May 9, 1854. HSA, 23, 333.

82. See the excellent recent English-language translation and introduction, Prince Hermann von Pückler-Muskau, *Letters of a Dead Man*, ed. and trans. Linda B. Parshall (Washington, DC: Dumbarton Oaks Research Library and Collection, 2016). Goethe, who was often stingy with his praise for contemporary authors, also thought well of Pückler-Muskau. See Wulf Wülfing, "Reiseliteratur und Realitäten im Vormärz. Vorüberlegungen zu Schemata und Wirklichkeitsfindung im frühen 19.

African and Middle Eastern travelogues in the 1840s under the pen name Semilasso. Despite differences in social standing and religious background, Heine states that he and the prince were kindred spirits—they "fit together" (*zusammenpassten*) because, "yes, we were both travelers on this earth, that was our earthly speciality."[83] For Heine, the prince represents a particular type of authorial persona associated with the imaginary traversing of different spaces, places, and times, and he thus comes into view as one of many peripatetic figures with which Heine identified over the course of his life, including the wandering Jew and the flaneur. Pückler-Muskau was "the travel-addicted Mr. Everwhere and Nowhere" (*der wandersüchtige Überall-und-Nirgends*), the "romantic Anacharsis, the most fashionable of all oddballs [*der fashionabelste aller Sonderlinge*], Diogenes on horseback."[84] The prince's perpetual movement is a point of contrast to the stasis of the French academicians: indeed, Heine asks readers to conjure up an image of him riding on a camel through the Middle Eastern desert rather than reposing at some notional oasis.[85]

Heine's mention of his meeting with Pückler-Muskau recalls the many scenes in *Lutezia* in which he finds himself in proximity to important contemporary figures. But rather than describing the meeting in any detail, Heine notes how he commemorates the event through the act of writing, for writing and then publishing this dedication proves that he and the prince had once been together. It is a common "custom of travelers" to inscribe and date their names on trees, rocks, or walls amid the "clutter of other inscriptions" (*Wust von Inschriften*), an act that marks the "authentic date of our temporal convergence" (*authentisches Datum unseres zeitlichen Zusammentreffens*).[86] Such an inscription—here in the form of the book and its dedication—is left behind for "those who come after," for future readers whom Heine playfully encourages to think about

---

Jahrhundert," in *Reise und soziale Realität am Ende des 18. Jahrhunderts,* ed. Wolfgang Griep and Hans-Wolf Jäger (Heidelberg: Winter, 1983), 371–94.

83. Heine, "Zuneigungsbrief," *Lutezia*, I, iv.
84. Heine, "Zuneigungsbrief," *Lutezia*, I, xv.
85. Heine, "Zuneigungsbrief," *Lutezia*, I, xv.
86. Heine, "Zuneigungsbrief," *Lutezia*, I, v.

how exactly he and the prince might have "fit together" (*zusammen passten*).⁸⁷ At least on the semantic level, this convergence (*Zusammentreffen*) and the affinity between the two (*zusammenpassen*) bears some similarity to the collection, compilation, and arrangement (*Zusammenstellung*) of Heine's anthology, where each article is dated and marks a specific point in time. Clustered together, the articles and preface are differently dated texts, yet nearly all have the same physical location: Paris, the city of cities, or spectral "Lutezia," a palimpsest of the old and new. The book version adds one more ephemeral encounter with a literary luminary to those memorialized in the articles, and Heine leaves his mark on the city anew.

His demonstrative gesture of signing and dating likewise draws our attention to the peculiar format of the book version and to his deliberate gesture of signing originally anonymous articles. The travelers' inscription marks the convergence of two people, while republication tags the articles, already dated once in the 1840s, with a second publication date, now from 1854, or 1855 for the French translation. As with the practice of leaving inscriptive markings for other travelers to chance across, Heine sends his doubly dated articles out to an indeterminate future. This preface thus uses the technique of republication to mark and remark a present that points to a time and a materiality beyond itself, to a future installment.

Heine's marking of the time and place of their meeting is a gesture of history writing and of marking the historical moment of the present as well as the more than ten years that have intervened since the articles' publications. Dating events also helps to anticipate the time and place of a (re)encounter: now that the book is finished, Heine is eager to provide the prince with his own copy. Delivering the epistolary dedication (along with the book) presents its own difficulties, though, and Heine closes the preface with uncertainty about where to address it: "Where is he now? In the Occident or in

---

87. "Those who come after us and see the wreath in this book through which I am weaving together our two names will at least gain an authentic date of our temporal coincidence [*gewinnen wenigstens ein authentisches Datum unseres zeitlichen Zusammentreffens*], and they may conjecture as they like to what extent the author of the *Briefe eines Verstorbenen* and the reporter [*der Berichterstatter*] of *Lutezia* fit together." Heine, "Zuneigungsbrief," *Lutezia*, I, vi.

the Orient? In China or in England? In pants from Nanking or from Manchester? In the Middle East or in Transpomerania? Do I need to address my book to Kyritz, or to Timbuktu, poste-restante?"[88] The bodily copresence of the past meeting stands in marked contrast to Heine's professed ignorance as to the peripatetic prince's current location. As an addressee, the prince becomes an elusive target, and as an addressed object, Heine's book likewise is set in motion, out for delivery to an uncertain location. The prince becomes a figure for future reception; he is one privileged future reader among many, but one whose location is indeterminate.[89] Seen in light of Heine's poetics of (anti) portraiture, there would seem to be a certain spectral quality to the prince's characterization. He is hard to pin down in space and time—not fully there, but also not fully "then," if you will, and not fully at a determinate spot in time, instead straddling past, present, and future. Although the prince is quite stylish, Heine professes uncertainty as to his current appearance—is he wearing Nanking or Manchester pants? Returning to Heine's analogy of his writing to the daguerreotype, it is almost as if the prince is nearly unphotographable, for he never sits in one place long enough to have his portrait taken.[90]

Heine's ideal of writing on the move is also informed by the semantics of life and death, as he returns to Pückler-Muskau's most famous book, the *Briefe eines Verstorbenen*. Despite supposedly being dead, the prince is the "most living of all dead men," having outlived many people who are "living in title only" (*Titularlebendige*).[91] The prince is a relic of a different age who nonetheless is more relevant than many of the figures that Heine described in his articles for the *Allgemeine Zeitung*. Heine associates travel and life with

---

88. Heine, "Zuneigungsbrief," *Lutezia*, I, xviii.
89. On the prince as representing future readers, see also Phelan, *Reading Heinrich Heine*, 206–8.
90. It is common knowledge at the time that the exposure time of early photography is rather long and required the subject to sit still for long periods of time, hence Benjamin's quip, "everything about these early images was meant to last" (*Alles an diesen frühen Bildern war angelegt zu dauern*). Walter Benjamin, "Eine Kleine Geschichte der Photographie," in *Das Kunstwerk im Zeitalter seiner technischen Reproduzierbarkeit* (Frankfurt: Suhrkamp, 1963), 45–64, 52.
91. Heine, "Zuneigungsbrief," *Lutezia*, I, xvii.

a dynamic style of authorship and also with a kind of historical afterlife that straddles pre- and post-1848 periods. To be sure, informed readers would have known that he was confined to bed and flirting with death ("nailed down to his mattress," as he put it in a letter to the prince from May of 1854[92]). Yet despite his and the prince's figural (and impending actual) deaths, they remain in motion. The trope of "dead, yet still moving" applies to the model of history writing at work in *Lutezia* more generally, with Heine sending off (and resending) ephemeral snapshots of bygone moments into unknown futures. Breaking with any naive assertion of liveliness and presence, Heine comes down as much on the side of the dead as the living, seeking to bestow on his own discourse a kind of relevance and actuality that transcends the narrow concerns of the present moment. The dead are interesting because they bring a different time with them into the present and future. This dated, signed inscription represents one further alternative to naive portraiture, for, rather than relying on a notion of the embodied copresence of the author and prince, it places their persons and their authorial voices at various kinds of temporal and historical remove. Being hard to pin down temporally and spatially helps to model future reception, even though it does not do away with the contingency associated with such reception. Heine (re)sends his ephemeral snapshots of past presents out into an unknown future, from one dead man to another. This is hardly an unironic assertion of literary immortality, but one should expect nothing of the sort from Heine. The prince is a figure for the kindred reader who truly understands the author and also for one who appreciates the contingencies of small, occasional, ephemeral forms. To the extent that Heine's characterization of the prince and his corresponding self-characterization as fellow traveler are two further *Virtuosenfratzen*, Heine sends off two more caricature-like sketches as pieces of flotsam and jetsam on the sea of print—two more ironic masks, to shift the metaphor, that do anything but anchor the personalities in any kind of fixed form.

---

92. Heinrich Heine to Prince Hermann von Pückler-Muskau, May 9, 1854. HSA, 23, 333.

Though Heine's "daguerrotypic" images are of past times, some of the effects of their seriality belong to the future: in the face of a future that is hard to predict, seriality persuades us that more is to come, even if we must wait an unknown amount of time. While Heine jokingly compares his articles to the *Iliad*, the serial juxtaposition of individual articles and tableaus presents an alternative to the linear logic of the epic in which one thing follows directly and necessarily from another; again, we encounter the fault line between travel writing and high historical narration. Heine's history writing is premised on the difficulty, if not impossibility, of predicting what is coming next, and also on the conviction that something is coming. The knowledge about the future that Heine writes from here is perhaps more bullish than the French preface about an authorial afterlife that does not end in utter disintegration, yet the two prefaces are not incompatible, for both write the future through the fleeting materiality of contemporary histories and their precarious, uncertain journeys to future readers.

Afterword

Serial Literature's Untimely Afterlives?

> The Pre-March era [1830–1848] is a veiled time. Indecipherable like the present and hard to recognize.
>
> *Der Vormärz ist eine verschleierte Zeit. Unkenntlich wie die Gegenwart und schwer zu erkennen.*
>
> —Reinhart Koselleck to Carl Schmitt,
> letter, April 30, 1962

In closing, I would like to add one more figure to our gallery of nineteenth-century writers and editors whose works straddle book and journal formats and take on differently timed afterlives. The Austrian writer Adalbert Stifter (1805–1868) first published most of his work in journals, and early on in his career he incorporated adapted aspects of Jean Paul's "foolish" tone into such pieces. Yet in reworking and expanding the size and scope of his writings, he increasingly aspired to a Goethean notion of the completed work.¹ Like many contemporary writers, Stifter's ultimate benchmark of literary success was a single-author works edition, yet he continued to write for journals until his death. These tensions between continuation and completion and between journal and book formats can be seen in the posthumous volumes of *Vermischte Schriften* (Mixed writings) (1870), which are part of the multivolume works edition *Adalbert Stifters Werke* (1869–1870) and which collect fragments and sundry periodical texts, including several short essays published just a few years earlier in the illustrated family weekly *Die Gartenlaube für Österreich* (The garden bower for Austria) (1866–1869). The piece "New Year's Eve" (*Der Sylvesterabend*) takes us back to the commemoration of the new year through "small" products of serial print considered in parts I and II of this book and to questions of literary legacy. In this middlebrow family journal, Stifter appears as a specifically Austrian writer, but one adept at stock forms from the periodical press. This piece appears in *Die Gartenlaube*'s final issue of the year and begins with speech reportedly overheard during the last hours of the year:

> "New Year's Eve is here," people say, "a year is up in a few hours and a new one begins."
> "It is an important segment of time [*Zeitabschnitt*]," the others say,
> "It's brought the one thing and the other, what will the new one bring."
> And, as many ask, "What is time?"²

These anonymous, anodyne statements evoke the tone, if not the content, of year-end reflections, but these overheard fragments might just as well serve as a personalization of the ubiquitous ways that journals and newspapers mark the passing of the year—one journal has a poem about time, another predicts what will come in the new year, and yet another offers more general reflections on time, et cetera.

Turning from what other people/journals have to say, Stifter shifts to a first-person perspective: "When I speak of something so

---

1. Johannes John calls this aspiration the "utopia of the finished text." Johannes John, "Die Utopie des 'fertigen' Textes," *Stifter-Jahrbuch* 20 (2006): 105.
2. Adalbert Stifter, "Der Sylvesterabend," in *Vermischte Schriften*, vol. 2 (Pesth: Heckenast, 1870), 310.

enormous as a period of time, I ask, 'How can one cut it up [*abschneiden*] and cut it apart [*zerschneiden*]?'"³ Continuing, he writes that time is perhaps the most unknowable part of life: "It is the secret of all of creation, we are enveloped in it, no heartbeat, no gaze of the eyes, no twitch of a fever takes place outside of it, we cannot step out of it, and do not know what it is."⁴ These ruminations are evocative of Augustine's famous reflections on time in the *Confessions*, and they fit well with the popular pedagogy of the journal—indeed, the journal format performs the very work of segmenting through its periodic, serialized publication. Stifter wraps up this section by returning to the conceit of reported speech, giving the floor to a kind of no-nonsense common man:

> "Wait a moment," someone will say, "what's the point of these idle questions, what's the point of this idle talk that people don't even understand in the first place [*wozu das müssige Gerede, das man nicht einmal überall versteht*] and that there isn't even a solution for and probably isn't even necessary in the first place? What's the point?"
> The man is right, I will never find the solutions to these questions, and yet I ask these questions time and again, and even write them down here in a New Year's Eve speech, and will ask these questions again, and people will ask them with me who travel down similar paths, and the others will have to forgive us, all the people who, when sitting in front of the image of Sais, don't feel the twitch in their fingers to at least partially raise the veil.⁵

Ruminating about time is idle (*müssig*) and perhaps even foolish. Though Stifter's piece is not outright humorous in tone, "idle" (*müssig*) and "foolish" (*närrisch*) are not far apart in the moral compass of the provincial *Bildungsbürger*, and the fool is associated with certain kinds of periodical-based entertainment that we have seen throughout the book. Indeed, calling these reflections a new year's "speech" brings to mind Jean Paul's end-of-the-year addresses and the perpetuation of such stock genres through the periodical press. This passage is organized around a notion of repetition and recurrence, with the

---

3. Stifter, "Der Sylvesterabend," 310.
4. Stifter, "Der Sylvesterabend," 310.
5. Stifter, "Der Sylvesterabend," 315–16.

first-person narrator underlining the repetitive quality of his reflections on time. Stifter thereby envisions a process of ongoing observation, a process of past, present, and future temporal reflection that measures and cuts up time, as well as related processes pursued by others. Even if these undertakings are "idle," they are collective and involve multiple participants, as Stifter envisions journal readers undertaking similar observations in tandem. Even if time remains inscrutable, we can find an approximate understanding of it by marking it in different ways and by breaking it into different segments, not least through techniques that Stifter draws attention to in "writing down" (and publishing) his "speech."

It is at this point that the essay pivots to territory more familiar to some of the family journal's readers: "I return to the middle-class celebration of New Year's Eve" (*Ich kehre zu dem bürgerlichen Sylvesterabende zurück*). The piece proceeds to sketch how people spend the end of the year, whether by gathering with one's family and exchanging gifts, meeting in the local *Gasthaus*, or passing a lonely night without company. This impressionistic surveying of different figures and social types corresponds to *Die Gartenlaube*'s ideal of mirroring and figurally unifying different aspects of Austrian society.[6] Stifter closes with a gesture of well-wishing that is rather stock, yet it exhibits nicely how writing helps to observe and commemorate certain periods of time:

> And before I put down the quill, I write on the sheet [*Und ehe ich die Feder niederlege, schreibe ich noch auf das Blatt*]: a joyous new year for all who read these lines, and for all who do not read it, and may heaven provide that the good that befalls certain people persist and that the deep pain that has come in certain hearts be softened.[7]

This somewhat curious move of directing new year's wishes to people who do not receive them represents an oblique gesture toward future reception, with the arrival of the wishes with certain audiences at

---

6. On this function in the German *Gartenlaube*, see Kirsten Belgum, *Popularizing the Nation: Audience, Representation, and the Production of Identity in "Die Gartenlaube," 1853–1900* (Lincoln, NE: University of Nebraska Press, 1998).

7. Stifter, "Der Sylvesterabend," 320.

some future moment occurring via circuitous and indirect pathways that no longer coincide with this particular year (indeed, this is a feature of this text that is reinforced by its publication in the posthumous works edition). The wishes might well arrive with those who need it by some other means or at some other point in time, at the next holiday or the next year's New Year's Eve. The reference to a lack of present reception and to forms of circulation that remain outside the control of the author opens up a space for repetition and reencounter. Here we have a rather impassive sense of literary legacy that is open to the possible reception of minor works, simple "sheets," rather than insistent about the enduring greatness of larger works.[8] Despite Stifter's literary fame at this late stage in his career, it is striking that he so readily and comfortably inhabits a mode of journal-based writing. Stifter sends his wishes off into the world and out onto the sea of print, uncertain of where or when it will arrive. Taken together with the essay's reflections on time, this closing remark continues the process of the ongoing marking of time through patterns of repetition and continuation, a process that would seem to run counter to any kind of finality or completion. This gesture complements the function of collected works to promote a sense of literary legacy based on future encounter, yet the gesture is not organized around a notion of the completed work or set of works. Even if it is foolish to write about time, such folly is hard to resist and calls out for more: more imitators, more writing, more images, and more attempts to lift the veil and perceive time in its smallest and largest segments.

Reflections on the timeliness and untimeliness of serial forms—including on their indeterminate or untimely afterlives—prompt considerations as to serial literature's place in the writing of literary history. The promise of more to come or future reencounter is all too pertinent to literary historiography, which tasks itself with managing the terms and justification for future rereadings of shifting literary

---

8. This scene is an example of what Ulrike Vedder identifies as scenes of successful and failed transfer and inheritance in Stifter's writing, scenes that operate "beyond intention" and that eschew direct and intentional transfer. Ulrike Vedder, "Erbschaft und Gabe, Schriften und Plunder. Stifters testamentarische Schreibweise," in *History, Text, Value. Essays on Adalbert Stifter*, ed. Michael Minden, Martin Swales, and Godela Weiss-Sussex (London: University of London Press, 2003), 31.

corpora. Of course, foregrounding periodical culture and serialization brings into view key, often underthematized features of nineteenth-century media ecologies and is of merit if only for that reason. Yet theorizing the textual and medial heterogeneity that one encounters on the pages of periodicals, newspapers, and magazines can be both productive and daunting: the corpus is potentially unlimited, and one runs the risk of focusing on one set of objects almost arbitrarily over others. What, then, are the actual (or just potential or possible) afterlives of nineteenth-century serial print, and what roles should such afterlives play in the writing of literary history? Is the study of serial formats a subcategory of the broader literary tradition and its patterns of transmission, or should it be a more privileged thread? How does the focus on seriality negotiate the challenge of discerning the relationships among various kinds of more or less interrelated texts in comparison to other literary-historical approaches? How do serial forms bring a sense of nineteenth-century life and experience more into view, on the one hand, and reveal the difficulties involved in doing so, on the other? In offering partial, case-specific answers to these questions, this book has attempted to show how serial forms complicate conceptions of the self-standing work and authorial oeuvre; how the migration from journal to book to works edition prompts reflection on the literary field more broadly; how republication can function as an important technique of authorial promotion and diminution alike; how early and mid-nineteenth-century modes of history writing draw on the peculiarities of serialized cultural journalism; and how format and genre conceits such as the tableau, caricature, and physiognomic portrait train readers to be on the lookout for more to come. Studying serial literature shifts our attention from individual monumental works to the ongoing flow of variously sized forms, genres, and formats and thus expands the range of materials we are interested in as literary historians.

Another way to pose the question of literary-historical relevance is to ask how the study of the serial print of past centuries might shed light on the temporal awareness of our digital age. Do certain aspects of nineteenth-century serial culture converge with our present-day experience of digital ephemeralities? Any consideration of the contemporary relevance of nineteenth-century print is immediately confronted with the ubiquity of such material in digital archives.[9] Indeed, the writing of parts of this book would have not been possible without digitization projects at the Universities of Bielefeld, Jena, Munich and at the Austrian and German national libraries. With most nineteenth-century print being in the public domain, such digitized material is ripe for various projects, including digital humanities and curation projects and topic-specific databases.[10] If we think back to Ludwig Börne's thought experiment about the perishing of Parisian readers in a future natural disaster which began part I of this book,[11] we might conclude that this digital archive in fact disproves his vision of the disappearance of the newspapers and journals that nineteenth-century readers held in their hands: instead, we have embarked on a preservation project that can continue to make nineteenth-century serial print available and ever more searchable. Even as certain key aspects of nineteenth-century life are lost to us, we do have many journals and papers from the era at our disposal, contrary to Börne's vision of incinerated print. As James Mussell puts it, digitization returns "newspapers and periodicals, previously neglected due to their complicated bibliographical condition, to their central place in [the nineteenth-century] corpus of print."[12] Even though certain aspects of this media ecology have been superseded—leading journals have ended their run, and new media regimes have emerged—digitization redeems serial print's promise to continue and to reemerge. Digitization makes print timely again, one might argue, for it allows us to access the central place of it in the lives of nineteenth-century readers. Serial forms help us to rethink the archive and our inventories of it. Here, too, the

---

9. Mussell, *The Nineteenth-Century Press*.
10. "As digitization creates processable data, content and metadata from different publications can be cross-searched and compared. Unlike holdings in print archives, digital resources can be accessed by many people at the same time, from wherever they are ... and whenever they want." Mussell, *The Nineteenth-Century Press*, 58.
11. Börne imagines a Paris engulfed, Pompeii-like, by natural disaster and Parisians frozen in their entombed poses as they are reading their daily papers.
12. Mussell, *The Nineteenth-Century Press*, 1.

trope that we tracked throughout the book of reencountering old papers seems to find new purchase. Digitization complicates and even counteracts the material and figural ephemerality of newspapers. Access to the archive allows us to find proof of how serial cultures of various sorts saturate the nineteenth century, a concern of recent studies of serial forms by Clare Pettitt, Claudia Stockinger, and others.[13]

At the same time, though, so many of the practices and media ecologies of print continue to withhold themselves from view, and new forms of access do not make this material any less foreign. We are far removed from the world of nineteenth-century print; part of my book's project has been to bring it closer, but it is still a difficult if not impossible task to recreate the print diet of the typical nineteenth-century reader and the conscious or unconscious points of reference that readers, editors, artists, and writers brought to texts. Here Koselleck's remark (in a letter to Carl Schmitt) that the *Vormärz* era (1830–1848) remains an "indecipherable," "veiled time" is salient. For at the very time Koselleck wrote this to his notorious mentor, he was working on his massive habilitation dealing with exactly this period. If there was anyone who had access to historical knowledge about the *Vormärz*, it would have been Koselleck! Yet he expresses the essential historical insight that great swaths of the past (and of the present, as he observes) are lost to us. This insight would seem to confirm a certain strand of Börne's thought experiment: it is nearly impossible to work our way into the life worlds of the past, let alone into those of our contemporaries. In this line of thinking, the lives and afterlives of serial print become precarious, tenuous, and contingent, and the mass of materials that exist in print and digital archives amplifies an awareness of loss.

Reflections on the unrecognizability of the past and present prompt us to do new things with serial print and to undertake historiographical thought experiments that linger with the foreignness and untimeliness of the material. These are historiographical choices that do not start with the book- and work-based biases of

---

13. See Pettitt, *Serial Forms*; and Stockinger, *An den Ursprüngen populärer Serialität*.

more traditional scholarship but instead aim for a more accurate sense of reading practices and publishing techniques, yet that simultaneously also recognize that we access this material differently than nineteenth-century readers. Recent scholarship has experimented with different ways of encountering serial forms and imagining structures of reading and archival strategies that engage with the particularities of serial print. As James Mussell has pointed out, an irony of nineteenth-century serials is that we stand at a historical remove where we can witness the end of publication formats predicated on serial continuation, that is, on not ending. This makes our perspective as readers fundamentally different from that of past readers. As Mussell puts it, "From our vantage point in the present, we have the last [installment of given periodicals] and so are able to do what its nineteenth-century readers could not: step outside the series and see the periodical or newspaper as a whole."[14] This seeing as a whole is a historicizing gesture to be sure, and perhaps Mussell exaggerates the point; nineteenth-century editors and historians of journalism could indeed have surveyed a range of short-lived journal projects and evaluated what did and didn't work in recent decades. Yet approaching serial forms from the perspective of their ends prompts us to consider afterlives that do not adhere to the logic of continuation inherent in these forms. Viewing the journal as a whole, discretely bounded run is different from looking at how serialization and periodicity structures its contents. If certain organs of serial print are predicated on not ending, what do we do when they end? This was the thought experiment undertaken by Jean Paul, in the context both of his eulogy for the *Morgenblatt* in the journal's very first issue and of his conception of a works edition that would somehow be continued after his death.

Other scholars similarly manipulate the parameters of serial form in order to get at the particularities of periodical literature. Jon Klancher, for example, explores how the shift of journals into bookish volumes of collected issues and then into digital archives causes something to "happen" to periodicals that wrests them

---

14. Mussell, "Repetition," 345.

from the ways that they were consumed issue to issue.[15] To be sure, the common practice of anthologizing journal issues into a continuously paged, bound volume at the end of the year belies the contrast of ephemeral journal and permanent book, yet, as Klancher notes, anthologizing often changes the appearance of the issue, cutting out advertising and removing at times up to almost half the pages of given issues. (This is part of what Laurel Brake speaks of when referencing the "stripping, disciplining and institutionaliz[ing]" of various kinds of texts.[16]) Similar alterations occur with the migration of the printed page to digital readers. The loss of certain features of journal issues in these processes is also analogous to the loss of materiality in the process of digitization.[17] It is in this context that Klancher proposes that we return to single issues as our object of study, in effect drawing in small draughts from the sea of print and breaking up the flow of multi-issue formats in the process. This approach runs counter to treating issues and texts as interlinked series of materials and thus as broader serial shapes of time as I have sought to do in this book, yet Klancher's proposed style of reading nonetheless makes seriality visible in its absence, as he reads against rather than with certain rules established by print and digital archives. If the nineteenth century is an age of mass print in which serial culture occupies large swaths of public debate and consumption, taking a microperspective can be instructive and is in line with recent work in literary historiography that emphasizes the sometimes outsize cultural labor achieved by small forms.[18]

A recent book similarly limits its focus to a short range of irregular Napoleonic era journals printed in Germany from 1813 to 1815, exploring how such journals shape a sense of irregular temporalities.[19] These journals mirror the chaotic uncertainty of

---

15. Jon Klancher, "What Happened to the Periodical?" *Studies in Romanticism* 59, no. 4 (2020): 507–18.

16. Brake, *Print in Transition, 1850–1910*, 29.

17. On "lossiness" as a key feature of serial print, see Mark W. Turner, "Seriality, Miscellaneity, and Compression in Nineteenth-Century Print," *Victorian Studies* 62, no. 2 (2020): 283–94.

18. See for example Tautz, *Translating the World*.

19. See Brehm et al., *Zeit/Schrift 1813–1815*.

wartime, but they also lend structure to temporal frameworks in their own way and warrant the finetuned attention of microanalysis. In a collective undertaking, David Brehm, Nicola Kaminski, Volker Mergenthaler, Nora Ramtke, and Sven Schöpf uncover such times at work in contemporaneous formats, genre rubrics, title vignettes, and more. They explore time-specific occurrences in the unfolding runs of specific journals and papers, revealing points of convergence and concentration between different journals that at times run parallel to unfolding events (*Ereignisgeschichte*) but also have their own logics that facilitate reader experiences with nonlinearity, simultaneity, contiguity, and incoherence.[20] In an interesting formatting decision, the authors opt to present their research in a book, the pages of which take on the appearance of an irregular twenty-three installment, sixteen-page quarto journal, with articles by different authors existing side by side and serialized across multiple "issues" (which replace the chapter rubrics of conventional edited volumes). The decision to present contemporaneous scholarship in the costume of an anachronistic historical format serves to make the complex temporalities manifested by these historical journals even more salient. This format also remediates text passages and images from different journals under examination, using "headlines and ultrashort excerpts" that draw attention to the reflexes of serial print to mark time.[21] This project is a radically microperspectival deep dive into the print archive that allows the authors and readers to intuit by analogy the complexity, irregularity, and multidirectional times at work in other historical media ecologies.

Koselleck's suggestion that past and present are similarly unrecognizable invites us to consider how the untimeliness of the past might illuminate the untimeliness of the present. The foreignness of past historical epochs was certainly a problem that occupied Koselleck and Schmitt in relation to the pre– and post–World War II eras, but this problem can also be extended to the divide between print and technical media. Media theorists are often keen to stress differences between pre- and post-electric and electronic media,

---

20. Brehm et al., *Zeit/Schrift 1813–1815*, xiii.
21. Brehm et al., *Zeit/Schrift 1813–1815*, xii.

yet certain shared strategies of negotiating and organizing print and digital archives nonetheless persist, whether it is through techniques of managing the flow, feed, or stream of constant information, through the perception of accelerated news cycles, or through necessary strategies of selection and curation. Print and digital media likewise both enable the ability to reencounter variously timed ephemeralities. Here the work of media theorist Wendy Hui Kyong Chun is instructive, for she identifies a basic ephemerality at the core of digital media that arises not only through the internet's constant self-regeneration but also through the simple yet counterintuitive fact of the material decay of digital media: "Digital media [are] not always there. We suffer daily frustrations with digital sources that just disappear. Digital media [are] degenerative, forgetful, eraseable."[22] Computer memory is impermanent and volatile, and the decay and planned (or unplanned) obsolescence of digital archives provide a new perspective on a more general problem pertaining to all media. Here Chun positions herself against views that take digital media to be the newest panacea for archiving previously unstable media, views that assert that "the always there-ness of digital media [could] make things more stable, more lasting."[23]

Along with exploring how material technologies create media times of their own (a key component of recent media theory à la Wolfgang Ernst), Chun also stresses the temporalities at work in human interface and use.[24] In contrast to the broadcast model of television and radio, users consume web content across a range of heterogeneous temporal frames. The ways in which digital archives store information condition or alter its "liveness" or timeliness. To be sure, digital media capture and circulate exponentially more traces of minute ephemera of the everyday, allowing ever more individuals to weigh in with their time-specific opinions, emotions, and desires and

---

22. Chun argues that web-based digital media create "enduring ephemerals" by archiving time-specific materials that can be accessed at different times. Wendy Hui Kyong Chun, "The Enduring Ephemeral, or the Future Is a Memory," *Critical Inquiry* 35, no. 1 (2008): 169.
23. Chun, "The Enduring Ephemeral," 153.
24. For Ernst, the human falls out the more the technological operations of media become incongruous with forms of human experience.

leave a trace of these in a common web-based archive. At the same time, however, digital media archive these interventions and make it possible to access them at nonsimultaneous, heterogenous points in time: "The lag between a digital object's creation and its popular or scholarly uptake—its nonsimultaneous dissemination... grounds [new media] as new."[25] In a sense, then, the live, the ephemeral, and the event are lying in wait, sometimes becoming outdated or obsolete, and sometimes suddenly and without notice becoming more timely than ever, giving new meaning to untimeliness. This, then, is the compelling paradox of digital media: they speed up the production and dissemination of content, but they also persist in ever-shifting forms in the online archive. Chun calls this a form of "enduring ephemerality" particular to the digital and distinct from earlier technical media such as television,[26] but the untimely preservation and recirculation of once current, now expired ephemeralities is a central feature of the print landscape as well, both at the time and in its literary- and media-historical resonances. Analogous to the universal medium of the computer, serial print is the universal medium of the nineteenth-century information age, remediating other media—the visual image, theater, performance, and more—and provides timely and untimely points of comparison to digital media.

All of these approaches are interested in the untimely afterlives of different media and read media ensembles as dynamic constellations open for multiple inroads and kinds of use. These constellations appear different to each user depending on what they are looking at and exhibit in varyingly radical ways the contingency of literary-historical choices. It is a common gesture in serial literature to refer to the "future historian" who will have the proper overview to survey the source materials collected in serial print and achieve conclusive historical knowledge, to disentangle "the thousandfold intertwined knot [*Knäuel*] of written and oral traditions," as Bertuch and Böttiger put it. Perhaps such future historians never

---

25. Chun, "The Enduring Ephemeral," 153.
26. "Networked new media does not follow the same logic of seriality as television; flow and segmentation do not quite encompass digital media's ephemerality." Chun, "The Enduring Ephemeral," 153.

came, perhaps the task was simply too large, or perhaps the corpus too massive to survey, and indeed, many such expectations for future readers peter out amid the flow of ever more materials. In this context, it would be presumptuous to position ourselves as the very future historians capable of providing disentangled systematic overviews even as we chart new inroads into media constellations of the past and track specific shapes of time. Throughout this book I have worked with the metaphor of multiple literary-historiographical horizons: the horizon of reader orientation toward a classicizing work, the horizon of the kindred reader attuned to authorial sentiment, the horizon of the philological editor of the critical edition, the horizon of author-based republication across different formats, the horizon of future republication and reception, and the horizon of the never-ending proliferation of serial entertainment and cultural journalism. Each of these horizons opens up on the basis of the choices we make as readers and scholars, and each tracks certain shapes of times and closes itself off to others. Throughout this book, I have examined writers and editors who are especially attuned to the horizons of serial literature, to the temporal footprints of different publishing formats, to questions of authorial control, and to questions of untimely history writing. All cast out into the sea of print in search of shapes of time and provide us with a more differentiated vision of time and its medial filiations.

One final word on Börne's thought experiment about Paris as an archaeological site that served as the point of entry for this book: the paradox of the simultaneous ephemerality and the endurance of serial print occasions us to consider the world of print as it was serially reproduced day in and day out throughout the nineteenth century and beyond, but it also invites us to think about how we reencounter the past in the future, both as a material absence and as an actual material artifact. Put differently, the trope of print ephemerality helps to imagine both the presence and absence and both the accessibility and inaccessibility of bygone historical presents in the future. The future history of today's newspapers is a story about these papers' ends, but it is also a story about their continuation. The past both withholds and discloses itself through the material traces of print as publications migrate across formats, from journal to book, from microfiche to pdf, or from digital pagination to XML. Börne ultimately was after a specifically political promise inherent to reading serial print—that reading the newspaper on a daily basis is a form of democratic participation—but the promise of repetitive patterns of print can be read as a media-archaeological promise as well. As long as we continue to sift through the ephemera of the past, we are bound to discover differently timed patterns of life, the world, and media, either in artifacts that have long since disintegrated, in preserved print matter, or in the remediated digital archive.

BIBLIOGRAPHY

Primary Sources

Journals

Anzeiger des Teutschen Merkurs. Ed. Christoph Martin Wieland. Weimar: Verl. der Gesellschaft, 1773–1789.

Deutsches Museum. Ed. Friedrich Schlegel. Vienna: Camesinasche Buchhandlung, 1812–1813.

Die Gartenlaube für Österreich: Wochenschrift für Familie und Volk, Freiheit und Fortschritt. Ed. Heinrich Sacher-Masoch. Graz: 1866–1869.

Historischer Almanach fürs Jahr 1790, enthaltend die Geschichte der Großen Revolution in Frankreich. Ed. Lorenz Westenrieder and J. C. F. Schulz. Braunschweig: Schulbuchhandlung, 1790.

Die Horen, eine Monatsschrift. Ed. Friedrich Schiller. Tübingen: Cotta, 1798–1800.

Intelligenzblatt zum Journal des Luxus und der Moden. Ed. Friedrich Justin Bertuch and Georg Melchior Kraus. Weimar: Verl. des Landes-Industrie-Comptoirs, 1786–1827.

Intelligenzblatt zum Morgenblatt für gebildete Stände. Tübingen: Cotta, 1807–1865.
Journal des Luxus und der Moden (JLM). Ed. Friedrich Justin Bertuch and Georg Melchior Kraus. Weimar: Verl. des Landes-Industrie-Comptoirs, 1786–1827. [*Journal der Moden* (1786), *Journal für Luxus, Mode und Gegenstände der Kunst* (1813–1814), *Journal für Literatur, Kunst, Luxus und Mode* (1814–1826).]
London und Paris. Ed. F. J. Bertuch and Karl August Böttiger. Weimar: Verl. des Landes-Industrie-Comptoirs, 1798–1815. [*Paris, Wien und London* (1811), *Paris und Wien* (1812), *London, Paris und Wien* (1814).]
Das Morgenblatt für gebildete Stände. Tübingen: Cotta, 1807–1865. [*Morgenblatt für gebildete Leser* (1837–1865).]
Die Propyläen. Eine Periodische Schrift. Ed. Johann Wolfgang von Goethe and Johann Heinrich Meyer. Tübingen: Cotta, 1798–1800.
The Spectator. Ed. Joseph Addison and Richard Steele. London: 1711–1712.
Der Teutsche Merkur. Ed. Christoph Martin Wieland. Weimar: Verl. der Gesellschaft, 1773–1789.
Die Wage. Eine Zeitschrift für Bürgerleben, Wissenschaft, und Kunst. Ed. Ludwig Börne. Frankfurt: Hermann, 1818–1821.
Vaterländisches Museum. Ed. Friedrich Perthes. Hamburg: Perthes, 1810–1811.
Zeitschwingen, oder Des deutschen Volkes fliegende Blätter. Ed. Ludwig Börne. Offenbach: Verl. der Expedition der Zeitschwingen, 1817–1819.
Zeitung für Einsiedler. Ed. Achim von Arnim, Clemens Brentano, and Joseph Görres. Heidelberg: Mohr and Zimmer, 1808.

Other Primary Sources

Adelung, Johann Christian. *Grammatisch-kritisches Wörterbuch der Hochdeutschen Mundart.* Vol. 1. Leipzig: Breitkopf, 1793.
Börne, Ludwig. *Gesammelte Schriften.* 15 vols. Vols. 1–8, Hamburg: Hoffmann and Campe, 1829–1832. Vols. 9–14, Hamburg, Offenbach, Paris, 1832–1834 (*Briefe aus Paris*). Vol. 15, Paris, 1837. [Abbreviated as GS in citations with volume and page number.]
Börne, Ludwig. *Sämtliche Schriften.* 5 vols. Ed. Inge Rippman and Peter Rippmann. Dreieich: Melzer, 1977. [Abbreviated as SS in citations with volume and page number.]
Büchner, Georg. *Werke und Briefe.* Munich: Hanser, 1980.
Campe, Joachim Heinrich. "Beantwortung dieses Einwurfs." *Braunschweigisches Journal* 1, no. 1 (1788): 19–44.
Carlyle, Thomas. "Review of William Taylor, *Historic Survey of German Poetry.*" *Edinburgh Review* 53, no. 105 (1831): 179–80.

Goethe, Johann Wolfgang von. *Goethes Werke*. 133 vols. H. Böhlau: Weimar, 1887–1919. [Abbreviated as WA in citations with part number followed by the volume and page number.]
Goethe, Johann Wolfgang von. *Masken des römischen Carnevals*. Weimar and Gotha: Ettinger, 1790.
Goethe, Johann Wolfgang von. *Das römische Carneval*. Weimar and Gotha: Ettinger, 1789.
Goethe, Johann Wolfgang von. *Sämtliche Werke nach Epochen seines Schaffens*. 21 vols. Munich: Hanser, 1992. [Abbreviated as MA in citations with volume and page number.]
Hegel, G. W. F. *Vorlesungen über die Ästhetik*. Vol. 13 of *Werke in zwanzig Bänden*. Ed. Eva Muldenhauer and Karl Markus Michel. Frankfurt: Suhrkamp, 1970.
Hegel, G. W. F. *Vorlesungen über die Philosophie der Geschichte*. Vol. 12 of *Werke in zwanzig Bänden*. Ed. Eva Muldenhauer and Karl Markus Michel. Frankfurt: Suhrkamp, 1970.
Heine, Heinrich. *Französische Zustände*. Hamburg: Hoffmann und Campe, 1833.
Heine, Heinrich. *Historisch-kritische Gesamtausgabe der Werke*. 16 vols. Ed. Manfred Windfuhr. Hamburg: Hoffmann und Campe, 1973–1997. [Abbreviated as DHA in citations with part number followed by the volume and page number.]
Heine, Heinrich. "Kampf und Kämpfer." *Zeitung für die Elegante Welt* 43, no. 36 (September 6, 1843): 874–878.
Heine, Heinrich. *Ludwig Börne: A Memorial*. Trans. Jeffrey L. Sammons. Rochester, NY: Camden House, 2006.
Heine, Heinrich. *Lutezia: Berichte über Politik, Kunst und Volksleben*. Vols. 2–3 of *Vermischte Schriften*. Hamburg: Hoffmann und Campe, 1854.
Heine, Heinrich. "Preface to the French Edition of *Lutezia*." In *The Romantic School and Other Essays*, ed. Jost Hermand and Robert C. Holub, 295–302. New York: Continuum, 1985.
Heine, Heinrich. *Säkularausgabe: Werke, Briefwechsel, Lebenszeugnisse*. 27 vols. Berlin: Akademie, 1970–. [Abbreviated as HSA in citations with volume and page number.]
Heine, Heinrich. "Various Conceptions of History." In *The Romantic School and Other Essays*, ed. Jost Hermand and Robert C. Holub, 289–60. New York: Continuum, 1985.
Heine, Heinrich. *Werke und Briefe*. 10 vols. Ed. Hans Kaufmann and Gotthard Erler. Berlin: Aufbau, 1961–1964.
Horace. *Odes and Epodes*. Ed. and trans. Niall Rudd. Cambridge, MA: Harvard University Press, 2004.
Jean Paul. *Dämmerungen für Deutschland*. Tübingen: Cotta, 1809.
Jean Paul. *Der Komet, oder Nikolaus Markgraf, eine komische Geschichte*. 3 vols. Berlin: Reimer, 1820–1822.
Jean Paul. *Herbst-Blumine oder gesammelte Werkchen aus Zeitschriften*. 3 vols. Stuttgart and Tübingen: Cotta, 1810, 1815, 1820.

Jean Paul. *Jean Pauls Briefe und bevorstehender Lebenslauf*. Gera and Leipzig: Heinsius, 1799.
Jean Paul. "Konjektural-Biographie." In *Jean Pauls Briefe und bevorstehender Lebenslauf*, 289–450. Gera and Leipzig: Heinsius, 1799.
Jean Paul. *Museum*. Stuttgart and Tübingen: Cotta, 1814.
Jean Paul. *Politische Fastenpredigten während Deutschlands Marterwoche*. Cotta: Stuttgart and Tübingen, 1817.
Jean Paul. *Jean Pauls Sämtliche Werke, historisch-kritische Ausgabe*. Ed. Eduard Berend et al. Weimar: Böhlau, 1927–. [Abbreviated as SW HKA with part and volume number followed by page number.]
Jean Paul. *Sämmtliche Werke*. 65 vols. Berlin: Reimer, 1826–1838. [Abbreviated as Reimer I in citations with installment and part number followed by volume number and publication date.]
Jean Paul. *Sämtliche Werke in 10 Bänden*. 10 vols. Ed. Norbert Miller. Munich/Vienna: Hanser, 1974–1985. [Cited in footnotes with no abbreviation, with part and volume number followed by page number.]
Marlet, Jean-Henri. *Tableaux de Paris*. Paris: 1821–1824.
Marx, Karl. "The Eighteenth Brumaire of Louis Bonaparte." In *Marx: Later Political Writings*, ed. Terrell Carver, 31–127. Cambridge: Cambridge University Press, 1996.
Mercier, Louis-Sébastien. *Panorama of Paris: Selections from Mercier's Tableau de Paris*. University Park: Pennsylvania State University Press, 1999.
Mercier, Louis-Sébastien. *Tableau de Paris*. Vol. 2. Amsterdam: 1782.
Moritz, Karl Philipp. *Anthousa, oder Roms Alterthümer. Ein Buch für die Menschheit*. Berlin: Maurer, 1791.
Moritz, Karl Philipp. *Reise eines Deutschen in Italien in den Jahren 1786 bis 1788*. Berlin: Maurer, 1792.
Moritz, Karl Philipp. "Über die Würde des Studiums der Altertümer." In *Karl Philipp Moritz Werke*, vol. 2, 1045–48. Frankfurt: Deutscher Klassiker Verlag, 1997.
Moritz, Karl Philipp. "Versuch einer Vereinigung aller schönen Künste und Wissenschaften unter dem Begriff des in sich selbst Vollendeten." In *Karl Philipp Moritz Werke*, vol. 2, 943–49. Frankfurt: Deutscher Klassiker Verlag, 1997.
Stifter, Adalbert. "Der Sylvesterabend." In *Vermischte Schriften*, vol. 2, 310–20. Pesth: Heckenast, 1870.

Secondary Sources

Anderson, Benedict. "Nationalism, Identity, and the Logic of Seriality." In *The Spectre of Comparisons: Nationalism, Southeast Asia, and the World*, 29–44. London: Verso, 1998.
Apgar, Richard B. "Flooded: Periodicals and the Crisis of Information around 1780." In *Market Strategies and German Literature in the Long Nineteenth*

Century, ed. Vance Byrd and Ervin Malakaj, 25–54. New York: De Gruyter, 2020.
Arburg, Hans-Georg von. *Kunst-Wissenschaft um 1800. Studien zu Georg Christoph Lichtenbergs Hogarth-Kommentaren*. Göttingen: Wallstein, 1998.
Arendt, Hannah. *On Revolution*. New York: Penguin, 2006 [1963].
Aretz, Heinrich. *Heinrich von Kleist als Journalist. Untersuchungen zum "Phöbus", zur "Germania" und den "Berliner Abendblättern."* Stuttgart: Akademischer Verlag, 1984.
Bade, Heidemarie. *Jean Pauls politische Schriften*. Tübingen: Niemeyer, 1974.
Baker, Keith Michael, and Dan Edelstein. "Introduction." In *Scripting Revolution: A Historical Approach to the Comparative Study of Revolutions*, ed. Keith Michael Baker and Dan Edelstein, 1–24. Stanford, CA: Stanford University Press, 2015.
Bakhtin, Mikhail. *Problems of Dostoevsky's Poetics*. Trans. Caryl Emerson. Minneapolis: University of Minnesota Press, 1984.
Bakhtin, Mikhail. *Rabelais and His World*. Trans. Hélène Isowlsky. Bloomington: Indiana University Press, 1984.
Baudelaire, Charles. "The Painter of Modern Life." In *The Painter of Modern Life and Other Essays*, 1–42. New York: Phaidon, 1964 [1863].
Beck, Andreas, and Volker Mergenthaler, ed. *Journalförmige Bücher—buchförmige Journale. Pfennig-Magazin zur Journalliteratur*. Vol. 8. Hanover: Wehrhahn, 2022.
Becker, Ernst Wolfgang. *Zeit der Revolution!—Revolution der Zeit? Zeiterfahrungen in Deutschland in der Ära der Revolutionen 1789–1848/49*. Göttingen: Vandenhoeck und Ruprecht, 1999.
Beiser, Frederick C. *The German Historicist Tradition*. Oxford: Oxford University Press, 2011.
Belgum, Kirsten. *Popularizing the Nation: Audience, Representation, and the Production of Identity in "Die Gartenlaube," 1853–1900*. Lincoln, NE: University of Nebraska Press, 1998.
Benedict, Barbara. *Making the Modern Reader: Cultural Mediation in Early Modern Literary Anthologies*. Princeton, NJ: Princeton University Press, 1996.
Benjamin, Walter. "Der Eingetunkte Zauberstab: Zu Max Kommerell's 'Jean Paul.'" In *Gesammelte Schriften*, vol. 3, ed. Rolf Tiedemann and Hermann Schweppenhäuser, 409–17. Frankfurt: Suhrkamp, 1972.
Benjamin, Walter. "Eine Kleine Geschichte der Photographie." In *Das Kunstwerk im Zeitalter seiner technischen Reproduzierbarkeit*, 45–64. Frankfurt: Suhrkamp, 1963.
Benjamin, Walter. "Wider ein Meisterwerk: Zu Max Kommerell, 'Der Dichter als Führer in der deutschen Klassik.'" In *Gesammelte Schriften*, vol. 3, ed. Rolf Tiedemann and Hermann Schweppenhäuser, 252–59. Frankfurt: Suhrkamp, 1972.
Benne, Christian. "'Kein Einfall sollte untergehen': Nachlassbewusstsein und Nachlass-Selbstbewusstsein bei Jean Paul." In *Nachlassbewusstsein: Literatur,*

Archiv, Philologie, 1750–2000, ed. Kai Sina and Carlos Spoerhase, 217–46. Göttingen: Wallstein, 2017.

Berend, Eduard. "Jean Paul, der meistgelesene Schriftsteller seiner Zeit?" In *Jean Paul*, ed. Uwe Schweikert, 155–69. Darmstadt: Wissenschaftliche Buchgesellschaft, 1974.

Berend, Eduard. *Prolegomena zur historisch-kritischen Gesamtausgabe von Jean Pauls Werken*. Berlin: Verlag der Akademie der Wissenschaften, 1927.

Berger, Karol. *Bach's Cycle, Mozart's Arrow: An Essay on the Origins of Musical Modernity*. Berkeley: University of California Press, 2007.

Berhorst, Ralf. *Anamorphose der Zeit. Jean Pauls Romanästhetik und Geschichtsphilosophie*. Tübingen: Niemeyer, 2002.

Bies, Michael. "Wieder das Fabrikenwesen. Goethe und das Handwerk der Klassik." In *Der Streit um Klassizität: Polemische Konstellationen vom 18. Zum 21. Jahrhundert*, ed. Daniel Ehrmann and Norbert Christian Wolf, 47–66. Munich: Fink, 2021.

Bies, Michael, and Wolfgang Hottner. *"(Ist fortzusetzen.)" Anschlüsse, Fortführungen und Enden in Goethes späten Werken*. Freiburg: Rombach, 2024.

Blanke, Horst Walter. "Historische Zeitschriften." In *Von Almanach bis Zeitung. Ein Handbuch der Medien in Deutschland 1700–1800*, ed. Ernst Fischer, Wilhelm Haefs, and York-Gothart Mix, 71–88. Munich: Beck, 1999.

Blättler, Christine. "Überlegungen zu Serialität als ästhetischem Begriff." *Weimarer Beiträge* 49, no. 4 (2003): 502–16.

Blumenberg, Hans. *Lebenszeit und Weltzeit*. Frankfurt: Suhrkamp, 1986.

Blumenberg, Hans. *Quellen, Ströme, Eisberge*. Ed. Ulrich von Bülow and Dorit Krusche. Frankfurt: Suhrkamp, 2012.

Böck, Dorothea. "Archäologie in der Wüste. Jean Paul und das ‚Biedermeier'—Eine Provokation für das Fach (ante portas)." In *Atta Troll tanzt noch Selbstbesichtigungen der literaturwissenschaftlichen Germanistik im 20. Jahrhundert*, ed. Petra Boden, Holger Dainat, and Ursula Menzel, 241–69. Berlin: Akademie, 1997.

Böck, Dorothea. "Satirische Raffinerien für Menschenkinder aus allen Ständen: Überlegungen zur Genesis von Jean Pauls Kunstmodell." In *Greizer Studien*, ed. Harald Olbrich et al., 149–208. Greiz: Staatliche Museen Greiz, 1989.

Böhmer, Sebastian, Christiane Holm, Veronika Spinner, and Thorsten Valk, ed. *Weimarer Klassik. Kultur des Sinnlichen*. Berlin: Deutscher Kunstverlag, 2012.

Booß, Rutger. *Ansichten der Revolution: Paris-Berichte deutscher Schriftsteller nach der Juli-Revolution 1830; Heine, Börne, u.a.* Cologne: Pahl-Rugenstein, 1977.

Borchert, Angela. "Charles Baudelaire. Die Karikatur und die Genese einer Poetik des Flüchtigen." In *Flüchtigkeit der Moderne. Die Eigenzeiten des Ephemeren im langen 19. Jahrhundert*, ed. Sean Franzel, Michael Bies, and Dirk Oschmann, 61–88. Hanover: Wehrhahn, 2017.

Borchert, Angela. "Die Produktion von Karikatur in der Karikatur: Zeichnungs-, Schreib- und Druckszenen in der französischen und deutschen illustrierten

Satire-Journale (1830–1848)." *Colloquia Germanica* 49, nos. 2–3 (2016): 201–34.
Borchert, Angela. "Einleitung." In *Das "Journal des Luxus und der Moden": Kultur um 1800*, ed. Angela Borchert and Ralf Dressel, 11–20. Heidelberg: Winter, 2004.
Borchert, Angela. "Ein Seismograph des Zeitgeistes: Kultur, Kulturgeschichte und Kulturkritik im *Journal des Luxus und der Moden*." In *Das "Journal des Luxus und der Moden": Kultur um 1800*, ed. Angela Borchert and Ralf Dressel, 74–104. Heidelberg: Winter, 2004.
Bosse, Heinrich. *Autorschaft ist Werkherrschaft. Über die Entstehung des Urheberrechts aus dem Geist der Goethezeit*. Paderborn: Fink, 2014 [1981].
Boutin, Aimée. *City of Noise: Sound and Nineteenth-Century Paris*. Champaign, IL: University of Illinois Press, 2015.
Brake, Laurel. *Print in Transition, 1850–1910: Studies in Media and Book History*. London: Palgrave, 2001.
Brehm, David, et al. *Zeit/Schrift 1813–1815 oder Chronopoetik des 'Unregelmäßigen*. Hanover: Wehrhahn, 2022.
Briese, Olaf. "'Schutzmittel 'für' die Cholera': Geschichtsphilosophische und politische Cholera-Kompensation bei Heine und seinen Zeitgenossen." *Heine Jahrbuch* 32 (1993): 9–26.
Bringemeier, Martha. *Ein Modejournalist erlebt die Französische Revolution*. Münster: Coppenrath, 1981.
Bronfen Elisabeth, Christiane Frey, and David Martyn. "Vorwort." In *Noch einmal Anders. Zu einer Poetik des Seriellen*, ed. Elisabeth Bronfen, Christine Frey, and David Martyn, 7–16. Zurich and Berlin: Diaphanes, 2016.
Brylowe, Thora. "Two Kinds of Collections: Sir William Hamilton's Vases, Real and Represented." *Eighteenth-Century Life* 32, no. 1 (2008): 23–56.
Bunzel, Wolfgang. "Publizistische Poetik. Goethes Veröffentlichungen in Almanachen und Taschenbüchern." In *Almanach- und Taschenbuchkultur des 18. und 19. Jahrhunderts*, ed. York-Gothart Mix, 63–76. Wiesbaden: Harrassowitz, 1996.
Busch, Werner. *Das sentimentalische Bild. Die Krise der Kunst im 18. Jahrhundert und die Geburt der Moderne*. Munich: Beck, 1993.
Byrd, Vance. *A Pedagogy of Observation: Nineteenth-Century Panoramas, German Literature, and Reading Culture*. Lewisburg, PA: Bucknell University Press, 2017.
Byrnes, Joseph F. *Catholic and French Forever: Religious and National Identity in Modern France*. University Park: Pennsylvania State University Press, 2005.
Cahn, Michael. "*Opera Omnia*: The Production of Cultural Authority." In *History of Science, History of Text*, ed. Karine Chemla, 81–94. Dordrecht: Springer, 2004.
Campbell, Timothy. *Historical Style: Fashion and the New Mode of History, 1740–1830*. Philadelphia: University of Pennsylvania Press, 2016.
Campe, Rüdiger. "To Be Continued: Einige Beobachtungen zu Goethes *Unterhaltungen*." In *Noch einmal anders: Zu einer Poetik des Seriellen*, ed. Elisabeth

Bronfen, Christiane Frey, and David Martyn, 119–36. Zürich: Diaphanes, 2016.

Campe, Rüdiger. "Writing; The Scene of Writing." *MLN* 136, no. 5 (2021): 971–83.

Canguilhem, Georges. "Fontenelle, philosophe et historien des sciences." In *Études d'histoire et de philosophie des sciences*, 51–56. Paris: Libraire philosophique J. Vrin, 1968.

Cilleßen, Wolfgang. "Modezeitschriften." In *Von Almanach bis Zeitung. Ein Handbuch der Medien in Deutschland 1700–1800*, ed. Ernst Fischer, Wilhelm Haefs, and York-Gothart Mix, 207–24. Munich: Beck, 1999.

Cilleßen, Wolfgang, and Rolf Reichardt. "Nachgestochene Caricaturen. Ein Journal und sein bildgeschichtlicher Hintergrund." In *Napoleons Neue Kleider*, ed. Wolfgang Cilleßen, Rolf Reichardt, and Christian Deuling, 6–35. Berlin: G&H Verlag, 2006.

Cilleßen, Wolfgang, Rolf Reichardt, and Christian Deuling, ed. *Napoleons Neue Kleider. Pariser und Londoner Karikaturen im klassischen Weimar*. Berlin: G&H Verlag, 2006.

Chakkalakal, Silvy. *Die Welt in Bildern: Erfahrungen und Evidenz in Friedrich J. Bertuchs Bilderbuch für Kinder*. Göttingen: Wallstein, 2014.

Cheesman, Tom. *The Shocking Ballad Picture Show: German Popular Literature and Cultural History*. Oxford: Berg, 1994.

Chun, Wendy Hui Kyong. "The Enduring Ephemeral, or the Future Is a Memory." *Critical Inquiry* 35, no. 1 (2008): 148–71.

Clark, Christopher. *Time and Power: Visions of History in German Politics, from the Thirty Years' War to the Third Reich*. Princeton, NJ: Princeton University Press, 2019.

Clark, Frazer S. *Zeitgeist and Zerrbild. Word, Image, and Idea in German Satire, 1800–1848*. Bern: Peter Lang, 2006.

Clark, William. *Academic Charisma and the Origins of the Research University*. Chicago: University of Chicago Press, 2007.

Collenberg-Plotnikov, Bernadette. *Klassizismus und Karikatur. Eine Konstellation der Kunst am Beginn der Moderne*. Berlin: Gebr. Mann, 1998.

Cook, Roger. *By the Rivers of Babylon: Heinrich Heine's Late Songs and Reflections*. Detroit: Wayne State University Press, 1998.

Cooper, Daniel. "Portraiture." In *Propaganda and Mass Persuasion: A Historical Encyclopedia, 1500 to the Present*. Ed. Nicholas J. Cull, David Culbert, and David Welch, 305–7. Santa Barbara, CA: ABC-CLIO, 2003.

Crane, Susan A. *Collecting and Historical Consciousness in Early Nineteenth-Century Germany*. Ithaca, NY: Cornell University Press, 2000.

Cuno, James. "Introduction." *French Caricature and the French Revolution, 1789–1799* 13–24. Los Angeles: Grunwald Center for the Graphic Arts, 1988. Exhibition catalogue.

Danelzik-Brüggemann, Christoph. *Ereignisse und Bilder. Bildpublizistik und politische Kultur in Deutschland zur Zeit der Französischen Revolution*. Berlin: Akademie Verlag, 1996.

D'Aprile, Ivan-Michelangelo. *Die Erfindung der Zeitgeschichte. Geschichtsschreibung und Journalismus zwischen Aufklärung und Vormärz.* Berlin: Akademie Verlag, 2013.

De Bruyn, Günter. "Dämmerungen. Jean Paul und die Politik." *Sinn und Form* 38, no. 6 (1986): 1147–62.

Deinet, Klaus. "Heinrich Heine und Frankreich—eine Neueinordnung." *Internationales Archiv für Sozialgeschichte der deutschen Literatur* 32, no. 1 (2007): 112–52.

Deuling, Christian. "Early Forms of Flânerie in the German Journal *London und Paris* (1798–1815)." In *The Flâneur Abroad: Historical and International Perspectives*, ed. Richard Wrigley, 94–117. Newcastle: Cambridge Scholars Press, 2014.

Deuling, Christian. "Die Karikatur-Kommentare in der Zeitschrift *London und Paris* (1798–1815)." In *Napoleons Neue Kleider*, ed. Wolfgang Cilleßen, Rolf Reichardt, and Christian Deuling, 79–93. Berlin: G&H Verlag, 2006.

Dickey, Laurence. "Philosophizing about History in the Nineteenth Century: *Zusammenhang* and the 'Progressive Method' in German Historical Scholarship." In *The Cambridge History of Philosophy in the Nineteenth Century (1790–1870)*, ed. Allen W. Wood and Songuk Susan Hahn, 793–816. Cambridge: Cambridge University Press, 2012.

Diers, Michael. "Bertuchs Bilderwelt. Zur populären Ikonographie der Aufklärung." In *Friedrich Justin Bertuch (1747–1822). Verleger, Schriftsteller und Unternehmer im klassischen Weimar*, ed. Gerhard R. Kaiser and Siegfried Seifert, 434–64. Tübingen: Niemeyer, 2000.

Diers, Michael. "Ewig und drei Tage. Erkundungen des Ephemeren—zur Einführung." In *Mo(nu)mente: Formen und Funktionen ephemerer Denkmäler*, ed. Michael Diers, 1–10. Berlin: Akademie, 1993.

Doane, Mary Ann. *The Emergence of Cinematic Time: Modernity, Contingency and the Archive.* Cambridge, MA: Harvard University Press, 2002.

Eco, Umberto. "Interpreting Serials." In *The Limits of Interpretation*, 83–100. Bloomington, IN: University of Indiana Press, 1990.

Ehrmann, Daniel, and Norbert Christian Wolf. "Einführung." *Der Streit um Klassizität: Polemische Konstellationen vom 18. Zum 21. Jahrhundert*, ed. Daniel Ehrmann and Norbert Christian Wolf, 1–29. Munich: Fink, 2021.

Eickenrodt, Sabine. *Augenspiel: Jean Pauls optische Metaphorik der Unsterblichkeit.* Göttingen: Wallstein, 2006.

Erlin, Matt. *Necessary Luxuries: Books, Literature, and the Culture of Consumption in Germany, 1770–1815.* Ithaca, NY: Cornell University Press, 2014.

Ernst, Wolfgang. *Chronopoetics: The Temporal Being and Operativity of Technical Media.* Trans. Anthony Enns. London: Rowman and Littlefield, 2016.

Esposito, Elena. *Die Verbindlichkeit des Vorübergehenden: Paradoxien der Mode.* Trans. Allesandra Corti. Frankfurt: Suhrkamp, 2004.

Esterhammer, Angela. *Print and Performance in the 1820s: Improvisation, Speculation, Identity.* Cambridge: Cambridge University Press, 2020.

Falk, Rainer. "Sehende Lektüre. Zur Sichtbarkeit des Textes am Beispiel von Goethes *Römischem Carneval*." In *Ästhetische Erfahrung: Gegenstände, Konzepte, Geschichtlichkeit*, Freie Universität Berlin, 2006. Last accessed January 21, 2021. http://www.sfb626.de/veroeffentlichungen/online/aesth_erfahrung/aufsaetze/falk.pdf.

Fehrenbach, Frank. "'Bravi i morti!' Emphasen des Lebens in Goethes *Italienischer Reise*." In *Vita aesthetica. Szenarien ästhetischer Lebendigkeit*, ed. Armen Avenessian, Winfried Menninghaus, and Jan Völker, 57–75. Berlin: Diaphanes, 2009.

Ferstenberg, Helen. "Heinrich Heine und George Canning." *Heine-Jahrbuch* 35 (1996): 113–27.

Fischer, Bernard. "Einleitung." In *Morgenblatt für gebildete Stände/gebildete Leser (1807–1865): Register der Honorarempfänger/Autoren und Kollationsprotokolle*, ed. Bernhard Fischer, 9–24. Munich: Saur, 2000.

Fischer, Bernard. "Friedrich Justin Bertuch und Johann Friedrich Cotta. Die 'Phalanx' der Buchhändler." In *Friedrich Justin Bertuch (1747–1822). Verleger, Schriftsteller und Unternehmer im klassischen Weimar*, ed. Gerhard R. Kaiser and Siegfried Seifert, 395–407. Tübingen: Niemeyer, 2000.

Fischer, Bernard. "Johann Friedrich Cottas *Damencalender* ('Taschenbuch für Damen')." In *Kupferstich und Letternkunst. Buchgestaltung im 18. Jahrhundert*, ed. Peter-Henning Haischer et al., 539–70. Heidelberg: Winter, 2017.

Fischer, Bernhard. "Paris, London und Anderswo. Zur Welterfahrung in Hermann Hauffs *Morgenblatt* der 1830er Jahre." *Jahrbuch der Deutschen Schillergesellschaft* 51 (2007): 329–73.

Fleming, Paul. *The Pleasures of Abandonment: Jean Paul and the Life of Humor*. Würzburg: Königshausen und Neumann, 2006.

Fleming, Paul. "The Promises of Childhood: Autobiography in Goethe and Jean Paul." *Goethe Yearbook* 14 (2007): 27–38.

Foucault, Michel. "Of Other Spaces." *Diacritics* 16 (1986): 22–27.

Foucault, Michel. "What Is an Author." In *The Foucault Reader*, ed. Paul Rabinow, 101–20. New York: Pantheon, 1984.

Frank, Gustav, and Stefan Scherer. "Zeit-Texte. Zur Funktionsgeschichte und zum generischen Ort des Feuilletons." *Zeitschrift für Germanistik* 22, no. 3 (2012): 524–39.

Frank, Gustav, Madleen Podewski, and Stefan Scherer. "Kultur—Zeit—Schrift. Literatur- und Kulturzeitschriften als 'kleine Archive.'" *Internationales Archiv für Sozialgeschichte der Literatur* 34 (2009): 1–45.

Franzel, Sean. "Constructions of the Present and the Philosophy of History in the Lecture Form." In *Performing Knowledge, 1750–1850*, ed. Mary Helen Dupree and Sean Franzel, 295–322. Franzel. Berlin: De Gruyter, 2015.

Franzel, Sean. "Koselleck's Timely Goethe?" *Goethe Yearbook* 26 (2019): 283–99.

Franzel, Sean. "Serial Inventories: Cataloguing the Age of Paper." In *Network@1800: Non-Linear Transatlantic Histories*, ed. Birgit Tautz and Crystal Hall. Liverpool: University of Liverpool Press, 2023.

Franzel, Sean. "Von Magazinen, Gärböttichen und Bomben: Räumliche Speichermetaphern der medialen Selbstinszenierung von Zeitschriften." In *Archiv/Fiktionen. Verfahren des Archivierens in Kultur und Literatur des langen 19. Jahrhunderts*, ed. Daniela Gretz and Nicolas Pethes, 207–30. Freiburg: Rombach, 2016.

Franzen, Jonathan. *The Kraus Project: Essays by Karl Kraus*. New York: Farrar, Straus and Giroux, 2013.

Frederick, Samuel. *Narratives Unsettled: Digression in Robert Walser, Thomas Bernhard, and Adalbert Stifter*. Evanston, IL: Northwestern University Press, 2012.

Fritzsche, Peter. *Stranded in the Present: Modern Time and the Melancholy of History*. Cambridge, MA: Harvard University Press, 2004.

Fröhlich, Vincent. *Der Cliffhanger und die serielle Narration. Analyse einer transmedialen Erzähltechnik*. Bielefeld: Transcript, 2015.

Fuchs, Eduard. *Die Karikatur der europäischen Völker. Teil 1. Vom Altertum bis zum Jahre 1848*. Munich: Langen, 1921.

Fuhrmann, Manfred. "Fasnacht als Utopie: Vom Saturnalienfest im alten Rom." *Narrenfreiheit: Beiträge zur Fasnachtsforschung* 51 (1980): 29–42.

Gailus, Andreas. "Poetics of Containment: Goethe's Conversations of German Refugees and the Crisis of Representation." *Modern Philology* 100, no. 3 (2003): 436–74.

Gamper, Michael. *Der große Mann: Geschichte eines politischen Phantasmas*. Göttingen: Wallstein, 2016.

Gamper, Michael. "Gegenwärtige Politik des Vergangenen: Politische Nachträglichkeit bei Heinrich Heine." In *Gleichzeitigkeit des Ungleichzeitigen: Formen und Funktionen von Pluralität in der ästhetischen Moderne*, ed. Sabine Schneider and Heinz Brüggemann, 89–104. Munich: Wilhelm Fink, 2010.

Gamper, Michael, and Helmut Hühn. "Einleitung." In *Zeit der Darstellung. Ästhetische Eigenzeiten in Kunst, Literatur und Wissenschaft*, ed. Michael Gamper and Helmut Hühn, 7–23. Hanover: Wehrhahn, 2014.

Garber, Jörn. "Die Zivilisationsmetropole im Naturzustand: Das revolutionäre Volk von Paris als Regenerations- und Korruptionsfaktor der 'Geschichte der Menschheit.'" In *Rom-Paris-London: Erfahrung und Selbsterfahrung deutscher Schriftstellern in den fremden Metropolen*, ed. Conrad Wiedemann, 420–56. Stuttgart: Metzler, 1988.

Gelderloos, Carl. *Biological Modernism: The New Human in Weimar Culture*. Evanston, IL: Northwestern University Press, 2020.

Gerhardt, Katja. "Goethe und 'das Römische Carneval.' Eine Betrachtung zu Text und Bild." *Weimarer Beiträge* 42, no. 2 (1996): 289–96.

Geulen, Eva. "Serialization in Goethe's Morphology." *Compar(a)ison* 2 (2008): 53–70.

Gibhardt, Boris Roman. *Vorgriffe auf das schöne Leben: Weimarer Klassik und Pariser Mode um 1800*. Göttingen: Wallstein, 2019.

Gilgen, Peter. *Lektüren der Erinnerung: Lessing, Kant, Hegel*. Munich: Fink, 2012.

Gilman, Sander L. "Heine's Photographs." In *Paintings on the Move: Heine and the Visual Arts*, ed. Susanne Zantop, 92–116. Lincoln: University of Nebraska Press, 1989.
Gleißner, Stephanie, et al. *Optische Auftritte. Marktszenen in der medialen Konkurrenz von Journal-, Almanachs- und Bücherliteratur.* Hanover: Wehrhahn, 2019.
Goetschel, Willi. *Heine and Critical Theory.* London: Bloomsbury, 2019.
Goff, Alice. *The God Behind the Marble: Transcendence and the Art Object in the German Aesthetic State.* Chicago: University of Chicago Press, 2024.
Göttsche, Dirk. "Challenging Time(s): Memory, Politics, and the Philosophy of Time in Jean Paul's *Quintus Fixlein*." In *(Re-)writing the Radical: Enlightenment, Revolution, and Cultural Transfer in 1790s Germany, Britain, and France*, ed. Maike Oergel, 219–38. New York: De Gruyter, 2012.
Göttsche, Dirk. *Zeit im Roman. Literarische Zeitreflexion und die Geschichte des Zeitromans im späten 18. und im 19. Jahrhundert.* Munich: Fink, 2001.
Graczyk, Annette. *Das literarische Tableau zwischen Kunst und Wissenschaft.* Munich: Fink, 2004.
Graevenitz, Gerhart von. "Memoria und Realismus: Erzählende Literatur in der deutschen 'Bildungspresse' des 19. Jahrhunderts." In *Memoria: Vergessen und Erinnern*, ed. Anselm Haverkamp and Renate Lachmann, 282–304. Munich: Fink, 1993.
Graevenitz, Gerhart von. *Theodor Fontane: ängstliche Moderne. Über das Imaginäre.* Konstanz: Konstanz University Press, 2014.
Gretz, Daniela, ed. *Medialer Realismus.* Freiburg: Rombach, 2011.
Gretz, Daniela, Marcus Krause, and Nicolas Pethes, ed. *Reading Miscellanies—Miscellaneous Readings.* Hanover: Wehrhahn, 2022.
Gretz, Daniela, and Nicolas Pethes, ed. *Archiv/Fiktionen: Verfahren des Archivierens in Literatur und Kultur des langen 19. Jahrhunderts.* Freiburg: Rombach, 2016.
Grossman, Jeffrey. "Fractured Histories: Heinrich Heine's Responses to Violence and Revolution." In *Contemplating Violence: Critical Studies in Modern German Culture*, ed. Carl Niekerk and Stefani Engelstein, 67–87. Amsterdam: Rodopi, 2010.
Hagel, Ulrike. *Elliptische Zeiträume des Erzählens: Jean Paul und die Aporien der Idylle.* Würzburg: Königshausen und Neumann, 2003.
Hagemann, Karen. *Revisiting Prussia's Wars against Napoleon: History, Culture, and Memory.* Cambridge: Cambridge University Press, 2015.
Hagen, Waltraud. *Die Drucke von Goethes Werken.* Berlin: Akademie, 1971.
Haischer, Peter-Henning. *Historizität und Klassizität. Christoph Martin Wieland und die Werkausgabe im 18. Jahrhundert.* Heidelberg: Winter, 2011.
Haischer, Peter-Henning, and Charlotte Kurbjuhn. "Faktoren und Entwicklung der Buchgestaltung im 18. Jahrhundert." In *Kupferstich und Letternkunst. Buchgestaltung im 18. Jahrhundert*, ed. Peter-Henning Haischer et al., 3–94. Heidelberg: Winter, 2017.

Hansen, Volkmar. *Heinrich Heines politische Journalistik in der Augsburger "Allgemeinen Zeitung."* Augsburg: Stadt Augsburg, 1994. Exhibition catalogue.
Hartog, François. *Regimes of Historicity: Presentism and Experiences of Time.* Trans. Saskia Brown. New York: Columbia University Press, 2015.
Heady, Katy. *Literature and Censorship in Restoration Germany: Repression and Rhetoric.* Rochester, NY: Camden House, 2009.
Hebekus, Uwe. "Goethes Feste. Allegorien der Geschichte." In *Goethes Feste*, ed. Uwe Hebekus, 273–302. Frankfurt: Insel, 1993.
Hecht, Wolfgang. "Goethes Maskenzüge." In *Studien zur Goethezeit*, ed. Helmut Holtzhauer and Bernhard Zeller, 127–42. Weimar: Böhlau, 1968.
Hell, Julia. *The Conquest of Ruins: The Third Reich and the Fall of Rome.* Chicago: University of Chicago Press, 2019.
Helms, Hans G. "Jean Paul, ein politischer Autor." *Text + Kritik*, special volume (1983): 118–23.
Heringman, Noah. *Deep Time: A Literary History.* Princeton, NJ: Princeton University Press, 2023.
Hocks, Paul, and Peter Schmidt. *Literarische und politische Zeitschriften 1789–1805.* Stuttgart: Metzler, 1975.
Hoffmann, Christhard. "History versus Memory: Heinrich Heine and the Jewish Past." In *Heinrich Heine's Contested Identities: Politics, Religion, and Nationalism in Nineteenth-Century Germany*, ed. Jost Hermand and Robert Holub, 25–48. New York: Peter Lang, 1999.
Hohendahl, Peter Uwe. "Literary Criticism in the Epoch of Liberalism." In *A History of German Literary Criticism, 1730–1980*, ed. Peter Uwe Hohendahl, 179–276. Lincoln: University of Nebraska Press, 1988.
Höhn, Gerhard. "Eternal Return or Indiscernible Progress? Heine's Conception of History after 1848." In *A Companion to the Works of Heinrich Heine*, ed. Roger Cook, 169–200. Rochester, NY: Camden House, 2002.
Hollmer, Heide, and Albert Meier. "Kunstzeitschriften." In *Von Almanach bis Zeitung. Ein Handbuch der Medien in Deutschland 1700–1800*, ed. Ernst Fischer, Wilhelm Haefs, and York-Gothart Mix, 157–75. Munich: Beck, 1999.
Holm, Christiane, and Günter Oesterle. "Andacht und Andenken. Zum Verhältnis zweier Kulturpraktiken um 1800." In *Erinnerung, Gedächtnis, Wissen, Studien zur kulturwissenschaftlichen Gedächtnisforschung*, ed. Günter Oesterle, 433–48. Göttingen: Vandenhoeck und Ruprecht, 2005.
Hölscher, Lucian. *Zeitgärten. Zeitfiguren in der Geschichte der Neuzeit.* Göttingen: Wallstein, 2020.
Hopwood, Nick, Simon Schaffer, and Jim Secord. "Seriality and Scientific Objects in the Nineteenth Century." *History of Science* 48, nos. 3–4 (2010): 251–80.
Hosfeld, Rolf. *Heinrich Heine: Die Erfindung des europäischen Intellektuellen.* Munich: Siedler, 2014.

Hughes, Linda K., and Michael Lund. *The Victorian Serial*. Charlottesville: University of Virginia Press, 1991.
Hunfeld, Barbara. "Eine neue Jean-Paul-Werkausgabe." *Geschichte der Germanistik* 31/32 (2007): 111–16.
Hunt, Lynn. *Measuring Time, Making History*. Budapest: Central European University Press, 2008.
Huyssen, Andreas. *Miniature Metropolis: Literature in an Age of Photography and Film*. Cambridge, MA: Harvard University Press, 2015.
John, Johannes. "Die Utopie des 'fertigen' Textes." *Stifter-Jahrbuch* 20 (2006): 99–115.
Jordheim, Helge. "Against Periodization: Koselleck's Theory of Multiple Temporalities." *History and Theory* 51 (2012): 151–71.
Jordheim, Helge. *Der Staatsroman im Werk Wielands und Jean Pauls. Gattungsverhandlungen zwischen Poetologie und Politik*. Tübingen: Niemeyer, 2007.
Jordheim, Helge. "'Unzählbar viele Zeiten.' Die Sattelzeit im Spiegel der Gleichzeitigkeit des Ungleichzeitigen." In *Begriffene Geschichte. Beiträge zum Werk Reinhart Kosellecks*, ed. Hans Joas and Peter Vogt, 449–80. Frankfurt: Suhrkamp, 2011.
Jost, Jacob Sider. *Prose Immortality: 1711–1819*. Charlottesville: University of Virginia Press, 2015.
Jürgensen, Christoph. *Federkrieger: Autorschaft im Zeichen der Befreiungskriege*. Stuttgart: Metzler, 2018.
Kaiser, Gerhard R. "Friedrich Justin Bertuch—Versuch eines Porträts." In *Friedrich Justin Bertuch (1747–1822) Verleger, Schriftsteller und Unternehmer im klassischen Weimar*, ed. Gerhard R. Kaiser and Siegfried Seifert, 15–39. Tübingen: Niemeyer, 2000.
Kaiser, Gerhard R. "'Jede große Stadt ist eine Moral in Beispielen.' Bertuchs Zeitschrift 'London und Paris.'" In *Friedrich Justin Bertuch (1747–1822). Verleger, Schriftsteller und Unternehmer im klassischen Weimar*, ed. Gerhard R. Kaiser and Siegfried Seifert, 547–76. Tübingen: Niemeyer, 2000.
Kaminski, Nicola. "'Nachdruck des Nachdrucks' als Werk(chen)organisation oder Wie D. Katzenberger die *Kleinen Schriften von Jean Paul Friedrich Richter* anatomiert." *Jahrbuch der Jean Paul Gesellschaft* 52 (2017): 29–70.
Kaminski, Nicola. "25. Oktober 1813 oder Journalliterarische Produktion von Gegenwart, mit einem Ausflug zum 6. Juli 1724." In *Aktualität: Zur Geschichte literarischer Gegenwartsbezüge vom 17. Bis zum 21. Jahrhundert*, ed. Stefan Geyer and Johannes F. Lehmann, 241–70. Hanover: Wehrhahn, 2018.
Kaminski, Nicola, and Volker Mergenthaler. *Zuschauer im Eckfenster 1821/22 oder Selbstreflexion der Journalliteratur im Journal(text). Mit einem Faksimile des "Zuschauers" vom April/Mai 1822*. Hanover: Wehrhahn, 2015.
Kaminski, Nicola, Nora Ramtke, and Carsten Zelle. "Zeitschriftenliteratur/Fortsetzungsliteratur: Problemaufriß." In *Zeitschriftenliteratur/Fortsetzungsliteratur*, ed. Nicola Kaminski, Nora Ramtke, and Carsten Zelle, 7–39. Hanover: Wehrhahn, 2014.

Karla, Anna. "Die verschlafene Revolution von 1789. Französisch-Deutsches Revolutionserzählen im Modus der Zeitgenossenschaft." In *Sattelzeit: Historiographische Revisionen*, ed. Elisabeth Découltot and Daniel Fulda, 198–217. Berlin: De Gruyter, 2016.

Karla, Anna. *Revolution als Zeitgeschichte. Memoiren der Französischen Revolution in der Restaurationszeit*. Göttingen: Vandenhoeck & Ruprecht, 2014.

Kauffmann, Kai. *"Es ist nur ein Wien!" Stadtbeschreibungen von Wien 1700–1873. Geschichte eines literarischen Genres der Wiener Publizistik*. Wien: Böhlau, 1994.

Kelleter, Frank. "Five Ways of Looking at Popular Seriality." In *Media of Serial Narrative*, ed. Frank Kelleter, 7–36. Columbus, OH: Ohio State University Press, 2017.

Kirchner, Joachim. *Das deutsche Zeitschriftenwesen. Seine Geschichte und seine Probleme*. Vol. 1. Wiesbaden: Harrassowitz, 1958.

Kittler, Friedrich A. "Die Laterna magica der Literatur: Schillers und Hoffmanns Medienstrategien." *Athenäum* 4 (1994): 219–37.

Kittler, Friedrich A. *Die Nacht der Substanz*. Bern: Benteli, 1989.

Kittler, Friedrich A. *Gramophone, Film, Typewriter*. Trans. Geoffrey Winthrop-Young and Michael Wutz. Stanford, CA: Stanford University Press, 1999.

Klancher, Jon. "What Happened to the Periodical?" *Studies in Romanticism* 59, no. 4 (2020): 507–18.

Klausmeyer, Bryan. "Fragmenting Fragments: Jean Paul's Poetics of the Small in 'Meine Miszellen'" *Monatshefte* 108, no. 4 (2016): 485–509.

Kleinert, Annemarie. "Die französische Konkurrenz des *Journal des Luxus und der Moden*." In *Das "Journal des Luxus und der Moden": Kultur um 1800*, ed. Angela Borchert and Ralf Dressel, 195–216. Heidelberg: Winter, 2004.

Kleinert, Annemarie. *Die frühen Modejournale in Frankreich: Studien zur Literatur der Mode von den Anfängen bis 1848*. Berlin: Erich Schmidt, 1980.

Knorr, Birgit. "Georg Melchior Kraus (1737–1806). Maler-Pädagoge-Unternehmer." PhD diss., University of Jena, 2003.

Koch, Ursula E. *Der Teufel in Berlin. Von der Märzrevolution bis zu Bismarcks Entlassung. Illustrierte politische Witzblätter 1848–1890*. Cologne: Leske, 1991.

Koepke, Wülf. "Jean Paul's Battles with the Censors and his *Freiheits-Büchlein*." In *Zensur und Kultur, Censorship and Culture*, ed. John A. McCarthy and Werner von der Ohe, 99–110. Tübingen: Niemeyer, 1995.

Koerner, Joseph Leo. *Bosch and Breugel: From Enemy Painting to Everday Life*. Princeton, NJ: Princeton University Press, 2016.

Koschorke, Albrecht. *Körperströme und Schriftverkehr. Mediologie des 18. Jahrhunderts*. Munich: Fink, 1999.

Koselleck, Reinhart. "Constancy and Change of All Contemporary Histories. Conceptual-Historical Notes." In *Sediments of Time: On Possible Histories*, trans. and ed. Sean Franzel and Stefan-Ludwig Hoffmann, 100–117. Stanford, CA: Stanford University Press, 2018.

Koselleck, Reinhart. "Daumier and Death." *The Practice of Conceptual History: Timing History, Spacing Concepts*, trans. Todd Samuel Presner et al., 265–84. Stanford, CA: Stanford University Press, 2002.

Koselleck, Reinhart. "Does History Accelerate?" In *Sediments of Time: On Possible Histories*, trans. and ed. Sean Franzel and Stefan-Ludwig Hoffmann, 79–99. Stanford, CA: Stanford University Press, 2018.

Koselleck, Reinhart. "Einleitung." In *Geschichtliche Grundbegriffe. Historisches Lexikon zur politisch-sozialen Sprache in Deutschland*, vol. 1, xiii–xxvii. Stuttgart: Klett-Cotta, 1972.

Koselleck, Reinhart. "Einleitung." In *Zeitschichten: Studien zur Historik*, 9–19. Frankfurt: Suhrkamp, 2000.

Koselleck, Reinhart. "Goethe's Untimely History." In *Sediments of Time: On Possible Histories*, trans. and ed. Sean Franzel and Stefan-Ludwig Hoffmann, 60–78. Stanford, CA: Stanford University Press, 2018.

Koselleck, Reinhart. "Historia Magistra Vitae: The Dissolution of the Topos into the Perspective of a Modernized Historical Process." In *Futures Past: On the Semantics of Historical Time*, trans. Keith Tribe, 26–42. New York: Columbia University Press, 2004.

Koselleck, Reinhart. "Historical Criteria of the Modern Concept of Revolution." In *Futures Past: On the Semantics of Historical Time*, trans. Keith Tribe, 43–57. New York: Columbia University Press, 2004.

Koselleck, Reinhart. "On the Need for Theory in the Discipline of History." In *The Practice of Conceptual History: Timing History, Spacing Concepts*, trans. Todd Samuel Presner et al., 1–18. Stanford, CA: Stanford University Press, 2002.

Koselleck, Reinhart. "Sediments of Time." In *Sediments of Time: On Possible Histories*, trans. and ed. Sean Franzel and Stefan-Ludwig Hoffmann, 3–9. Stanford, CA: Stanford University Press, 2018.

Koselleck, Reinhart, et al. "Revolution, Rebellion, Aufruhr, Bürgerkrieg." In *Geschichtliche Grundbegriffe. Historisches Lexikon zur politisch-sozialen Sprache in Deutschland*, 653–788. Vol. 5. Stuttgart: Klett-Cotta, 1972.

Koselleck, Reinhart, and Carl Schmitt. *Der Briefwechsel, 1953–1983*. Ed. Jan Eike Dunkhase. Frankfurt: Suhrkamp, 2019.

Kouvelakis, Stathis. *Philosophy and Revolution: From Kant to Marx*. Trans. G. M. Goshgarian. London: Verso, 2003.

Kracauer, Siegfried. "Time and History." *History and Theory* 6, no. 6 (1966): 65–78.

Krajewski, Markus. *Paper Machines: About Cards and Catalogues, 1548–1929*. Trans. Peter Krapp. Cambridge, MA: MIT Press, 2011.

Krämer, Sibylle. "The Cultural Techniques of Time Axis Manipulation: On Friedrich Kittler's Conception of Media." *Theory, Culture & Society* 23, nos. 7–8 (2006): 93–109.

Krausse, Joachim. "Ephemer." In *Ästhetische Grundbegriffe. Historisches Wörterbuch in sieben Bänden*, ed. Karlheinz Barck et al., 240–60. Vol. 2. Stuttgart: Springer, 2001.

Kreienbock, Jörg. *Malicious Objects, Anger Management, and the Question of Modern Literature*. New York: Fordham University Press, 2012.
Kremer, Roman B. "Miszellen." In *Historisches Wörterbuch der Rhetorik*, ed. Gert Ueding, 711–16. Vol. 10. Berlin: De Gruyter, 2012.
Kubler, George. *The Shape of Time: Remarks on the History of Things*. New Haven, CT: Yale University Press, 1962.
Kuhles, Doris, and Ulrike Standke. *Journal des Luxus und der Moden. Analytische Bibliographie mit sämtlichen 517 schwarzweißen und 976 farbigen Abbildungen der Originalzeitschrift*. 3 vols. Munich: Saur, 2003.
Kunzle, David. "Goethe and Caricature: From Hogarth to Töpffer." *Journal of the Warburg and Courtauld Institutes* 48 (1985): 164–88.
Labuhn, Wolfgang. *Literatur und Öffentlichkeit im Vormärz. Das Beispiel Ludwig Börne*. Königstein: Forum Academicum, 1980.
Lämke, Ortwin. *Heines Begriff der Geschichte: Der Journalist Heinrich Heine und die Julimonarchie*. Stuttgart: Metzler, 1997.
Landwehr, Achim. *Geburt der Gegenwart. Eine Geschichte der Zeit im 17. Jahrhundert*. Frankfurt: Fischer, 2014.
Lauster, Martina. *Sketches of the Nineteenth Century: European Journalism and Its Physiologies, 1830–50*. New York: Palgrave MacMillan, 2007.
Lepenies, Wolf. *Das Ende der Naturgeschichte. Wandel kultureller Selbstverständlichkeiten in den Wissenschaften des 18. und 19. Jahrhunderts*. Munich: Hanser, 1976.
Lüdemann, Susanne. "Vom Römischen Karneval zur ökonomischen Automate. Massendarstellung bei Goethe und E.T.A. Hoffmann." In *Massenfassungen: Beiträge zur Diskurs- und Mediengeschichte der Menschenmenge*, ed. Susanne Lüdemann and Uwe Hebekus, 107–23. Munich: Fink, 2010.
Luhmann, Niklas. *Art as a Social System*. Trans. Eva M. Knodt. Stanford, CA: Stanford University Press, 2000.
Luhmann, Niklas. "Temporalisierung von Komplexität: Zur Semantik neuzeitlicher Zeitbegriffe." In *Gesellschaftsstrukur und Semantik*, 235–300. Vol. 1. Frankfurt: Suhrkamp, 1980.
MacLeod, Catriona. "The German Romantic Reading Public: *Taschenbücher* and Other Illustrated Books." In *The Enchanted World of German Romantic Books 1770–1850*, ed. John Ittmann, 198–207. New Haven, CT: Yale University Press, 2017.
MacLeod, Catriona. "Schattenriß (Silhouette)." *Goethe-Lexicon of Philosophical Concepts* 1, no. 1 (2021): 74–82.
MacLeod, Catriona. "Skulptur als Ware. Gottlieb Martin Klauer und das *Journal des Luxus und der Moden*." In *Das "Journal des Luxus und der Moden": Kultur um 1800*, ed. Angela Borchert and Ralf Dressel, 261–80. Heidelberg: Winter, 2004.
MacLeod, Catriona. "Sweetmeats for the Eye: Porcelain Miniatures in Classical Weimar." In *The Enlightened Eye: Goethe and Visual Culture*, ed. Evelyn K. Moore and Patricia Anne Simpson, 41–72. Amsterdam: Rodopi, 2007.

Mainardi, Patricia. *Another World: Nineteenth-Century Illustrated Print Culture*. New Haven, CT: Yale University Press, 2017.

Mainberger, Sabine. *Die Kunst des Aufzählens. Elemente zu einer Poetik des Enumerativen*. Berlin: De Gruyter, 2003.

Martens, Wolfgang. *Die Botschaft der Tugend. Die Aufklärung im Spiegel der deutschen Moralischen Wochenschriften*. Stuttgart: Metzler, 1967.

Martus, Steffen. *Werkpolitik. Zur Literaturgeschichte kritischer Kommunikation vom 17. bis ins 20. Jahrhundert mit Studien zu Klopstock, Tieck, Goethe und George*. Berlin: De Gruyter, 2007.

Maskarinec, Malika. "Introduction." In *Truth in Serial Form: Serial Formats and the Form of the Series (1850-1930)*. Ed. Malika Maskarinec, 1-22. Berlin: De Gruyter, 2023.

Matala de Mazza, Ethel. *Der populäre Pakt: Verhandlungen der Moderne zwischen Operette und Feuilleton*. Frankfurt: Fischer, 2018.

Matala de Mazza, Ethel. "Die fehlende Hauptsache: Exekutionen der Julimonarchie in Heines *Lutezia*." In *Heinrich Heine: Ein Wegbereiter der Moderne*, ed. Paolo Chiarini and Walter Hinderer, 309–28. Würzburg: Königshausen and Neumann, 2009.

Mayer, Hans. "Der unzuverlässige Jean Paul." In *Politische Fastenpredigten während Deutschlands Marterwoche*, by Jean Paul, 141–53. Frankfurt: Insel, 1966.

McGillen, Petra. "Andauernder Effekt: Medienkonkurrenz und Rhetorik in Heinrich Heines Napoleon-Schriften." In *Zwischen Gattungsdisziplin und Gesamtkunstwerk: Literarische Intermedialität 1815–1848*, ed. Stefan Keppler-Tasaki and Wolf Gerhard Schmidt, 203–21. Berlin: De Gruyter, 2015.

McGillen, Petra S. *The Fontane Workshop: Manufacturing Realism in the Industrial Age of Print*. New York: Bloomsbury, 2019.

McLuhan, Marshall. *Understanding Media: The Extensions of Man*. Cambridge, MA: MIT Press, 1994.

McNeely, Ian. *The Emancipation of Writing: German Civil Society in the Making, 1790s–1820s*. Berkeley: University of California Press, 2003.

McNeil, Peter. "Fashion and the Eighteenth-Century Satirical Print." In *The Fashion History Reader: Global Perspectives*, ed. Giorgio Riello and Peter McNeil, 257–62. London: Routledge, 2010.

Mende, Fritz. *Heinrich Heine: Studien zu seinem Leben und Werk*. Berlin: Akademie-Verlag, 1983.

Meyer, Reinhart. *Novelle und Journal: Titel und Normen. Untersuchungen zur Terminologie der Journalprosa, zu ihren Tendenzen, Verhältnissen und Bedingungen*. Stuttgart: Steiner, 1987.

Mielke, Christine. *Zyklisch-serielle Narration: Erzähltes Erzählen von 1001 Nacht bis zur TV-Serie*. Berlin: De Gruyter, 2006.

Miller, Norbert. "Jean Paul versus Goethe. Der Dichter und die Forderung des Tages. Jean Pauls Vermischte Schriften als Teil seiner Wirkungsgeschichte." In *Sämtliche Werke in 10 Bänden*, ed. Norbert Miller, 459–96. Vol. II/4. Munich/Vienna: Hanser, 1974–1985.

Miller, Norbert, and Wilhelm Schmidt-Biggemann. "Kommentar zu den Vermischten Schriften." In *Sämtliche Werke in 10 Bänden*, ed. Norbert Miller, 457–730. Vol. II/4. Munich/Vienna: Hanser, 1974–1985.

Moran, Daniel. *Toward the Century of Words: Johann Cotta and the Politics of the Public Realm in Germany, 1795–1832*. Berkeley: University of California Press, 1990.

Morgenthaler, Walther. "Die Gesammelten und die Sämtlichen Werke: Anmerkungen zu zwei unterschätzten Werktypen." *Textkritische Beiträge* 10 (2005): 13–26.

Mosse, George L. *The Nationalization of the Masses: Political Symbolism and Mass Movements in Germany from the Napoleonic Wars through the Third Reich*. New York: Fertig, 1975.

Müller, Götz. "'Ich vergesse den 15.November nie.' Intertextualität und Mehrfachbesetzung bei Jean Paul." *Jean Paul im Kontext. Gesammelte Aufsätze*, ed. Götz Müller, 125–39. Würzburg: Königshausen und Neumann, 1996.

Müller-Krumbach, Renate. "'Da ich den artistischen Theil ganz zu besorgen habe.' Die Illustrationen für das *Journal des Luxus und der Moden* von Georg Melichor Kraus." In *Das "Journal des Luxus und der Moden": Kultur um 1800*, ed. Angela Borchert and Ralf Dressel, 212–26. Heidelberg: Winter, 2004.

Müller-Sievers, Helmut. *The Cylinder: Kinematics of the Nineteenth Century*. Berkeley: University of California Press, 2012.

Müller-Sievers, Helmut. "Kinematik des Erzählens: Zum Stand der amerikanischen Fernsehserie." *Merkur* 64, no. 794 (2015): 19–29.

Multigraph Collective. "Anthologies." In *Interacting with Print: Elements of Reading in the Era of Print Saturation*, 33–48. Chicago: University of Chicago Press, 2018.

Multigraph Collective. *Interacting with Print: Elements of Reading in the Era of Print Saturation*. Chicago: University of Chicago Press, 2018.

Multigraph Collective. "Spacing." In *Interacting with Print: Elements of Reading in the Era of Print Saturation*, 260–73. Chicago: University of Chicago Press, 2018.

Mussell, James. *The Nineteenth-Century Press in the Digital Age*. London: Palgrave Macmillan, 2012.

Mussell, James. "Repetition: Or, 'In Our Last.'" *Victorian Periodicals Review* 48, no. 3 (2015): 343–58.

Nährlich-Slatewa, Elena. "Das groteske Leben und seine edle Einfassung. 'Das Römische Karneval' Goethes und das Karnevalskonzept von Michail M. Bachtin." In *Goethe Jahrbuch* 106 (1989): 181–202.

Nash, Andrew. "The Culture of Collected Editions: Authorship, Reputation, and the Canon." In *The Culture of Collected Editions*, ed. Andrew Nash, 1–15. Basingstoke & New York: Palgrave Macmillan, 2003.

Naumann, Ursula. *Predigende Poesie. Zur Bedeutung von Predigt, geistliche Rede und Predigertum für das Werk Jean Pauls*. Nürnberg: Verlag Hans Carl, 1976.

Neumann, Peter Horst. "Die Werkchen als Werk: Zur Form- und Wirkungsgeschichte des Katzenberger-Korpus von Jean Paul." *Jahrbuch der Jean Paul Gesellschaft* 10 (1970): 151–86.
Norman, Larry F. "Multiple Classicisms." In *Classicisms*, ed. Larry F. Norman and Anne Leonard, 13–30. Chicago: Smart Museum of Art, 2017.
Nutt-Kofoth, Rüdiger. "Editionsphilologie als Mediengeschichte." *Editio* 20 (2006): 1–23.
Nutz, Maximilian. "Das Beispiel Goethe. Zur Konstituierung eines nationalen Klassikers." In *Wissenschaftsgeschichte der Germanistik im 19. Jahrhundert*, ed. Jürgen Fohrmann and Wilhelm Voßkamp, 605–37. Stuttgart: Metzler, 1994.
Obenaus, Sibylle. *Literarische und politische Zeitschriften 1830–48*. Stuttgart: Metzler, 1986.
Oellers, Norbert. "Ludwig Börne." In *Deutsche Dichter des 19. Jahrhunderts. Ihr Leben und Werk*, ed. Benno von Wiese, 124–48. Berlin: Erich Schmidt, 1969.
Oergel, Maike. *Zeitgeist—How Ideas Travel: Politics, Culture, and the Public in the Age of Revolution*. Berlin: De Gruyter, 2019.
Oesterle, Günter. "Suchbilder kollektiver Identitätsfindung. Die öffentliche Feste während der Französischen Revolution und ihre Wirkung auf die Deutschen." In *Vergangene Zukunft: Revolution und Künste 1789 bis 1989*, ed. Erhard Schütz und Klaus Siebenhaar, 129–52. Bonn: Bouvier, 1992.
Oesterle, Günter, and Ingrid Oesterle. "'Gegenfüßler des Ideals'—Prozeßgestalt der Kunst—'Mémoire processive' der Geschichte: Zur ästhetischen Fragwürdigkeit von Karikatur seit dem 18. Jahrhundert." In *"Nervöse Auffangsorgane des inneren und äußeren Lebens": Karikaturen*, ed. Klaus Herding and Günter Otto, 87–130. Gießen: Anabas, 1980.
Oesterle, Günter, and Ingrid Oesterle. "Karikatur." *Historisches Wörterbuch der Philosophie*, ed. Joachim Ritter, 696–701. Vol. 4. Basel and Stuttgart: Schwabe, 1976.
Oesterle, Ingrid. "Der 'Führungswechsel der Zeithorizonte' in der deutschen Literatur: Korrespondenzen aus Paris, der Hauptstadt der Menschheitsgeschichte, und die Ausbildung der geschichtlichen Zeit 'Gegenwart.'" In *Studien zur Ästhetik und Literatur der Kunstperiode*, ed. Dirk Grathoff, 11–76. Frankfurt: Peter Lang, 1985.
Oesterle, Ingrid. "'Es ist an der Zeit!' Zur kulturellen Konstruktionsveränderung von Zeit gegen 1800." In *Goethe und das Zeitalter der Romantik*, ed. Walter Hinderer, 91–120. Würzburg: Königshausen und Neumann, 2002.
Olson, Nancy. *Garvani: The Carnival Lithographs*. New Haven, CT: Yale University Art Gallery, 1979.
Ortlieb, Cornelia. "Schöpfen und Schreiben: Weimarer Papierarbeiten." In *Weimarer Klassik: Kultur des Sinnlichen*, ed. Sebastian Böhmer, Christiane Holm, Veronika Spinner, and Thorsten Valk, 76–85. Berlin: Deutscher Kunstverlag, 2012.
Osterhammel, Jürgen. *Die Verwandlung der Welt. Eine Geschichte des 19. Jahrhunderts*. Munich: Beck, 2011.

Ozouf, Mona. *Festivals and the French Revolution*. Cambridge, MA: Harvard University Press, 1991.
Ozouf, Mona. "Space and Time in the Festivals of the French Revolution." *Comparative Studies in Society and History* 17, no. 3 (1975): 372–84.
Pabst, Stephan. "Kultur der Kopie. Antike im Zeitalter ihrer Reproduzierbarkeit." In *Weimarer Klassik. Kultur des Sinnlichen*, ed. Sebastian Böhmer, Christiane Holm, Veronika Spinner, and Thorsten Valk, 136–45. Berlin: Deutscher Kunstverlag, 2012.
Patten, Robert L. *George Cruikshank's Life, Times, and Art*. Vol. 1. New Brunswick, NJ: Rutgers University Press, 1992.
Pauly, Yvonne. "Überblickskommentar." In *Anthousa oder Roms Alterthümer*. Vol. 4.1 of *Sämtliche Werke*, ed. Yvonne Pauly, 339–418. Berlin: De Gruyter, 2005.
Peters, John Durham. *The Marvelous Clouds: Towards a Philosophy of Elemental Media*. Chicago: University of Chicago Press, 2015.
Pethes, Nicolas. *Vermischte Schriften. Jean Pauls Roman-Anthologie D. Katzenbergers Badereise (1809)*. Hanover: Wehrhahn, 2022.
Pettitt, Clare. *Serial Forms: The Unfinished Project of Modernity, 1815–1848*. Oxford: Oxford University Press, 2020.
Pettitt, Clare. *Serial Revolutions 1848: Writing, Politics, Form*. Oxford: Oxford University Press, 2022.
Pfotenhauer, Helmut. "Das Leben Schreiben- das Schreiben Leben: Jean Paul als Klassiker der Zeitverfallenheit." *Jahrbuch der Jean Paul Gesellschaft* 35–56 (2000/2001): 46–58.
Pfotenhauer, Helmut. *Jean Paul: das Leben als Schreiben*. Munich: Hanser, 2013.
Phelan, Anthony. *Reading Heinrich Heine*. Cambridge: Cambridge University Press, 2007.
Piper, Andrew. *Dreaming in Books: The Making of the Bibliographical Imagination in the Romantic Age*. Chicago: University of Chicago Press, 2009.
Piper, Andrew. "Rethinking the Print Object: Goethe and the Book of Everything." *PMLA* 121, no. 1 (2006): 124–38.
Piper, Andrew. "Transitional Figures: Image, Translation and the Ballad from Broadside to Photography." In *Book Illustration in the Long Eighteenth Century: Reconfiguring the Visual Periphery of the Text*, ed. Christina Ionescu, 157–91. Cambridge: Cambridge Scholars Publishing, 2011.
Pirholt, Mattias. "Goethe's Exploratory Idealism." In *Beyond Autonomy in Eighteenth-Century British and German Aesthetics*, ed. Karl Axelsson, Camilla Flodin, and Mattias Pirholt, 217–38. New York and London: Routledge, 2021.
Pirholt, Mattias. *Grenzerfahrungen. Studien zu Goethes Ästhetik*. Heidelberg: Winter, 2018.
Plachta, Botho. "Goethe über das lästige Geschäft des Editors." In *Autor-Autorisation-Authentizität*, ed. Thomas Bein, Rüdiger Nutt-Kofoth, and Bodo Plachta, 229–38. Tübingen: Niemeyer, 2004.

Pompe, Hedwig. *Famas Medium: Zur Theorie der Zeitung in Deutschland zwischen dem 17. und 19. Jahrhundert*. Berlin: De Gruyter, 2012.

Popkin, Jeremy D. "Editor's Preface." In *Panorama of Paris: Selections from Mercier's Tableau de Paris*, ed. Jeremy D. Popkin, 1–20. University Park, PA: Pennsylvania State University Press, 1999.

Prawer, Siegbert S. "Heine and the Photographers." In *Paintings on the Move: Heine and the Visual Arts*, ed. by Susanne Zantop, 75–90. Lincoln: University of Nebraska Press, 1989.

Preisendanz, Wolfgang. "Der Funktionsübergang von Dichtung und Publizistik bei Heine." In *Die nicht mehr schönen Künste: Grenzphänomene des Ästhetischen*, ed. Hans Robert Jauß, 343–74. Munich: Wilhelm Fink, 1968.

Proescholdt, Catherine W. "Johahnn Christian Hüttner (1766–1847): A Link Between Weimar and London." In *Goethe and the English-Speaking World*, ed. Nicholas Boyle and John Guthrie, 99–110. Rochester, NY: Camden House, 2001.

Pückler-Muskau, Prince Hermann von. *Letters of a Dead Man*. Ed. and trans. Linda B. Parshall. Washington, DC: Dumbarton Oaks Research Library and Collection, 2016.

Purdy, Daniel L. *The Tyranny of Elegance: Consumer Cosmopolitanism in the Era of Goethe*. Baltimore, MD: Johns Hopkins University Press, 1998.

Ramtke, Nora. "Zeitschrift und Zeitgeschichte. *Die Zeiten* (1805–1820) als chronopoetisches Archiv ihrer Gegenwart." *IASL* 45, no. 1 (2020): 112–34.

Ramtke, Nora, and Séan Williams. "Approaching the German Anthology, 1700–1850." *German Life and Letters* 70, no. 1 (2017): 1–21.

Rang, Florens Christian. *Historische Psychologie des Karnevals*. Ed. Lorenz Jäger. Berlin: Brinkman and Bose, 1983 [1927/1928].

Reichardt, Rolf. "The French Revolution as a European Media Event." *European History Online (EGO)*, Leibniz Institute of European History (IEG), August 27, 2012. Last accessed January 27, 2021. http://www.ieg-ego.eu/reichardtr-2010-en.

Reichardt, Rolf, and Hubertus Kohle. *Visualizing the Revolution: Politics and Pictorial Arts in Late Eighteenth-Century France*. London: Reaktion, 2008.

Rennie, Nicholas. *Speculating on the Moment: The Poetics of Time and Recurrence in Goethe, Leopardi, and Nietzsche*. Göttingen: Wallstein, 2005.

Rieder, John. *Science Fiction and the Mass Cultural Genre System*. Middletown, CT: Wesleyan University Press, 2017.

Riha, Karl. *Die Beschreibung der "Großen Stadt." Zur Entstehung des Großstadtmotivs in der deutschen Literatur (ca. 1750–1850)*. Bad Homburg: Gehlen, 1970.

Rippmann, Inge. "'Die Zeit läuft wie ein Reh vor uns her.' Der Zeitschriftsteller als Geschichtsschreiber." In *"Die Kunst—eine Tochter der Zeit". Neue Studien zu Ludwig Börne*, ed. Inge Rippmann and Wolfgang Labuhn, 130–69. Bielefeld: Aisthesis, 1998.

Roche, Daniel. *The Culture of Clothing: Dress and Fashion in the 'Ancien Régime.'* Trans. Jean Birrell. Cambridge: Cambridge University Press 1994.

Rosenblum, Robert. "The Origin of Painting: A Problem in the Iconography of Romantic Classicism." *Art Bulletin* 39, no. 4 (1957): 279–90.
Rosenkranz, Karl. *Ästhetik des Häßlichen*. Stuttgart: Reclam, 1990 [1853].
Rothöhler, Simon. *Theorien der Serie zur Einführung*. Hamburg: Junius, 2020.
Sammons, Jeffrey L. "Introduction." In *Ludwig Börne: A Memorial*, trans. Jeffrey L. Sammons. Rochester, NY: Camden House, 2006.
Sandor, Andras. "The Oak Tree and the Ax: Delaroche's Painting and Heine's Montage." In *Painting on the Move: Heinrich Heine and Visual Arts*, ed. Susanne Zantop, 51–73. Lincoln, NE: University of Nebraska Press, 1989.
Saul, Nicholas. *Prediger aus der neuen romantischen Clique. Zur Interaktion von Romantik und Homiletik um 1800*. Würzburg: Königshausen and Neumann, 1999.
Schäfer, Armin. "Jean Pauls monströses Schreiben." *Jahrbuch der Jean Paul Gesellschaft* 37 (2002): 216–34.
Schaffrick, Matthias. "Ambiguität der Autor-Werk-Herrschaft (Bosse, Luhmann, Jean Paul)." *Autor und Werk. Wechselwirkungen und Perspektiven* 3 of Textpraxis, ed. Svetlana Efimova. *Digitales Journal für Philologie* (2018). Last accessed March 13, 2023. https://www.textpraxis.net/matthias-schaffrick-autor-werk-herrschaft.
Schanze, Helmut. "Heines Medien." In *Zwischen Gattungsdisziplin und Gesamtkunstwerk: Literarische Intermedialität 1815–1848*, ed. Stefan Keppler-Tasaki and Wolf Gerhard Schmidt, 374–94. Berlin: De Gruyter, 2015.
Scherer, Stefan and Claudia Stockinger, "Archive in Serie. Kulturzeitschriften des 19. Jahrhunderts." In *Archiv/Fiktionen. Verfahren des Archivierens in Kultur und Literatur des langen 19. Jahrhunderts*, ed. Daniela Gretz and Nicolas Pethes, 253–76. Freiburg: Rombach, 2016.
Schievelbusch, Wolfgang. *Culture of Defeat: On National Trauma, Mourning, and Recovery*. New York: Picador, 2004.
Schmid, Pia. "'. . . Das Rad der Kleider-Moden mauerfest und täglich neue überraschende Phänomene.' Die Französische Revolution im *Journal des Luxus und der Moden* 1789–1795." In *Französische Revolution und deutsche Öffentlichkeit. Wandlungen in Presse und Alltagskultur am Ende des 18. Jahrhunderts*, ed. Holger Böning, 419–38. Munich: Saur, 1992.
Schmid, Ulrich. "Buchmarkt und Literaturvermittlung." In *Zwischen Restauration und Revolution 1815–1848. Hanser Socialgeschichte der deutschen Literatur*, ed. Gert Sautermeister and Ulrich Schmid, 60–93. Munich: Hanser, 1998.
Schmidt, Georg. "Inszenierungen und Folgen eines Musensitzes: Goethes Maskenzüge 1781–84 und Carl Augusts politische Ambitionen." *Ständige Konferenz Mitteldeutsche Barockmusik* (2002): 101–18.
Schmidt-Funke, Julia A. *Karl August Böttiger (1760–1835). Weltmann und Gelehrter*. Heidelberg: Winter, 2006.
Schmitz-Emans, Monika. "*Der Komet* als ästhetische Programmschrift—poetologische Konzepte, Aporien, und ein Sündenbock." *Jahrbuch der Jean-Paul-Gesellschaft* 35/36 (2001): 59–92.

Schneider, Helmut J. "The European Machine God: The Image of Napoleon Bonaparte in the Political Writings of Jean Paul." In *Inspiration Bonaparte? German Culture and Napoleonic Occupation*, ed. Seán Allan and Jeffrey L. High, 181–99. Rochester, NY: Camden House, 2021.

Schramm, Wilhelm von. "Einleitung." In *Jean Pauls Sämtliche Werke, historisch-kritische Ausgabe*. Vol. I/14. Weimar: Hermann Böhlaus Nachfolger, 1939.

Schumacher, Doris. *Kupfer und Poesie. Die Illustrationskunst um 1800 im Spiegel der zeitgenössischen deutschen Kritik*. Cologne: Böhlau, 2000.

Schütterle, Michael. *"Untadeliche Schönheit." Kommentarband zum Rudolstädter Faksimile von Johann Wolfgang von Goethe: "Das Römische Carneval."* Rudolstadt: Hain 1993.

Schwab, Heinrich W. "Musikbeilagen in Almanachen und Taschenbüchern." In *Almanach- und Taschenbuchkultur des 18. Und 19. Jahrhunderts*, ed. York-Gothart Mix, 167–201. Wiesbaden: Harrassowitz Verlag, 1996.

Seifert, Hans-Ulrich. "Die Französische Revolution im Spiegel der deutschen periodischen Zeitschriften." In *La Révolution Française vue des deux côtés du Rhin*, ed. André Dabezie, 161–97. Aix-en-Provence: University of Provence Press, 1990.

Seifert, Siegfried. *"Archiv der Moden des Leibes und des Geistes. Zur Wiederspiegelung der Französischen Revolution von 1789 bis 1795 im Weimarer Journal des Luxus und der Moden."* *Leipziger Jahrbuch zur Buchgeschichte* 23 (2015): 61–125.

Seifert, Siegfried. "Goethe/Schiller und die 'nivellirenden Naturen.' Literarische Diskurse im 'klassischen Weimar.'" In *Das Schöne und das Triviale*, ed. Gert Theile, 79–92. Munich: Fink, 2003.

Sengle, Friedrich. *Biedermeierzeit. Deutsche Literatur im Spannungsfeld zwischen Restauration und Revolution 1815–1848*. Vol 2. Stuttgart: Metzler, 1972.

Senzel, Dennis. "Werkchen, die zum Werk werden. Zu Jean Pauls *Wochenschrift*." *Colloquia Germanica* 49, nos. 2–3 (2016): 119–36.

Seyhan, Azade. *Heinrich Heine and the World Literary Map: Redressing the Canon*. New York: Palgrave Macmillan, 2019.

Sherman, Stuart. *Telling Time: Clocks, Diaries, and English Diurnal Form, 1660–1785*. Chicago: University of Chicago Press, 1996.

Silbermann, Alphons. "Die Kulturzeitschrift als Literatur." *Internationales Archiv für Sozialgeschichte der deutschen Literatur* 10 (1985): 94–112.

Simmel, Georg. "The Philosophy of Fashion." In *Simmel on Culture: Selected Writings*, ed. David Frisby and Mike Featherstone, 187–205. London: Sage, 1997.

Sina, Kai. *Kollektivpoetik. Zu einer Literatur der offenen Gesellschaft in der Moderne mit Studien zu Goethe, Emerson, Whitman und Thomas Mann*. Berlin: De Gruyter, 2019.

Slauter, Will. "Periodicals and the Commercialization of Information in the Early Modern Era." In *Information: A Historical Companion*, ed. Ann Blair et al., 128–50. Princeton, NJ: Princeton University Press, 2021.

Sperber, Jonathan. *Revolutionary Europe: 1780–1850*. Harlow, UK: Pearson, 2000.

Spoerhase, Carlos. *Das Format der Literatur: Praktiken materieller Textualität zwischen 1740 und 1830*. Göttingen: Wallstein, 2018.

Spoerhase, Carlos. "Was ist ein Werk? Über philologische Werkfunktionen." *Scientia Poetica* 11 (2007): 276–344.

Springer, Peter. "Denkmalsrhetorik." In *Historisches Wörterbuch der Rhetorik*, ed. Gert Ueding, 527–36. Berlin: De Gruyter, 2013.

Stalnaker, Joanna. "The New Paris in Guise of the Old: Louis Sébastien Mercier from Old Regime to Revolution." *Studies in Eighteenth-Century Culture* 35 (2006): 223–42.

Starobinski, Jean. *1789: The Emblems of Reason*. Trans. Barbara Bray. Cambridge, MA: MIT Press, 1988.

Sternke, René. *Böttiger und der archäologische Diskurs*. Berlin: Akademie, 2008.

Stierle, Karlheinz. *Der Mythos von Paris: Zeichen und Bewusstsein der Stadt*. Munich: Carl Hanser, 1993.

Stockinger, Claudia. *An den Ursprüngen populärer Serialität: Das Familienblatt "Die Gartenlaube."* Göttingen: Wallstein, 2018.

Swellander, Michael. "Understanding the Present: The Representation of Contemporary History in Ludwig Börne, Heinrich Heine, and Georg Büchner." PhD diss., Columbia University, 2019.

Tatlock, Lynne. "The Afterlife of Nineteenth-Century Popular Fiction and the German Imaginary: The Illustrated Collected Novels of E. Marlitt, W. Heimburg, and E. Werner." In *Publishing Culture and the "Reading Nation": German Book History in the Long Nineteenth Century*, ed. Lynne Tatlock, 118–53. Rochester, NY: Camden House, 2010.

Tautz, Birgit. *Translating the World: Toward a New History of German Literature Around 1800*. State College, PA: Pennsylvania State University, 2018.

Taws, Richard. *The Politics of the Provisional: Art and Ephemera in Revolutionary France*. University Park, PA: Penn State University Press, 2013.

Thierse, Wolfgang. "'Das Ganze aber ist das, was Anfang, Mitte und Ende hat.' Problemgeschichtliche Beobachtungen zur Geschichte des Werkbegriffs." In *Ästhetische Grundbegriffe. Studien zu einem historischen Wörterbuch*, ed. Karlheinz Barck, Martin Fontius, and Wolfgang Thierse, 378–414. Stuttgart: Metzler, 1990.

Turner, Mark W. "Periodical Time in the Nineteenth Century." *Media History* 8, no. 2 (2002): 183–96.

Turner, Mark W. "Seriality, Miscellaneity, and Compression in Nineteenth-Century Print." *Victorian Studies* 62, no. 2 (2020): 283–94.

Turner, Mark W. "The Unruliness of Serials in the Nineteenth Century (and in the Digital Age)." In *Serialization in Popular Culture*, ed. Thijs van den Berg and Rob Allen, 11–32. London: Taylor and Francis, 2014.

Uhlig, Ludwig. "Goethes *Römisches Carneval* im Wandel seines Kontexts." *Euphorion* 72, no. 1 (1978): 74–85.

University of Würzburg. "Projektdetails." Last accessed March 12, 2023. http://www.jean-paul-portal.uni-wuerzburg.de/neue-werkausgabe/pilotband-hesperus/projektdarstellung/projektdetails/.
Unseld, Siegfried. *Goethe and His Publishers*. Trans. Kenneth J. Northcott. Chicago: University of Chicago Press, 1996.
Valk, Thorsten. "Weimarer Klassik. Kultur des Sinnlichen." In *Weimarer Klassik. Kultur des Sinnlichen*, ed. Sebastian Böhmer et al., 11–23. Berlin: Deutscher Kunstverlag, 2012.
Vedder, Ulrike. "Erbschaft und Gabe, Schriften und Plunder. Stifters testamentarische Schreibweise." In *History, Text, Value. Essays on Adalbert Stifter*, ed. Michael Minden, Martin Swales, and Godela Weiss-Sussex, 22–34. London: University of London Press, 2003.
Vismann, Cornelia. *Akten: Medientechnik und Recht*. Frankfurt: Fischer, 2000.
Vogl, Joseph. *Kalkül und Leidenschaft. Poetik des ökonomischen Menschen*. Munich: Sequenzia, 2002.
Vogl, Joseph. "Luxus." *Ästhetische Grundbegriffe. Historisches Wörterbuch in sieben Bänden*, ed. Karlheinz Barck et al., 694–708. Vol. 3. Stuttgart: Metzler, 2001.
Voisine, Jacques. "Heine als Porträtist in der *Lutezia*." In *Internationaler Heine-Kongreß Düsseldorf 1972*, ed. Manfred Windfuhr, 219–26. Hamburg: Hoffmann and Campe, 1973.
Wald, James. "Periodicals and Periodicity." In *Companion to the History of the Book*, ed. Jonathan Rose and Simon Eliot, 421–33. Hoboken: Wiley, 2008.
Walz, Christa. *Jeanette Wohl und Ludwig Börne: Dokumentation und Analyse des Briefwechsels*. Frankfurt: Campus, 2001.
Wegner, Reinhart. "Augenblicke. Autonomie und Selbstreferenzialität sprachlicher Formen beim Betrachten von Bildern." In *Europäische Romantik. Interdisziplinäre Perspektiven der Forschung*, ed. Helmut Hühn und Joachim Schiedermair, 83–97. Berlin: De Gruyter, 2015.
Wellbery, David. "Form und Idee. Skizze eines Begriffsfeldes um 1800." In *Morphologie und Moderne. Goethes 'Anschauliches Denken' in den Geistes- und Kulturwissenschaften seit 1800*, ed. Jonas Maatsch, 17–42. Berlin: De Gruyter, 2014.
White, Hayden. *Metahistory: The Historical Imagination in Nineteenth-Century Europe*. Baltimore: Johns Hopkins University Press, 1973.
Wieland, Magnus. *Vexierzüge: Jean Pauls Digressionspoetik*. Hanover: Wehrhahn, 2013.
Wies, Ruth. "Das *Journal des Luxus und der Moden* (1786–1827), ein Spiegel kultureller Strömungen der Goethezeit." PhD diss., University of Munich, 1953.
Wild, Reiner. "Einführung," In Johann Wolfgang von Goethe, *Sämtliche Werke nach Epochen seines Schaffens* [MA], vol. 4.1, 915–39. Munich: Hanser, 1992.
Williams, Séan M. *Pretexts for Writing: German Romantic Prefaces, Literature, and Philosophy*. Lewisburg, PA: Bucknell University Press, 2019.

Wimmer, Mario. "World History in Six Installments: Epistemic Seriality and the Epistemology of Series." In *Truth in Serial Form: Serial Formats and the Form of the Series (1850–1930)*, ed. Malika Maskarenic, 55–82. Berlin: De Gruyter, 2023.

Winthrop-Young, Geoffrey. "Introduction to the *Journal of Luxury and Fashion* (1786)." *Cultural Politics* 12, no. 1 (2016): 23–31.

Wülfing, Wulf. "Reiseliteratur und Realitäten im Vormärz. Vorüberlegungen zu Schemata und Wirklichkeitsfindung im frühen 19. Jahrhundert." In *Reise und soziale Realität am Ende des 18. Jahrhunderts*, ed. Wolfgang Griep and Hans-Wolf Jäger, 371–94. Heidelberg: Winter, 1983.

Wülfing, Wulf. *Schlagworte des Jungen Deutschland: Mit einer Einführung in die Schlagwortforschung*. Berlin: Erich Schmidt, 1982.

Wurst, Karin A. *Fabricating Pleasure: Fashion, Entertainment, and Cultural Consumption in Germany, 1780–1830*. Detroit: Wayne State University Press, 2005.

Wurst, Karin A. "Fashioning a Nation: Fashion and National Costume in Bertuch's *Journal des Luxus und der Moden* (1786–1827)." *German Studies Review* 28, no. 2 (2005): 367–86.

Yonan, Michael. "Porcelain as Sculpture: Medium, Materiality, and the Categories of Eighteenth-Century Collecting." In *Sculpture Collections in Europe and the United States 1500–1930: Variety and Ambiguity*, ed. Malcolm Baker and Inge Reist, 174–93. Amsterdam: Brill, 2021.

Zammito, John. "Koselleck's Philosophy of Historical Time(s) and the Practice of History." *History and Theory* 43, no. 1 (2004): 124–35.

Zantop, Susanne. "Verschiedenartige Geschichtsschreibung: Heine und Ranke." *Heine Jahrbuch* 23 (1984): 42–68.

Zantop, Susanne. *Zeitbilder: Geschichte und Literatur bei Heinrich Heine und Mariano José de Larra*. Bonn: Bouvier, 1988.

Index

Note: Page numbers in italic type indicate illustrations.

Académie Française, 340–42, 345
acceleration of time, 46
Addison, Joseph, 2, 67, 221, 238, 247
Alexander the Great, 154
Allgemeine deutsche Bibliothek, 245
Allgemeine Zeitung (General newspaper), 3, 142, 145, 275, 277, 324, 327–28, 332, 336, 340, 344–45, 352
almanacs, 6, 17, 32, 70, 76, 82, 109, 145, 244
Anderson, Benedict, 9
Anna Amalia (duchess), 74
Annalen des Luxus und der Moden (Annals of luxury and fashion), 58
Antiqua typeface, 79, 81, 100, *101*, 121, 164

antiquity: aesthetic principles of, 31, 97; fashion and, 128–29; French Revolutionary imitation of, 179; French Revolution compared to, 104–6; and gift giving, 128–33; Goethe and, 78–79, 97, 100, 102–5, 128; *Modejournal* and, 128–30; modernity in relation to, 61, 88, 97, 187–88; Moritz and, 61, 102, 104–9, 112, 125, 128, 130, 135; Napoleonic monuments and, 181, 186–87; popular culture and, 78, 97, 102–3, 125–26, 128–30; present compared to, 33, 45, 56, 61, 97, 102, 149–50; visual accounts of, 102–3, 106–7, 128. *See also* classical models/classicism

Apgar, Richard B., 152n26
Der Apotheker (The apothecary), 263
Archenholz, Johann Wilhelm von, 61
Archiv, 216
archives, journals as, 26–28, 59, 86–91, 220
Arendt, Hannah, 5
Aristophanes, 175
Arndt, Ernst Moritz, 205, 210, 215
Arnim, Achim von, 219
Ästhetik des Häßlichen (Aesthetics of the ugly), 153
Athenäum (Athenaeum), 3, 49, 51, 153
Augsburger Allgemeine Zeitung, 297
Augustine, 357
authorship: forms of, 5–6; Heine and, 348, 350, 353; Jean Paul and, 38, 194–95, 197, 202, 202n11, 213, 227–28, 237–71; and the significance of a life's work, 38–39, 245–46. *See also* works editions

Bakhtin, Mikhail, 111n59, 156
Balzac, Honoré de, 65
Battle of Jena—Auerstedt, 199, 225, 250, 252
Baudelaire, Charles, 65
Benjamin, Walter, 11, 269
Benne, Christian, 239
Berend, Eduard, 255, 257–58, 260–61, 268
Berlin Academy of Arts, 106, 107
Berliner Abendblätter, 49, 153
Die Berlinische Monatsschrift (The Berlin monthly), 2
Bertuch, Carl, 179
Bertuch, F. J., 19, 28, 37–38, 46–72, 76, 78–82, 80n80, 84, 88–89, 91–95, 97–101, 120–21, 124–25, 134, 141, 144, 146, 148–49, 151–52, 154, 156, 157, 167, 179–80, 189, 367
Beschreibung der vorzüglichsten Volksfeste, Unterhaltungen, Spiele und Tänze der meisten Nationen in Europa (Descriptions of the most exquisite popular festivals, entertainments, games, and dances of most of the nations of Europe), 141
Bibliothèque Nationale, 165–66
Bilderbuch für Kinder (Picturebook for children), 71
bildungsroman, 18
biology, models of time based on, 14–20
Blumenberg, Hans, 17, 20, 29
Böck, Dorothea, 193n5
Bonaparte, Napoleon: conflicting attitudes toward, 77, 143–44, 149, 167–68, 179; Jean Paul on, 38, 192, 193, 209, 211, 222, 225–26; journalistic attacks on, 37, 49, 77, 153, 157–58, 180; monuments associated with, 179, 181–88; occupation of Germany by, 38, 49, 84, 179–80, 199–201, 208, 211–12, 222; public image of, 179
books, as luxury, 79–82, 95–96, 100–101, 120
Borchert, Angela, 50, 125, 128
Börne, Ludwig: background of, 283; and caricature, 189; characteristics of the work of, 46; and contemporary history, 39, 42, 44–45, 273–74, 276–77, 285, 293–94; and cultural journalism, 41–42, 46–47, 275–76, 283–84, 309; as editor, 1, 39, 283, 285–87; and ephemerality, 44, 285, 293, 307–8, 361, 368–69; eulogy for Jean Paul, 239–40, 268–69; and fashion, 51; Heine and, 273, 277, 283, 284, 309, 311–12, 336n52; and historiography, 279–81, 294–95, 308–14; and images, 42, 44, 46, 278; Jean Paul as influence on, 223, 277–78, 285; and the letter genre, 297–305; and miscellaneity, 289; and politics, 283–84, 297, 309–15; reception of, 278, 285, 293, 309; republication of his works, 39, 259, 278, 288–93; and seriality, 39, 45, 276–78, 285, 292–93, 306, 308, 315; and time, 1, 39, 186, 305–8; and works editions, 285, 289

Börne, Ludwig, works: "Aphorisms and Miscellanies," 259; *Briefe aus Paris* (Letters from Paris), 39, 278, 284, 285, 297–305, *301*, *303*, 309, 311, 314–15, 327; "Depictions," 42; "From Paris: Reading-Cabinets [*Lese-Kabinette*]," 41–42; *Gesammelte Schriften* (Collected writings), 285, 287, 289–90, *291*, 299–300, *301*, 308, 312–13; "Last Will and Testament of the *Zeitschwingen*," 287, 290; *Sämtliche Schriften*, 302; *Scenes from Paris*, 47; *Schilderungen aus Paris* (Scenes from Paris), 47, 278, 289, 299, 304; "Tableaus of Paris," 42
Böttiger, K. A., 19, 28, 46–49, 52, 60, 65–70, 77–78, 92, 97–98, 125–34, 141, 144–46, 148–49, 151, 154, 157, 167, 189, 257, 367; "Painted and Written New Year's Presents of the Ancient Romans," 130–32; "The Saturnalia Feast," 126–27; "Venus and the Graces, with Good Wishes for the Year 1796," 128–30
Brake, Laurel, 35, 364
Braudel, Fernand, 22
Brehm, David, 365
Brentano, Clemens, 219
Büchner, Georg, 278
Byrd, Vance, 29

Cabinet de Mode, 55
calendars, 62, 88–89, *90*, 96, 107, 109
Campbell, Timothy, 57n13
Campe, J. H., 120, 297, 312, 328
canalization, of printed matter, 151–53, 164, 166
caricature: ancient satire as precursor of, 131, 151; Börne and, 189; and classicism, 45, 154–58, 179; and contemporary history, 45; as cultural journalism, 37–38, 147, 154, 189; emergence of, 146; fashion compared to, 77; French Revolution as subject of, 77; Heine and, 189, 317, 322, 337–39; historical value of, 147–48; in *London und Paris*, 148, 153–54, 156; monuments as subject of, 179–88; political, 146–48, 153; of street criers, 160–61; temporality of, 188–89; and ugliness, 153–54, 157, 160, 165, 179, 189. *See also* satire
Carlyle, Thomas, 4n6, 317; *On Heroes, Hero-Worship, and the Heroic in History*, 322
carnival: periodicals likened to, 141–42; politics likened to, 127, 142; in popular culture, 123, 127–28; as subject for journals, 95–96, 124, 126–27, 140, 142; techniques of, 146–47; temporality of, 103, 114, 118, 142. *See also* public festivals; Roman carnival; Saturnalia
censorship, 167, 168, 180, 182, 200, 222–23, 229, 275, 283–84, 287–88, 300, 328–29
Le Charivari, 142
Chodowiecki, Daniel, 76
Christianity, and time/history, 16, 203, 208, 217–18, 221, 265, 295
Christo, 183
Chun, Wendy Hui Kyong, 366–67
Clark, Christopher, 8
classical models/classicism: of beauty, 30, 37–38; caricature and, 45, 154–58, 179; Goethe and, 138; in journal images, 81, 84, *85*; in popular culture, 77–78, 98; public festivals and, 105, 173, 178; of time, 18, 33, 45, 98, 109, 116, 118. *See also* antiquity; neoclassicism
coherence. *See* organicism; unity/coherence/wholeness
Colonne der grossen Armee, 181–83, *184*, 186–88
communism, 344–45, 348
contemporary history (*Zeitgeschichte*): Börne and, 4, 39, 42, 44–45, 273–74, 276–77, 285, 293–94; caricature and, 45; carnival and, 142; concept of, 280; and concepts of time, 203; criticisms of, 216; cultural journalism and, 5, 180n86, 201, 214–16,

contemporary history (*continued*)
218–19; Heine and, 39, 273, 276–77, 319, 321, 329–30; Jean Paul and, 194, 201, 214–24, 228, 236–37, 252; of Napoleonic era, 181; public festivals as subject for, 103
continuation, 32–33, 45–46
Corday, Charlotte, 215, 223n75
Cotta, Johann Friedrich, 26, 80n80, 145, 171n, 195, 214, 219, 247, 275, 297, 327, 328
counterpieces, 28, 59–61, 69, 123
Cousin, Victor, 340
Crane, Susan, 201–2
cries, of merchants and news hawkers, 159–65, *162*, 168
Cruikshank, Isaac, 148, 149
cultural journalism: Bertuch and, 37; Börne and, 41–42, 46–47, 275–76, 283–84, 309; caricature as, 37–38, 147, 154, 189; classicism and caricature in, 45; and contemporary history, 5, 180n86, 201, 214–16; emergence of, 2, 275; genres and conventions of, 10–11; Heine and, 5, 275–76, 309, 327, 340; history and entertainment mingled in, 48; lectures and speeches as subject of, 340; Mercier's tableaus influential on, 29; Napoleon as target of, 37, 38, 49, 77, 153, 157–58; on print culture, 45–46; public festivals as subject of, 171–78; significance of, 47; temporalization of, 26. *See also* journals

D'Aprile, Iwan, 216
Darwin, Charles, 15
Daunou, Pierre, 341, 345
Delacroix, Eugène, *Liberty Leading the People*, 335
Desaix, Louis, 183, 186–87
Deutsche Blätter, 216
Deutsches Museum (German museum) [1776–1791], 218
Deutsches Museum (German museum) [1812–1813], 218

Dickens, Charles, 65
Diderot, Denis, 127, 306
digital age, 360–62, 364–67
Dinocrates, 154
Directory (French government), 144, 157–58, 167–68, 170, 172, 174, 178
Drawing School. *See* Weimar Princely Free Drawing School

Eighteenth Brumaire, 167–68, 170
Emerson, Ralph Waldo, 140
England und Italien, 61
Englische Miszellen (English miscellanies), 26, 195
Enlightenment, 2, 17, 22, 58, 78, 103, 218, 294
Entwicklung (development), 18–19
ephemerality: Börne and, 44, 285, 293, 307–8, 361, 368–69; digital media and, 366–67; digitization as antidote to, 361–62; Jean Paul on, 203–4; of journals, 167–68; *London und Paris* and, 152; monuments and, 179–88; of newspapers, 44–45, 286; organic wholeness/completeness contrasted with, 17–18; print media associated with, 16–18, 170–71; public festivals and, 173, 176, 178
Ephemerides, 17
Erlin, Matt, 79
Ernst, Wolfgang, 366
Esposito, Elena, 16–17
Ettiger (Gotha), 99
Europäische Annalen (European annals), 145, 214

fashion: and antiquity, 128–29; caricature/satire in relation to, 76–77; comparative histories of, 57–60; historiographical import of, 63; imagery associated with, 70–78; journals and, 5, 37, 50–51, 55–63, 82, *83*, *85*; and the new, 37, 50, 57; politics as, 50–51, 62–63, 72; print media and, 50; and time, 74. *See also* luxury
festivals. *See* public festivals

feuilletons, 11, 26, 156, 318, 327
Fichte, Johann Gottlieb, 49, 200, 211, 217; *Reden an die deutsche Nation* (Addresses to the German nation), 210
Fischer, Bernhard, 79, 80n80
flow metaphor: text and images, 4, 11–13, 24, 29–31, 49, 51, 61, 103, 112, 123, 125, 151–53, 154, 189; time, 12, 14, 28–29, 70, 142, 151–52, 203–8, 280. See also canalization
Forster, Georg, 297
Foucault, Michel, 27
Les Français peints par eux-mêmes (The French, painted by themselves), 65
France. See Bonaparte, Napoleon; Directory (French government); French official culture; French Revolution; July Revolution
Frankfurt Museum, 229
Französische Miszellen (French miscellanies), 26, 195
Der Freimüthige (The candid one), 220
French official culture, as target of satire and caricature, 157–58, 178
French Revolution: antiquity in relation to, 104–6, 179; Börne on, 310–12; calendar revision instigated by, 62, 88–89; caricature and, 146; carnival likened to, 33, 127; as fashion, 62–63, 72; German attitudes toward, 49, 60, 65, 77, 86, 97, 105, 146, 158, 217; Goethe's *Römische Carnival* and, 92, 96–97, 104–5, 118, 136; Heine on, 311–12, 317, 318, 323; historiography of, 5, 22, 37, 46–47, 52, 317, 324, 340; imagery based on, 71–72, 73, 76–77; Jean Paul and, 200, 203, 223, 225; journalistic coverage of, 3, 5, 21, 47, 49–50, 52, 60, 61, 64, 86, 96n10, 104; and the new, 88, 118; print media linked to, 42, 47, 105, 145n8; and public festivals, 105, 172–75; and time, 5, 22, 33, 37, 46, 50, 88, 97, 200

Friedensblätter, 216
Fuchs, Eduard, 153
future: authors' envisioning of their works', 36, 38–39; Enlightenment and modern conceptions of, 22; Jean Paul and, 192, 214–24, 234, 236; the past's value for predicting, 22, 46; serial forms' shaping of perceptions of, 4, 19, 34

Gamper, Michael, 320n12
Die Gartenlaube für Österreich (The garden bower for Austria), 10, 356, 358
Garvani, Paul (pen name of Sulpice Guillaume Chevalier), 142
Gebrauchsliteratur (use-oriented literature), 212, 220–22, 240, 256. See also moral weeklies
Geist der Zeit (Spirit of the time), 215
Gelderloos, Carl, 19–20
Gentz, Friedrich, 215
Geulen, Eva, 93n3
gift giving, and antiquity, 128–33
Gilgen, Peter, 217
Gillray, James, 148, 149
Goethe, Johann Wolfgang von: and antiquity, 78–79, 97, 100, 102–5, 128; and Bertuch, 94; criticisms of caricature, 154, 156–57; criticisms of journals, 51–52, 69, 125, 132, 154; and the French Revolution, 136–37; and history/time, 23–24, 218; images from masked procession sponsored by, 74–75, 75; Italian travels of, 93, 299; on literary works as monuments, 242; and the *Modejournal*, 55, 93–95, 132, 140; and neoclassicism, 92; and organicism, 31; and print formats, 37, 38, 93; *Propyläen* journal, 3, 51; and Pückler-Muskau, 349n82; reception of, 270; republication of his works, 94, 119, 124–25, 134–42; and works editions, 124, 136–42, 253, 255–56, 258–60; *xenia* produced by, 132–33, 140

Goethe, Johann Wolfgang von, works: *Ausgabe letzer Hand* (Edition of the last hand), 124–25, 136, 138, 139, 197, 240–41, 243, 255–56, 258–60; *Auszüge aus einem Reise-Journal* (Excerpts from a travel journal), 101; "Excerpts from a Travel Journal," 298; "Fragments from Italy," 138; *Goethe's Neue Schriften* (Goethe's new writings), 124, 136–37, 139, 141; "The Good Women," 138; *Der Groß-Cophta* (The Grand Kofta), 136; *Italienische Reise* (Italian journey), 94, 110, 124, 138; *Des Joseph Balsamo, genannt Cagliostro, Stammbaum* (The family tree of Joseph Balsamo, a.k.a. Cagliostro), 136, 138; *Das römische Carneval*, 33, 37, 80, 81, 92–105, 109–25, *113, 117, 127, 133–42,* 302; *Sämtliche Schriften* (Complete writings), 138; *Unterhaltungen deutscher Ausgewanderten* (Conversations of German émigrés), 136–37, 138; *Werther*, 137; *Wilhelm Meister*, 49

Goetschel, Willi, 322
Görres, Joseph, 219
Göschen (publisher), 79, 100
Göttsche, Dirk, 8, 203
Graevenitz, Gerhard von, 2, 19
guillotine, 64, 123
Guizot, François, 340
Gutzkow, Karl, 259; *Öffentliche Charaktere* (Public figures), 322

Hartog, François, 183
Hegel, G. W. F., 21, 31, 192, 211, 216, 217, 277, 279, 280, 308, 317, 322, 325, 336, 343
Heine, Heinrich: anti-portraiture of, 335–39, 342–44, 349, 352–53; Börne and, 273, 277, 283, 284, 309, 311–12, 336n52; and caricature, 189, 317, 322, 337–39; and contemporary history, 39, 273, 276–77, 319, 321, 329–30; and cultural journalism, 5, 275–76, 309, 327, 340; and fashion, 51; and the French Revolution, 311–12, 317, 318, 323; and historiography, 279–81, 309, 316–46, 351, 354; and images, 278, 321, 337–39; irony in the work of, 317, 322, 346–49, 353; Jean Paul as influence on, 223, 277–78; on literary history, 241; and politics, 142, 297, 311–12, 344–45; portraits of historical figures by, 334–39; reception of, 278, 311–12, 347–48; reflection on his own death, 347, 353; republication of his works, 39, 259, 278, 317–18, 320–21, 328–29, 332–33, 344–54; and seriality, 39, 276–78, 317, 320–22, 331–32, 334, 337–38, 345–46, 354

Heine, Heinrich, works: *Book of Songs*, 348; "Communism, Philosophy, and Clergy," 344; *Französiche Zustände* (Conditions in France), 39, 297, 316–17, 319, 323, 326–33, 335, 337–38; *Heinrich Heine über Ludwig Börne* (Heinrich Heine on Ludwig Börne), 273; *Lutezia*, 39, 316–17, 318n6, 320–22, 335–38, 340, 344, 346, 350, 353; *Reisebilder* (Travel pictures), 278, 334; *Der Salon*, 334; "Verschiedenartige Geschichtsauffassung" (Various conceptions of history), 324, 326, 329, 331

Helms, Hans G., 224n
Heraclitus, 28, 280
Herder, Johann Gottfried von, 78, 98, 125, 205, 218
Herz, Markus and Henriette, 283
heterochronicity, 27, 204, 206, 208, 314
Der hinkende Teufel zu Berlin (The limping devil of Berlin), 96, 141
historicism, 50
history/historiography: academic/traditional, 8, 21, 39, 276–77, 279, 310, 319–22, 324, 339–44 (*see also* philosophical approaches to); Börne and, 279–81, 294–95, 308–14; and

the conception of time, 14–15, 21–24; fashion as model for, 63; of the French Revolution, 5, 22, 37, 46–47, 52, 317, 324, 340; Heine and, 279–81, 309, 316–46, 351, 354; impersonal approach to, 335–39, 342–44; journals dedicated to, 145; linear conceptions of, 15, 22; modern conception of, 22; past-present comparisons in, 57–58, 60–61; pedagogical conception of, 219, 324, 342; philosophical approaches to, 216–18, 308, 318, 321–22, 325 (*see also* academic/traditional); progress-oriented model of, 7, 15, 22, 158, 217, 280–81, 295, 317, 324–25; typological conceptions of, 22. *See also* contemporary history; literary history
Hogarth, William, 76, 146
Hohendahl, Peter Uwe, 318
Holm, Christiane, 84
Homer, 128
Horace, 178, 242
Die Horen (The Horae), 3, 49, 137, 145, 153
Huber, Theresa, 210
Hughes, Linda, 19
Hugo, Victor, *Les Miserables*, 327
Humboldt, Wilhelm von, 318
Hunt, Lynn, 46
Hüttner, Johann Christian, 148
Huyssen, Andreas, 35n92

idealism, 18, 21, 23, 31, 217–18, 280, 308, 318
images: Börne and, 42, 44, 46, 278; fashion-related, 70–78; French Revolution as subject of, 71–72, 73, 76–77; of Goethe's *Römische Carneval*, 95, 111–14, 139–40; Heine and, 278, 321, 337–39; in *London und Paris*, 148, 161, *162*; in *Modejournal*, 70–78, 73, 75, 82, 148; in periodicals, 29–30, 52; of public festivals, 110, 112, 172–73
irregular periodicity, 33–34, 308

Italien und Deutschland, in Rücksicht auf Sitten, Gebräuche, Litteratur, und Kunst (Italy and Germany, regarding mores, customs, literature, and art), 61, 101

Jean Paul (pen name of Johann Paul Friedrich Richter): Börne and, 285; and contemporary history, 194, 201, 214–24, 228, 236–37, 252; death of, 261; and fashion, 51; and the French Revolution, 200, 203, 223, 225; incompletion as feature of works of, 224, 237, 252, 255, 257–59, 261–62, 264, 267; on literary works as monuments, 84, 224, 226–29, 232, 236–37, 242; and miscellaneity, 25, 38–39, 194–96, 211, 214, 228, 237, 242, 256, 261, 270–71; on politics, 193–94, 199–202, 208–9, 211–13, 215, 224–29, 224n, 233n88, 249–50; reception of, 191–92, 201, 210, 239–40; reflections on authorship and his own work, 38, 194–95, 197, 202, 202n11, 213, 227–28, 237–71, 363; reflections on his own life and death, 38, 192, 194, 197, 238–39, 243–47, 249, 251, 261–66, 363; republication of his works, 35, 196–97, 202, 202n11, 208–9, 211–13, 229, *230–31*, 232, 240–43; satire, irony, and humor in the works of, 38–39, 191–92, 194–97, 202, 203, 208, 210, 214, 225–26, 232–34, 239, 241, 243, 245, 250, 260, 262, 264, 266–68; and seriality, 191–94, 196, 208, 214, 227–28, 239, 242, 244–45, 253, 257, 261, 263–65, 269–71; sermons as a genre employed by, 200, 202, 207, 209–12, 228; Stifter and, 355, 357; and time, 38, 192–93, 197, 200–224, 233, 236, 249; twilight/threshold in time conception of, 202, 206–12; and works editions, 197, 224n, 240–45, 253, 255–61, 268–69

Jean Paul (pen name of Johann Paul Friedrich Richter), works: "Abschiedsrede bey dem künftigen Schlusse des Morgenblatts" (Farewell speech on the occasion of the future end of the *Morgenblatt*), 247, *248*, 249–51, 264, 266; "Ausschweife für künftige Fortsetzungen von vier Werken" (Digressions for future continuations of four works), 261–66, 270; *Dämmerungen für Deutschland* (Twilights for Germany), 199, 201, 207–11, 217, 222, 225, 226, 229, 260; "December 31, 1810 presents: My Awakening at the New Year's Ball in the Casino Hall," 234; *Dr. Katzenbergers Badereise* (Dr. Katzensberger's trip to the spa), 215; *Friedens-Predigt an Deutschland gehalten von Jean Paul* (Peace sermon to Germany held by Jean Paul), 199, 209–11, 234, 260; "Germanisms and Gallicisms and Catholicisms," 222; *Herbst-Blumine, oder gesammelte Werkchen aus Zeitschriften* (Autumn flora, or collected little works from journals), 196, 251–52; *Jean Pauls Briefe und bevorstehender Lebenslauf* (Jean Paul's letters and impending course of life), 243, 260; *Jean Paul's sämmtliche Werke* (Jean Paul's complete works), 240–41, *255*; *Der Komet* (The comet), 260, 262; "Konjektural-Biographie" (Conjectural biography), 243–47, 249, 264, 266; *The Marvelous Society on New Year's Eve*, 233n91; *Museum* (Museum), 196, 229, 233, 236; "My Miscellanies" (*Meine Miszellen*), 195–96; *Nachdämmerungen für Deutschland* (After twilights for Germany), 199, 207–8, 219; *Nachlass*, 258, 268; "On God in History and in Life," 217–18; *Papierdrache*, 262–64, 266–68, 270; *Politische Fastenpredigten während Deutschlands Marterwoche* (Political Lenten sermons during Germany's holy week), 196, 199–200, 208–12, 225; "Programm der Feste oder Aufsätze, welche der Verfasser in jedem Monat des künftigen Morgenblattes 1810 den Lesern geben will" (Program of festivals or articles that the author intends to give to readers in each month of the coming 1810 *Morgenblatt*), 227, 229, 232–34, *235*, 236–37; "Proposal for Political Festivals of Mourning," 225; reception of, 267–71; *Selberlebensbeschreibung*, 205, 209, 243; *Titan*, 260; *Die unsichtbare Loge*, 265

Jena Romantics, 49

Journal des Luxus und der Moden (*Modejournal*) [Journal of luxury and fashion (Fashion journal)], 3, 37–38, 47, 49–95, 73, *83*, 87, *90*, 97, 99, 101, 112, 119–21, 123–34, 140–41, 145, 148–49, 159, 171–72, 180, 227

Journal für Literatur, Kunst, Luxus und Mode (Journal for literature, art, luxury, and fashion), 180

Journal für Luxus, Mode und Gegenstände der Kunst (Journal for luxury, fashion, and objects of art), 180

journals: as archives, 26–28, 59, 86–91, 220; criticisms of, 51–52, 98, 278; ephemerality of, 167–68; facets of, 47, 50, 56, 149; and fashion, 5, 37, 50–51, 55–63, 82, *83*, *85*; and luxury, 5, 30, 37, 79–84, 121; and miscellaneity, 194–95, 219–20; names of, 26–27; newspapers compared to, 4; permanence of, 120–21; public festivals as subject for, 140, 152, 157, 171–78; rise and significance of cultural, 3, 5, 47–48; and seriality, 195; time thematized and structured by, 5, 49, 133–34, 158–59, 220; topics of, 158–60. *See also* cultural journalism; newspapers; periodicals

July Monarchy, 316, 342, 347
July Revolution (1830), 273–74, 277, 279, 284, 297, 300, 313, 326–34
Juvenal, 149, 151

Kaminski, Nicola, 365
Kant, Immanuel, 58, 205, 217, 283, 318
Karla, Anna, 301
Kelleter, Frank, 7
Kittler, Friedrich, 12–13
Klancher, Jon, 363–64
Klauer, G. M., 78, 134
Kleist, Heinrich von, 49, 220
Klopstock, Friedrich Gottlieb, 137
Koerner, Joseph Leo, 16n42
Kommerell, Max, 269
Koselleck, Reinhart, 7–8, 21–24, 137–38, 145n8, 147, 189, 193, 218, 280, 324, 355, 362, 365
Kracauer, Siegfried, 11, 13–14
Krämer, Sibylle, 12
Kraus, Georg Melchior, 49, 52, 55, 57, 64, 71–72, 79, 81, 82, 84, 92, 95, 98, 99, 120, 121, 124, 134, 154; "Aufzug des Pulcinellen-Königs" (after drawing by Schütz), *113*
Kraus, Karl, 278
Kubler, George, 13–14, 32, 236
Kugler, Franz, *Geschichte Friedrich des Großen* (History of Friedrich the Great), 322

Lämke, Ortwin, 325n24
Landes-Industrie-Comptoir, 53–55, 71, 134, 154, 180
Laube, Heinrich, 300n29
Leipzig fall book fair, 244–47
Lessing, Gotthold Ephraim, 137, 204, 212
letters and correspondence reports, 297–302
Lichtenberg, Georg Christian, 76, 148
linearity: periodicals' hindrance of, 26; time conceived in terms of, 7, 14, 22, 203–5, 280. *See also* progress
Lippert, P. D., 107

Lips, Johann Heinrich, 116; title page illustration for Goethe's *Das römische Carneval*, 116, *117*
literary history: afterlives of works in, 134–42, 267–71, 346–54, 358–59; book-centered bias of, 6, 35; construction of authorship in, 245–46; digital preservation and, 361–62, 364; horizons of perspective in, 92–93, 136, 140, 242, 253, 267–71, 346, 368–69; place of serial literature in, 6, 359–60, 362–64
London und Paris, 19, 37–38, 46–47, 51, 52, 58, 60, 67–68, 70, 77, 144, 148–89, *150*, *162*, *169*, 312
Louis Philippe, King of France, 341–42, 347
Luhmann, Niklas, 16
Lund, Michael, 19
luxury: books as, 79–82, 95–96, 100–101, 120; images of, 29–30; journals and, 5, 30, 37, 79–84, 121; large and small print forms of, 81, 91, 100–101, 106–7, 129, 133–34, 141, 148. *See also* fashion

MacLeod, Catriona, 78, 98
Magasin Encyclopédique, 126
Marat, Jean-Paul, 86, 215, 223n75
Marie Antoinette, 86
Marlet, Jean-Harlet, "Lecture des Journaux aux Thuileries," 42, *43*
Martens, Wolfgang, 221
Martus, Steffen, 137
Marx, Karl, 105, 279, 280, 308, 340, 346
Masken des römischen Carnevals (booklet), 121, *122*, 123
Matala de Mazza, Ethel, 345
Mayer, Hans, 201, 237
McLuhan, Marshall, 1–2
Menippus, 156
Mercier, Louis-Sebastien, 37, 64–69, 127, 160–61, 161n46, 173; *Le Nouveau Paris*, 64, *65*; *Le Tableau de Paris*, 29, 41, 64, 66, 127, 312
Mergenthaler, Volker, 365

Meyer, J. H., 81, 98; "Versuch in der Verhäßlichungskunst, dem großen Lobredner derselben gewidmet" (Attempt in the art of uglifying, dedicated to the great eulogist of it), 154, 155, 156
Michelet, Jules, 276, 317, 340
Mignet, François, 276, 340–45, 347
Millin, Aubin-Louis, 126, 165, 165n55
miscellaneity: Börne and, 289; historical roots of, 194; Jean Paul and, 25, 38–39, 194–96, 211, 214, 228, 237, 242, 256, 261, 270–71; journals and, 194–95, 219–20; and seriality, 25–26, 196; significance of, 25–26, 38–39; and time, 220
Modejournal. See Journal des Luxus und der Moden
modernity: antiquity in relation to, 61, 88, 97, 187–88; character of, 11, 28, 30, 103; print media associated with, 2, 10–11, 28, 44, 317, 320; social and political concepts associated with, 22; time conceptions associated with, 2, 7, 16–17, 37, 200, 203, 223, 314. *See also* the new
Moniteur, 215, 222–23, 229, 287–88, 307
Monument des Generals Desaix, 183, 185, 186–88
monuments, as ephemeral or subject to caricature, 179–88
moral miscellanies, 196, 213
moral weeklies, 2, 3, 25, 26, 67, 151, 194, 202, 220–22, 233, 263. *See also Gebrauchsliteratur*
Moran, Daniel, 145
Morgenblatt für gebildete Stände (Morning pages for the educated classes), 3, 25, 26, 41, 45, 47, 51, 171n, 192, 194, 195, 206, 210, 219, 220, 227, 229, 232–34, 235, 238, 242, 247, 248, 249–53, 254, 260–63, 267, 270, 275, 287, 327, 334, 363
Moritz, Karl Philipp, 30, 31, 61, 97, 101–5, 112, 116, 124, 125, 128, 130, 135, 225; *Anthousa, oder Roms Alterthümer* (Anthousa, or Rome's antiquities), 104, 106–9, *108*, 115, 135; *Götterlehre* (Doctrine of the gods), 107; *Reise eines Deutschen in Italien in den Jahren 1786 bis 1788* (Travels of a German in Italy in the years 1786 to 1788), 101; "Über die bildende Nachahmung des Schönen," 139; *Vorbegriffe zu einer Theorie der Ornamente* (Preliminary ideas toward a theory of the ornament), 102, 139
Müller, Adam, 220
Müller-Sievers, Helmut, 20, 34, 269
Mussell, James, 25, 361, 363

Napoleon. *See* Bonaparte, Napoleon
Nash, Andrew, 257
Die Nationalfeste, Feierlichkeiten, Ceremonie und Spiele aller Völker, Religionen und Stände (The national festivals, ceremonies, and games of all peoples, religions, and estates), 141
National Museum, 208
Naumann, Ursula, 209n36
Nemesis, Zeitschrift für Politik und Geschichte (Nemesis, journal for politics and history), 214
neoclassicism, 30, 38, 92, 97, 128, 138
Der Neue Teutsche Merkur (The new German mercury), 125
Neuste Weltkunde (Newest world news), 145, 214
the new: fashion and, 37, 50, 57; French Revolution and, 88, 118; modernity's emphasis on, 22; periodicals and, 32, 37; tableaus and, 67. *See also* modernity; present
newspapers: ephemerality of, 44–45, 286; and freedom of the press, 168–70, *169*; hawkers of, 159, 164–65, 168; journals compared to, 4; rise of modern, 3, 144–45; timeliness of, 222–23. *See also* journals; periodicals

Nicolai, Christoph Friedrich, 245
Niebuhr, B. G., 317
Nietzsche, Friedrich, 215
Norman, Larry F., 99

Oesterle, Günter, 84
Oesterle, Ingrid, 204n18, 276, 280
Offenbach, Jacques, 11
organicism: in aesthetics, 18, 31, 36, 52, 91, 97, 135, 157, 257; in conceptions of a person's life, 260; in conceptions of time, 18–19. *See also* unity/coherence/wholeness
Oserhammel, Jürgen, 27
Ovid, 128
Ozouf, Mona, 104n38

Pabst, 98
Pandora (fashion calendar), 58, 88–89
Panorama, 27
Paris, Wien, und London—ein fortgehendes Panorama dieser drei Hauptstädte (Paris, Vienna and London—a continuous panorama of these three capitals), 179–81, 183
Paris Academy, 334
Pariser Laufberichte (Paris walking reports), 66
Der Pariser Zuschauer (The Parisian spectator), 66
past: predictive value of, 22, 46, 324; serial forms' engagement with, 21; trope of contrasting the present and, 33, 57–58, 60–61. *See also* antiquity
Pericles, 340
periodicals: as archival storage, 26–28; books compared to, 4; carnival likened to, 141–42; characteristics of, 4, 24–36; commodity status of, 6; images in, 29–30, 52; in late eighteenth and nineteenth centuries, 2–3, 144–45; miscellaneity of, 25–26; and the new, 32, 37; periodicity of, 31–36; routinization promoted by, 4–5; scholarship and, 6–7, 9–10; and sequential viewing, 28–29; seriality of, 4–5; time thematized and structured by, 1–2, 4–5, 7, 10–12, 32. *See also* journals; moral weeklies; newspapers; print media; seriality/serial forms
periodicity, 31–36. *See also* irregular periodicity
Perthes, Friedrich, 208, 218, 219, 220
Pettitt, Clare, 84, 362
Pfotenhauer, Helmut, 267, 268n86, 270n93
Phelan, Anthony, 319n10
philology, 267–68
Phöbus, 220
photography, 322, 337–39
Piper, Andrew, 139
Pirholt, Mattias, 72
Plutarch, 60
pocketbooks. See *Taschenbücher*
politics: Börne and, 283–84, 297, 309–15; caricature and, 146–48, 153; as fashion, 50–51, 62–63; Heine and, 297, 311–12, 344–45; Jean Paul and, 193–94, 199–202, 208–9, 211–13, 215, 224–29, 224n, 233n88, 249–50; journalism and, 144–45, 214–15. *See also* French Revolution
Polybius, 144
Posselt, E. L., 214
predictability: in classical models of time, 45; in past-future relationship, 22, 46, 324; temporal disruptions to, 34
prepublication, 34, 35, 202, 209
present: antiquity compared to, 33, 45, 56, 61, 97, 102, 149–50; caricature concerned with, 147; cultural journalism's engagement with, 37, 38, 42, 44–45; in transitional periods, 8, 205; trope of contrasting the past and, 57–58, 60–61. *See also* modernity; the new; *Zeitgeschichte*
print media: digital media compared to, 366–67; digitization of, 361–62; *Entwicklung* (development) and, 18–19; ephemerality of, 16–18, 170–71; fashion and, 50; French

print media (*continued*)
Revolution linked to, 42, 47, 105, 145n8; in late eighteenth and nineteenth centuries, 145–46; periodicity in, 31–36; structuring of time by, 12–14; and time, 12–14, 46–47, 204, 207. *See also* journals; newspapers; periodicals
progress, historical understanding based on the concept of, 7, 15, 22, 158, 217, 280–81, 295, 317, 324–25. *See also* linearity
Propyläen (Propylaea), 3, 51
public festivals: aesthetic coherence of, 106–7, 172–73; classicism and, 105, 173, 178; comparative treatment of, 104; ephemerality of, 173, 176, 178; French Revolution and, 105, 172–75; images of, 110, 112, 172–73; journalistic coverage of, 33, 140, 152, 157, 171–78, 171n; *London und Paris*'s coverage of, 171–78, *177*; as subject for contemporary history, 103; temporality of, 105, 109, 114. *See also* carnival; Roman carnival; Saturnalia
Pückler-Muskau, Hermann von, 322, 349–53, 349n82; *Briefe eines Verstorbenen* (Letters of a dead man), 298, 349, 352

Ramberg, Johann Heinrich, 76
Ramtke, Nora, 365
Rang, Florens Christian, 142
Ranke, Leopold von, 276, 277, 308, 324
reading, 41–45, 61–62, 71
Reign of Terror, 49, 60, 65, 86
Reimer, G. A., 253, 256, 260–61
reproduction, 134
republication: authors' approaches to, 346; Börne and, 39, 259, 278, 288–93; forms and contexts of, 34–36; Goethe and, 94, 119, 124–25, 135–42; Heine and, 39, 259, 278, 317–18, 320–21, 328–29, 332–33, 344–54; and irregular periodicity, 34; Jean Paul and, 35, 196–97, 202, 202n11, 208–9, 211–13, 229, *230–31*, 232, 240–43; time conceptions influenced by, 39, 212–13. *See also* prepublication; works editions
Restoration (France), 226, 283–84
revolution: Börne and, 284, 294, 297, 300, 306–8, 310–15; conceptions of time shaped by, 33, 45–46, 88; Heine and, 316, 319, 347; historiography of, 5, 39. *See also* French Revolution; July Revolution
Richter, Johann Paul Friedrich. *See* Jean Paul
Rieder, John, 20n56
Rippmann, Inge, 302
Rippmann, Peter, 302
Roman carnival, 33, 37, 92–93, 103–5, 109–27, 134–42
Romanticism, 31, 218, 294, 347. *See also* Jena Romantics
Rosenkranz, Karl, 153
Rousseau, Jean-Jacques, 58, 103
Rowlandson, Thomas, 146
Russian Miscellanies, 195

Sachsen-Eisenach, Johann Ernst von, 58
satire: ancient, 77, 131, 151; fashion compared to, 76–77; French Revolution as subject of, 62; in moral weeklies, 26; in prints, 76. *See also* caricature; *xenia*
Saturnalia, 103, 109, 112, 114, 124, 126–27, 130, 135
Schiller, Friedrich, 3, 49, 98, 125, 132–33, 137, 145, 318; *Sämtliche Werke* (Complete works), 259
Schlegel, August Wilhelm, 3
Schlegel, Friedrich, 3, 49, 218
Schleiermacher, Friedrich, 210
Schlosser, F. C., 308, 310, 311
Schmitt, Carl, 224n, 362, 365
Schneider, Helmut J., 226n81
Schöpf, Sven, 365
Schütz, Christian Georg, 95, 99; "Aufzug des Pulcinellen-Königs" (print after), *113*

Seifert, Siegfried, 63n30
sequential viewing, 28–29
serial culture, 4–5, 31, 103, 220–21, 360, 362, 364
seriality/serial forms: aesthetics of, 106–7; as archival storage, 26–28; and autonomy/individuality, 31; Börne and, 39, 45, 276–78, 285, 292–93, 300–302, 306, 308, 315; characteristics of, 4, 178; classicism and, 99; concept of, 9; criticisms of, 31; digitization and, 361–62, 364; Goethe and, 93–94, 93n3, 110–13, 118; Heine and, 39, 276–78, 317, 320–22, 331–32, 334, 337–38, 345–46, 354; and images, 29–30; Jean Paul and, 191–94, 196, 208, 214, 227–28, 239, 242, 244–45, 253, 257, 261, 263–65, 269–71; journals and, 195; literary history and, 6, 359–60, 362–64; miscellaneity and, 25–26, 196; open vs. closed, 9, 51, 69–70; periodicity of, 31–36; scholarship on, 19–20; and sequential viewing, 28–29; small forms associated with, 6, 28, 189; tableaus as form of, 65–66, 166; time structured by, 11–15, 17, 19–20, 99; untimeliness of, 15, 21, 39, 280, 359, 362; waiting as component of, 285; works editions and, 260–61. *See also* periodicals
serial viewing, 64, 74, 103, 111, 116
sermons, as genre employed by Jean Paul, 200, 202, 207, 209–12, 228
Simmel, Georg, 58
Sina, Kai, 139–40
small forms of publication: Börne and, 278; caricature as, 148; *Goethe's Das römische Carneval* as, 80, 99–101, 121, 133, 137–38; Heine and, 278, 337; Jean Paul and, 196; and luxury, 81, 91, 100–101, 106–7, 129, 133–34, 141, 148; miscellany as, 25; positive and negative qualities of, 80–81, 99, 189; scholarship on, 9, 11; seriality associated with, 6, 28, 189; significance of, 189; visuality associated with, 28
spectacles. *See* public festivals
The Spectator, 2, 67, 221, 238, 247, 263
Spoerhase, Carlos, 139, 300
Steele, Richard, 2, 67, 151, 221, 238, 247
Stierle, Karlheinz, 284
Stifter, Adalbert, 192, 355–59; *Adalbert Stifters Werke*, 356; *Vermischte Schriften* (Mixed writings), 356
Stockinger, Claudia, 362
Strauß, Anton, 138
stream metaphor. *See* flow metaphor
street criers, 159–65, *162*, 168

tableaus, 28, 29, 37, 41, 63–70, 152, 166
tableaux mouvants, 29, 51, 68, 102, 182
Talma, F. J., 295
Taschenbuch der alten und neuen Masken (Pocketbook of old and new masks), 141
Taschenbücher (pocketbooks), 5, 6, 29, 70, 76, 80, 109, 140, 191, 193, 196, 209, 215, 244, 252
Taschenbuch für das Carneval (Pocketbook for carnival), 141
Taschenbuch für Freunde und Freundinnen des Carnevals mit Illuminierten Kupfern (Pocketbook for male and female friends of carnival with illuminated plates), 141
The Tatler, 2
Tatler (magazine), 151
Tautz, Birgit, 48
Taws, Richard, 28n, 44, 173
temporalization, 7–8
Der Teutsche Merkur (The German mercury), 3, 49, 93, 101, 139, 145, 298
Thiers, Adolphe, 276, 317, 340
A Thousand and One Nights, 320
Thucydides, 340

time: biological models of, 14–20; Börne and, 1, 39, 186, 305–8; caricature and, 188–89; Christian conceptions of, 16, 203, 208, 217–18, 221, 265, 295; classicizing shape of, 18, 33, 45, 98, 109, 116, 118; contemporary history and, 203; flow as metaphor of, 12, 14, 28–29, 70, 142, 151–52, 203–8, 280; French Revolution and, 5, 22, 33, 37, 46–47, 50, 88, 97, 200; Heine and, 39; heterochronicity and, 27, 204, 206, 208; historical models of, 14–15, 21–24; Jean Paul and, 38, 192–93, 197, 200–224, 233, 236, 249; late eighteenth- and early nineteenth-century conceptions of, 7–8; linear conceptions of, 7, 14, 22, 203–5, 280; miscellaneity and, 220; modern/new, 2, 7, 16–17, 37, 200, 203, 223, 314; Napoleon's occupation of Germany on influence of concepts of, 200; periodicals' thematizing and structuring of, 1–2, 4–5, 7, 10–12, 32, 49, 133–34, 158–59, 220; plural character of, 205, 207–8; print media and, 12–14, 46–47, 204, 207; public festivals as measure of, 105, 109, 114; republication as occasion for reconceiving, 39, 212–13; revolutions' effect on conceptions of, 33, 45–46, 88; seriality and, 11–15, 17, 19–20, 99; simultaneity in, 4, 13–14, 20, 22–23; Stifter and, 356–58; street criers as measure of, 163, 163n49; as threshold/twilight, 202, 206–12; untimely (various and conflicting) senses of, 15, 21, 23, 28, 39, 280, 359, 362, 365, 367–68; writing/reading and, 203–5. *See also* continuation; ephemerality; future; history/historiography; irregular periodicity; past; periodicity; present

Turner, Mark W., 285n

twilight, as metaphor in Jean Paul's writings, 202, 207–12

Über Land und Meer (Across land and sea), 27

ugliness, caricature associated with, 153–54, 157, 160, 165, 179, 189

Unger (publisher), 99, 100n26

unity/coherence/wholeness: aesthetic, 18, 31, 36, 81, 91, 99, 105–6, 110–11, 116, 135, 192; ephemerality contrasted with, 17–18; Goethe's *Römische Carnival* and, 102–3, 105–6, 109–11, 115–16, 135; historical/temporal, 19, 21–22, 91, 318; of works editions, 257–58. *See also* organicism

Das Universum (The Universe), 27

Unterhaltungsliteratur, *Unterhaltungsblätter* (journals for literary entertainment), 60, 149, 191, 203

untimeliness, 15, 21, 23, 28, 39, 280, 359, 362, 365, 367–68

urban sketches, 2, 10, 29, 37, 41, 64–66, 160–61

Vaterländisches Museum (Patriotic museum), 218, 219, 220

Vedder, Ulrike, 359n

Vormärz (Pre-March era [1830–1848]), 192, 201, 275n4, 276, 284, 326, 355, 362

Die Wage, Eine Zeitschrift für Bürgerleben, Wissenschaft und Kunst (The scale, a journal for public life, science, and art), 293–96, 304

Wedgwood, Josiah, 78, 134

Wedgwood vases, 30

Wegner, Reinhart, 107

Weimar, Germany, 49, 52–54

Weimar Princely Free Drawing School, 52, 53, 55, 72, 81, 116

wholeness. *See* organicism; unity/coherence/wholeness

Wieland, C. M., 3, 49, 79, 82, 100, 101, 137, 246

Wiener Zeitschrift für Kunst, Literatur, Theater und Mode (Viennese journal

for art, literature, theater, and fashion), 3
Winckelmann, Johann Joachim, 78, 102, 125, 156
Winckler, Fredrich Theophil, 148, 157–58, 160–61, 163–65, 174–78, 181
Wohl, Jeanette, 284, 298
works editions: authors' approaches to, 38, 255–60; Börne and, 285, 289; Goethe and, 124, 136–42, 253, 255–56, 258–60; Jean Paul and, 197, 224n, 240–45, 253, 255–61, 268–69; and literary history, 35; representation of author's life and works in, 259–61, 288–89; and seriality, 260–61; Stifter and, 356
writing time, 6, 11–12, 23, 102–3, 114, 142, 314, 322

xenia (satirical verses), 131–33, 140

Young Germany, 283, 292, 326

Zeichnungen zu einem Gemälde des jetzigen Zustandes von Paris (Sketches for a painting of the current condition of Paris), 66
Die Zeiten, oder Archiv für die neueste Staatengeschichte und Politik (The times, or archive for the newest state history and politics), 214
Zeitgeschichte. See contemporary history
Zeit/Schrift (Brehm et al.), 226n80, 364–65
Zeitschriftsteller, 5, 12, 275, 293–95, 297, 305
Die Zeitschwingen (The wings of time), 286–87, 290, 295, 307
Zeitung für die Elegante Welt (Paper for the elegant world), 3, 47, 51, 220, 344–45
Zeitung für Einsiedler (Paper for hermits), 219
Der Zuschauer (The spectator), 220

Milton Keynes UK
Ingram Content Group UK Ltd.
UKHW012149111023
430419UK00005B/380